T0295917

Tasks, Skills, and Institutions

UNU World Institute for Development Economics Research (UNU-WIDER) was established by the United Nations University as its first research and training centre and started work in Helsinki, Finland, in 1985. The mandate of the institute is to undertake applied research and policy analysis on structural changes affecting developing and transitional economies, to provide a forum for the advocacy of policies leading to robust, equitable, and environmentally sustainable growth, and to promote capacity strengthening and training in the field of economic and social policy making. Its work is carried out by staff researchers and visiting scholars in Helsinki and via networks of collaborating scholars and institutions around the world.

United Nations University World Institute for
Development Economics Research—UNU-WIDER
Katajanokanlaituri 6B, 00160 Helsinki,
Finland
www.wider.unu.edu

Tasks, Skills, and Institutions

The Changing Nature of Work and Inequality

Edited by

CARLOS GRADÍN
PIOTR LEWANDOWSKI
SIMONE SCHOTTE
AND
KUNAL SEN

A study prepared by the United Nations University World Institute for Development Economics Research—UNU-WIDER

OXFORD
UNIVERSITY PRESS

Great Clarendon Street, Oxford, OX2 6DP,
United Kingdom

Oxford University Press is a department of the University of Oxford.
It furthers the University's objective of excellence in research, scholarship,
and education by publishing worldwide. Oxford is a registered trade mark of
Oxford University Press in the UK and in certain other countries

Published in the United States of America by Oxford University Press
198 Madison Avenue, New York, NY 10016, United States of America

British Library Cataloguing in Publication Data
Data available

Library of Congress Control Number: 2023930856

ISBN 978–0–19–287224–1

DOI: 10.1093/oso/9780192872241.001.0001

Printed and bound by
CPI Group (UK) Ltd, Croydon, CR0 4YY

Foreword

Polarization in the labour markets of post-industrial economies is a twenty-first century trend. While jobs and earnings in middle-income occupations are decreasing, low- and high-income occupations conversely see increases. The 'lost' middle jobs, characterized by performing routine tasks at a higher level, are mirrored by a surge in highly creative jobs at the top end and low-skilled service jobs at the bottom end of the pay scale. This intensifying change is viewed by labour market specialists as symptomatic of globalization and automation of middle-income jobs, with the resulting polarization feeding income inequality. The changing nature of jobs and work has been at the centre of recent analyses explaining the distribution of earnings in wealthy countries but was regrettably understudied in the Global South.

To address the knowledge gap, UNU-WIDER pulled together a team of country experts for the sizeable research project, The Changing Nature of Work and Inequality. The research team carried out in-depth examinations of 11 developing countries in Africa, Asia, and Latin America—teasing out to what extent changes in jobs and wages are polarizing work and fuelling inequality.

This book contains the knowledge distilled from the body of multidisciplinary research work over three years. I sincerely thank the chapter authors for their scholarly contributions, including all the extraordinary effort it took to put together the data needed for the country studies, and my fellow editors—Carlos Gradín, Piotr Lewandowski, and Simone Schotte—for their editorial skills in bringing this rich research to publication.

UNU-WIDER gratefully acknowledges the support and financial contributions received for this project from the governments of Finland, Sweden, and the United Kingdom. Without such vital funding our research and policy advisory work would be impossible.

Kunal Sen
Director UNU-WIDER
Helsinki, November 2022

Acknowledgements

This book is the result of a collective effort that included institutions and researchers all over the world. We are grateful to all of them. The results were enriched with comments from participants in several meetings, including the intermediate online workshop, the IPD-JICA Employment Task Force Meeting, special sessions at the 2020 Jobs and Development conference, the 2021 LACEA annual meeting, the 2021 IEA World Congress, the 16th IRSA International Conference, and the 2022 WIDER Development conference in Bogotá, among others.

We would also like to acknowledge the Development Policy Research Unit at the University of Cape Town for hosting the inception workshop that was key for launching this project. The project has also benefited from the research assistance provided by Marc Riudavets, as well as the support provided by Iina Kuuttila and Tram Nguyen on the project management, and Timothy Shipp on communications.

The Editors
Carlos Gradín, Piotr Lewandowski, Simone Schotte, and Kunal Sen

Contents

IV. CONCLUSIONS

List of Figures

List of Tables

List of Abbreviations

AAGR	average annual growth rate
AFC	Asian financial crisis
BIDS	Bangladesh Institute of Development Studies
CAF	Centre for Analysis and Forecasting
CASEN	Encuesta de Caracterización Socioeconómica Nacional (Chile)
CGE	computable general equilibrium
CGSS	China General Social Survey
CHIP	China Household Income Project Survey
CNAE	National Classification of Economic Activities (Brazil)
CPIAL	Consumer Price Index for Agricultural Laborers (India)
CPIIW	Consumer Price Index for IndustrialWorkers (India)
CS-RTI	country-specific RTI
CULS	China Urban Labor Survey
DASP	Distributive Analysis Stata Package
DFL	DiNardo et al. (1996)
DIE	German Development Institute
ENAHO	Encuesta Nacional de Hogares (Peru)
ENPE	Enquête Nationale sur la Population et l'Emploi
EPH	Encuesta Permanente de Hogares (Argentina)
FinnOC	Finnish Overseas Consultants
FVA	foreign value-added
GDP	gross domestic product
GeFam	Family and Gender Economics Study Group
GIC	growth incidence curve
GLSS	Ghana Living Standards Survey
GVC	global value chain
HICs	high-income countries
HKUST	Hong Kong University of Science and Technology
HOS	Heckscher–Ohlin–Samuelson
IBS	Institute for Structural Research (Poland)
ICT	information and communication technology
IHDS	Indian Human Development Survey
ILO	International Labour Organization
INDEC	National Institute of Statistics and Censuses (Argentina)
INS	National Statistics Institute (Tunisia)
INSS	National Institute of Social Security (Brazil)
IRD	Institute for Research and Development
ISCO	International Standard Classification of Occupations

LICs	low-income countries
LMICs	lower-middle-income countries
LOOCV	leave-one-out cross-validation
MENA	Middle East and North Africa
MICs	medium-income countries
MW	minimum wage
NCO	National Classification of Occupations (India)
NSS	National Sample Surveys (India)
O*NET	Occupation Information Network (US)
OECD	Organisation for Economic Co-operation and Development
OLS	ordinary least squares
PALMS	Post-Apartheid Labour Market Series (South Africa)
PIAAC	Programme for the International Assessment of Adult Competencies (OECD)
PEAC	Presidential Economic Advisory Council (South Africa)
PEP	Partnership for Economic Policy
PLFS	Periodic Labour Force Survey (India)
PNAD	National Household Sample Survey (Brazil)
PNADC	Continuous National Household Sample Survey (Brazil)
PPP	purchasing power parity
RBTC	routine-biased technical change
RIF	recentred influence function
RTI	routine-task intensity
SAKERNAS	Survey Angkatan Kerja Nasional (National Labour Force Survey, Indonesia)
SASCO	South African Standard Classification of Occupations
SDGs	Sustainable Development Goals
StatsSA	Statistics South Africa
STBC	skilled-bias technological change
STEP	Skills Toward Employment and Productivity (World Bank)
UIBE-GVC	University of International Business and Economics - Global Value Chain
UK	United Kingdom
UMICs	upper-middle-income countries
UN	United Nations
UNU	United Nations University
UNU-WIDER	UNU World Institute for Development Economics Research
US	United States
VASS	Viet Nam Academy of Social Sciences
WHO	World Health Organization
WID	World Inequality Database
WTO	World Trade Organization

Notes on Contributors

Paola Ballon is a Senior Economist at the Social Sustainability and Inclusion Global Practice of the World Bank and Research Associate at the Smith School of Enterprise and the Environment, Oxford University, United Kingdom. She is an Associate Editor of Oxford Development Studies, former researcher of the Oxford Poverty and Human Development Initiative, and UNU-WIDER. She has served as Technical Adviser for poverty reduction to the Ministry of Economics and Finance in Mozambique. Her areas of research are the measurement and analysis of multidimensional poverty, female empowerment, water security, and multidimensional exclusion.

Haroon Bhorat is Professor of Economics and Director of the Development Policy Research Unit at the University of Cape Town, South Africa. He serves on the Presidential Economic Advisory Council (PEAC) and holds a prestigious SARChI Chair in Economic Growth, Poverty and Inequality Research. He sits on the UN/WHO's High Level Commission on Health Employment and Economic Growth and was a member of the World Bank's Advisory Board of the Commission on Global Poverty. He served as economic advisor to two past Ministers of Finance, and previous South African Presidents Thabo Mbeki and Kgalema Motlanthe, formally serving on the Presidential Economic Advisory Panel.

Sayema Haque Bidisha is a Professor in the Department of Economics, University of Dhaka, Bangladesh. She holds an MSc from the University of Bath and obtained her PhD in Labour Economics from the University of Nottingham. Her research interest lies in labour economics and development economics. She worked on a number of research projects on labour market, gender and women empowerment, migration and remittance earning, credit and food security, poverty and vulnerability, skill and education, etc. In addition, Dr Bidisha has also worked closely with the Government of Bangladesh in preparing various policy documents and government flagship projects.

Jorge Dávalos is a research director at the Partnership for Economic Policy (PEP) Network and an Associate Professor at Universidad del Pacifico in Lima, Peru. He is a consultant for international organizations, including the ILO research department. He has published in the fields of international migration, trade and labour market outcomes, environmental economics, and management sciences.

Sergio Firpo is Instituto Unibanco Professor of Economics at Insper in São Paulo, Brazil. He received his PhD in Economics from the University of California at Berkeley, United States, in 2003. He was an assistant professor of economics at the University of British Columbia, Canada (2003–06) and at the Pontifical Catholic University of Rio de Janeiro, Brazil (2004–08), and an associate professor at the Sao Paulo School of Economics (2008–15) before joining Insper in January 2016. His main research interests are microeconometrics, policy evaluation, labour economics, development economics, and empirical political economy.

Carlos Gradín holds a PhD in economics (Autonomous University of Barcelona, 1999). He is Professor of Applied Economics at the University of Vigo, Spain, and has been a Research Fellow at UNU-WIDER, Helsinki, Finland. His main research interests are poverty, inequality, and discrimination. He is especially interested in inequalities between population groups and deals with enhancing the empirical evidence as well as methodological tools for the measurement and understanding of those issues.

Putri Riswani Halim is a researcher at Center for Sustainable Development Goals Studies, Padjadjaran University, Indonesia and a PhD student at the Department of Economics of Padjadjaran University. Her research is in the area of development economics, particularly on inequality and labour market studies.

Saloni Khurana is a PhD scholar at Indian Institute of Foreign Trade, Delhi, India. Her research interests include empirical development economics, labour, and international trade. Her ongoing research examines the interlinkages between skills, international trade, and employment.

Minh-Phuong Le is a development economics PhD student supervised by Mohamed Ali Marouani at the Paris 1 Panthéon Sorbonne University, France. Her research interests are broad, including productivity and resource allocation, impact evaluation of industrial policies, and jobs and earnings inequality. Phuong's thesis, financed by the Research Institute for Development (IRD), focuses on firms' and workers' vulnerability in the times of crisis as well as wage inequality in developing countries. She is affiliated with (1) UMR Développement et Sociétés, Université Paris 1 Panthéon-Sorbonne and Institut de Recherche pour le Développement, Paris, France; (2) Centre for Analysis and Forecasting (CAF), Viet Nam Academy of Social Sciences (VASS), Ha Noi, Viet Nam.

Piotr Lewandowski is a labour economist, a President of the Board at the Institute for Structural Research (IBS), Warsaw, Poland, and a Research Fellow at the IZA, Bonn, and RWI Essen, Germany. His research interests include the impact of technology on labour markets, structural and occupational change, job quality, minimum wage, energy poverty, and the labour market effects of climate and energy policies.

Kezia Lilenstein is an Associate Programme Officer at UNU-WIDER and co-ordinates the Southern Africa - Towards Inclusive Economic Development (SA-TIED) programme based at the National Treasury, Pretoria, South Africa. At the time of writing, she was a researcher at the Development Policy Research Unit in the School of Economics, University of Cape Town, South Africa. Her research interests include youth unemployment, poverty, inequality, and labour markets.

Kanika Mahajan is Assistant Professor of Economics at Ashoka University, India. Her primary research interests include gender, labour, and agriculture. As part of her research agenda on gender and labour, she is currently working on issues around stagnation of women's labour force participation in urban India and gender wage gaps in urban labour markets explained by application behaviour of men and women to jobs. Her other projects in the area of gender examine links between economic shocks and women's employment, gender and sanitation, and violence against women.

Tanveer Mahmood is a Lecturer at the Department of Economics, University of Dhaka, Bangladesh. Prior to that he worked as a Research Associate at Bangladesh Institute of Development Studies (BIDS) for three years. He earned his Bachelor's and Master's degree from the Department of Economics, University of Dhaka. His research interest lies in applied econometrics, labour economics, and development economics.

Mohamed Ali Marouani is Representative of the Institute of Research for Development (IRD) in Tunisia and Associate Professor in Economics at Paris 1 Pantheon-Sorbonne University, France. He is Research Fellow of the Economic Research Forum and of the Migration Institute. His research focuses on structural change, migration, and the socio-economic impact of crises in the MENA region.

Michelle Marshalian is an Economist at the Regional Development and Multi-level Governance division of the Centre for Entrepreneurship, SMEs, Regions and Cities (CFE) where she manages the OECD project on Enhancing Innovation in Rural Regions. She uses microdata for firm and labour analysis and develops partnerships for access to timely and granular resources to fill the gap of information in data-poor regions. In addition, she manages an advisory committee on rural innovation consisting of academics and industry representatives.

Roxana Maurizio is Researcher at the National Scientific and Technical Research Council, CONICET, and at the Instituto Interdisciplinario de Economía Política (IIEP-BAIRES), Buenos Aires, Argentina. Her areas of interest are labour economics, income distribution, poverty, and social policies in Latin America.

Ana Paula Monsalvo is a researcher and assistant professor at the University of General Sarmiento, Buenos Aires, Argentina. She is technical advisor at the Instituto Nacional de Estadística y Censos. Her areas of research are labour market issues, income distribution, and poverty.

Morné Oosthuizen is a researcher at the Development Policy Research Unit in the School of Economics, University of Cape Town, South Africa. His research interests include intergenerational transfers, economic demography, and the demographic dividend; poverty; inequality; and labour markets.

Albert Park is a development and labour economist who is an expert on China's economic development. He is Chief Economist of the Asian Development Bank (ADB) and Chair Professor of Economics, Social Science, and Public Policy at Hong Kong University of Science and Technology (HKUST). In recent years he has published articles in leading economics journals on firm performance, poverty and inequality, migration and employment, health and education, and the economics of ageing in China. Professor Park has played a leadership role in numerous survey research projects in China.

Alysson Portella is a post-doctoral researcher at Insper Institute of Education and Research, in São Paulo, Brazil. His research concentrates mostly on wage and education inequality, with a focus on racial discrimination. He is associated with the Center of Racial Studies at Insper. He holds a PhD in Business Economics from the same institution, an MA in Economics from UFMG, Brazil, and a BA in Economics from Federal University of Rio Grande do Sul (UFRGS), Brazil.

Mahir A. Rahman is a Research Associate at Bangladesh Institute of Development Studies (BIDS). He has also worked as a Lecturer at the Department of Economics, East West University, Bangladesh. He earned his Bachelor's and Master's degree from the Department of Economics, University of Dhaka. His research interest lies in behavioural and experimental economics, labour economics, and development economics.

Flavio Riva is a PhD student in Public Administration and Government at Fundação Getulio Vargas, in São Paulo, Brazil. His research is focused on impact evaluations in education. He holds an MA and a BA in Economics from the São Paulo School of Economics at Fundação Getulio Vargas.

Simone Schotte is a development economist focusing on inequality, social stratification, and labour markets research. She is a Project Director at Finnish Overseas Consultants (FinnOC), Kerava, Finland, and has been a Research Associate at UNU-WIDER as well as a consultant to the World Bank. She holds a PhD from the University of Göttingen, Germany, and her research has been published in journals such as *World Development*, *Journal of Economic Inequality*, *Journal of Development Studies*, *Kyklos*, *International Migration Review*, among others.

Kunal Sen is Director of UNU-WIDER, Helsinki, Finland, and Professor of Development Economics, Global Development Institute, University of Manchester, UK (on leave). He has over three decades of experience in academic and applied development economics research. He has performed extensive research on the political economy of growth and development, international finance, the dynamics of poverty, social exclusion, female labour force participation, and the informal sector in developing economies. His research has focused on India, East Asia, and sub-Saharan Africa. He was awarded the Sanjaya Lall Prize in 2006 and the Dudley Seers Prize in 2003 for his publications.

Amy Thornton is a post-doctoral research fellow at the Southern African Labour and Development Research Unit and African Centre for Excellence in Inequality Research based at the University of Cape Town, South Africa. Previously, Amy worked as a researcher at the Development Policy Research Unit, University of Cape Town. Her research interests are labour economics, economic demography, and household surveys with a regional focus on South Africa.

Giovanna Úbida is a PhD student in Economics at Insper Institute of Education and Research, in São Paulo, Brazil. She is also a member of GeFam (Family and Gender Economics Study Group). Her research is in applied econometrics and microeconomics of development.

Chunbing Xing is a professor of economics at School of Agricultural Economics and Rural Development, Renmin University of China. His research area is China's labour market focusing on migration, education, wage structure, and income distribution. He has published over 50 journal articles in the fields of rural–urban migration, wage determination, and education policies.

Arief Anshory Yusuf is Professor of Economics at the Department of Economics, Padjadjaran University, Indonesia, Research Affiliate at Department of International Development of King's College London, United Kingdom, and Honorary Senior Lecturer at Crawford

School of Public Policy of the Australian National University. His research focuses on economic development, particularly on poverty and inequality as well as on the interlinkage between the economy and the environment. He is also well known for his expertise in economic modelling, particularly computable general equilibrium (CGE) modelling.

Gabriela Zapata-Román is an economist, with a PhD from the Global Development Institute of the University of Manchester, UK. She is currently a Research Fellow at the Interdisciplinary Research Center for the Study of the Economy and Society of The Universidad Central de Chile. At the time of this study, Gabriela was a Postdoctoral Research Fellow at Universidad Diego Portales, Chile, working on the project 'Structural transformations and their effects on inequalities in the Chilean labour market', project number 3210480, funded by the Chilean National Research and Development Agency (ANID). Her research topics are structural transformations and inclusive growth, gender and labour market inequality, inequality of opportunities and educational achievements, and intergenerational mobility.

PART I
INTRODUCTION

1

Introduction

The Changing Nature of Work and Inequality

Carlos Gradín, Piotr Lewandowski, Simone Schotte, and Kunal Sen

1.1 Introduction

Concerns about the evolution of income inequality within countries have become an important element of public debate all over the world. Its reduction has been elevated to a key global target that is integral to achieving the Sustainable Development Goals (Goal 10: Reduce inequality within and among countries). Yet, income inequality is a complex phenomenon. It results from the interplay between how household members obtain their primary incomes—in large parts being derived from their participation in the labour market—under the prevailing institutional framework, and how this income is redistributed by the actions of the state. To that effect, the public sector shapes the distribution of earnings by collecting taxes and paying social benefits, but also by configuring the institutional framework under which market incomes are obtained in the first place. The latter may involve a combination of policy measures that, for example, regulate labour relations, favour the acquisition of skills or the access to technology, and facilitate trade.

In the last decade, increasing attention has been paid to the concentration of incomes at the very top of the distribution—namely among the richest 1 per cent—which to a large extent originates from the accumulation of capital income by a minority of very affluent people. However, this focus tends to overshadow the component of earnings inequality that arguably remains most consequential for 'the other 99 per cent' of the population: changes in the labour market requirements and remuneration of skills, education, and job tasks. Labour earnings represent by far the largest source of incomes for most people and thus determine their relative income position. Even though the relationship between earnings and income inequality is mediated by tax-based redistributive policies, there are limits to what these can achieve if labour markets become highly unequal. This applies even more in presence of regressive tax-benefit reforms, as observed in several countries, as well as in contexts characterized by limited state capacity and a high incidence of informality, situations still prevalent in most of the developing world. Therefore, understanding the factors that drive the trends in earnings inequality

Carlos Gradín et al., *Introduction*. In: *Tasks, Skills, and Institutions*. Edited by Carlos Gradín, Piotr Lewandowski, Simone Schotte, and Kunal Sen, Oxford University Press. © UNU-WIDER (2023).
DOI: 10.1093/oso/9780192872241.003.0001

is vital to understanding and tackling inequalities in a much broader sense. Essentially, it is impossible to achieve more equal societies without a functional and inclusive labour market.

These considerations are at the heart of this book, which summarizes the findings of the research project on the 'Changing Nature of Work and Inequality' that UNU-WIDER launched in 2019.[1] The book provides in-depth analyses of the trends in earnings inequalities in 11 major developing countries and emerging economies, located throughout the main developing regions: Tunisia (Northern Africa), Ghana (Western Africa), South Africa (Southern Africa), Bangladesh and India (South Asia), China and Indonesia (East Asia), and Argentina, Brazil, Chile, and Peru (Latin America). These countries are at different levels of development, either lower-middle- or upper-middle-income countries (except Chile which was upgraded to a high-income country in 2006, during the period of analysis). They have followed different development paths and inequality trajectories. Still, all of them already had a substantial and growing part of their workforce receiving a wage outside of agriculture at the beginning of the study period, around 2000, with a few showing an outstanding manufacturing sector as well. A requisite for the selection was that all of them must have accessible microdata (household or labour force surveys) of sufficient quality to undertake this type of study, with consistent methodologies over a period that at least covers most of the last two decades. As explained in the data chapter, these studies are demanding in terms of data requirements. It is necessary to follow a detailed classification of occupations over a substantial time span to observe the distributional changes and identify how they connect with changes in the occupational structure.

Particular attention is paid to extending the most conventional explanations of changes in earnings inequality, based on the relative scarcity or abundance of skilled versus unskilled labour. We focus on recent theories that put the changing nature of work—the tasks performed by workers in their jobs, rather than their skills—at the centre. Accordingly, this book addresses two core questions: (i) what are the main drivers of the trend in earnings inequality in the developing world? and (ii) is the changing nature of work making labour markets more polarized or unequal in developing countries? By looking at these questions in a variety of countries that differ not only in their geographic location but also in their development paths, this book strives to provide nuanced and context-sensitive answers to these questions. The world is moving in the direction of rapid automation that will radically transform labour markets around the world.[2] Understanding how

---

[1] The project website provides more detailed information about the objectives, the research team, as well as the resulting working papers: https://www.wider.unu.edu/project/changing-nature-work-and-inequality.

[2] A good example, but in the context of developed countries, is the recent report by Oxford Economics (2019): *How robots change the world: What automation really means for jobs and productivity*. Available at: http://resources.oxfordeconomics.com/how-robots-change-the-world.

this technological process interplays with inequalities in the labour market for different types of workers or various industries in the Global South today will also help anticipate its effects in the near future, giving relevant stakeholders room to react appropriately to these changes.

1.2 What drives earnings inequality?

In recent decades, growing earnings inequality within countries has been linked to technological advancement and international trade. This link has traditionally been explained by the higher relative demand for skilled workers that new technologies bring out. Suppose this demand is not matched by the supply of skilled workers, whether they come from the national educational system or immigration. In that case, their earnings will increase faster than those of low-skilled workers, pushing inequality up. This is, in essence, what has become known as the 'skilled-bias technological change' (STBC). It has been identified as the main driver of inequality in the United States (US) and other industrialized countries. The 'skill-biased technological change' increases the earnings of highly skilled workers relative to less skilled ones, resulting in a widening earnings gap between workers of different skill levels.

More recently, it has been argued that the STBC dynamics alone cannot explain the patterns found in the inequality trends, specifically polarization. Jobs and earnings in middle-income occupations have declined in the US and other industrialized countries, while they have increased among both low- and high-income occupations (Autor et al. 2006; Goos et al. 2014). The discussion shifted from skills to tasks performed by workers and their relationship with technological progress and globalization.

A key insight emerging from this new strand of literature is that the effects of trade patterns and technical change on labour demand depend on the type of task content involved.[3] In this approach, tasks are understood as units of work activity that produce output (Autor 2013), typically defined at the occupational level, while skills denote the human capability to perform these tasks, typically approximated by workers' education. As skills do not necessarily map onto tasks one-to-one, this new approach can provide a more nuanced perspective on how the twin forces of trade and technology are shaping the nature of work around the world, going beyond the traditional notion of skills.

According to the 'routine-biased technological change' (RBTC) hypothesis, technical change does not necessarily compress demand for all low-skilled workers. It mainly affects the demand for workers involved in routine tasks that are

---

[3] A review of the contributions of this literature to understanding earnings inequality is provided in Chapter 2.

easier to codify and automate, and hence more likely to be replaced by machines or to be outsourced to economies with lower wages. Since in developed countries those tasks are usually most prevalent in the middle of the occupational structure, middle-income jobs have been most affected by these trends. At the same time, employment and wages increased in creative jobs for highly qualified professionals whose skills complement new technologies and who benefit from globalized markets. Employment also rose in highly personalized service jobs that require face-to-face contact and pay relatively low wages, which makes automation challenging and unprofitable. As a result, the RBTC has been identified as the main driver of recent trends in rising job and wage polarization in the US and other industrialized countries (Autor et al. 2003; Spitz-Oener 2006; Goos et al. 2014). However, in developing countries and emerging markets, evidence on how the nature of work is changing remains scarce and is decidedly mixed (World Bank 2019).

In the next two sections, we describe these two explanations in more detail.

1.3 Skills and earnings inequality

The relationship between technology and wage inequality has been of long-standing interest among economists. In the 1990s, in response to a documented increase in wage inequality in the US in the 1970s, a series of papers pointed out the role of technological change—especially the development of micro-computers—in explaining the increase in wage inequality (e.g. Bound and Johnson 1992; Katz and Murphy 1992). These papers noted that highly skilled workers—especially those with more schooling—are more likely to use computers on the job, suggesting that computer technology is complementary to human capital (Card and DiNardo 2002). This hypothesis—that a rapid increase in technology caused a rise in the demand for skilled workers, contributing to increased wage inequality—became known as the 'skilled-biased technological change' (SBTC) hypothesis.[4]

We provide a graphical exposition of the SBTC hypothesis in Figure 1.1. According to the SBTC hypothesis, the wage premium of skilled labour over unskilled labour is given by the intersection of the curves denoting relative demand for skilled labour and relative supply of skilled labour. We denote the wage premium as w, the relative demand for skilled labour as D^{SL} and the relative supply of skilled labour as S^{SL}. As is standard in a model of labour demand and labour supply, the relative demand for skilled labour is downward sloping (see Acemoglu 2002). We

---

[4] While the earlier literature treated technological change as mostly exogenous, linked to changes in the organization of the workplace and the introduction of general-purpose technologies, more recent literature, especially in relation to developing countries, argued that SBTC may be induced by trade integration (see, for example, Wood 1994; Robbins 1995). See Sen (2008) for a review.

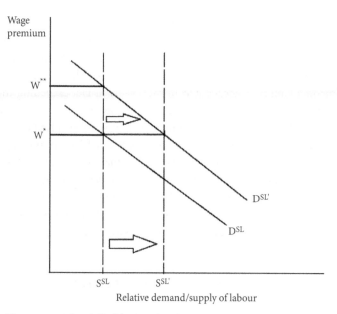

Figure 1.1 The skilled bias technological change hypothesis
Source: Authors' elaboration.

take the relative supply of skilled labour as inelastic in the short run. The equilibrium wage premium is denoted by w^*. Now consider an exogenous increase in the relative demand for labour due to SBTC. The relative demand for labour curve shifts to $D^{SL'}$. As is clear from Figure 1.1, the equilibrium wage premium increases to w^{**}, leading to higher wage inequality. Therefore, for a given relative supply of skilled labour, an increase in the relative demand for skilled labour increases the wage premium and therefore, wage inequality.

Now consider an increase in the relative supply of skilled labour curve over the long run from S^{SL} to $S^{SL'}$ as the increase in the wage premium induces more individuals to become skilled (possibly due to an increased preference for more education among those who are less educated). This would imply a rightward shift in the relative supply of labour curve, leading to a downward adjustment of the wage premium. If the shift rightwards of the relative supply of labour is large enough, the wage premium may return to its old equilibrium w^*. This implies that whether wage inequality increases with SBTC would depend on how the relative supply of skilled labour responds over time—if there is an increase in the number of educated workers in the workforce over time, the effect of SBTC on wage inequality will be greatly muted.

The empirical literature on the validity of the SBTC hypothesis remains largely confined to developed countries, with limited evidence on the applicability of the SBTC argument to developing countries. In survey papers reviewing the global evidence on SBTC, Berman et al. (1998) and Berman and Machin (2000) find a global trend of SBTC, where 'industries in developing countries sequence through the technologies historically used by technological leaders' (Berman and Machin 2000: 4). In particular, Berman and Machin find that the demand for skill in middle-income countries accelerated in the 1980s, in fact exceeding the rate in high-income countries. They also find that there was less persuasive evidence for the validity of SBTC for low-income countries. This is not surprising as most low-income countries have large agricultural sectors, where SBTC is unlikely to occur. It is far more likely that SBTC takes place in manufacturing and services sectors, where computerization can play a more important role. In this book, we contribute to the sparse empirical literature on SBTC in developing countries by presenting case studies of the role of skills and tasks in the evolution of wage inequality in a variety of lower-middle- and upper-middle-income countries.

1.4 Tasks and earnings inequality

The 'routine-biased technological change' (RBTC) hypothesis emerged to explain a key puzzle unaddressed by the SBTC—job and wage polarization that has been visible in the OECD countries since the 1980s. Middle-skilled jobs usually comprise structured, repetitive tasks that often demand being exact or accurate rather than solving problems or managing other people. These routine tasks could be cognitive, as in clerical jobs, or manual, as in blue-collar jobs. Computerization, progress in information and communication technologies (ICT) and digitally controlled robotics allowed the automation of repetitive, structured tasks, both manual and cognitive. The global adoption of ICT facilitated the offshoring of such jobs (Blinder and Krueger 2013). At the same time, these technologies and globalization complemented highly-skilled workers who performed non-routine tasks that require problem solving, analysis or interpretation of information, guiding, coaching, or motivating other people. Finally, automation rarely affects low-paid work as algorithm-driven technologies have struggled with spatial awareness and the mobility often required in these jobs. The growth of services increased employment in non-routine manual occupations, while the rising supply of workers who would have taken routine jobs in the past slowed down wage growth (Autor and Dorn 2013).

In developed countries, exposure to computerization and ICT contributed to the de-routinization of work—the declining role of routine tasks in particular occupations and the declining share of routine-intensive occupations in total employment (Autor et al. 2003; Spitz-Oener 2006). These processes translated into a U-shaped pattern in wage developments in the OECD countries: the middle-skilled, medium-paid occupations were most negatively affected (Goos et al. 2014). Polarization—a pattern consistent with RBTC but unaddressed by

SBTC—explained a substantial share of changes in wage inequality in developed countries (Goos and Manning 2007).

The polarization literature focused on occupations as the unit of analysis. This reflects the measurement of tasks at the occupational level. The US Occupation Information Network (O*NET), which includes detailed descriptions of occupational demands, has been the primary data source for researchers studying polarization. However, these data reflect the realities of the US technology level, labour market, and division of work. They offer a good approximation of occupational demands and routine-task intensity in other high-income countries but bias the assessment of routine-task intensity in low- or middle-income countries (Lo Bello et al. 2019; Caunedo et al. 2021; Lewandowski et al. 2022). As a result, the polarization literature focused on the US and other high-income countries.

Understanding the cross-country differences in occupational routine-task intensity is vital in studying polarization and wage inequality in low- or middle-income countries. Employers endogenously assign tasks to workers in view of the prevalent economic structure and available resources. Given that, we should expect that specific occupations utilize different skill sets and perform different tasks in low-, middle-, and high-income countries. For example, poorer countries that are further away from the technology frontier and have a less educated workforce can be expected to have a larger share of workers performing routine-intensive tasks (World Bank 2019). Moreover, while the shift away from manual and routine work towards non-routine work is a key feature of labour markets worldwide, the speed of this process may diverge substantially between countries. That is, some countries may be catching up faster than others, depending on the pace of economic growth, technology adoption, and educational attainment. In addition, structural changes such as industrialization and the growth of the service sector will play a role by altering the demand for different types of jobs (Bárány and Siegel 2018). The degree of trade integration also matters, as globalization tends to imply the outsourcing of routine-intensive tasks from high-wage countries to low-wage countries (Grossman and Rossi-Hansberg 2008; Hummels et al. 2018). The emerging, survey-based evidence shows that occupations in low- or middle-income countries are indeed more routine-intensive than similar occupations in high-income countries (Lo Bello et al. 2019; Caunedo et al. 2021; Lewandowski et al. 2022).

1.5 The contribution and structure of the book

This book contributes to this emerging strand of literature by providing a nuanced and context-sensitive developing-country perspective. The country analyses that this book presents were conducted by a good combination of both senior and experienced junior researchers, mostly from the developing world and resident in the analysed countries. Each country study provides an in-depth assessment of national trends in earnings inequality, which are assessed against changes in the supply of higher skilled workers and education premia, on the one hand, and changes in the occupational structure and the remuneration of tasks, on the other, while being mindful of broader macroeconomic trends and institutional developments. To ensure the cross-country comparability of results, much effort went into harmonizing national occupational codes to the international standard classification of occupations (ISCO-88), and a common methodological framework was adopted to investigate the main drivers that explain the trends in earnings inequality in each of the 11 countries (even if this framework was applied with flexibility to cater for the needs of each country). The effort has been worthwhile: this book now provides a unique, comparative assessment of how the nature of work is changing in 11 major developing countries, and the role that these changes play in shaping societies.

Given the scarcity of databases that allow the distribution of earnings and the tasks performed by individual workers to be study together, we have found innovative ways to push the boundaries of existing research and make the most of the information that is available in each of the countries under study. Critically, existing analyses of the effects of technology and globalization on employment and inequality largely rely on data for the US, where periodically updated descriptions of the specific tasks associated with each occupation have been collected through the O*NET since 2003. These studies, however, need to assume that occupations are identical around the world in the tasks they require. In view of sizeable structural differences, this is almost certain to be problematic for less-developed countries, which are the focus of this book. Therefore, to relax this assumption, this book adopts a novel approach that combines survey data (collected in 46 low-, middle- and high-income countries) and cross-country regressions to construct country-specific measures of occupational routine-task intensity, accounting for cross-country differences along four key dimensions: economic development, technology use, specialization in global value chains, and skills supply. In this book we show that the common assumption that occupations are identical around the world tends to lead to an overestimation of the non-routine task content of jobs in developing and emerging economies and to overly optimistic conclusions regarding the convergence of the nature of work in these countries towards the most advanced economies. The use of country-specific measures of routine-task intensity, along with the standard O*NET measures, thus allows the country studies to critically assess these potential discrepancies and provide a richer and more context-sensitive assessment.

The book is organized as follows. It is structured in four sections: introduction, cross-country analyses, country studies, and concluding remarks. In the introductory Part I, this introduction will be followed by Chapter 2, where we describe the main data and common methods used in this project by the different country studies to analyse their respective countries in a comparative way and make the most of the limited available data. In Part II, Piotr Lewandowski, Albert Park, and Simone Schotte present, in Chapter 3, their approach to measuring the routine content of tasks performed by workers in their jobs, providing a key input to country studies: a measure of routine-task intensity (country-specific RTI) for each occupation adapted to the special characteristics of each country (in terms of development, globalization, technological advancement, and skills supply), overcoming the need to rely on the same measure designed for the US economy which may not be fully appropriate in the context of less advanced economies. Chapter 4 synthesizes the main findings from the 11 country studies and discusses the patterns found across countries. Part III includes the 11 country studies following the common methodological framework. Finally, in Part IV we provide some final concluding remarks with an emphasis on policy implications and some lessons for future research.

References

Acemoglu, D. (2002). 'Technical Change, Inequality and the Labor Market'. *Journal of Economic Literature*, 40(1): 7–72. https://doi.org/10.1257/0022051026976

Autor, D.H. (2013). 'The "Task Approach" to Labor Markets: An Overview'. *Journal for Labour Market Research*, 46(3): 185–99. https://doi.org/10.1007/s12651-013-0128-z

Autor, D.H., and D. Dorn (2013). 'The Growth of Low-Skill Service Jobs and the Polarization of the US Labor Market'. *American Economic Review*, 103: 1553–97. https://doi.org/10.1257/aer.103.5.1553

Autor, D.H., F. Levy, and R. Murnane (2003). 'The Skill Content of Recent Technological Change: An Empirical Exploration'. *Quarterly Journal of Economics*, 118: 4. https://doi.org/10.1162/003355303322552801

Autor, D.H., L.F. Katz, and M.S. Kearney (2006). 'The Polarization of the U.S. Labor Market'. *American Economic Review*, 96: 189–94. https://doi.org/10.1257/000282806777212620

Bárány, Z.L., and C. Siegel (2018). 'Job Polarisation and Structural Change'. *American Economic Journal: Macroeconomics*, 10(1): 57–89. https://doi.org/10.1257/mac.20150258

Berman, E., J. Bound, and S. Machin (1998). 'Implications of Skill-Biased Technological Change'. *Quarterly Journal of Economics*, 113(4): 1245–79. https://doi.org/10.1162/003355398555892

Berman, E., and S. Machin (2000). 'Evidence of Factor Biased Technological Change in Developing Countries', mimeo.

Blinder, A.S., and A.B. Krueger (2013). 'Alternative Measures of Offshorability: A Survey Approach'. *Journal of Labor Economics*, 31: 97–128. https://doi.org/10.1086/669061

Bound, J., and G. Johnson (1992). 'Changes in the Structure of Wages in the 1980s: An Evaluation of Alternative Explanations'. *American Economic Review*, 82: 371–92.

Card, D., and J. DiNardo (2002). 'Skill-Biased Technological Change and Rising Wage Inequality: Some Problems and Puzzles'. *Journal of Labor Economics*, 20(4): 733–81. https://doi.org/10.1080/00036840802599933

Caunedo, J., E. Keller, and Y. Shin (2021). 'Technology and the Task Content of Jobs across the Development Spectrum'. NBER Working Paper 28681. Cambridge, MA: National Bureau of Economic Research. https://doi.org/10.3386/w28681

Goos, M., and A. Manning (2007). 'Lousy and Lovely Jobs: The Rising Polarization of Work in Britain'. *The Review of Economics and Statistics*, 89: 118–33. https://doi.org/10.1162/rest.89.1.118

Goos, M., A. Manning, and A. Salomons (2014). 'Explaining Job Polarisation: Routine-Biased Technological Change and Offshoring'. *American Economic Review*, 104: 2509–26. https://doi.org/10.1257/aer.104.8.2509

Grossman, G., and E. Rossi-Hansberg (2008). 'Trading Tasks: A Simple Theory of Offshoring'. *American Economic Review*, 98(5): 1978–97. https://doi.org/10.1257/aer.98.5.1978

Hummels, D., J.R. Munch, and C. Xiang (2018). 'Offshoring and Labor Markets'. *Journal of Economic Literature*, 56(3): 981–1028. https://doi.org/10.1257/jel.20161150

Katz, L.F., and K.M. Murphy (1992). 'Changes in Relative Wages 1963–1987: Supply and Demand Factors'. *Quarterly Journal of Economics*, 107(1): 35–78. https://doi.org/10.2307/2118323.

Lewandowski, P., A. Park, W. Hardy, Y. Du, and S. Wu (2022). 'Technology, Skills, and Globalization: Explaining International Differences in Routine and Nonroutine Work Using Survey Data'. *The World Bank Economic Review*, 36(3): 687–708. https://doi.org/10.1093/wber/lhac005

Lo Bello, S., M.L. Sanchez Puerta, and H. Winkler (2019). 'From Ghana to America: The Skill Content of Jobs and Economic Development'. IZA Discussion Papers 12259. Bonn: Institute of Labor Economics (IZA). https://doi.org/10.1596/1813-9450-875

Oxford Economics (2019). *How Robots Change the World: What Automation Really Means for Jobs and Productivity*. Oxford: Oxford Economics Ltd.

Robbins, D. (1995). *Trade, Trade Liberalization and Inequality in Latin America and East Asia: Synthesis of Seven Country Studies*. Cambridge, MA: Harvard Institute for International Development.

Sen, K. (2008). *Trade Policy, Inequality and Performance in Indian Manufacturing*. London: Routledge, UK. https://doi.org/10.4324/9780203894378

Spitz-Oener, A. (2006). 'Technical Change, Job Tasks, and Rising Educational Demands: Looking Outside the Wage Structure'. *Journal of Labor Economics*, 24: 235–70. https://doi.org/10.1086/499972

Wood, A. (1994). *North–South Trade, Employment and Inequality: Changing Fortunes in a Skill-Driven World*. Oxford: Clarendon Press. https://doi.org/10.1093/0198290152.001.0001

World Bank (2019). *World Development Report 2019: Digital Dividends*. Washington, DC: The World Bank. https://doi.org/10.1596/978-1-4648-0671-1

2

Data and Methodology

Carlos Gradín, Piotr Lewandowski, Simone Schotte, and Kunal Sen

2.1 Introduction

In order to address the main research questions of the 'Changing Nature of Work and Inequality' project—the findings of which are summarized in this book—the project team has compiled data on labour earnings, occupational classifications, and job tasks. The country teams addressed the scarcity of databases that allow the distribution of earnings and the characteristics of jobs to be studied together, and harmonized them across countries to the widest extent possible, making the most of the limited information available. This was achieved through three main contributions. First, household or labour force survey data were prepared to allow for this type of analysis. In some cases, this involved combining various data sources in a given country, correcting them for missing information, or focusing the analysis on specific subpopulations with more reliable data. Second, the national classifications of occupations were mapped into the internationally used classification of the International Labour Organization (ILO), namely ISCO-88. Third, to capture the differences in tasks performed by workers in comparable occupations in different countries, an econometric methodology combining micro- and macro-data was developed to derive country-specific measures of routine-task content. By relaxing the strict but often used assumption that occupations are identical around the world, the studies presented in this book provide a more nuanced diagnostic of labour market structures and factors behind earnings inequality. The studies also used the widely utilized task measures based on the US Occupation Information Network (O*NET) database (even if in some cases the detailed results are not reported in this book, they are available in the working paper versions on the project website[1]). Beyond these efforts concerning data and measurement, the country analyses in this project have adopted a common methodological framework, but with flexibility to adjust to the needs of each country. The approaches used bring together various analytical techniques that allow a better description of the magnitude and nature of the change in earnings inequality to be drawn up, particularly of the role of skills and the task composition of occupations.

---

[1] Project website: https://www.wider.unu.edu/project/changing-nature-work-and-inequality.

Carlos Gradín et al., *Data and Methodology*. In: *Tasks, Skills, and Institutions*. Edited by Carlos Gradín, Piotr Lewandowski, Simone Schotte, and Kunal Sen, Oxford University Press. © UNU-WIDER (2023).
DOI: 10.1093/oso/9780192872241.003.0002

In this chapter, we provide an overview of the data and key variables and briefly explain the main methods used and their implementation. More technical details can be found in the online methodological appendix (Gradín and Schotte 2020) and in the project working papers.

2.2 Data for earnings distributions and occupations

The analyses undertaken in this book are highly demanding in terms of data. They require information from a nationally representative sample of workers about their earnings, occupation (at a detailed level), and other characteristics (such as education and demographics). Although some of the processes analysed here, such as the effects of trade and technology, may affect mainly specific groups or workers (in particular, for example, those based in urban areas, working in the manufacturing sector, or paid employees), having information on the entire distribution of earnings provides a better understanding of the real impact of these phenomena in shaping the earnings distribution in a specific country. Ideally, the information on earnings and employment should come from the same source—which then allows an analysis of the joint distribution (that is, to associate changes in the employment composition with changes in earnings)—and be consistent over the period of analysis and across countries. Finally, comparable information on occupations and tasks is needed to quantify job demands and the routine intensity of occupations in various countries.

Nowadays, most developing countries have consolidated a statistical system that includes either labour force surveys or household living conditions surveys, or both. These, however, pose some limitations for the type of analyses undertaken in this project.

First, adequate information about earnings is often lacking for some population groups, particularly self-employed workers, especially those in rural areas working predominantly in small-scale agriculture. For example, in Argentina the survey sample covers only workers in urban areas. However, this constitutes a minor concern, as the country is highly urbanized, with 92 per cent of the overall population living in the urban parts of the country. In other cases, the sample includes all workers, but lacks information to consistently estimate the earnings of specific groups—such as family microenterprises, operating in the informal sector, in the subsistence economy, or on a seasonal or other irregular basis. The fact that most countries rely on consumption expenditure as the main household welfare measure to estimate poverty or inequality may partly explain why comparatively less effort is put into collecting the necessary information to estimate earnings. For these reasons, in some of the chapters, we had to restrict the analysis to only urban workers (e.g. Argentina), to paid employees (e.g. Tunisia), or to exclude self-employed in the agriculture sector (e.g. Ghana), for example. In some cases, the country teams have explored options to fill part of the data gap using different imputation techniques (e.g. Ghana and India).

Second, a number of challenges exist with regard to coding the self-reported main job performed by workers, particularly in developing countries, in a consistent way over time. First, to uniquely assign a worker to a specific occupation, researchers generally need to focus on the worker's main economic activity and ignore second or third jobs. Second, it may be possible to classify a given job in different categories, and the final decision will be based on a subjective assessment of the level of skill that the job requires, drawing on the limited information available. Third, the coding of occupations is often done using a national classification that needs to be mapped into an International Standard Classification of Occupations (ISCO). As all analyses in this book cover a period starting from the early 2000s or before, we use the ISCO-88 revision as the main reference. The mapping between different national and international classifications mainly relied on information provided by national statistical authorities and the ILO, but in some countries it also involved discretionary choices based on the researchers' knowledge of the country-specific context.

Finally, information on the specific task content of different occupations has not been systematically collected in most countries. The next section discusses in more detail how the project addressed this key issue.

2.3 The task content of occupations

A tasks approach to labour market analysis can contribute to a better understanding of the link between structural changes in employment and inequality trends. As explained in the introduction, in this context, tasks are understood as units of work activity that are typically defined at the occupational level. Workers will allocate their labour based on how the labour market remunerates the tasks performed in different occupations (Autor et al. 2003) and the level of formal education required for the competent performance of the tasks and duties involved. The main focus in the literature has been on the dichotomy between routine tasks, which are easier to codify and automate, and non-routine tasks, which largely comprise cognitive analytical or interpersonal tasks that are less likely to be replaced by machines or to be outsourced. Autor et al. (2003) argue that—in industrialized, high-income countries such as the United States (US)—the price for performing a standardized set of computational tasks has dropped substantially with the advancement of computerization and information technology. In consequence, employers have strong economic incentives to substitute labour by technology to perform these workplace tasks. At the same time, workers in analytic, problem-solving, and creative tasks that typically draw heavily on information as an input, and whose skills become increasingly productive as the price of computing falls, benefit substantially. However, these effects may be less pronounced in developing countries where an abundance of labour and a scarcity of capital prevail.

In order to apply the task approach to the 11 countries under study, we define two methods to quantify the occupational routine-task intensity (RTI). First, we assume that occupations are identical in all countries, and we apply the widely adopted measure based on the US dataset O*NET. Second, we assume that occupations differ between countries, and we utilize the method developed by Lewandowski et al. (2022) based on survey data.

2.3.1 O*NET measure

Because information on the specific task content of different occupations has not been systematically collected in most countries, existing studies largely rely on occupational task data for the US to analyse task demand in countries around the world. In the US, periodically updated descriptions of the specific tasks associated with each occupation have been provided by the Department of Labor since 2003 through O*NET (Table 2.1). Acemoglu and Autor (2011) used the O*NET data to construct what have now become standard indices of different

Table 2.1 Task items in O*NET used to calculate task content measures

Task content	Non-routine cognitive analytical	Non-routine cognitive interpersonal	Routine cognitive	Routine manual	Non-routine manual
Task items	Analysing data/ information Thinking creatively Interpreting information for others	Establishing and maintaining personal relationships Guiding, directing, and motivating subordinates Coaching/developing others	Importance of repeating the same tasks Importance of being exact or accurate Structured vs. unstructured work— reversed	Pace determined by speed of equipment Controlling machines and processes Spend time making repetitive motions	Operating vehicles, mechanized devices, or equipment Spending time using hands to handle, control or feel objects, tools or controls Manual dexterity Spatial orientation

Source: Authors' compilation based on Acemoglu and Autor (2011).

job tasks—non-routine cognitive analytical, non-routine cognitive interpersonal, routine cognitive, routine manual, and non-routine manual.

The literature (Autor and Dorn 2009, 2013; Goos et al. 2014) has also proposed a composite measure of RTI which increases with the relative importance of routine tasks. To calculate the RTI of occupation i, we use the formula proposed by Hardy et al. (2018):

$$RTI_i = \ln\left(\frac{r_{cognitive,\,i} + r_{manual,\,i}}{2}\right) - \ln\left(\frac{nr_{analytical,\,i} + nr_{personal,\,i}}{2}\right), \qquad (1)$$

where $r_{cognitive,i}$, $r_{manual,i}$, $nr_{analytical,i}$, and $nr_{personal,i}$ are the routine cognitive, routine manual, non-routine cognitive analytical, and non-routine cognitive personal task levels of occupation i, respectively.[2]

However, relying on the US O*NET task data to study task demand in other countries requires the assumption that the task content of each occupation is identical to that in the US. Although the O*NET data have been applied to other countries—usually the developed countries (Arias et al. 2014; Goos et al. 2014; Hardy et al. 2018; Lewandowski et al. 2020)—this assumption is problematic for less-developed countries. Given that tasks are endogenously assigned by employers in view of the prevalent economic structure and available resources and given that sizeable structural differences persist, we should expect that specific occupations utilize different skill sets and perform different tasks in low-, middle-, and high-income countries.

2.3.2 Country-specific measure

In recent years, the analysis of cross-country differences in task demand has been greatly facilitated by the increasing availability of national surveys collecting information on the tasks performed by individual workers. Lewandowski et al. (2022), de la Rica et al. (2020), and Marcolin et al. (2019) proposed measures based on the data from the OECD's Programme for the International Assessment of Adult Competencies (PIAAC), covering a set of high- or middle-income countries. Lewandowski et al. (2022) and Lo Bello et al. (2019) proposed measures based on the data from the World Bank's Skills toward Employment and Productivity (STEP).

The starting point for this project is the methodology developed by Lewandowski et al. (2022) who used PIAAC, STEP, and the China Urban Labor Survey (CULS) to define country-specific task measures which are consistent with

---

[2] For each task, the lowest score in the sample is added to the scores of all individuals, plus 0.1, to avoid non-positive values in the logarithm.

Table 2.2 Survey task items from US PIAAC selected to calculate task content measures consistent with O*NET occupation task measures

Task content	Non-routine cognitive analytical	Non-routine cognitive interpersonal	Routine cognitive	Manual
Task items	Solving problems Reading news (at least once a month) Reading professional journals (at least once a month)h Programming (any frequency)	Supervising others Making speeches or giving presentations (any frequency)	Changing order of tasks—reversed (not able) Filling out forms (at least once a month) Making speeches or giving presentations—reversed (never)	Physical tasks

Notes: The cut-offs for the 'yes' dummy are in parentheses. See Lewandowski et al. (2022) for more details on the full wording of questions, the definitions of cut-offs, and the criteria for selecting task items.
Source: Authors' illustration based on Lewandowski et al. (2022).

and comparable to the Acemoglu and Autor (2011) measures based on the O*NET data. The definitions of their measures are shown in Table 2.2.

Lewandowski et al. (2022) also define a composite measure of RTI, which increases with the importance of the routine content of work, and decreases with the importance of the non-routine content of work, using the formula:

$$RTI = ln\left(r_{cog}\right) - ln\left(\frac{nr_{analytical} + nr_{personal}}{2}\right), \tag{2}$$

where r_{cog}, $nr_{analytical}$, and $nr_{personal}$ are routine cognitive, non-routine cognitive analytical, and non-routine cognitive personal task levels, respectively.[3]

In Chapter 3 of this book, Lewandowski et al. calculate these country-specific occupational-level RTI measures for 46 low-, middle-, and high-income countries, and estimate models relating the routine-task intensity of occupations to four key factors defined for each country: (1) development level, measured by the gross domestic product (GDP) per capita (in purchasing power parity); (2) technology use, approximated by the number of internet users per 100 inhabitants; (3) globalization, quantified by a measure of specialization in global value chains

---

[3] For each task, the lowest score in the sample is added to the scores of all individuals, plus 0.1, to avoid non-positive values in the logarithm.

(GVCs); and (4) supply of skills, measured by the average years of schooling.[4,5] The survey data required to calculate the country-specific task measures are still not available for many economies—including Argentina, Brazil, Bangladesh, India, South Africa, and Tunisia, among the countries studied in this book. Therefore, they use regression models to predict country-specific occupational RTI scores in countries with no available survey data. A comparison between the survey-based and predicted values in countries with available data shows that the predictions are very close to the survey results for most countries. Given the narrower range of the predicted RTIs as compared to the survey results, our predictions provide a conservative estimate of the within-occupation differences in RTI levels across countries.

In the country case studies, the derived country-specific RTI values are combined with employment information from household or labour-force surveys (merged at the ISCO 2-digit level), to study changes in the average RTI of work in a given country over time. The observed patterns are also compared to the trends obtained by applying US O*NET task data.

Importantly, differences in the level of development, technology use, specialization in global value chains, and skills supply are not the only factors explaining the difference between the O*NET task measures and the provided country-specific RTIs. Even though the survey task content measures have been defined in a way that is consistent with those using O*NET, an important discrepancy to be aware of is that the differences in RTI between occupations are lower according to the country-specific measures drawing on survey data than according to the O*NET measures (see Lewandowski et al. 2022). Nonetheless, the ordering of occupations is largely consistent across the two measures.

---

[4] The data on GVC participation come from the RIGVC UIBE (2016) database. Lewandowski et al. (2020) use the backward linkage-based measure, defined as the foreign value-added share in production of final goods and services (Wang et al. 2017). The authors also interact this measure with GDP per capita (log) in order to account for the possibility that globalization reduces routine tasks in rich countries and increases them in poor countries. All other variables are obtained from the World Development Indicators database (World Bank 2020). All variables are demeaned using the unweighted average in the sample of countries with survey data.

[5] The regressions are fitted separately by 1-digit ISCO level occupation, adding fixed effects for occupation sub-categories at the 2-digit ISCO level. For each occupation, Lewandowski et al. (2020) select the best model from a set of seven alternatives which differ in the combination of explanatory variables. They use two model selection criteria. First, they select models that best fit the data, in particular, that have the highest predictive power based on the leave-one-out cross-validation (LOOCV). The chosen models exhibit the lowest root mean square errors, the lowest mean absolute errors, and the highest pseudo-R2 (with two exceptions) among all alternatives considered for each occupation. Second, the specifications are consistent with the occupation-specific regressions estimated at a worker level by Lewandowski et al. (2022).

2.4 Earnings inequality

Earnings inequality refers to the extent to which earnings are concentrated among only a few workers. Maximum inequality is reached when all earnings are obtained by one single worker, while minimum inequality is reached when all workers have the same earnings. In the case studies used in this book, we analyse trends in earnings inequality using two main analytical tools (that may or not be reported in the corresponding chapters).

First, we graphically compare the extent to which the earnings of workers at different pay levels have changed over the study period, using growth incidence curves (GICs) as a visual tool. The GICs map the annual growth rate in earnings for different percentiles of the distribution.[6] This gives us a general idea of whether the growth pattern over time was pro-poor (equalizing, when the earnings of the poorest workers grew the most), pro-rich (disequalizing, when the earnings of the most affluent workers grew the most), or mixed.

Second, we use standard inequality measures to quantify the changes in inequality over time. The most commonly used is the Gini index, taking values between 0 and 1 (or 100), with higher values indicating higher inequality. It is defined mathematically based on the Lorenz curve and provides a numerical summary measure that can be compared across time and between countries, and it is known to be most sensitive to changes in the middle of the distribution but less well-suited to pick up changes at the extremes. For that reason, it can be complemented with other inequality measures.

2.5 Role of tasks and skills in changing earnings inequality

The country studies presented in this book investigate the relationship between changes in employment and in earnings, on the one hand, and in the task composition of occupations, on the other. Below we provide condensed snapshots of each of the three main approaches used to investigate these changes.

2.5.1 Job and earnings polarization

In the presence of job polarization, we would expect to see employment growing more strongly in both low- and high-paying occupations while declining in middle-paying occupations, producing a hollowing out of middle-class jobs. Similarly, in the presence of earnings polarization, we would expect to see earnings

---

[6] The qth earnings percentile is that level of earnings that leaves q per cent of workers with earnings below that level. For example, the 50th percentile, also known as the median, leaves half of workers with earnings below (and the other half above).

growing more strongly in jobs at both ends of the earnings distribution at the expense of the middle. Given that polarization can be represented by a U-shaped pattern in the relationship between changes in employment or earnings and initial earnings across occupations, it can be tested either graphically or using a simple econometric test of a quadratic relationship. The country studies follow both approaches, in line with the previous literature.

First, the studies may use graphical tools such as mapping changes in employment shares or in real earnings (in percentage points) that correspond to each skill percentile (obtained by ranking occupations by average earnings in the initial year). They may also use scatterplots of the log change in employment shares and change in log mean earnings for each level of log earning in the initial year.

Second, most studies test whether the latter specification can be fitted by a quadratic relationship using a simple OLS regression (Goos and Manning 2007; Sebastián 2018). Specifically, each country study estimates the following models:

$$\Delta \log (E_{j,t}) = \beta_0 + \beta_1 \log (y_{j,t-1}) + \beta_2, \log (y_{j,t-1})^2, \tag{3}$$

$$\Delta \log (y_{j,t}) = \varphi_0 + \varphi_1 \log (y_{j,t-1}) + \varphi_2 \log (y_{j,t-1})^2, \tag{4}$$

where $\Delta \log (E_{j,t})$ and $\Delta \log (y_{j,t})$ are respectively the change in log employment share and in log mean labour earnings of occupation j between survey wave $t-1$ and t, $\log (y_{j,t-1})$ is the logarithm of the mean labour earnings in occupation j in survey wave $t-1$, and $\log (y_{j,t-1})^2$ is the square of initial log mean labour earnings.

Both equations are estimated by weighting each occupation by its initial employment share to avoid results being biased by compositional changes in small occupation groups. Evidence in support of a polarization pattern will be obtained if the relationship is U-shaped, with growth being stronger at both ends of the earnings distribution of jobs. That is, if β_1 is negative and β_2 is positive in the case of job polarization and, similarly, if φ_1 is negative and φ_2 is positive for earnings polarization.

2.5.2 Earnings inequality across occupations

To explore the role played by occupations in explaining aggregate inequality trends—as measured by the Gini index—the country studies estimate the contribution of inequality within and between occupations to overall inequality in each survey year. Given that the Gini index cannot be easily decomposed into the sum of both terms, the analyses presented in this book use the Shapley decomposition technique proposed by Shorrocks (2013) applied to our specific study context:

$$G = G_B + G_W;$$
$$\text{with } G_B = \tfrac{1}{2}[G(y_b) + G - G(y_w)] \ \text{and} \ G_W = \tfrac{1}{2}[G(y_w) + G - G(y_b)], \tag{5}$$

where G denotes the Gini index, y_b is a vector in which the earnings of all workers in each occupation are replaced by the average earnings in that occupation, and y_w is a vector in which the earnings of all workers are re-scaled so that all occupations have the same average earnings.

In this regard, the 'between-occupation component' captures inequality that originates in average earnings differentials between workers who are employed in different occupations and who are thus performing different sets of tasks (assuming there is no inequality within occupations, that is, all workers earn the occupational average). In contrast, the 'within-occupation component' captures inequality that originates in earnings differentials among workers who are employed in the same occupation and who are thus performing similar tasks, but who may differ in other personal or job characteristics, such as skills, experience, geographic location, or formality status. That is, inequality is estimated after eliminating between-occupation earnings differentials (by re-scaling all earnings to the population average).

Total inequality will be the sum of both between- and within-components. If the share of overall inequality that is due to the between-component is large and increases over time, it reveals that differences among occupations do play a fundamental role in driving the inequality trend. Notably, this can be due to two different trends. First, changes in the earnings gap between occupations may impact the overall distribution of earnings. If, for example, incomes grow faster in high-paying occupations than in low-paying occupations, while the structure of employment remains unchanged, this will result in an increase in overall earnings inequality. Second, changes in the structure of employment can also affect inequality trends. If, for example, employment grows faster in low- and high-paying occupations than in middle-paying occupations, while the earnings differences between occupations remain stable, this would result in a pattern of job polarization, and overall inequality will tend to rise. To disentangle whether changes in average earnings or changes in employment structure are driving the trend in inequality between occupations, the country studies may repeat the analysis with counterfactual distributions in which either the occupational shares or the occupational mean earnings are kept constant.

To further explore the relevance of the task composition of occupations in explaining trends in inequality between occupations, the country case studies may calculate, in addition, a concentration index. This index is calculated analogously to the Gini index estimated on the average earnings by occupations, with the only difference being that occupations are sorted by their RTI (from highest to lowest) instead of their average earnings.[7] Both indices are identical when occupations are equally ordered by average earnings and by RTI. The ratio between the concentration and the Gini index is a measure of the association between RTI and average earnings (based on the Gini metrics).

On the contrary, if it is the within-component that increases over time, this reveals a situation in which occupations are not playing a fundamental role in the inequality trend, and this is rather due to other factors, such as differences in skills among workers, bargaining power, etc. that occur within some or all occupations.

2.5.3 Disentangling inequality drivers: reweighting and RIF-regression decomposition

Overview

While the two approaches discussed above are focused on the role of occupations on inequality, in a final step, most country studies follow a more general approach to disentangle the contribution of different potential drivers of changes in the distribution of earnings. The particular focus here is on the roles of worker skills (education) and the tasks content of occupations (RTI), as these underlie the two main competing explanations of recent changes in earnings distributions.

The approach aims to produce a decomposition of the change in earnings at different percentiles over time into 'composition' and 'earnings structure' components. The main idea is to separate the direct effect on earnings of changes in the composition of workers by characteristics, if the earnings structure were to remain constant over time, from changes in the earnings structure itself, if the composition of workers remained the same. The main worker characteristics considered here are their education, the RTI in their occupations, and demographic characteristics such as age, gender, or ethnicity. In our main specification, we explicitly ignore other possible worker attributes strongly correlated with their occupations that could be relevant, but if considered would wipe out part of the full effect of RTI (such as occupational group, sector, industry, region, etc.).

The composition component of the decomposition is the direct expected effect on earnings due to the workforce becoming, for example, better educated, working more often in least routine occupations, or more formal, along changes in its demographics (e.g. higher shares of women or younger workers, etc.). It is possible

---

[7] The concentration index is defined as twice the area between the concentration curve and the diagonal (while the Gini index is twice the area between the Lorenz curve and the diagonal). While the Lorenz curve plots the cumulative distribution of occupational earnings for each cumulative proportion of employment, with occupations sorted by mean earnings, the concentration curve does the same but with workers sorted from highest to lowest RTI instead. Unlike the Lorenz curve, the concentration curve is not necessarily convex and may fall above the diagonal.

that inequality increases just because there are now more highly skilled workers, or less routine workers, even if each of these categories of workers keeps receiving similar relative earnings as they used to. This composition effect is potentially important given that structural change along the demographic dynamics in developing countries often implies large changes in the composition of the workforce due to rapid population growth, migration flows, demographic transitions that take place at some point of the development process, changes in social norms that push women to work out of their homes, a rapid expansion of education enhancing the supply of skills, improvements in infrastructure allowing better connectivity, etc. This approach will measure the extent to which these changes in the composition, assuming nothing else changed, are associated with the observed change in inequality.

The earnings structure component of the decomposition refers to the change in earnings due to changes in the earnings structure, that is, how the labour market remunerates each category of workers (high or low skill, working in less or more routine occupations, etc.). This relates to the common explanation of changes in inequality following changes in the skill premium, the relatively higher remuneration of workers with higher skills (for example with secondary or with tertiary education, compared with the remuneration received by workers with none or only primary education). If the skill premium is driving inequality, as suggested by the 'skilled-bias technological change' (STBC) approach, we will expect to identify that the returns to education are playing a role in inequality changes through the earnings structure effect. This component also relates to the role of tasks. If earnings grow faster at either most and least routine occupations, as derived from the 'routine-biased technological change' (RBTC) or task approach, and this is having an impact on earnings inequality, which is not clearly determined, we will also identify a large earnings structure component associated with occupational RTI.

The total change in earnings at each quantile is just the net effect of adding up all composition and earnings structure effects (including one for the intercept that refers to categories being omitted in the regressions to avoid multicollinearity), taking into account that some may tend to increase earnings while others tend to decrease them. From the decomposition of changes in (log) earnings at different quantiles, one can also infer the impact on inequality of these partial effects, applying the same logic as in the analysis of the GIC for the observed changes.

If one particular composition effect (e.g. more educated workers, or less routine jobs) or one particular structural effect (e.g. changes in the education premium over time, or in the remuneration of routine jobs) tends to increase the earnings of workers at the lowest percentiles while decreasing (or increasing less) the earnings of those at the top, for example, this means that the effect is equalizing, and we expect that it will contribute to reduce inequality. On the contrary, if an effect tends to increase the earnings of those in the highest percentiles at a greater rate, the effect will be disequalizing and we expect it will increase inequality.

The total change in inequality will be the net result of adding the total effects at all quantiles. However, we also directly look at the effect of each factor on the change in an inequality measure such as the Gini index or an inter-quantile ratio following the same exercise discussed above for the change in earnings, by decomposing the change in the inequality measure instead (which should reflect what is observed at the quantile level).

For example, Figure 5.1 in Chapter 5 shows a clear pro-poor pattern of the earnings structure effect associated with changes in the returns to education in Ghana between 2005/06 and 2012/13 (among all workers except farm self-employed). This is so, because the change in the returns of education is associated with significant increases in earnings at the bottom percentiles (between the 5th and 45th), while it contributes to a decline in earnings at the higher percentiles, particularly the 95th. As a result, the earnings structure effect of education is found to have contributed to a decline of the Gini index by 0.37 Gini points (Table 5.3). Since this reduction is larger than the one actually observed (0.28 Gini points, from 0.571 to 0.544), it means that the declining education premium alone can entirely explain the decline in inequality in Ghana in that period. There are other effects contributing to increases and declines of inequality in the same period, but never as big as the effect of education returns, and the net effect only accounts for an increase of 0.09 Gini points.

It is worth noting some important features of this approach for a correct interpretation. Decompositions are just 'accounting' exercises that do not seek the identification of causal effects or make predictions but are rather trying to identify statistical associations between patterns observed in the changes in earnings distribution with patterns observed in the distribution of characteristics among workers. It is well known that some of the assumptions that are needed to identify causality with these decompositions are not held in practice (see extensive discussion in Fortin et al. 2011). In particular, we ignore the potential endogeneity of some of the explanatory factors (that could be affected by unobserved factors also shaping inequality), as well as the possible general equilibrium effects that occur when, for example, changing the composition of a characteristic would also affect its returns. In that sense, we look at direct or short-run effects of changes in the composition of exogenous characteristics before workers react to them changing their behaviour, ignoring that these could trigger more structural changes in their returns (and vice versa). For example, it is possible that there are more skilled workers in the labour market, and, at the same time, the education premium is falling as a result. The decomposition exercise will separate the effect on inequality of the increase in education (keeping constant the education premium) from the effect on inequality of the fall in the skill premium (keeping constant the share of skilled workers) as if they were independent from each other.

Implementation

To undertake this decomposition exercise, we follow the methodology developed by Firpo et al. (2007, 2009), also extensively described in Fortin et al. (2011) and Firpo et al. (2018), that extended the Oaxaca-Blinder decomposition method, originally applied to decompose an average wage differential, to changes in any statistic of interest (including percentiles and inequality measures).

The main idea is to break the total change in a statistic v (such as the Gini index or a quantile) over time, $\Delta_o^v = v\left(F_{y_1|t=1}\right) - v\left(F_{y_0|t=0}\right)$, into two main components, namely the composition (Δ_X^v) and the earnings structure (Δ_S^v) effects.

For that, we compare the initial ($F_{y_0|t=0}$) and final ($F_{y_1|t=1}$) distributions observed over a period of time with a counterfactual or hypothetical distribution in which either only the characteristics or only the returns change, but not both. In the analysis of this book, we take the counterfactual in which characteristics are alike in the final distribution, but they are remunerated as in the initial distribution ($F_{y_0|t=1}$):

$$\Delta_o^v = v\left(F_{y_1|t=1}\right) - v\left(F_{y_0|t} = 0\right) = \left[v\left(F_{y_1|t=1}\right) - v\left(F_{y_0|t=1}\right)\right] + \left[v\left(F_{y_0|t=1}\right) - v\left(F_{y_0|t=0}\right)\right]$$

$$= \Delta_S^v + \Delta_X^v \qquad (6)$$

Therefore, the initial and counterfactual distributions both share the same characteristic returns and only differ from each other in the composition of the workforce (e.g. having more workers with higher education, female, in the formal sector, working in less routine occupations ...), allowing us to interpret the difference in a statistic (earnings at each percentile or the Gini index) estimated in these two distributions as being the result of a composition effect (change in the proportion of workers in each category, while keeping their remuneration by category of workers constant). On the other hand, the final distribution and the counterfactual one share the same composition of the workforce but differ in the way these are remunerated in the labour market, allowing us to interpret the difference as the change in earnings or in inequality produced by changes in the earnings structure; that is, how the labour market remunerates each category of workers (while keeping the composition constant over time).

This aggregate decomposition into composition and earnings structure effects is best done, under certain common assumptions, using a reweighting method approach, where the new weights can be estimated using a probability model (logit in our case). This means that the sample in the initial distribution is reweighted so that the distribution of characteristics is the same as in the final period. For that, the reweighted initial distribution will tend to increase the weight of workers with those characteristics that increased over time (such as having secondary or tertiary education), while keeping the earning returns workers get from those characteristics in the initial year. These reweighting factors are obtained from the probabilities of workers observed in the pooled sample of both years belonging to the final and initial distributions conditional on their characteristics, estimated using a logistic regression.

In a second stage, the two aggregate components are further subdivided into the contribution of the different factors. This is done using the statistical concept of the recentred influence function (RIF) of any statistic, which indicates by how much that statistic changes if we marginally increase the population with a certain earnings level. By running a regression of the RIF values on workers' characteristics, we estimate the expected change in each earnings percentile (or in overall inequality) after marginally increasing the proportion of workers with a given characteristic (that will depend on where in the earnings distribution these workers are). A similar counterfactual exercise as the one done to obtain the aggregate effects will allow the detailed effects to be obtained. In this case two Oaxaca-Blinder exercises are necessary, one that compares the initial distribution and the counterfactual, and another that compares the counterfactual and the final distributions. The first exercise will produce the detailed composition effect, while the second will produce the detailed earnings structure effect.[8]

References

Acemoglu, D., and D.H. Autor (2011). 'Skills, Tasks and Technologies: Implications for Employment and Earnings'. In O.C. Ashenfelter and D. Card (eds), *Handbook of Labor Economics*. Vol. 4, pp. 1043–171. Amsterdam: Elsevier. https://doi.org/10.1016/S0169-7218(11)02410-5

Arias, O.S., C. Sánchez-Páramo, M.E. Dávalos, I. Santos, E.R. Tiongson, C. Gruen, N. de Andrade Falcão, G. Saiovici, and C.A. Cancho (2014). 'Back to Work: Growing with Jobs in Eastern Europe and Central Asia'. Europe and Central Asia Reports. Washington, DC: The World Bank. https://doi.org/10.1596/978-0-8213-9910-1

Autor, D., and D. Dorn (2009). 'This Job is "Getting Old": Measuring Changes in Job Opportunities Using Occupational Age Structure'. *American Economic Review: Papers and Proceedings*, 99(2): 45–51. https://doi.org/10.1257/aer.99.2.45

Autor, D., and D. Dorn (2013). 'The Growth of Low-Skill Service Jobs and the Polarization of the US Labor Market'. *American Economic Review*, 103(5): 1553–97. https://doi.org/10.1257/2020aer.103.5.1553

Autor, D.H., F. Levy, and R. Murnane (2003). 'The Skill Content of Recent Technological Change: An Empirical Exploration'. *Quarterly Journal of Economics*, 118: 4. https://doi.org/10.1162/003355303322552801

de la Rica, S., L. Gortazar, and P. Lewandowski (2020). 'Job Tasks and Wages in Developed Countries: Evidence from PIAAC'. *Labour Economics*, 101845. https://doi.org/10.1016/j.labeco.2020.101845

---

[8] Additionally, from each exercise we obtain an error term, respectively, the reweighting and specification errors.

Firpo, S., N.M. Fortin, and T. Lemieux (2007). 'Decomposing Wage Distributions using Recentered Influence Function Regressions'. Unpublished manuscript, Vancouver: University of British Columbia.

Firpo, S., N.M. Fortin, and T. Lemieux (2009). 'Unconditional Quantile Regressions'. *Econometrica*, 77(3): 953–73. https://doi.org/10.3982/ECTA6822

Firpo, S., N.M. Fortin, and T. Lemieux (2011). 'Occupational Tasks and Changes in the Wage Structure'. IZA Discussion Paper 5542. Bonn: Institute of Labor Economics (IZA). https://doi.org/10.2139/ssrn.1778886

Fortin, N.M., T. Lemieux, and S. Firpo (2011). 'Decomposition Methods in Economics'. In O.C. Ashenfelter and D. Card (eds), *Handbook of Labor Economics*, pp. 1–102. Amsterdam: North Holland. https://doi.org/10.1016/S0169-7218(11)00407-2

Firpo, S., N.M. Fortin, and T. Lemieux (2018). 'Decomposing Wage Distributions Using Recentered Influence Function Regressions'. *Econometrics*, 6(2): 1–40. https://doi.org/10.3390/econometrics6020028

Goos, M., and A. Manning (2007). 'Lousy and Lovely Jobs: The Rising Polarization of Work in Britain'. *The Review of Economics and Statistics*, 89(1): 118–33. https://doi.org/10.1162/rest.89.1.118

Goos, M., A. Manning, and A. Salomons (2014). 'Explaining Job Polarization: Routine-Biased Technological Change and Offshoring'. *American Economic Review*, 104: 2509–26. https://doi.org/10.1257/aer.104.8.2509

Gradín, C., and S. Schotte (2020). 'Implications of the Changing Nature of Work for Employment and Inequality in Ghana'. WIDER Working Paper 119/2020. Helsinki: UNU-WIDER. https://doi.org/10.35188/UNU-WIDER/2020/876-4

Hardy, W., R. Keister, and P. Lewandowski (2018). 'Educational Upgrading, Structural Change and the Task Composition of Jobs in Europe'. *Economics of Transition*, 26(2): 201–31. https://doi.org/10.1111/ecot.12145

Lewandowski, P., A. Park, and S. Schotte (2020). 'The Global Distribution of Routine and Non-Routine Work'. WIDER Working Paper 75/2020. Helsinki: UNU-WIDER. https://doi.org/10.35188/UNU-WIDER/2020/832-0

Lewandowski, P., A. Park, W. Hardy, Y. Du, and S. Wu (2022). 'Technology, Skills, and Globalization: Explaining International Differences in Routine and Nonroutine Work Using Survey Data'. *The World Bank Economic Review*, 36(3): 687–708. https://doi.org/10.1093/wber/lhac005

Lo Bello, S., M.L. Sanchez Puerta, and H.J. Winkler (2019). 'From Ghana to America: The Skill Content of Jobs and Economic Development'. Policy Research Working Paper 8758. Washington, DC: The World Bank. https://doi.org/10.1596/31354

Marcolin, L., S. Miroudot, and M. Squicciarini (2019). 'To Be (Routine) or not to Be (Routine), that Is the Question: A Cross-Country Task-Based Answer'. *Industrial and Corporate Change*, 28(3): 477–501. https://doi.org/10.1093/icc/dty020

RIGVC UIBE (2016). *UIBE GVC Index*. Beijing: Research Institute for Global Value Chains, University of International Business and Economics.

Sebastián, R. (2018). 'Explaining Job Polarisation in Spain from a Task Perspective'. *SERIEs*, 9: 215–48. https://doi.org/10.1007/s13209-018-0177-1

Shorrocks, A.F. (2013). 'Decomposition Procedures for Distributional Analysis: A Unified Framework Based on the Shapley Value'. *Journal of Economic Inequality*, 11(1): 99–126. https://doi.org/10.1007/s10888-011-9214-z

Wang, Z., S. Wei, X. Yu, and K. Zhu (2017). 'Measures of Participation in Global Value Chains and Global Business Cycles'. NBER Working Paper 23222. Cambridge, MA: National Bureau of Economic Research. https://doi.org/10.3386/w23222

World Bank (2020). *World Development Indicators*. Washington, DC: The World Bank. Available from https://databank.worldbank.org/source/world-development-indicators (accessed 25 June 2019).

PART II
CROSS-COUNTRY ANALYSIS

3

Global Divergence in the De-routinization of Jobs

Piotr Lewandowski, Albert Park, and Simone Schotte

3.1 Introduction

The shift from routine-intensive jobs to non-routine work has been a critical feature of twenty-first-century labour markets. It has been driven by technological progress and globalization and has contributed to rising wage polarization in many countries (Autor et al. 2003; Goos et al. 2014). Over the past decade, a growing body of research has studied the evolution of the task content of jobs. It investigated patterns over time and across countries, the relative importance of demand and supply factors, and the consequences of these processes for wage inequality (Acemoglu and Autor 2011; Firpo et al. 2011; Autor 2013).

Theory suggests that employers endogenously assign tasks based on the demand and supply of different skills given available technologies (Acemoglu and Autor 2011; Autor and Handel 2013). As a consequence, workers in a specific occupation in low- and middle-income countries may perform different tasks than workers in comparable occupations in high-income countries. With globalization, poorer countries may specialize in routine tasks, and richer countries may specialize in non-routine tasks (Grossman and Rossi-Hansberg 2008). In previous research, the task content of jobs, namely the role of routine vs non-routine and cognitive vs manual tasks, has been typically measured at the occupation level. However, most countries have not systematically collected information on the task content of occupations. Hence, the majority of past studies use the US Occupation Information Network (O*NET) occupational data to analyse task demand around the world (Arias et al. 2014; Fonseca et al. 2018; Hardy et al. 2018; Reijnders and de Vries 2018) or to assess the suitability of jobs to working from home (Dingel and Neiman 2020). This approach requires assuming that the task content of each occupation everywhere in the world is the same as in the US. It may be problematic given the large cross-country differences in technology, economic structures, and labour force skills (Hsieh and Klenow 2010; Niebel 2018; Eden and Gaggl 2020).

Corroborating this concern, Lewandowski et al. (2022) presented evidence of substantial differences in the task content of work within occupations across

Piotr Lewandowski, Albert Park and Simone Schotte, *Global Divergence in the De-routinization of Jobs.* In: *Tasks, Skills, and Institutions.* Edited by Carlos Gradín, Piotr Lewandowski, Simone Schotte, and Kunal Sen, Oxford University Press.
© UNU WIDER (2023). DOI: 10.1093/oso/9780192872241.003.0003

countries. They found that sector and country differences in technology use, workers' skills, and globalization (measured by foreign value-added (FVA) share) are all related to cross-country differences in the task content of jobs, both across and within particular occupations. Lo Bello et al. (2019) also showed that jobs in low- and middle-income countries are more routine intensive than in high-income countries. Even among developed countries, there are differences in the task content of occupations and wage premia associated with performing less routine-intensive tasks (de la Rica et al. 2020). Lewandowski et al. (2022) relied on adult skill use surveys collected in 47 countries, including low-, middle-, and high-income economies. However, such data are (as yet) unavailable for several large emerging economies such as Argentina, Brazil, Bangladesh, India, Nigeria, and South Africa. As a result, they are insufficient to quantify the global allocation of routine and non-routine work fully, nor to test whether de-routinization and wage polarization have occurred in low- and middle-income countries to an extent comparable with developed economies.

In this chapter, we relax the assumption that occupations are identical worldwide. We study the global evolution and distribution of routine and non-routine work from 2000 to 2017, making two main contributions. First, building upon earlier work (Lewandowski et al. 2022), we develop a regression-based methodology to predict the country-specific task content by occupational group in many countries where no task survey data are yet available. This enables a more accurate picture of work in low- and middle-income countries than assuming that occupational tasks are identical worldwide. Our second contribution is to establish stylized facts on the patterns and evolution of the global distribution of routine and non-routine work since the early 2000s. To this end, we merge country-specific occupational task measures with employment structure data for 87 countries from 2000 to 2017. Our country sample includes 25 low- or lower-middle-income countries, 24 upper-middle-income countries, and 38 high-income countries. In 2017, the countries in our sample jointly accounted for over 2.5 billion workers, equivalent to approximately 75 per cent of global employment. We analyse the changing distribution of tasks over time, both by holding country–occupation routine-task intensity (RTI) fixed over time and by allowing the task content of occupations to evolve. Using country-specific task measures, we show that in countries with lower economic and technological development levels, workers tend to perform more routine-intensive tasks compared to those in more advanced countries, even within the same occupations. These cross-country within-occupation gaps are sizeable and are mainly attributable to differences in technology.

Three key stylized facts emerge. First, accounting for cross-country differences in RTI, the de-routinization of work has occurred much more slowly in low- and middle-income countries compared to high-income countries. In contrast, the assumption that occupations are identical worldwide leads to an improbable result that the reallocation of labour away from routine and towards non-routine work has occurred at a similar pace in all country groups.

Second, we find that the gap in average RTI between low- and middle-income countries, on the one hand, and high-income countries, on the other, is much larger than suggested using O*NET. Moreover, this gap has widened over time, so the nature of work in poorer countries has not converged to that in high-income countries, despite their increasing integration into global value chains and rising technology levels. We attribute this pattern to between-occupation effects—poorer countries exhibit higher employment shares of routine-intensive occupations— and within-occupation effects—in poorer countries, occupations require more routine tasks.

Third, we show that the assumption that occupations are identical world-wide leads to the finding that, between the early 2000s and the middle 2010s, low- and middle-income countries became the dominant supplier of non-routine work. In contrast, accounting for cross-country within-occupation differences in tasks reveals that high-income countries have remained the dominant provider of non-routine work, while routine work has remained concentrated in low- and middle-income countries. Overall, our findings corroborate theories of allocation of tasks that suggest that a higher level of technology and a more sophisticated role in global value chains is associated with less routine intensive work. They also show that ignoring this property and assuming that occupations are identical around the world would underestimate the role of routine work in low- and middle-income countries.

The remainder of the chapter is structured as follows. Section 3.2 introduces the data and methodology. Section 3.3 presents stylized facts regarding the global evolution and distribution of task content of jobs. Section 3.4 concludes.

3.2 Data and methodology

3.2.1 Measuring the task content of jobs using survey data

Economists have studied the changes in the task content of jobs—within and between occupations—as a key method to track changes in the nature of work attributed to technological progress and globalization, particularly offshoring (Autor et al. 2003; Spitz-Oener 2006). Most previous research studying the evolution of the task content of jobs focuses on developed countries (Goos et al. 2014; Hardy et al. 2018) or middle-income countries (Arias et al. 2014; Reijnders and de Vries 2018). That research assumed that occupational task demands are identical across countries and can be quantified using the task content measures proposed by Autor et al. (2003) and Acemoglu and Autor (2011) based on the US O*NET data.

The increasing availability of surveys collecting information on tasks performed by individual workers has facilitated more detailed studies of occupational task demand (Arntz et al. 2017). Using these new data, researchers developed several approaches to measure country-specific, worker-level job tasks (Lo Bello et al. 2019; de la Rica et al. 2020; Caunedo et al. 2021; Lewandowski et al. 2022). In particular, Lewandowski et al. (2022) developed survey-based, harmonized task measures of non-routine cognitive analytical, non-routine cognitive interpersonal, routine cognitive, and manual tasks. These measures were consistent with the widely used Acemoglu and Autor (2011) measures based on the O*NET data (definitions shown in Table 2.2 in Chapter 2). They also combined them into a composite measure of RTI, which increases with the importance of routine work content and decreases with the importance of non-routine content. Previous studies on high-income countries (Autor and Dorn 2013; Goos et al. 2014) often used RTI. It captures the differences in the task demand across occupations, and quantifies the potential substitutability of human work in various jobs with routine-replacing technologies based on algorithms.

Applying the methodology proposed by Lewandowski et al. (2022), we calculate country-specific RTI using worker-level data from three large-scale surveys available for 47 countries (Table 3.1):

- the OECD's Programme for the International Assessment of Adult Competencies (PIAAC), covering high- or middle-income countries;
- the World Bank's Skills toward Employment and Productivity (STEP) surveys, conducted in the middle- and low-income countries;
- the China Urban Labor Survey (CULS), collected by the Institute of Population and Labor Economics of the Chinese Academy of Social Science; CULS included a module based on STEP.

For each country, we calculate the average RTI by 1- and 2-digit occupations according to the International Standard Classification of Occupations (ISCO-08) classification. We also use the 2017 release of O*NET and Acemoglu and Autor's (2011) methodology to define task content and RTI values under the assumption that occupations are identical worldwide. We standardize all task variables, including the RTI, using relevant means and standard deviations in the US. The final measures refer to the US average and standard deviations in 2000.[1]

In the US, the correlation between the survey-based RTI and the O*NET RTI is very high, so the survey measure successfully captures the variation in the routine intensity of work across occupations (Lewandowski et al. 2022). First, the

---

[1] Following Acemoglu and Autor (2011), we use survey weights (at the 3-digit ISCO level) from the US 2000 census for the standardization of O*NET tasks. However, to ensure consistency with the ILOSTAT data we use in our cross-country study, we adjusted the census weights (at the 1-digit level) to match the occupational structure in the ILOSTAT data for the US in 2000.

Table 3.1 Allocation of countries to income groups

Low- and lower middle-income countries	Upper middle-income countries	Bottom high-income countries	Top high-income countries
Covered by survey data			
Armenia	China	Chile	Austria
Bolivia	Ecuador	Czechia	Belgium
Cambodia	Kazakhstan	Cyprus*	Canada
Colombia*	Mexico	Estonia	Denmark
Georgia	Peru	Greece	Estonia
Ghana	Romania	Hungary	Finland
Indonesia	Turkey	Italy	France
Kenya		Lithuania	Germany
Laos		Poland	Ireland
Macedonia*		Russia	Israel
		Slovenia	Japan
		South Korea	Netherlands
		Spain	New Zealand
			Norway
			Singapore
			Sweden
			United Kingdom
			United States
Covered by model-based predictions			
Bangladesh	Albania	Croatia	Australia
Egypt, Arab Rep.	Argentina	Latvia	Hong Kong SAR,
El Salvador	Azerbaijan	Portugal	China
Guatemala	Belarus	Slovakia	Luxembourg
Honduras	Botswana	Uruguay	Switzerland
India	Bulgaria		
Kyrgyz Republic	Brazil		
Mongolia	Dominican		
Morocco	Republic		
Nigeria	Iran, Islamic Rep.		
Pakistan	Jamaica		
Paraguay	Malaysia		
Philippines	Mauritius		
Sri Lanka	Namibia		
Vietnam	South Africa		
Zambia	Thailand		
	Tunisia		
	Venezuela		
Share in total employment of countries in a given group (in %)			
62	85	98	93

Note: The allocation of countries to low- and lower middle-, upper middle-, and high-income groups follows the World Bank Analytical Classification. The additional split of high-income countries to the bottom and top subgroups follows Lewandowski et al. (2022). Data from countries marked with * are used only in regressions shown in Table 3.2 and Figure 3.1, as the data on occupational structure in these countries between 2000–2017 are not available for them.
Source: Authors' elaboration based on World Bank data.

survey questions on the repetitive and structured component of work—used to calculate the routine cognitive measure—successfully capture the general routine aspect of work. Second, the survey questions on solving problems at work, programming, or supervising others—used to create the non-routine cognitive measures—successfully capture this aspect of work. Both approaches—survey and O*NET—identify plant and machine operators and assemblers (ISCO 8), and elementary occupations (ISCO 9) as the most routine-intensive occupations, followed by craft and related trades workers (ISCO 7)—see Lewandowski et al. (2022). They also show that managers (ISCO 1) and professionals (ISCO 2) are the least routine-intensive occupations, followed by technicians (ISCO 3). Clerical workers (ISCO 4) and sales and services workers (ISCO 5) are in the middle of the RTI distribution: O*NET suggests that clerical jobs are slightly more routine-intensive than sales and service jobs. In contrast, the survey-based measure finds the opposite.

Achieving the distribution of the survey RTI across occupations in the US that is consistent with the distribution of O*NET RTI in the US ensures that the concept of the routine intensity of work as measured with survey data is in line with the idea used in the literature on developed countries (Acemoglu and Autor 2011; Autor and Handel 2013). However, the critical difference between the O*NET and the survey-based measures is that the latter allows measuring differences in occupational task demand across countries.

3.2.2 Predicting the country-specific task content of jobs

To predict the task content of occupations in countries with no available survey data on tasks, we estimate a set of ordinary least squares (OLS) regressions that relate the *RTI* of occupation j in country c to four key factors defined for each country: (1) development level, measured by the gross domestic product (*GDP*) per capita (in purchasing power parity, natural logarithm); (2) technology use (*T*), approximated by the number of internet users per 100 inhabitants; (3) globalization (*G*), quantified by foreign value-added share of domestic output (FVA share); and (4) supply of skills (*S*), measured by the average years of schooling. We add fixed effects, γ_{kj}, for 2-digit ISCO sub-occupations k that belong to a given 1-digit occupation j. Formally:

$$RTI_{kjc} = \beta_{j0} + \beta_{j1}\,GDP_c + \beta_{j2}T_c + \beta_{j3}G_c + \beta_{j4}S_c + \gamma_{kj} + \varepsilon_{kjc}. \qquad (1)$$

The task content of occupations can change over time depending on the country's overall endowments (Autor et al. 2003; Spitz-Oener 2006) and will likely not be reactive to short-term business cycle fluctuations. Therefore, to fit the regression model, we take averages of the explanatory variables for 2011–16 since most STEP/PIAAC/CULS survey data come from this period. We use globalization variables from 2011 as more recent data are not available.[2]

For each occupation, we select the model that fits the data best from a set of seven alternatives that differ in explanatory variables. We use leave-one-out cross-validation, and select models that exhibit the lowest root mean square errors, the lowest mean absolute errors, and (with two exceptions) the highest pseudo-R^2.[3] We prioritize specifications consistent with the findings of worker-level regressions in Lewandowski et al. (2022). They found that technology and skills are significant correlates of workers' routine intensity of tasks in all occupations. Globalization is particularly relevant for the content of work in occupations predominantly employed in tradable sectors, such as plant and machine operators. For agricultural workers (ISCO 6), we condition RTI on development level and average years of schooling. The estimation results are reported in Table 3.2.

Our regression results show that higher technology use is associated with lower RTI in all non-farming occupations (Table 3.2). A higher supply of skills and a higher level of development partly mediate this effect. In occupations typical for tradable sectors (ISCO 7-9), workers in countries more specialized in GVCs perform more routine-intensive tasks, especially in less developed countries. We also find a negative relationship between development level and the RTI of agricultural workers (ISCO 6).

Next, we use the estimated coefficients to predict the RTI by 1- and 2-digit occupations for each country, conditional on the level of economic development, skill supply, technology endowment, and participation in GVCs.

The predicted, country-specific values of task content show substantial cross-country differences in RTI for specific occupations, matching the patterns observed in the survey data (Lewandowski et al. 2022).[4] Work in particular occupations is generally more routine-intensive in less developed countries—a negative relationship exists between development level and occupational RTI (Figure 3.1). It is most pronounced in high-skilled occupations (ISCO 1—managers, ISCO 2—professionals, ISCO 3—technicians): skilled workers in richer countries perform less routine-intensive tasks than those in poorer countries. We attribute most of

[2] The data on FVA share come from the University of International Business and Economics (Beijing) Global Value Chains (UIBE-GVC) database. Other data come from the World Development Indicators database by the World Bank.
[3] Estimation results of all specifications as well as models at the 2-digit ISCO level are available upon request.
[4] The predicted values are close to the survey results for most countries covered by PIAAC/STEP/CULS but show a narrower range. Our predictions thus provide a conservative estimate of the within-occupation differences in RTI levels across countries.

Table 3.2 The estimated occupation-specific models of correlates of RTI

	Managers (ISCO 1)	Professionals (ISCO 2)	Technicians (ISCO 3)	Clerical workers (ISCO 4)	Sales and services workers (ISCO 5)	Agricultural workers (ISCO 6)	Crafts-men (ISCO 7)	Machine operators (ISCO 8)	Elementary occ. (ISCO 9)
GDP per capita (ln)	0.039 (0.074)	0.091 (0.056)	0.068 (0.063)	0.236*** (0.070)	0.105 (0.067)	−0.229*** (0.090)	0.266*** (0.072)	0.198** (0.090)	−0.044 (0.079)
FVA share (%)							1.276*** (0.359)	1.590*** (0.457)	0.621 (0.395)
FVA share × GDP per capita (ln)							−0.604 (0.577)	−0.949 (0.737)	0.783 (0.640)
Internet use (%)	−1.152*** (0.309)	−1.389*** (0.236)	−1.242*** (0.264)	−1.318*** (0.294)	−1.331*** (0.282)		−1.678*** (0.304)	−1.476*** (0.370)	−0.642* (0.332)
Average years of schooling	0.025 (0.021)	0.076*** (0.016)	0.073*** (0.018)	0.091*** (0.020)	0.064*** (0.019)	−0.035 (0.031)	0.064*** (0.020)	0.088*** (0.025)	0.075*** (0.022)
Fixed-effects 2-digit level	YES	YES	YES	YES	YES	NO	YES	YES	YES
Observations	164	246	205	164	164	44	200	112	227
Adjusted R^2	0.368	0.390	0.330	0.158	0.201	0.408	0.233	0.197	0.128

Note: *** $p<0.01$, ** $p<0.05$, * $p<0.1$. Robust standard errors in parentheses. Constant not shown.
Source: Authors' estimations based on PIAAC, STEP, CULS, World Bank, and UIBE-GVC data.

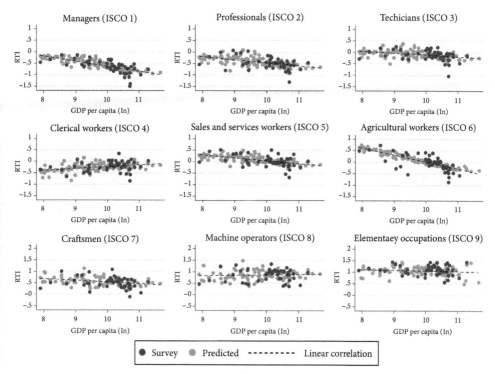

Figure 3.1 Predicted routine-task intensity levels by 1-digit occupations
Source: Authors' estimations based on PIAAC, STEP, CULS, World Bank, and UIBE-GVC data.

the cross-country variance in RTI in these occupations to differences in technology, as better access to technology in the more-developed countries is associated with a lower routine intensity of tasks performed by workers.

The relationship between GDP per capita and RTI is mixed for occupations typical for service sectors. Among sales and services workers (ISCO 5), those in more affluent countries do less routine-intensive work. Again, we attribute these differences mainly to lower technology use in less-developed countries. Among clerical workers (ISCO 4), there is no clear-cut relationship between the development level and RTI. However, clerical workers in the poorest countries in our sample perform less routine-intensive tasks, which may be associated with a lower supply of skills in these countries. Indeed, clerical workers are the only occupational group for which the cross-country differences in skill supply make the largest contribution to international differences in RTI.

There is no clear-cut relationship between development level and RTI among workers in occupations typical for manufacturing and other tradable sectors (ISCO 8—plant and machine operators, ISCO 7—craft and related trades workers). However, compared to other occupations, we find a larger dispersion of RTI among countries at a similar development level (Figure 3.1), related to differences in countries' participation in global value chains. Globalization plays the most crucial role for these occupations in predicting cross-country task differences. Routine jobs are easier to offshore, so poorer countries may specialize in them (Grossman and Rossi-Hansberg 2008). Indeed, a higher FVA share in domestic production is associated with a higher RTI among less-developed countries and a lower RTI among more-developed countries. Among workers in elementary occupations (ISCO 9), which are more often demanded in non-tradable sectors, the dispersion of RTI at a given development level is less pronounced (Figure 3.1). Differences in skills play a much greater role, while differences in GVC specialization play a much smaller role than among plant and machine operators.

3.2.3 Investigating the evolution of task content over time across country groups

Having predicted the occupation-specific RTI in various countries, we investigate the evolution of task content over time. We merge the country-specific and O*NET 2017 RTI values with ILOSTAT data on employment structures from 2000 to 2017. Our sample includes 87 countries (Table 3.1) comprising approximately 2.5 billion workers in 2015–17, corresponding to 75 per cent of global employment.[5]

Of the countries covered by the ILOSTAT data, we include those where data for all explanatory variables in equation (1) are available.[6] To avoid extrapolating beyond the range used to build the model, we omit nine economies with a GDP per capita below Kenya ($2,687 purchasing power parity (PPP), on average, between 2011 and 2016), the poorest country in the PIAAC/STEP/CULS sample. The starting point is 2000, or the earliest available employment data. The end point is 2017, or the most recent available data. We omit countries with no data available before 2005 or from 2014 on.

Based on the World Bank classifications in 2010–11, we define four income groups: low- and lower-middle-income countries, LIC-LMICs (25 countries), upper-middle-income countries, UMICs (24), bottom high-income countries,

---

[5] Due to data availability, our sample covers a lower share of total employment in low- and lower-middle income countries (62 per cent, see Table 3.1) and in upper-middle income countries (85 per cent) than in high-income countries (96 per cent). As a result, our sample is likely to overstate the extent of non-routine work globally.

[6] We omit seven oil exporting countries, and five countries classified as tax havens (according to Financial Secrecy Index for 2011).

bottom-HICs (17), and top high-income countries, top-HICs (21, Table 3.1). The countries in each income group remain fixed across years for comparability purposes.

We calculate the average RTI in a given country and year as a weighted average of the country-specific RTI across occupations, using occupation employment shares as weights.[7] For countries covered by the survey data, we use occupation-specific average RTIs calculated as described in Section 3.2.1. For the remaining countries, we use values predicted in line with the framework presented in Section 3.2.2. For skilled agricultural, forestry, and fishery workers (ISCO 6), we use predicted RTI values at the 1-digit level for all countries because the sample sizes in ISCO 6 are small in some countries covered by STEP, which is an urban survey.

First, we hold the occupational RTI constant over time so that shifts in the employment structure are the only drivers of change. Second, we allow for intertemporal changes in occupational task content. We predict the country- and occupation-specific RTIs using averages of explanatory variables across 2001–05, except for the globalization variable, which is available only for 2004.[8] For O*NET, we use the 2003 dataset. We then apply a weighted average. From 2000–02, we use the RTI predicted for 2001–05 (O*NET 2003); for any year t in 2003–17, we assign a weight $\frac{2017-t}{14}$ to the RTI predicted for 2001–05 (O*NET 2003), and a weight $\frac{t-2003}{14}$ to the RTI predicted for 2011–16 (O*NET 2017). As these time-variant estimates require assuming that the estimated cross-country models (2) hold over time, we treat these as complementary to our baseline results.

We apply a shift-share decomposition to analyse to what extent the cross-country differences in average RTI values can be attributed to differences in occupational structures, and to what extent to differences in occupation-specific RTI values. We decompose the difference between the average RTI in a given country group c, RTI_c, and the average in top high-income countries, RTI, into the

---

[7] Whenever possible, we use data at the 2-digit occupation level. However, we use 1-digit level data if the employment structure at the 2-digit level is not available in the survey data or in the ILOSTAT data, or if the share of workers unclassified at the 2-digit occupation level exceeds 5 per cent in a given year. If the share of workers unclassified at the 1-digit occupation level exceeds 5 per cent, we omit such year. We use a linear interpolation to fill other gaps in the ILOSTAT data. We use either ISCO-08 or ISCO-88, depending on the classification available in the ILOSTAT data for a given year and country. In order to convert all RTI measures to the ISCO-88 classification, we use the crosswalk prepared for the European Working Conditions Survey data.

[8] We have to predict the past levels of RTI as the survey data on the task content of jobs has so far been collected only once per country so direct measurement of changes in occupational RTI is not possible. An additional assumption behind our prediction is the independence of right-hand side variables, in particular technology adoption and participation in global value chains. There is some evidence for developing countries that participation in global value chains facilitates the adoption of advanced technologies, like Industry 4.0 (Delera et al. 2022). However, we are focused on basic ICT technologies. Nevertheless, our estimates of country-specific changes in occupational RTI can be interpreted as lower-bound estimates.

between-occupation, BO_c, within-occupation, WO_c, and interaction, INT_c, terms. Formally:

$$RTI_c - RTI = \sum_{j \in ISCO} \alpha_{j,c} rti_{j,c} - \sum_{j \in ISCO} \alpha_j rti_j = BO_c + WO_c + INT_c \quad (2)$$

$$BO_c = \sum_{j \in ISCO} rti_j \left(\alpha_{j,c} - \alpha_j \right) \quad (3)$$

$$WO_c = \sum_{j \in ISCO} \alpha_j \left(rti_{j,c} - rti_j \right) \quad (4)$$

$$INT_c = \sum_{j \in ISCO} \left(\alpha_{j,c} - \alpha_j \right) \left(rti_{j,c} - rti_j \right) \quad (5)$$

whereby:

- $rti_{j,c}$ and rti_j are the average values of RTI for workers in occupation j in country group c, and top high-income countries, respectively;
- $\alpha_{j,c}$ and α_j are the shares of workers in occupation j in total employment in country group c, and top high-income countries, respectively; and
- ISCO is the set of 1-digit ISCO-08 occupations.

Finally, we use the task measures merged with employment data to quantify the global allocation of routine and non-routine work. To this aim, we calculate the global distribution of RTI (weighted by total employment across all countries and occupations in our sample) at the end of our study period.[9] We define the threshold for the non-routine jobs as the 25th percentile of that distribution and classify all jobs with the RTI value below it as non-routine. We define the threshold for the routine jobs as the 75th percentile of that distribution and classify all jobs with the RTI value above it as routine. We apply the same thresholds at the beginning and end of our study period. This ensures that the definitions of routine and non-routine jobs are consistent over time.

Next, we calculate the shares of particular country groups in total, routine, and non-routine employment in each period. We conduct this analysis using our country-specific occupational task and O*NET task measures. This allows us to quantify how much the role of non-routine tasks in low- and middle-income countries is overestimated under the assumption that occupations are identical worldwide. The O*NET task content data are provided as point estimates and have been presented as such in previous research (Autor et al. 2003; Acemoglu and Autor 2011). For comparability, we also focus on the point estimates of country-specific RTI.

---

[9] As a starting point, we use the 2000 employment data, and for countries lacking 2000 data, we use the earliest available data. The end point is 2017, and for countries lacking 2017 employment data, we use the most recent available data. If a country has no data available before 2005, or from 2014 on, we do not include it in this analysis.

3.3 Results

3.3.1 The de-routinization of jobs has occurred much more slowly in LICs and MICs than in HICs

Since 2000, occupational structures around the world have evolved away from routine-intensive occupations and towards non-routine-intensive occupations. However, accounting for cross-country differences in the task content of occupations shows that the de-routinization occurred more slowly than would have been apparent under the assumption that occupations are identical worldwide. In particular, de-routinization in LICs and MICs occurred visibly more slowly than in HICs.

Using the country-specific measures and holding the occupational RTI values constant over time (to focus on changes in task content attributable to shifts in occupational structures), we find evidence of diverging trends (Figure 3.2a). In particular, in the group of LIC-LMICs, the average RTI has barely declined, while in the HICs, it has declined steeply. When we allow for changes in the task content of occupations over time, the decline in RTI between 2000–17 appears stronger. However, using the country-specific task measures, the decrease in RTI in LIC-LMICs is still much slower than for other country groups (Figure 3.2b).

In contrast, if one assumes that occupations are identical around the world and uses the O*NET-based task measures, the routine intensity of work appears much lower on average (0.27 in 2017 compared to 0.43 using country-specific task measures). Moreover, the trends in labour reallocation away from routine and toward non-routine tasks seem to be parallel across all country groups (Figure 3.2a). Assuming that occupations are identical worldwide leads to a substantial overestimation of the role of non-routine tasks in less-developed countries and their growth over time.

3.3.2 Gaps in the routine-task intensity of jobs between LICs/MICs and HICs have increased over time

The unequal trends in the de-routinization of jobs have created widening gaps in the task content of work in LICs and MICs as compared to HICs.

According to the country-specific measures (and holding the occupational RTI values constant over time), the differences between top-HICs and less-developed countries have increased by about 10 per cent of the initial gap in both LIC-LMICs and UMICs (Figure 3.3a). But in bottom HICs, the distance to the top HICs has barely changed. The shift-share decomposition analysis shows that a substantial share of these gaps (on average, 40 per cent for both LIC-LMICs and UMICs) is attributable to differences in the country-specific task content of comparable

(a)   Constant occupational task
       content, by country groups

(b)   Changing occupational task
       content, by country groups

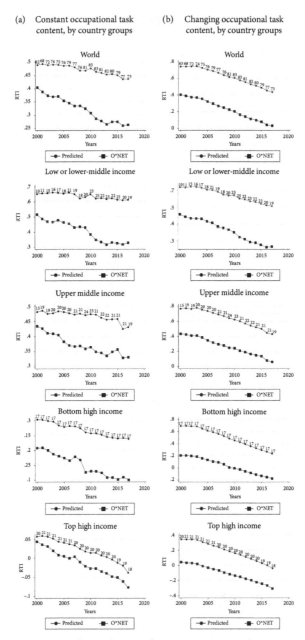

Figure 3.2 The evolution of average routine-task intensity according to country-specific and O*NET measures

Note: Labels indicate the number of countries per group with data available in a given year.

Source: Authors' estimations based on PIAAC, STEP, CULS, O*NET, World Bank, UIBE-GVC, and ILOSTAT data.

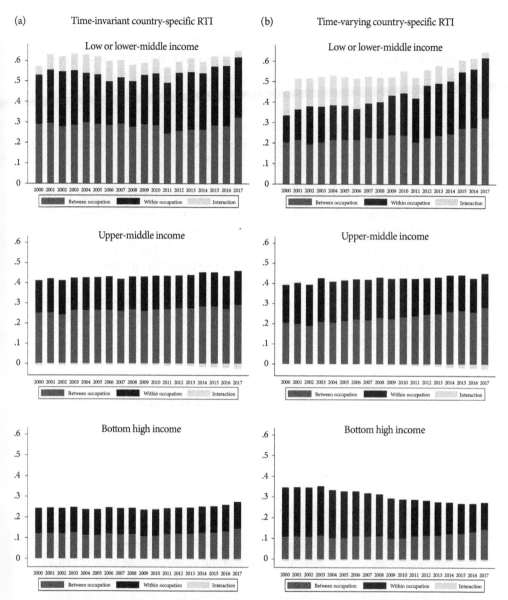

Figure 3.3 The shift-share decomposition of differences in the average routine-task intensity between particular country groups and the top-HICs, according to the time-invariant and time-varying country-specific RTI

Source: Authors' estimations based on PIAAC, STEP, CULS, World Bank, UIBE-GVC, and ILOSTAT data.

occupations (the within-occupation effect, Figure 3.3a). In our regression-based approach, we attribute most of these within-occupation differences to lower technology use in less developed countries. For LIC-LMICs, part of the gap in RTI with the top-HICs (11 per cent on average) is attributable to the interaction effect, which means that occupations that are more routine intensive than in top-HICs also have higher employment shares. This finding aligns with theories of trade and offshoring that imply that poorer countries with a less-productive labour force might specialize in more routine-intensive activities (Grossman and Rossi-Hansberg 2008; Reijnders and de Vries 2018).

Accounting for task content changes within occupations over time, we find that the gap in average RTI between LIC-LMICs and top-HICs widens even more (by 40 per cent of the initial gap, Figure 3.3b). The within-occupation effect has contributed substantially to this widening, suggesting that de-routinization within identical occupations has been slower in poorer countries. In bottom-HICs, the gaps to top-HICs have narrowed as occupational RTI in these countries has converged (Figure 3.3b). In contrast, assuming that occupations are identical worldwide leads to the conclusion that the gaps in RTI between country groups have remained virtually unchanged as the gaps are entirely due to differences in occupational structures.

3.3.3 HICs remain the dominant suppliers of non-routine work, while LICs and MICs remain the dominant suppliers of routine work

Accounting for cross-country differences in the task content of occupations, we find that the global allocation of routine and non-routine work has been much more stable than it would appear if occupations were identical worldwide.

According to the country-specific measures, non-routine workers remain concentrated in HICs, while routine workers remain concentrated in LICs and MICs (Figure 3.4). In 2017, 53 per cent of non-routine workers were either in the bottom or top HICs. However, the share of these countries in total employment in our sample was 24 per cent. In 2000, the concentration of non-routine work in HICs was even stronger (60 per cent). Although the share of LICs' and MICs' workers in global non-routine employment increased, they remained a minority. Using O*NET, that is, assuming that high-skilled occupations such as managers and professionals in LICs and MICs involve as many non-routine tasks as in HICs, implies that by 2017 LICs and MICs became the leading suppliers of non-routine work (Figure 3.4).

At the same time, LICs and MICs have consistently been the dominant suppliers of routine work: according to the country-specific measures, their share of routine work has remained stable at almost 90 per cent. According to the O*NET

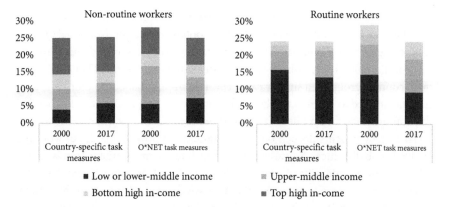

Figure 3.4 The distribution of routine and non-routine workers across country groups according to country-specific and O*NET measures, expressed as shares in global employment in 2000 and 2017 (in %)

Note: For each country, we use data from 2000, or the earliest available, and 2017, or the most recent available.
Source: Authors' estimations based on PIAAC, STEP, CULS, O*NET, World Bank, UIBE-GVC, and ILOSTAT data.

measures, the LICs' and MICs' share in global pool routine work was noticeably lower (80 per cent).

3.4 Conclusions

In this chapter, we have developed a methodology to predict the country-specific task content of occupations in a wide range of countries at all development levels. We have combined these measures with employment data in 87 countries representing more than 2.5 billion workers, or 75 per cent of global employment before the COVID-19 pandemic. We have shown that occupations in low- and middle-income countries are more routine intensive than in high-income countries, especially in high-skilled occupations (ISCO 1–3). These international differences in the RTI of occupations are mainly attributable to lower technology use in less-developed countries.

On this basis, we have established three new stylized facts about the evolution of occupational task content in countries at different stages of development, spanning the period 2000–17. First, the gross reallocation of labour away from routine work and toward non-routine work has occurred much more slowly in LICs and MICs than in HICs. Second, as a consequence, the gap between these country groups in work content, as measured with routine-task intensity, has widened. Finally, HICs have remained the dominant supplier of non-routine work, while LICs and MICs have remained the dominant supplier of routine work.

These stylized facts derived using our country-specific estimates of occupational task content contrast with the findings obtained using conventional O*NET task measures that assume that the task content of occupations is identical around the world. Analysis based on the latter has suggested that average RTI has declined in all country groups at a similar pace. The assumption that occupations are identical has also led to an implausible conclusion that by 2017 LICs and MICs became the dominant global supplier of non-routine work.

These new insights deepen our understanding of how the nature of work has evolved globally since the early 2000s. The finding of divergent trends in the relative routine intensity of work in developed and developing countries has important policy implications. First, the cross-country differences in the content of work are much larger than would be implied by cross-country differences in the supply of skills. Investment in skills in developing and emerging countries are most likely necessary for the convergence of work content and productivity to high-income countries (World Bank 2019). However, they are unlikely to be sufficient, considering that technology use and participation in global value chains are key factors behind differences in the task content of work. Second, assuming that occupations are identical worldwide may lead to an overestimation of the role of routine-replacing technological change, embodied in ICT and automation technologies, in explaining the evolution of wage inequality in low- or middle-income countries.

References

Acemoglu, D., and D.H. Autor (2011). 'Skills, Tasks and Technologies: Implications for Employment and Earnings'. In: O. Ashenfelter and D. Card (eds), *Handbook of Labor Economics*. Amsterdam: Elsevier, pp. 1043–1171. https://doi.org/10.1016/S0169-7218(11)02410-5

Arias, O.S., C. Sánchez-Páramo, M.E. Dávalos, I. Santos, E.R. Tiongson, C. Gruen, N. de Andrade Falcão, G. Saiovici, and C.A. Cancho (2014). Back to Work: Growing with Jobs in Europe and Central Asia | Europe and Central Asia Reports. https://doi.org/10.1596/978-0-8213-9910-1

Arntz, M., T. Gregory, and U. Zierahn (2017). 'Revisiting the Risk of Automation'. *Economics Letters*, 159: 157–60. https://doi.org/10.1016/j.econlet.2017.07.001

Autor, D.H. (2013). 'The "Task Approach" to Labor Markets: An Overview'. *Journal of Labour Market Research*, 46: 185–99. https://doi.org/10.1007/s12651-013-0128-z

Autor, D.H., and D. Dorn (2013). 'The Growth of Low-Skill Service Jobs and the Polarization of the US Labor Market'. *American Economic Review*, 103: 1553–97. https://doi.org/10.1257/aer.103.5.1553

Autor, D.H., and M.J. Handel (2013). 'Putting Tasks to the Test: Human Capital, Job Tasks, and Wages'. *Journal of Labor Economics*, 31: 59–96.

Autor, D.H., F. Levy, and R.J. Murnane (2003). 'The Skill Content of Recent Technological Change: An Empirical Exploration'. *Quarterly Journal of Economics*, 118: 1279–333. https://doi.org/10.1162/003355303322552801

Caunedo, J., E. Keller and Y. Shin (2021). Technology and the Task Content of Jobs across the Development Spectrum (No. w28681). National Bureau of Economic Research. https://doi.org/10.3386/w28681

de la Rica, S., L. Gortazar, and P. Lewandowski (2020). 'Job Tasks and Wages in Developed Countries: Evidence from PIAAC'. Labour Economics, 65: 101845. https://doi.org/10.1016/j.labeco.2020.101845

Delera, M., C. Pietrobelli, E. Calza, and A. Lavopa (2022). 'Does Value Chain Participation Facilitate the Adoption of Industry 4.0 Technologies in Developing Countries?' World Development, 152: 105788. https://doi.org/10.1016/j.worlddev.2021.105788

Dingel, J.I. and B. Neiman (2020). 'How Many Jobs Can Be Done at Home?' Journal of Public Economics, 189: 104235. https://doi.org/10.1016/j.jpubeco.2020.104235

Eden, M., and P. Gaggl (2020). 'Do Poor Countries Really Need More IT?' World Bank Economic Review, 34: 48–62. https://doi.org/10.1093/wber/lhy022

Firpo, S., N.M. Fortin, and T. Lemieux (2011). Occupational Tasks and Changes in the Wage Structure (No. 5542), IZA Discussion Papers. Institute of Labor Economics (IZA).

Fonseca, T., F. Lima, and S.C. Pereira (2018). 'Job Polarization, Technological Change and Routinization: Evidence for Portugal'. Labour Economics, 51: 317–39. https://doi.org/10.1016/j.labeco.2018.02.003

Goos, M., A. Manning, and A. Salomons (2014). 'Explaining Job Polarization: Routine-Biased Technological Change and Offshoring'. American Economic Review, 104: 2509–26. https://doi.org/10.1257/aer.104.8.2509

Grossman, G.M., and E. Rossi-Hansberg (2008). 'Trading Tasks: A Simple Theory of Offshoring'. American Economic Review, 98: 1978–97. https://doi.org/10.1257/aer.98.5.1978

Hardy, W., R. Keister, and P. Lewandowski (2018). 'Educational Upgrading, Structural Change and the Task Composition of Jobs in Europe'. Economics of Transition and Institutional Change, 26: 201–31. https://doi.org/10.1111/ecot.12145

Hsieh, C.-T., and P.J. Klenow (2010). 'Development Accounting'. American Economic Journal: Macroeconomics, 2: 207–23. https://doi.org/10.1257/mac.2.1.207

Lewandowski, P., A. Park, W. Hardy, Y. Du, and S. Wu (2022). 'Technology, Skills, and Globalization: Explaining International Differences in Routine and Nonroutine Work Using Survey Data'. The World Bank Economic Review, lhac005. https://doi.org/10.1093/wber/lhac005

Lo Bello, S., M.L. Sanchez Puerta, and H. Winkler (2019). From Ghana to America: The Skill Content of Jobs and Economic Development (No. 12259), IZA Discussion Papers. Institute of Labor Economics (IZA).

Niebel, T. (2018). 'ICT and Economic Growth—Comparing Developing, Emerging and Developed Countries'. World Development, 104: 197–211. https://doi.org/10.1016/j.worlddev.2017.11.024

Reijnders, L.S.M., and G.J. de Vries (2018). 'Technology, Offshoring and the Rise of Non-routine Jobs'. Journal of Development Economics, 135: 412–32. https://doi.org/10.1016/j.jdeveco.2018.08.009

Spitz-Oener, A. (2006). 'Technical Change, Job Tasks, and Rising Educational Demands: Looking outside the Wage Structure'. Journal of Labor Economics, 24: 235–70. https://doi.org/10.1086/499972

World Bank (2019). World Development Report 2019: The Changing Nature of Work. Washington, DC: World Bank.

4

Cross-country Patterns in Structural Transformation and Inequality in Developing Countries

Carlos Gradín, Piotr Lewandowski, Simone Schotte, and Kunal Sen

4.1 Heterogeneity in inequality trends

Before investigating the role of tasks and skills in shaping the distribution of earnings in developing countries, we collect the main facts on the evolution of earnings inequality. There is a large diversity in the level of observed earnings inequality and, more importantly, diverse inequality trends among the 11 countries studied in this book between the early 2000s and the late 2010s. We divide this period into two subperiods: from 2000/05 to 2010/13, and from 2010/13 to 2015/19, roughly before and after the Great Recession. Figure 4.1 shows the level of initial and final earnings inequality (as measured by the Gini index) in both subperiods, based on our country studies.

Only China and Indonesia witnessed a sustained increase in earnings inequality in both periods. Before the Great Recession, declining inequality was the norm in Latin American countries as well as African countries such as Ghana and Tunisia. South Asian countries (India and Bangladesh) recorded somewhat stagnant levels (with a modest fall and rise, respectively). After the Great Recession, half of the countries in our sample experienced widening earnings inequality. Inequality continued to increase in China and Indonesia. The declining trend reversed in Argentina, Brazil, and Ghana. In South Africa, inequality widened after being stable in the first period. However, inequality declined post-Great Recession in India and Bangladesh. The downward trend continued in Chile, Peru, and Tunisia. Even within particular regions, there was heterogeneity in these changes. As a result, four countries (Chile, India, Peru, and Tunisia) experienced no substantial rise in inequality over any period under analysis.

Carlos Gradín et al., *Cross-country Patterns in Structural Transformation and Inequality in Developing Countries.*
In: *Tasks, Skills, and Institutions.* Edited by Carlos Gradín, Piotr Lewandowski, Simone Schotte, and Kunal Sen, Oxford University Press. © UNU-WIDER (2023). DOI: 10.1093/oso/9780192872241.003.0004

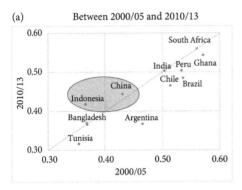
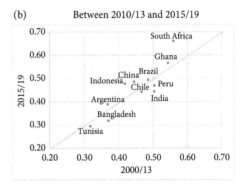

Figure 4.1 Earnings inequality trends in selected developing countries (Gini index)
Note: The Gini index in each case refers to the main sample of workers and years used in the corresponding country study.
Source: Authors' presentation based on country studies.

4.2 Skill supply and education premia

Educational attainment and literacy rates have generally increased globally over the past decades. This expansion in education is also visible in all country cases covered in this book. From an inequality perspective, an important question is whether the increasing supply of skilled workers has met market demands.

In recent decades, many advanced countries have seen the demand for skilled workers outpace the supply. The resulting surge in premia on higher levels of education contributed substantially to the net growth of earnings inequality in these countries. For example, in the US about two-thirds of the overall rise in earnings inequality from 1980 to 2005 have been attributed to an increased premium on higher education in general and post-secondary schooling in particular (Autor 2014).

Developing countries naturally had more room to expand their education supply over time as they generally started with much lower levels. A delay in the adoption of technology and the abundance of labour may have deferred the rise in demand for higher skills during the structural transformation process that many emerging economies exhibited during the last two decades. This may have resulted in declining returns to higher education. Indeed, the case studies included in this book show a tendency for the skill premia to go up in episodes of rising inequality and down in periods of declining inequality. However, this match is far from turning the skill premium into a perfect predictor of the trend in earnings inequality, indicating that other factors are in play.

The case studies of two Asian economies experiencing more sustained increasing inequality—China and Indonesia—find similar patterns as those described for more advanced countries. Most remarkably, in China, the wage premium for educated workers rose sharply in the 1990s and remained high thereafter, with education becoming the largest contributor to increases in wage inequality over the study period. Indonesia also saw a disproportionate increase in the returns to tertiary education, which contributed to rising earnings inequality between 2010 and 2015 (see Table 4.1). This process is also observed in Bangladesh but is not exclusive to fast-growing Asian economies. A similar pattern emerged in South Africa, where rising returns to post-high-school education accompanied the surge in inequality after 2010. The authors argue that schooling quality did not keep up with the country's strong expansion of high-school education. Consequently, secondary education lost its signalling effect for employers, reflected by a decline in the premium on secondary education, while the premium on post-secondary education increased.

In Latin America, the overall decline in income inequality during the 2000s has been associated with a narrowing earnings gap between high- and low-skilled workers. This pattern has been attributed to faster real-wage growth at the bottom of the wage distribution, driven by improvements in the minimum wage and an economic expansion that favoured low-skill-intensive service sectors (Guerra-Salas 2018; Messina and Silva 2019).

In line with these findings, the chapters on Argentina, Brazil, and Chile associate the decline in earnings inequality during the 2000s with a fall in the education premium. Similarly, in Ghana and Tunisia, substantial reductions in the premia on higher education contributed to decreasing trends in earnings inequality during the 2000s (see Table 4.1). India also witnessed a decline in the skill premium after 2004, but it did not seem to play a major role in explaining overall trends in earnings inequality.

Table 4.1 Changing premium to higher (secondary and tertiary) education

	Africa			Asia				Latin America			
	Ghana	South Africa	Tunisia	Bangladesh	China	India	Indonesia	Argentina	Brazil	Chile	Peru
2000/05–2010/13	↓	↑	↓	↔↑	↑	↓	↓	↓	↓	↓	↔
2010/13–2015/19	↓	↑	↔	↑	↑	↓	↑	↔↑	↓	↓	↔

Note: Symbols indicate a falling ↓, rising ↑, or stable ↔ premium on higher education. In Bangladesh, the premium on higher education for males remained relatively constant during the 2000s, while it increased for females. In Argentina, the premium on higher education fluctuated after 2012 and showed a modest increase toward the end of the study period.
Source: Authors' presentation based on country chapters.

Changes in education premia are not the sole determinants of earnings inequality trends and can be overcompensated by other effects. For example, in Brazil, Chile, and Ghana, the premia on secondary and tertiary education continued to fall during the 2010s, a period characterized by rising inequality (while a higher premium was consistent with the rise in inequality in Argentina). Similarly, in Indonesia, earnings inequality rose over the 2005–10 period, despite falling premia on higher education. Contrarily, in Bangladesh, earnings inequality fell sharply after 2010, despite rising premia on secondary and tertiary education. In Peru, inequality declined from 2011 to 2018 despite relatively constant education premia.

4.3 Changes in the composition and earnings of jobs

In several Western economies, economists have associated rises in earnings inequality with patterns of labour market polarization. There is scarce evidence on the extent to which similar—or even opposing—patterns exist in countries of the Global South. The country chapters in this book address this gap. They present evidence on how the composition of employment has changed across high-, medium-, and low-skill occupations since the turn of the century, and how the distribution of mean earnings by occupation has evolved.[1]

In line with the expansion in educational attainment, most chapters find an increase in the employment share of occupations that usually demand a higher skill level, particularly managers, professionals, and technicians. These occupations tend to be located at the upper end of the earnings distribution, so their growth widens inequality. Exceptions from this are Argentina in the 2000s and Tunisia in the 2010s (see Table 4.2), which saw a decline in high-skilled occupations mainly driven by a fall in the share of technicians. In Tunisia, this is attributed to shrinking activity in the transport and telecom sectors after the Revolution.

At the other end of the skill and earnings scale, there was a general decline of employment in agriculture. In some countries, upgrading to middle-skilled occupations followed (see Table 4.2). China is the only country that saw a strong manufacturing sector expansion over the study period (especially up to 2010), which was able to absorb a substantial share of workers into middle-skill occupations. In Latin American countries, the shift from low- to medium-skill occupations during the 2000s was largely facilitated by expanding opportunities in medium-skill service sector occupations, including communications, health services, financial services, and public administration.

---

[1] While closely related to the discussion on educational attainment and skill premia above, differences between occupations do not only reflect differentials in skill requirements and productivity but can also be influenced by other job characteristics, such as working conditions, sectoral differences (e.g. wage differentials between public and private sector workers), and the type of tasks being performed.

Table 4.2 Employment by occupational group

	Africa			Asia				Latin America			
	Ghana	South Africa	Tunisia	Bangladesh	China	India	Indonesia	Argentina	Brazil	Chile	Peru
2000/05–2010/13											
Low-skilled	↑	.	↑↓	↑	↓	↓	↑	↓	↓	↓	↓
Medium-skilled	↓	.	↓	↓	↑	↓	↓	↑	↑	↑	↑
High-skilled	↑		↑	↔	↑	↑	↑	↓	↑	↔	↑
2010/13–2015/19											
Low-skilled	↓	.	↑↓	↓	↓	↓	↑	↓	↓	↑	↔
Medium-skilled	↑	.	↑	↑	↑	↓	↓	↓	↔	↓	↔
High-skilled	↑	.	↓	↑	↔	↑	↑	↑	↑	↑	↔

Note: Symbols indicate a falling ↓, rising ↑, or stable ↔ employment. High-skilled occupations: ISCO 1 Managers, ISCO 2 Professionals and ISCO 3 Technicians. Medium-skilled occupations: ISCO 4 Clerks, ISCO 5 Service and sales workers, ISCO 6 Craft and related trades workers, ISCO 7 Plant and machine. Low-skilled occupations: ISCO 6 Skilled Agriculture, ISCO 9 Elementary Occupations. In Tunisia, the share of low-skilled workers decreased between 2000 and 2017, with an acceleration after 2010, when all workers are considered, but increased when looking at paid employees only.
Source: Authors' presentation based on country studies.

However, the decline of low-skilled agriculture employment has not necessarily involved shifting workers into middle-skilled occupations (see Table 4.2). In India, for example, low-skilled workers moving out of agriculture largely entered elementary jobs in the construction sector since there were few job opportunities in manufacturing (witnessing a falling employment share over time). Similarly, in Ghana, especially during the 2000s, the decline in the agriculture share was mirrored by an expansion in construction, mining, and a range of services such as trade, transport, hotels, and restaurants. Many of these were informal sector jobs. At the same time, the growth of industrial employment was relatively slow.[2]

The country studies used a simple regression model (see Chapter 2 for details on the methodology) to formally test for a quadratic relationship between initial, average occupational earnings and changes in employment or earnings over time—an often used test for the presence of job or wage polarization. Results are rather mixed (see Table 4.3). In the presence of job polarization, we would expect

[2] Overlapping with changes in the occupational composition, changes in the sectoral composition of employment are strongly related to inequality. Existing research suggests that employment growth in manufacturing tends to reduce income inequality, while a shift toward service sector employment tends to increase inequality in structurally developing countries (Baymul and Sen 2020), especially if driven primarily by the informal sector.

Table 4.3 Polarization test (quadratic relationship)

	Africa			Asia				Latin America			
	Ghana	South Africa	Tunisia	Bangladesh	China	India	Indonesia	Argentina	Brazil	Chile	Peru
Employment											
2000/05–2010/13	↑	.	↔	U	U	↔	U	↔	∩	↔	∩
2010/13–2015/19	↔	.	↔	↔∩	↔	U	↔	↔	U	↔	U
Earnings											
2000/05–2010/13	∩	.	L	U	U	↔	⟨⟩	∩	U	∩	U
2010/13–2015/19	↔	.	↔	U		∩	U	U	U	↔	↔

Note: Symbols indicate a negative ↓, positive ↑, U-shaped U, inverted-U-shaped ∩, and insignificant ↔ relationship with regard to earnings in the base period. In Bangladesh, the estimated relationship is insignificant when only paid employees are considered but inverted-U-shaped when all workers are considered. In Tunisia, the regression results suggest a U-shaped relationship, while the graphical results suggest the relationship to be L-shaped with highest growth at the bottom.
Source: Authors' presentation based on country studies.

to see employment growing more strongly in both low- and high-paying occupations while declining in middle-paying occupations. Indonesia in the 2000s is an example of this U-shaped pattern, which indicates inequality-enhancing occupational change. A similar pattern emerged in China in the same period, with the largest growth exhibited at the low–middle part of the distribution rather than at the bottom. Also, Bangladesh recorded stronger employment growth at the bottom, with significant growth in some top occupations. These three cases consistently correspond to episodes of rising inequality. A similar polarization pattern in employment occurred in Brazil, India, and Peru in the 2010s. However, only in Brazil did it correspond to an episode of a small increase in inequality, while inequality declined in the other two countries.

However, some countries recorded an inverted-U-shaped pattern indicating faster employment growth in middle-paying occupations than at the lower or upper extremes. Such an equalizing occupational change took place in Brazil and Peru during the 2000s, and Bangladesh during the 2010s, contributing to the overall downward trend of earnings inequality. In the remaining countries, no statistically significant relationship between changes in the composition of employment and initial earnings could be detected.

Polarization can also affect earnings. It has an ambiguous effect on overall earnings inequality, since stronger growth at the bottom is equalizing. In comparison, stronger growth at the top has an opposite effect, with the net effect depending on the intensity of both processes. This can partly explain why earnings polarization coincided with declining inequality in several countries. The simple econometric test identifies a quadratic U-shape relationship for a larger set of countries and periods, including Peru in the 2000s, Argentina and Indonesia in the 2010s, and Bangladesh, Brazil, and China over the full study span. However, in some cases (e.g. Brazil during the 2000s), only the downward part of the U is observed in the data, making this distributional change equalizing. In other cases (e.g. Indonesia in the 2010s), the largest growth occurred in the lower-middle rather than at the bottom of the earnings distribution.

An opposite, inverted U-shaped pattern indicating the strongest earnings growth in middle-paying occupations is detected in Argentina, Chile, and Ghana in the 2000s and in India during the 2010s. In all four countries this is observed along a decline in earnings inequality during the respective period.

4.4 Routine-task intensity

One of the core questions this volume attempts to address concerns the extent to which these dynamics in the composition and returns to occupations can be explained by the type of tasks workers perform. Since 2000, occupational structures around the world have evolved away from routine-intensive occupations and towards non-routine-intensive occupations. However, the cross-country analysis presented in Chapter 3 shows that the de-routinization of jobs occurred much more slowly in low- and middle-income countries than in high-income countries.

Accordingly, the individual country studies show mixed trends in the evolution of routine-task intensity (RTI), especially during the 2000s (see Table 4.4). While Brazil, Ghana, Indonesia, and Peru show a de-routinization of employment,

Table 4.4 Changes in RTI

	Africa			Asia				Latin America			
	Ghana	South Africa	Tunisia	Bangladesh	China	India	Indonesia	Argentina	Brazil	Chile	Peru
2000/05–2010/13	↓	.	↑	↑	↑	↓↑	↓	↔	↓	↑	↓
2010/13–2015/19	↓	.	↑↓	↓	↓	↓	↔↑	↓	↓	↓	↓

Note: Symbols indicate a falling ↓, rising ↑, or stable ↔ RTI. In India, the country-specific measure indicates a decline in the RTI during the 2000s, while the O*NET measure points to an increase. In Tunisia, the average RTI for paid employees increased over the 2010s according to the country-specific measure, while it decreased according to the O*NET measure. In Indonesia, the country-specific measure remained relatively constant in the 2010s, while the O*NET measure fell.
Source: Authors' presentation based on country studies.

Table 4.5 Relationship between employment and earnings with RTI

	Africa			Asia				Latin America			
	Ghana	South Africa	Tunisia	Bangladesh	China	India	Indonesia	Argentina	Brazil	Chile	Peru
2000/05–2010/13											
a) Employment											
Country-specific	↔	.	↔	↔	.	U	U	↔	↓	∩	↔
O*NET	↔	.	↔	↑	.	↔	↓	↔	↓	∩	↔
b) Earnings											
Country-specific	↔	.	↔	↔	.	↑	↔	↔	↑	↑	↔
O*NET	↔	.	↑	∩	.	↑	↔	↔	↑	∩	↔
2010/13–2015/19											
a) Employment											
Country-specific	↔	.	↔	↔	.	U	↔	↓	↔	↓	↔
O*NET	↔	.	↔	↔	.	↓	↔	↓	↔	U	↓
b) Earnings											
Country-specific	↔	.	↑	U	.	∩	↔	↔	↑	↑	↔
O*NET	↔	.	↑	↔	.	↑	↔	↔	↔	↑	↔

Note: Symbols indicate a negative ↓, positive ↑, U-shaped U, inverted-U-shaped ∩, and insignificant ↔ relationship with regard to RTI.
Source: Authors' presentation based on country studies.

in Bangladesh, China, Chile, and Tunisia, occupational change favoured more routine-intensive occupations. Since 2010, de-routinization appears to have picked up steam in most of the countries under study. The automation of these jobs or tasks could explain the outflux of workers from more routine-intense occupations. Interestingly, there is some weak evidence for an increase in routine-intensive jobs in Bangladesh during the 2000s, which could reflect a specialization in certain, more routine-intensive steps of production, potentially offshored from more developed countries.

In only a few countries is the relationship between changes in the composition and returns to occupations and the routine intensity of tasks performed on the job significant. Somewhat surprisingly, in several countries earnings growth has been fastest in more routine occupations (Table 4.5). This is the opposite of what we would expect if the demand for these jobs declined due to automation processes. For example, the chapter on India argues that this may point to a demand-supply mismatch. Other factors that may be at play include rising minimum wages at the lower end of the earnings spectrum and the effect of a major public works programme.

4.5 What drives earnings inequality?

Changes in the occupational composition of employment (e.g. job polarization) or in the occupational earnings structure (e.g. earnings polarization, or changes in the returns to routine-intense tasks) can contribute to overall changes in the distribution of earnings, which ultimately would materialize in changes in household income inequality.

The evidence presented in the case studies in this book strongly suggests that the average characteristics of occupations (including the average earnings associated with the demanded skills or the type of tasks performed by workers) are indeed very relevant in explaining overall earnings inequality at a given point in time. In most countries, inequality between occupations[3] is large (Figure 4.2a), and so is its contribution to the overall inequality (Figure 4.2b), except for Ghana.

While occupations are a critical factor behind inequality at a given time, we find little evidence that they contribute to changes in inequality in the low- and middle-income countries covered by this volume. In most countries, between-occupation inequality declined or was stagnant (except for Bangladesh and Indonesia). This decline mostly resulted from equalizing changes in average earnings across occupations over time. Changes of the occupational composition of employment were of lesser importance. Thus, changes in average earnings over time seem more important than changes in employment shares to determine the (non-increasing) trend in inequality between occupations in these countries.

More generally, the average characteristics of occupations do not seem to be driving the trend in inequality over time in our sample of countries. The share of overall inequality explained by the between-occupation component has declined or remained stable in most cases. This is very clear in South Africa, Ghana, and Brazil during both periods. Moreover, all studied countries, except Bangladesh, exhibited, in the long run, a decline in the share of overall inequality that can be attributed to inequality between occupations. Therefore, the trends in earnings inequality have been mostly driven by changes in inequalities within occupations, that is, were associated with changes in the earnings structure among workers performing similar tasks in their jobs, and can be associated with other personal characteristics such as worker skills, contract type, etc., or institutional factors (such as labour regulations).

Likewise, occupational differences in routine-task intensity (RTI) explain a large part of earnings inequality at a given time but only a minor share of changes

---

[3] Inequality that remains after all earnings have been equalized within occupations, see Chapter 2.

(a) Gini between occupations

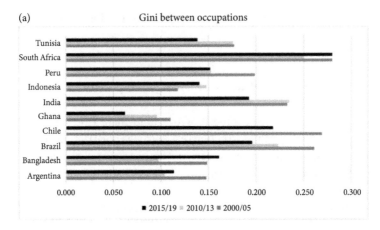

(b) As a share of overall inequality (Shapley decomposition)

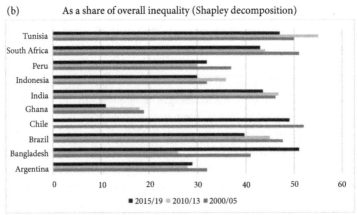

(c) Concentration index (country-specific RTI)
as a share of inequality between occupations

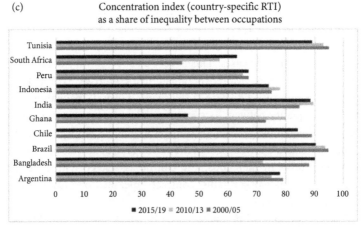

Figure. 4.2 Earnings inequality trends—inequality between occupations

Source: Authors' presentation based on country studies.

in inequality over time. Although more routine-intensive occupations tend to generate lower average earnings, this relationship is not perfectly monotonic—often, the least- and best-paying occupations are not necessarily the most and least routine, respectively. Moreover, the relationship between RTI and earnings has generally weakened over time in countries such as Tunisia, Ghana, Chile, or Brazil, and remained stable in the remaining countries. For example, the country study for Ghana shows an increase in the routinization of jobs among the best paid workers. Therefore, there are no strong signs that the returns to occupation tasks have been disequalizing overall.

In countries studied in this book, workers have generally become more skilled and gradually moved from routine to non-routine tasks between the early 2000s and the late 2010s. The market remunerations of these attributes have also evolved. To disentangle the role of these processes, the case studies have investigated drivers of inequality over time using a regression-based decomposition analysis (see Chapter 2).

Almost unanimously, the case studies concluded that the changes in the earnings structure drove the changes in inequality over time rather than changes in the composition of workers. The case studies, for example, confirmed the predominantly disequalizing effects of changes in the skill premia in the 2010s. It was the case in countries with increasing inequality (Brazil and China), and in countries with declining inequality (Chile, Bangladesh, Tunisia, and India), where these changes blunted the inequality decline. In this sense and in line with previous research, the skill premium seems to be partly associated with the change in the trend in inequality in recent years in various countries. The impact of the returns to education during the first period, *ceteris paribus*, seems to be more limited and the direction is mixed (disequalizing in Indonesia or India, equalizing in Ghana, Bangladesh, and China).[4] However, the mechanism behind the large contribution of changes in the earnings structure remains unclear partly because of the large contribution of the intercept. This means that omitted categories or other factors uncorrelated with the explanatory factors used in the regression could have played a role.

Changes in the composition of the workforce had a smaller, albeit in some countries noticeable, effect on inequality. The case studies document several inequality-widening changes in education and the distribution of (country-specific) RTI (Table 4.6). The most prominent example is Brazil in 2011–18, the only case in which the composition effect dominated in pushing inequality up. Compositional

---

[4] Among other factors that can explain the trend in inequality, the evolution of the returns to formality have shifted from helping to reduce inequality in Argentina in the first period, to contributing to the increase that followed in the second one. Similarly, the returns to working in the public sector had a disequalizing effect in Tunisia after the Revolution that contrasts with the equalizing effect in the previous period.

Table 4.6 Composition versus earnings structure effects in explaining the change in inequality (Gini) over time

	Africa			Asia				Latin America			
	Ghana	South Africa	Tunisia	Bangladesh	China	India	Indonesia	Argentina	Brazil	Chile	Peru
2000/05–2010/13											
a) Education											
Composition		.				↑			↑		
Structure	↓	.		↓	↓	↑	↑				
b) Country-specific RTI											
Composition		.				↑			↓		↑
Structure		.	↓	↑	↓	↓	↓	↑			
c) Other											
Composition		.	↑ (P)					↓ (F)	↓ (F)		
Structure		.	↓ (P)					↓ (F)	↑ (F)		
2010/13–2015/19											
a) Education											
Composition	↓	.		↑					↑	↑	
Structure		.	↑	↑	↑		↑		↑	↑	
b) Country-specific RTI											
Composition		.							↑	↑	
Structure	↑	.		↓	↑	↑	↓			↓	
c) Other											
Composition		.							↑ (F)		
Structure		.	↑ (P)					↑ (F)			

Note: Symbols indicate an equalizing ↓, disequalizing ↑, and insignificant ↔ relationship. F abbreviates formal employment, P abbreviates public-sector employment.
Source: Authors' presentation based on country studies (RIF regression-based decomposition of changes in the Gini index).

effects also mitigated the decline in inequality in Chile (2006–17). Compositional changes pertaining to informality also played a role in some countries. The increase in the share of workers in the formal sector played a role in the initial decline in inequality in Brazil and Argentina. At the same time, the later rebound in informality in Brazil widened inequality. In Tunisia, the drastic decline in the share of workers in the public sector blunted the fall in inequality between 2002–10, while its sharp increase after the revolution to tackle discontent and youth unemployment was rather neutral.

As suggested by the literature that motivated this book, changes in the earnings associated with the routine intensity of occupations have, *ceteris paribus*, widened inequality in episodes of rising inequality in Indonesia, China, and Ghana during the 2010s or in Bangladesh during the 2000s. It has also partly mitigated the decline of inequality in Argentina during the first period. But there is also strong evidence of the opposite effect in both periods. Changes in the returns to RTI contributed to declining inequality in Bangladesh, Chile, India, Tunisia, and China, or to avoiding a larger increase in Indonesia in the first period. Therefore, although changes in returns to routine job tasks seem to play a role in shaping earnings inequality in the Global South, the direction has not been unanimous.

Finally, various case studies, including the four countries in the Latin American region, Ghana, South Africa, and India, have discussed the potential effects of institutional factors that have not been considered in the decomposition analysis, particularly the minimum wage. They highlighted that the rise of the minimum wage (above the rise in prices) has pushed the earnings in the lower or middle parts of the distribution, especially in the 2000s, consistently with declines in inequality. Similarly, the stagnation or decline in the real minimum wage in the most recent years may have aggravated the trend in inequality in countries like Argentina, Brazil, or Ghana.

4.6 Conclusions

In this chapter we have discussed that there was no unanimous trend in earnings inequality in developing countries in the last two decades. Still, inequality has risen (or its fall has been mitigated) in several countries in the 2010s. The workforce has substantially changed in many countries over time, which has led in several cases to job polarization and/or earnings polarization. However, the evidence of de-polarization trends or no clear patterns can also be found.

Despite this large workforce transformation that developing countries exhibited in the 2000s and 2010s, earnings inequality between occupations have either declined or remained constant in most cases. The relationship between the RTI of jobs and their average earnings weakened. These changes in the composition of workers by education and job RTI have, *ceteris paribus*, contributed to increasing inequality. Still, they do not seem to be the main driving force. Changes in inequality can be primarily related to changes in the earnings structure (i.e. how the market remunerates worker characteristics). The shift in the direction of this structural effect is key to understanding the overall inequality trend. It seems to be driven by the change towards the disequalizing developments of education premia during the 2010s, contrasting with mixed developments (equalizing and disequalizing) in the 2000s. We find mixed evidence of changes in the returns to routine content of jobs (equalizing in some cases, disequalizing in others).

In any case, traditional factors explaining trends in earnings inequality, especially changes in the education premium, remain relevant in the countries studied. In some countries, we found evidence of job polarization or widening of earnings inequality driven by the evolution of the routine intensity of jobs. However, their role was smaller than that of the education premium. In addition, we have highlighted the potential influence of other local factors such as labour institutions (e.g. minimum wage).

References

Autor, D. H. (2014). 'Skills, Education, and the Rise of Earnings Inequality among the "Other 99 Percent". *Science*, 344(6186): 843–51. https://doi.org/10.1126/science.1251868

Baymul, C., and K. Sen (2020). 'Was Kuznets Right? New Evidence on the Relationship between Structural Transformation and Inequality'. *The Journal of Development Studies*, special section: 'Double Dividends and Mixed Blessings: Structural Transformation, Income Inequality and Employment Dynamics': 1643–62. https://doi.org/10.1080/00220388.2019.1702161

Guerra-Salas, J. F. (2018). 'Latin America's Declining Skill Premium: A Macroeconomic Analysis'. *Economic Inquiry*, 56(1): 620–36. https://doi.org/10.1111/ecin.12497

Messina, J., and J. Silva (2019). 'Twenty Years of Wage Inequality in Latin America'. IDB Working Paper 1041. Washington, DC: Inter-American Development Bank (IDB). https://doi.org/10.18235/0001806

PART III
COUNTRY STUDIES

5

Ghana

Employment and Inequality Trends

Carlos Gradín and Simone Schotte

5.1 Introduction

This chapter provides an in-depth examination of the employment and inequality trends in Ghana since the mid-2000s, using data from the Ghana Living Standards Survey (GLSS) collected in 2005/06, 2012/13, and 2016/17.[1]

Our analysis focuses on shifts in the structure of employment and in the distribution of earnings within and across workers' main occupations that can be linked to changes in the supply of and demand for skills, on the one hand, and to changes in the demand for and remuneration of routine versus non-routine tasks performed within specific occupations, on the other. The principal measures of routine-task intensity (RTI) used in our analysis are derived from data provided by the Ghana Skills Toward Employment and Productivity (STEP) Survey, which we merge with the GLSS survey data at the occupational level (see Chapter 4 for details).[2]

We detect substantial structural changes in the composition of employment from 2005/06 to 2016/17, characterized mainly by a pronounced move of employment out of agriculture, which was most pronounced in the first subperiod up to 2012/13. As in many other sub-Saharan African countries, this shift has been accompanied not by a rise in manufacturing employment but by an expansion of the service sector. These changes in the occupational structure imply a shift towards jobs demanding higher skills and involving less-routine tasks, resulting in a fall in average RTI, regardless of the measure used. While earnings inequality among non-farm workers has not changed greatly over the full study period, striking differences are observed by subperiod: we find a decline in inequality

---

[1] We focus on the working age population who did any work for pay, profit, or family gain in the previous seven days. See Gradín and Schotte (2020) for more details on the data, sample, definitions, and results.

[2] For comparative purposes, we also assessed the patterns observed when task measures are constructed from O*NET even if they are not always discussed here. The methods are explained in Chapter 2.

Carlos Gradín and Simone Schotte, *Ghana: Employment and Inequality Trends.* In: *Tasks, Skills, and Institutions.* Edited by Carlos Gradín, Piotr Lewandowski, Simone Schotte, and Kunal Sen, Oxford University Press. © UNU-WIDER (2023). DOI: 10.1093/oso/9780192872241.003.0005

during the first subperiod (2005/06–2012/13), in which the economy grew much faster, with the largest earnings growth at the bottom percentiles and the smallest growth at the top; and a rise in inequality during the second subperiod (2012/13–2016/17), in which the economy kept growing but at a slower pace and with a clear 'pro-rich' pattern. In both periods, the trends in inequality are primarily explained by changes in the earnings structure, while the composition effect is small. Specifically, the decline in inequality in the first subperiod can be associated with a substantial decline in the education premium, following improvements in the level of education across workers, while the rise in inequality in the second subperiod is explained by a combination of two effects: a smaller equalizing effect due to a slow-down in the decline of the education premium was coupled with a disequalizing effect due to changes in the remuneration of non-routine jobs, relative to more-routine occupations.

5.2 Employment trends and earnings inequality

5.2.1 Context

Ghana has made remarkable progress, being recognized as one of the 'most notable success stories' in sub-Saharan Africa (McKay et al. 2016: 85). It has managed a peaceful democratic transition, has maintained democratic stability, and has experienced strong and robust economic growth over the past three decades, attaining lower-middle-income status in 2007. Between 2005 and 2017, Ghana's gross domestic product (GDP) grew at an average annual rate of 6.6 per cent. Over the same time period, GDP per capita expanded from GHC3,091 to GHC4,994, growing at an average annual rate of 4.1 per cent, with the highest growth rate being recorded in 2011 (11.3 per cent) and the lowest in 2015 (–0.1 per cent).

During the growth spurt experienced around 2011, Ghana was one of only seven countries in the world, and the only country in sub-Saharan Africa, to achieve double-digit economic growth (IMF 2012). Importantly, this impressive growth performance is largely attributable to the discovery of oil and gas around that time, adding to the country's traditional main exports of gold and cocoa. Macroeconomic conditions worsened after 2013 in reaction to a fall in oil prices, weaker fiscal and monetary policies, and electricity rationing (GSS 2018), which slowed GDP growth to around 3 per cent between 2014 and 2016, picking up again in 2017.

Crude oil exports, mining, and financial intermediation—all sectors with a low labour absorption capacity—were the main factors driving economic growth in Ghana in the 2000s, while the labour-intensive sectors of agriculture and manufacturing grew much more slowly. In consequence, employment growth in Ghana has not kept up with its economic growth and the structure of the economy remains highly informal (Aryeetey and Baah-Boateng 2016). Importantly, the country's impressive growth rates and its shift away from the dominance of agriculture to services contributing the largest share to national output should not be interpreted as evidence of significant structural transformation (McKay and Aryeetey 2004; Aryeetey and Baah-Boateng 2016). Despite its declining share in the economy, agriculture remains the major source of employment in Ghana, followed by low-value service activities in the informal sector, which accounted for the largest proportion of newly created jobs over the past decades (Aryeetey and Baah-Boateng 2016).

Ghana's strong economic performance—accompanied by several social intervention programmes implemented over the last two decades (GSS 2018)—can be associated with a significant reduction in consumption poverty. The proportion of Ghanaians living below the international poverty line, set at US$1.90 a day (2011 purchasing power parity (PPP)) reduced by three-quarters from close to 50 per cent in the early 1990s to 24.5 per cent in 2005/06 and 12 per cent in 2012/13, one of the lowest poverty rates in the region (World Bank 2019). Similarly, the incidence of poverty measured by national standards reduced from 31.9 to 24.2 per cent over the seven-year period from 2005/06 to 2012/13. However, poverty reduction stalled in subsequent years. The country recently witnessed a slight increase in extreme poverty and in the incidence of poverty in rural areas, with the rural poverty headcount in 2016/17 being five times higher than that of urban areas. Historically, there has been large regional variation in the incidence of poverty—the Northern Region accounting for the highest share of people living in poverty, while Greater Accra contributes the lowest share—and regional gaps have widened in recent years. Nonetheless, a disaggregated picture reveals important disparities within regions, including sizeable pockets of poverty even in the better-off regions (GSS 2018).

Starting from a relatively low level in the 1990s, consumption inequality (based on per capita household consumption) has continuously widened in Ghana, as indicated by an increase in the Gini index of between 5 and 6 points from 1991/92 to 2016/17. In particular, the rise in inequality over the 12-year period from 2005/06 to 2016/17 has been concentrated largely in rural areas. A comparison of the growth rates in per capita consumption at different points of the wealth distribution suggests that the benefits of growth have not reached households in the poorest quintile (GSS 2018).

Earnings inequality among paid employees and non-farm self-employed workers in Ghana, as measured by the Gini index, showed a modest decline from 57.1 in 2005/06 to 56.6 in 2016/17, but with striking differences by subperiod. For the first subperiod (2005/06 to 2012/13), in which the economy grew much more quickly, we find a substantial decline in the Gini index of almost three points. During these

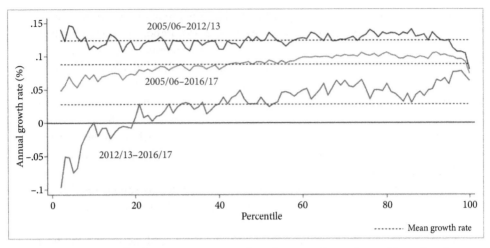

Figure 5.1 Growth of earnings among paid employees and non-farm self-employed workers, 2005/06–2016/17
Source: Authors' calculations.

years, in relative terms, growth in earnings was strongest at the bottom and weakest at the top of the distribution (see Figure 5.1). This was followed by a second period (2012/13 to 2016/17) in which the economy kept growing but at a slower pace, with a clear pro-rich pattern. While earnings were shrinking in the bottom quintile, higher earnings percentiles experienced positive growth, resulting in a rise in inequality (from 54.4 to 57.1).

5.2.2 Structural change: employment, the skill premium, and the minimum wage

Over the period from 2005/06 to 2016/17, Ghana experienced significant structural changes, characterized by a pronounced move of employment away from agriculture toward services, which was most pronounced in the first subperiod up to 2012/13. This was accompanied by an important expansion of the share of paid employees (from 19 to 30 per cent) in the workforce—observed for both men (from 29 to 41 per cent) and women (from 9 to 19 per cent)—along with a decline in agricultural self-employment (from 53 to 37 per cent).

As in other sub-Saharan African countries, the shift away from agriculture was associated with a considerable increase in the relative share of services, while the growth of employment in the industry sector has been comparatively slow. Particularly during the first subperiod (2005/06 to 2012/13), Ghana witnessed a sharp drop in the share of employment in agriculture (from 56 to 47 per cent), but also a decline in manufacturing (from 11 to 8 per cent), while the employment share expanded in construction, mining, and a large range of services such as trade, transport, hotels and restaurants, and other services. During the second subperiod (2005/06 to 2012/13), the agricultural share continued to decline but at a slower pace (from 47 to 44 per cent), whereas the manufacturing sector recovered part of its initial employment levels, and construction continued to expand. In addition, the country saw a particularly outstanding expansion of high-skilled services such as education and public administration. Accordingly, the formality rate among paid employees and non-farm self-employed workers fell from 30 per cent in 2005/06 to 26 per cent in 2012/13 and increased thereafter to 34 per cent in 2016/17. Based on previous cross-country evidence (Odusola et al. 2017; Baymul and Sen 2020), we would expect that this movement of workers from agriculture to services in Ghana would tend to be generally inequality-enhancing, being at odds with the reduction in inequality observed in the first subperiod.

In line with the sectoral changes in the occupational structure discussed above, in both subperiods we observe a movement towards jobs demanding higher skills, including managers (ISCO 1) and professionals (ISCO 2), which was counterbalanced during the first subperiod by a significant increase in the share of service and sales workers (ISCO 5), typically in informal activities, who tend to be low to medium skilled, as well as a rise in low-skilled elementary occupations.

These changes in the employment structure also implied a shift towards more non-routine occupations (the country-specific RTI from 0.70 to 0.62), an RTI measure that is clearly negatively correlated with earnings percentiles, except at the very top (Figure 5.2). This latter feature is accentuated in the last wave, with an increase in the share of routine occupations among top earners. The graphical evidence suggests that the relationship between the RTI of occupations and earnings has weakened over time. While those at the bottom of the distribution tend to be in highly routinized jobs, those at the top are not necessarily in occupations with the lowest RTI.

From 2005/06 to 2012/13, the fall in earnings inequality was mirrored by a substantial decline in the education premium at all levels, and for both men and women, following a general improvement in the level of education of workers (see Figure 5.3). However, it is worth noticing that the education premium continued to fall during the second period up to 2016/17. The rise in earnings inequality over this later period therefore must be explained by other factors.

Additionally, institutional factors might help to explain the different inequality trends observed in the two subperiods. In the context of Ghana, it is noteworthy that there was a substantial increase in the national minimum wage in real terms during the first subperiod (2005/06 to 2012/13), raising the floor of the distribution, while minimum wages stagnated in the second subperiod (2012/13 to 2012/13), even showing a moderate decline in real terms.

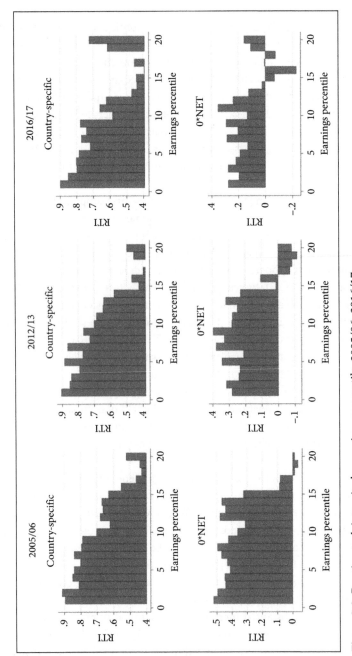

Figure 5.2 Routine-task intensity by earnings percentile, 2005/06–2016/17

Source: Authors' calculations based on GLSS 5, GLSS 6, and GLSS 7.

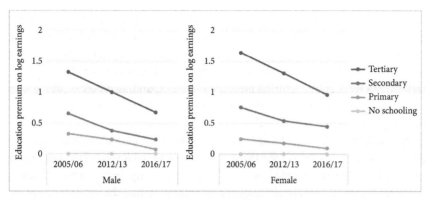

Figure 5.3 Education premium by gender and level of education, 2005/06–2016/17

Note: log weekly earnings are regressed in each year separately by gender on dummy variables for three education levels (tertiary, secondary, primary, with no schooling as base category), two age groups (ages 15 to 24 years and 45 to 64 years, with 25 to 44 years as base category), seven region dummies (with Greater Accra as base category), eight ethnic groups (with Ashanti-Akan as base category), and occupation units at the ISCO-88 two-digit level (with salespersons [ISCO 52] as base category). The figure shows the coefficient estimates on the education categories, which directly measure the returns to attaining a higher level of education in terms of (log) weekly earnings (i.e. the education premium) across survey waves separately by gender.

Source: Authors' calculations based on GLSS 5, GLSS 6, and GLSS 7.

5.3 The role of tasks and skills in changing earnings inequality

As previously discussed, earnings inequality declined during the first subperiod (2005/06 to 2012/13), characterized by strong pro-poor growth, and raised during the second subperiod (2012/13 to 2016/17), characterized by slower growth displaying a clear pro-rich pattern. The decline in the education premium over the full period may be associated with the fall in inequality in the first subperiod but cannot explain the subsequent rise. Moreover, observed shifts in the occupational structure seemed to counteract the inequality trends. In this section, we want to understand to what extent changes in earnings inequality were the result of changes in the nature of jobs performed by workers.

5.3.1 Job and earnings polarization

In the presence of job polarization, we would expect to see employment growing more strongly in both low- and high-paying occupations while declining in middle-paying occupations, producing a hollowing out of middle-class jobs. Similarly, in the presence of earnings polarization, we would expect to see earnings growing more strongly in jobs at both ends of the earnings distribution at the expense of the middle.

As previously documented, Ghana followed other developed and developing countries and experienced a decline in the average routinization of jobs. However, this may not necessarily imply a polarizing trend in Ghana given its position as a middle-income country, as well as its insertion in the global value chain, characterized by a weak manufacturing industry and an expanding oil sector, along with the relatively minor transformation of the economy, in which agriculture remains key despite the large shift of workers to the service sector.

We test for polarization (Table 5.1, first panel) using a simple econometric test of a quadratic relationship—at the three-digit occupational level—of the log change in employment share and the change in log mean earnings between survey waves, on initial log mean weekly earnings and its square, testing the significance of the parameters pointing to a U-shape (Goos and Manning 2007; Sebastián 2018).

Table 5.1 Check for employment and earnings polarization, 2005/06–2016/17

Earnings	Log change in employment share			Change in log mean earnings		
	2005/06–12/13	2012/13–16/17	2005/06–16/17	2005/06–12/13	2012/13–16/17	2005/06–16/17
(log) mean weekly earnings (t−1)	3.731*	−0.891	2.292	0.847**	−0.640	−0.424
	(2.227)	(0.909)	(2.131)	(0.370)	(0.971)	(0.591)
Sq. (log) mean weekly earnings (t−1)	−0.471	0.110	−0.260	−0.157***	0.043	−0.009
	(0.290)	(0.110)	(0.271)	(0.052)	(0.119)	(0.080)
Constant	−7.182*	1.728	−4.767	−0.369	1.905	2.219**
	(4.230)	(1.840)	(4.120)	(0.647)	(1.936)	(1.057)
Observations	104	97	97	104	97	97
Adj. R-squared	0.086	−0.014	0.075	0.175	0.198	0.331
RTI						
Country-specific	−0.534	−0.072	−0.634	0.102	0.104	0.357*
	(0.414)	(0.095)	(0.426)	(0.093)	(0.103)	(0.186)
RTI						
Sq. country-specific	0.314	0.057	0.479	−0.065	−0.012	−0.137
	(0.297)	(0.055)	(0.294)	(0.081)	(0.059)	(0.149)
RTI						
Constant	−0.168	−0.044	−0.176	0.700***	0.029	0.700***
	(0.175)	(0.064)	(0.189)	(0.044)	(0.059)	(0.073)
Observations	104	97	97	104	97	97
Adj. R-squared	0.007	−0.015	0.027	−0.007	0.011	0.074

Note: Standard errors in parentheses; ***$p<0.01$, **$p<0.05$, *$p<0.1$.
Source: Aauthors' calculations based on GLSS 5, GLSS 6, and GLSS 7.

Polarization in this context implies that the coefficient of log earnings is negative while the coefficient of its squared value is positive. Although the impacts of these polarization trends on inequality are not straightforward, they are mostly associated with periods of increasing inequality.

The first period in Ghana was characterized by declining inequality, and we actually observe an inverted-U-shaped pattern, a sign of depolarization, with both earnings and employment growing faster at the middle of the distribution. However, the quadratic term in the regression is only statistically significant with regard to the change in log mean earnings. This depolarizing employment shift towards middle-income occupations was more pronounced in the informal sector.

Figure 5.4 helps to graphically visualize the actual changes for paid employees. The inverted-U pattern is clearly visible, showing changes in earnings. However, while there was a large decline in employment at the bottom of the distribution, the improvement in the middle was less uniform than that found for earnings, and there was also an increase at the top.

The second period, however, was characterized by increasing inequality, and therefore it is more likely to show a polarizing pattern. Indeed, we observe a polarizing trend in both employment and earnings, although this is not statistically significant in the econometric regressions (see Table 5.2). Figure 5.4 shows that changes in employment occurred mostly in the middle, expanding employment in the lower-middle at the expense of the upper-middle. Changes in earnings tended to favour the lowest-paying jobs, which seems paradoxical in a period of growing inequality. This indicates that rising inequality was not the result of disequalizing changes in earnings across occupations but was due to other factors, which will be explored in more detail in Section 5.3.2.

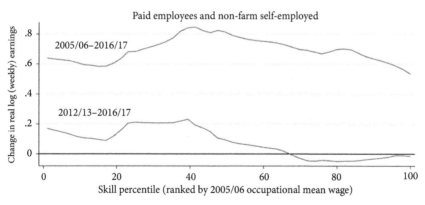

Figure 5.4 Changes in employment and earnings across skill percentiles
Source: Authors' calculations based on GLSS 5, GLSS 6, and GLSS 7.

Table 5.2 Gini index decomposed into inequality between and within occupations, 2005/06–2016/17

	Actual			Shares constant			Means constant		
	2005/06	2012/13	2016/17	2005/06	2012/13	2016/17	2005/06	2012/13	2016/17
1 Overall Gini	0.571	0.544	0.566	0.571	0.551	0.575	0.571	0.566	0.587
Shapley decomposition									
2 Between-occupation	0.110	0.096	0.062	0.110	0.109	0.064	0.110	0.136	0.134
% ratio	19	18	11	19	20	11	19	24	23
3 Within-occupation	0.462	0.448	0.504	0.462	0.442	0.512	0.462	0.430	0.453
% ratio	81	82	89	81	80	89	81	76	77

Note: ISCO-88, two digits.
Source: Authors' calculations based on GLSS 5, GLSS 6, and GLSS 7.

In the industrialized nations, the main hypothesis about what is behind polarization trends is that they are the result of earnings and employment growing faster in non-routine manual and cognitive jobs, which in countries such as the US tend to be allocated at the two extremes of the earnings distribution, while growth is slower in middle-income routine jobs that are most affected by automation and international trade competition. As shown above, in Ghana the relationship between RTI and earnings is less straightforward and tends to depend on the point in time and measure used. To check the extent to which changes in employment and earnings in Ghana were concentrated in jobs involving more or less routineintensive tasks, we also fit a quadratic regression of the log change in employment share and of the log change in earnings on the level of routine intensity, using the country-specific RTI measure (Table 5.1, second panel). Overall, we find that the routine-task content of occupations explains only a small share of the variance in changes in both employment and earnings at the occupational level.

5.3.2 Earnings inequality across occupations and its relationship to routine-task content

To further assess the role of tasks performed by workers in their jobs in explaining observed inequality trends, we turn our attention to the distribution of mean earnings by occupation. The average pay by occupation reflects the labour market rewards attached to each job. Differences between occupations do not necessarily perfectly reflect differentials in skill requirements and productivity but can also be influenced by other job characteristics, such as working conditions, sectoral differences (e.g. wage differentials between public and private sector workers), and the type of tasks being performed.

If changes in the rewards of certain occupations help to explain the trends in earnings inequality, this would be reflected in the gaps in average earnings between occupations. If, however, inequality changes are explained by other factors not related to the characteristics of occupations, such as differences in skills or other productivity-related attributes among workers performing similar jobs, this would be reflected in within-occupation inequality driving the overall earnings inequality patterns.

According to the Shapley decomposition that allows us to disaggregate the total Gini index into the contribution of inequality between and within occupations, we find that differences in average earnings across occupations explain 19 per cent of overall earnings inequality at the beginning of our study period (based on ISCO-88, two digits). While this share remained at a similar level during the first period, it declined substantially thereafter, accounting for only 11 per cent of overall inequality in the final year. This implies that differences in earnings within occupations explain the bulk of earnings inequality and that this feature has intensified over time (Table 5.2). This finding is robust across alternative specifications.

A further inspection of these changes reveals that the main driver for rising inequality within occupations in the second period was 523, 'Stall and market salespersons', which increased in size (from 18.7 to 21.1 per cent) and inequality (from 60.2 to 63.4). This is consistent with new workers joining the occupation falling at the bottom of the distribution, as one would expect from the type of structural transformation experienced by Ghana. This occupation witnessed changes in the same direction during the first period, but this was more than compensated for by opposite trends in other occupations (such as 741, 'Food processing and related trades workers', which declined in both size and inequality).

Accordingly, while the initial reduction in inequality was explained in similar proportions by earnings inequality declining between and within occupations (maintaining the relative contributions), the subsequent increase in inequality was entirely driven by a rise in inequality within occupations, partially offset by the continuing decline in between-occupation inequality as previously discussed.

To better understand the drivers behind the decline in inequality between occupations, we disentangle the direct role of changes in the composition of employment by occupation from the role of changes in mean earnings by occupation. We do this by analysing two counterfactual situations in which either occupation shares or mean earnings are held constant (Table 5.2).

Our findings show that the decline in between-occupation inequality in both subperiods is entirely due to a narrowing of the gap in average earnings across occupations. Moreover, this suggests both an equalizing effect of changes in mean earnings and a disequalizing effect of changes in the composition of employment that were more pronounced in the second subperiod, with the former dominating the latter in both periods, explaining the overall decline in inequality between occupations.

We isolate the effect of RTI, that is, the extent to which the degree of routinization of occupations is associated with this decline in earnings inequality between occupations, in a first simple approach, by looking at the concentration index. This index measures the extent to which average earnings of occupations tend to systematically increase with less routine intensity of jobs. In fact, the Gini concentration and between-group inequality indices are the same whether sorting occupations by average earnings or from highest to lowest RTI, in which case the concentration ratio (the ratio between both indices) would be 100 per cent.

The two occupation rankings are highly similar in the first survey wave, as indicated by the corresponding concentration ratios (varying between 73 per cent using the country-specific measure and 63 per cent using O*NET). However, while the country-specific measure suggests that this relationship further intensified over the first period, we observe a decline in the rank correlation between earnings and the O*NET RTI measure. However, during the second subperiod (and the entire period), the correlation unambiguously declines according to both measures (to a ratio of 46 and 21 per cent respectively), indicating that the relationship between the routine intensity of occupations and average earnings has weakened.

This decline likely reflects the fact that although the average RTI tends to be lower for occupations with higher earnings, this relationship is non-monotonic, and the least routine occupations are not necessarily the best-paid ones. This feature is exacerbated during the second subperiod, since there is an increase in the share of relatively routine occupations among the best-paying jobs.

5.3.3 Disentangling inequality drivers: the RIF-regression decomposition

To further investigate the role played by the routine-task content of occupations in shaping inequality, we use a RIF-regression decomposition approach to disentangle the relative importance of routine-task content in occupations, as opposed to the contribution of other competing explanations, particularly skills and demographic factors. The approach also allows us to disentangle whether the effect, if any, is channelled through changes in the composition of employment by occupation (composition effect) or in the associated earnings (wage structure effect). The former accounts for the first-round effect of compositional changes, such as the shift toward less-routine jobs or the increasing level of education among workers, before these changes have an effect on earnings. The latter accounts for the structural changes in earnings—that is, how the labour market retributes worker characteristics. Both effects, however, are interlinked, as the change in the structure of earnings may be the second-round (general equilibrium) effect of the changes in workforce composition. For example, the returns to education may fall as the result of an expansion in the supply of better-educated workers. But identifying which effects are more relevant helps us to better understand the nature of the inequality trend.

The results confirm some of the findings previously described. Changes in the demographic characteristics (i.e. in age composition and female employment) and education levels of the workforce, or in the structure of employment (i.e. the shift of workers towards less-routine occupations, changes in the share of formality), do not seem to directly explain the trend in inequality if the returns to these attributes are kept constant over time. If anything, changes in educational attainment, generally consisting of a rise in education levels, point in the opposite direction to the inequality trend. The decline observed in the share of workers in the formal sector in the first period, followed by an increase in the second period, also point in the opposite direction to the general inequality trend. That is, they show a disequalizing effect in the first subperiod, when inequality declined, and an equalizing effect in the second period, when inequality increased.

In consequence, it is the earnings structure effect (i.e. changes over time in the market returns to workers' characteristics, holding their composition constant), that explains the trend in inequality observed in the two examined subperiods. Specifically, the initial decline in inequality can be attributed largely to the strong equalizing effect of changes in the education premium, pointing to an effect in line with results for the declining inequality over the 2000s in many Latin American countries (e.g. Latin American chapters in this book). This indicates that the most conventional explanation of changes in earnings inequality based on the relative scarcity of skilled workers should not be understated. Changes in the returns to routine versus non-routine tasks additionally contributed to the decline in inequality if measured by O*NET, whereas the country-specific measure, which should better represent the task content of Ghanaian occupations, shows no significant effect in this first period (Table 5.3).

During the second subperiod, in which inequality substantially increased, the education premium continued to be inequality-reducing, but with a much lower intensity. The rise in inequality can be entirely attributed to changes in the returns to routine versus non-routine tasks at the occupation level, if measured by the country-specific index. However, our results using the O*NET RTI measure do not confirm this effect, indicating again that the way RTI is measured matters. It is noteworthy that the changes in the returns to formality of workers played no relevant part in driving the inequality trend in either subperiod.

The concentration index presented above tested for a monotonic relationship between earnings and RTI, pointing to a weaker relationship in the second subperiod of growing inequality. The regression-based decomposition presented here, apart from controlling for other characteristics, allows us to explore a more flexible non-monotonic relation between RTI and inequality (by including a quadratic term). Thereby, it captures the fact that the top-percentile occupations are not necessarily the least routine, and that this feature intensified over time, as previously discussed.

The Gini index summarizes the distributional changes along the entire distribution, reflecting the aggregate impact on inequality. However, it is important to disentangle how the different effects operate along the entire earnings distribution, as they are not necessarily uniform. For this purpose, we use the RIF-regression decomposition technique to decompose changes over time by (log) quantiles.

The aggregate decomposition of the change in earnings quantiles shows that the earnings structure effect drives the trend in both subperiods, over the entire distribution and not only at specific points (Figure 5.5).

The detailed decomposition of the earnings structure effect clearly shows a kind of polarizing effect of the change in country-specific RTI occupation returns during the first subperiod, contributing to reducing earnings in the middle of the distribution while increasing earnings at the bottom and part of the top, that has no significant net effect on the Gini index, as seen above (Figure 5.6). During

Table 5.3 RIF-regression decomposition of the change in earnings inequality (Gini index), 2005/06–2016/17

	RTI (country-specific)			RTI (O*NET)		
	2005/06–12/13	2012/13–16/17	2005/06–16/17	2005/06–12/13	2012/13–16/17	2005/06–16/17
Change	−0.028	0.021	−0.007	−0.028	0.021	−0.007
	(0.009)	(0.006)	(0.009)	(0.009)	(0.006)	(0.009)
Reweighting						
Composition	0.004	−0.009	−0.007	0.007	−0.009	−0.006
	(0.004)	(0.002)	(0.004)	(0.005)	(0.002)	(0.005)
Earnings	−0.032	0.030	0.000	−0.035	0.030	−0.001
structure	(0.010)	(0.006)	(0.010)	(0.011)	(0.006)	(0.011)
RIF						
Composition	0.008	−0.009	−0.003	0.010	−0.009	−0.002
	(0.004)	(0.002)	(0.004)	(0.004)	(0.002)	(0.004)
Specification	−0.004	0.000	−0.004	−0.003	0.000	−0.004
error	(0.002)	(0.001)	(0.002)	(0.002)	(0.001)	(0.003)
Earnings	−0.032	0.030	−0.001	−0.035	0.030	−0.001
structure	(0.010)	(0.006)	(0.010)	(0.010)	(0.006)	(0.011)
Reweighting	0.000	0.000	0.000	−0.001	0.000	0.000
error	(0.001)	(0.000)	(0.001)	(0.001)	(0.000)	(0.001)
Detailed composition						
Education	0.005	−0.005	−0.003	0.003	−0.005	−0.006
	(0.003)	(0.001)	(0.003)	(0.003)	(0.001)	(0.003)
Formality	0.002	−0.004	−0.002	0.003	−0.005	−0.002
	(0.001)	(0.001)	(0.001)	(0.001)	(0.001)	(0.001)
Detailed structure						
Age	−0.002	−0.007	−0.006	0.004	−0.006	−0.001
	(0.007)	(0.005)	(0.008)	(0.008)	(0.005)	(0.009)
Gender	0.013	−0.005	0.006	0.012	0.006	0.015
	(0.010)	(0.007)	(0.011)	(0.011)	(0.007)	(0.011)
Education	−0.037	−0.007	−0.036	−0.029	−0.009	−0.030
	(0.012)	(0.011)	(0.014)	(0.012)	(0.011)	(0.014)
Ethnic	0.006	0.000	0.000	0.008	0.001	0.003
	(0.009)	(0.006)	(0.010)	(0.010)	(0.006)	(0.010)
RTI	−0.002	0.034	0.035	−0.016	−0.003	−0.021
	(0.017)	(0.012)	(0.015)	(0.014)	(0.004)	(0.017)
Formality	−0.002	0.008	0.006	0.000	0.007	0.010
	(0.007)	(0.006)	(0.008)	(0.007)	(0.006)	(0.008)
Intercept	−0.008	0.008	−0.005	−0.014	0.034	0.022
	(0.030)	(0.021)	(0.029)	(0.031)	(0.018)	(0.030)

Note: Bootstrapped standard errors in parentheses (500 replications).
Source: Authors' calculations based on GLSS 5, GLSS 6, and GLSS 7.

(a)   2005/06–12/13

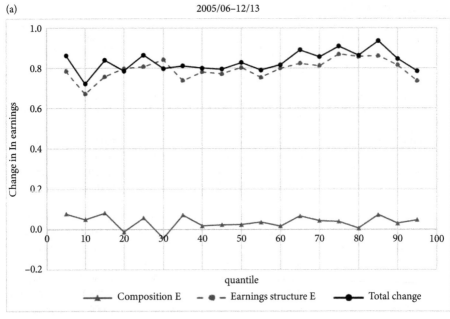

(b)   2012/13–16/17

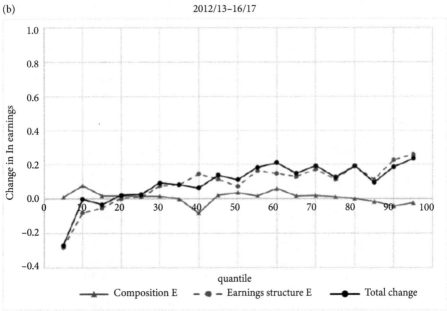

Figure 5.5 Reweighted RIF decomposition (country-specific RTI) of the change in earnings by quantile

Source: Authors' calculations based on GLSS 5, GLSS 6, and GLSS 7.

(a)

2005/06–12/13

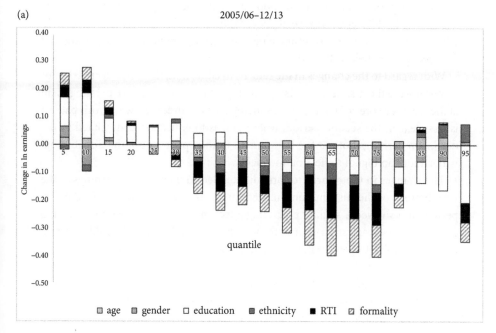

(b)

2012/13–16/17

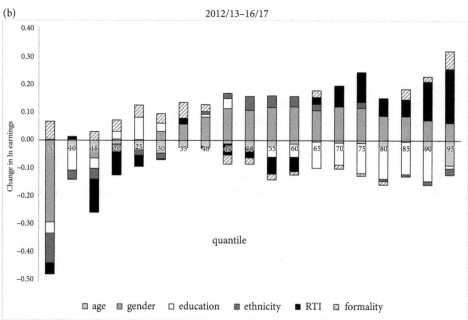

Figure 5.6 Detailed RIF decomposition (country-specific RTI) of the earnings structure effect by quantile

Source: Authors' calculations based on GLSS 5, GLSS 6, and GLSS 7.

the second period, the decomposition shows the clearly pro-rich profile of the change in the RTI effect on earnings quantiles, which explains the increase in Gini over these years, contributing to raising earnings above the 70th quantile and depressing them below the 60th.

With regard to the changes in the returns to education, there is a clear pro-poor profile during the first period, raising earnings at the bottom and depressing them at the top, therefore contributing to reducing the Gini index. However, this pattern is less clear in the second period, when returns to education contributed to the decline in earnings both at the bottom and in the upper half of the distribution, with a more ambiguous effect on inequality.

The changes in the returns to formality tended to increase the earnings at the very bottom of the distribution but decrease them everywhere else in the first period, and showed a slightly polarizing effect in the second period (increasing earnings at both extremes) but with no substantial effect on inequality overall. Running the RIF decomposition separately for formal and informal workers suggests that the role of the education premium in the first period and of the returns to RTI in the second period tends to be more intense among informal workers but applies to both groups. The null effect of returns to country-specific RTI in the first period is different, though, having an equalizing effect for informal workers and a disequalizing effect among formal workers.

5.4 Conclusion

We find that the entire period from 2005/06 to 2016/17 was characterized by substantial structural changes in the composition of employment in Ghana, driven primarily by a sharp reduction in the relative share of employment in agriculture, most pronounced in the first subperiod up to 2012/13. As in other sub-Saharan African countries, this shift was accompanied not by a rise in manufacturing employment but by an expansion of the service sector. These changes in the occupational structure imply a shift towards jobs demanding higher skills and involving less-routine tasks (RTI).

Earnings inequality among paid employees and non-farm self-employed workers in Ghana, as measured by the Gini index, did not change much over the entire period (2005/06 to 2016/17) but showed striking differences by subperiod. We observe a substantial decline in inequality during the first subperiod (2005/06 to 2012/13), in which the economy grew much more quickly, with the largest earnings increases taking place at the bottom percentiles and the smallest growth being experienced at the top percentiles. This was followed by a second period (2012/13 to 2016/17) in which the economy kept growing, but at a slower pace and with a clear pro-rich pattern.

We have shown that the decline in inequality in the first period involved a depolarizing trend, with both employment and earnings growing more strongly in middle-earnings occupations. This reduction in inequality was the combined result of declining inequality within occupations and narrowing gaps in average earnings among occupations. In contrast, the rise in inequality in the second period was entirely driven by a surge in inequality within occupations, to a large extent driven by some occupations with growing employment becoming more unequal, while inequality between occupations continued to decline. However, we did not find clear evidence that this increase in inequality was associated with a polarization in average earnings or employment by occupation, in terms of either occupation average earnings or task content.

Our RIF decomposition results indicate that in both periods the trends in inequality are primarily explained by changes in the earnings structure, while the composition effect is small. This means that shifts in employment per se had no substantial impact on inequality unless they contributed to changes in the earnings structure. The decline in earnings inequality during the first subperiod, indeed, can be associated with a substantial decline in the education premium, following a general improvement in the level of education across the workforce. The rise in inequality that followed in the second subperiod was possibly due to a combination of two effects. First, we observe a slow-down in the decline of the education premium—resulting in a smaller equalizing effect. Second, we find a disequalizing effect brought about by changes in the remuneration of non-routine jobs with a high demand for cognitive analytical and interpersonal tasks, relative to more-routine occupations.

In summary, we found evidence suggesting that traditional factors related to the relative scarcity of skills are key to understanding the trend in inequality in Ghana. This highlights the importance of continuing the expansion of education to ensure that the supply of skills outpaces the expected increasing demand, to prevent inequality skyrocketing in an already highly unequal country. However, we have also shown that even in a period in which the education premium falls, inequality can increase as the result of changes in the way routine and non-routine tasks performed by workers are remunerated in the labour market, and there are reasons to believe that this may be accentuated in the future as the country catches up with more advanced countries in incorporating technology. This happened in the context of a development process that, as in other sub-Saharan countries that can learn from the Ghanaian experience, has implied little real structural transformation and then little exposure to the potential effects of automation and international trade. Even if the workforce is becoming more skilled and performing less-routine jobs, the persistently low productivity of newly created jobs, whether routine or not, can be highly disequalizing and needs to be addressed.

References

Aryeetey, E., and W. Baah-Boateng (2016). 'Understanding Ghana's Growth Success Story and Job Creation Challenges'. In H. Bhorat and F. Tarp (eds), *Understanding the African Lions: Growth Traps and Opportunities in Six Dominant African Economies*,pp. 77–108. Washington, DC: Brookings Institution Press.

Baymul, C., and K. Sen (2020). 'Was Kuznets Right? New Evidence on the Relationship between Structural Transformation and Inequality'. *The Journal of Development Studies*, special section: 'Double Dividends and Mixed Blessings: Structural Transformation, Income Inequality and Employment Dynamics': 1643–62. https://doi.org/10.1080/00220388.2019.1702161

Goos, M., and A. Manning (2007). 'Lousy and Lovely Jobs: The Rising Polarization of Work in Britain'. *The Review of Economics and Statistics*, 89(1): 118–33. https://doi.org/10.1162/rest.89.1.118

Gradín, C., and S. Schotte (2020). Implications of the changing nature of work for employment and inequality in Ghana. WIDER Working Paper 119/2020. Helsinki: UNU-WIDER. https://doi.org/10.35188/UNU-WIDER/2020/876-4

GSS (2018). 'Ghana Living Standards Survey Round 7 (GLSS 7): Poverty Trends in Ghana, 2005–2017'. Accra: GSS. Available at: www2.statsghana.gov.gh (accessed 8 January 2020).

IMF (2012). 'Ghana: Poverty Reduction Strategy Paper'. IMF Country Report 12/203. Washington, DC: International Monetary Fund. https://doi.org/10.5089/9781475506594.002

McKay, A., and E. Aryeetey (2004). 'Operationalizing Pro-Poor Growth: A Country Case Study on Ghana'. Working Paper 32889. Washington, DC: World Bank. Available at: http://documents.worldbank.org/curated/en/310521468249924654/Operationalizing-pro-poor-growth-a-country-case-study-on-Ghana (accessed 15 March 2020).

McKay, A., J. Pirttilä, and F. Tarp (2016). Ghana: Poverty Reduction over Thirty Years'. In C. Arndt, A. McKay, and F. Tarp (eds), *Growth and Poverty in Sub-Saharan Africa*, pp. 69–88. Oxford: Oxford University Press.

Odusola, A., G.A. Cornia, H. Bhorat, and P. Conceição (eds) (2017). *Income Inequality Trends in Sub-Saharan Africa: Divergence, Determinants and Consequences*. New York: United Nations Development Programme (UNDP).

Sebastián, R. (2018). 'Technological Change and Employment Polarisation'. Thesis dissertation. Salamanca: University of Salamanca.

World Bank (2019). 'World Development Indicators'. Washington, DC: World Bank. Available at: https://databank.worldbank.org/source/world-development-indicators# (accessed 8 January 2020).

6

South Africa

Employment and Inequality Trends

Haroon Bhorat, Kezia Lilenstein, Morné Oosthuizen, and Amy Thornton

6.1 Introduction

The extent to which highly routine jobs can be replaced by computer or machine technology is an important explanation for the patterns behind growing inequality in industrialized economies (Goos et al. 2014). So far, this explanation has not been so thoroughly tested in developing country cases. In this chapter, we consider South Africa, a country with extreme labour market inequality (Wittenberg 2017a, b), the persistence and form of which has already been studied in a burgeoning literature. The role of structural transformation (Edwards and Lawrence 2008, Bhorat et al. 2016a, Bhorat et al. 2018), changing returns to education (Branson et al. 2012; Finn and Leibbrandt 2018), labour market institutions (Kerr and Wittenberg 2017; Bhorat et al. 2020), and other historical and social factors (Casale and Posel 2011; Mosomi 2019) in maintaining inequality in South Africa have been closely examined. With a special focus on gender, the goal of this chapter is to review some of the descriptive evidence for how well a routine-work explanation is associated with changes in the South African labour market using a measure of routine-task intensity.

Extreme gendered occupational sorting by women (Casale and Posel 2011) makes routine-biased technical change more relevant for men than women. Women cluster relatively evenly into non-routine work in the form of domestic work and personal care further down the wage distribution; and highly routine work in the form of clerks further up the wage distribution. The persistence of this clustering makes it difficult to apply a task-based logic to change in female employment and the persistence of the pattern has more to do with gender norms and discrimination in South Africa, than technology (Mosomi 2019). For men then, we find tasks are more relevant for explaining employment changes than wage changes. The influence of minimum wages and other state and institutional intervention in wage-setting means that changes in the wage structure are sometimes de-linked from changes in employment composition, especially at the bottom of the wage distribution. Even in terms of employment though, it is unlikely that routine work by itself represents a pivotal explanation for South African labour

Haroon Bhorat et al., *South Africa: Employment and Inequality Trends*. In: *Tasks, Skills, and Institutions*. Edited by Carlos Gradín, Piotr Lewandowski, Simone Schotte, and Kunal Sen, Oxford University Press. © UNU-WIDER (2023).
DOI: 10.1093/oso/9780192072241.003.0006

market inequality and instead falls into a supporting role for the more important drivers already identified in the literature. In particular, employment composition has been profoundly impacted by the rapid structural transformation of the economy from one based on agriculture, mining, and manufacturing to one that is finance and services-led (Bhorat et al. 2022); and routine work has, to an extent, interacted with this change.

The contraction of the South African primary and secondary sectors has complicated historical and context-specific explanations (Bhorat et al. 2022). However, it is not by chance that most new jobs in South Africa have been in the least-routine sector: services. The nature of many of the fastest-growing service jobs, (e.g. personal care, security work) make them difficult to offshore or outsource to a machine. This pattern of premature de-industrialization, or tertiarization, of the South African economy does not necessarily mean it is destined to overcome inequality, though. As high-skilled professional and technical service jobs have grown, so too have menial service jobs—security guards, personal care, street sweepers and garbage collectors.

In the future, non-routine work is perhaps going to be more important in South Africa, represented mainly by the services sector. Understanding how the services sector will challenge or maintain inequality is an important research agenda. At the bottom and middle of the wage distribution, the fact that service work is non-routine is 'protective', meaning it ensures the continued need for human beings to do these jobs. At the top end, growth in services, even so-called tradable services, has been pulled by growing local and global demand according to both South Africa's current comparative advantage and position as a destination of outsourced service work in the global value chain.

Following an introduction of our data in Section 6.2, we describe inequality in the South African labour market and provide an overview of its main drivers in Section 6.3. We investigate the evolution of earnings and employment across distributions of wages and skill focusing on gender in Section 6.4. A test of the association between routine work and earnings change controlling for other important drivers of inequality is carried out in Section 6.5. A decomposition of the role of routine work on the wage Gini is reported in Section 6.7. Section 6.8 concludes.

6.2 Data

The data used are version 3.2 of the Post-Apartheid Labour Market Series (PALMS) which is a harmonized series of South African labour force surveys for the years 1995–2015 curated by DataFirst at the University of Cape Town (Kerr et al. 2017). The original data for the series come from annual nationally representative cross-sectional labour force surveys collected by Statistics South Africa (StatsSA), the national statistics bureau, since 1995. These were the

October Household Surveys (1995–99), Labour Force Surveys (2000–07), and the Quarterly Labour Force Surveys (2008–current). Earnings information for the Quarterly Labour Force Surveys is sourced from the Labour Market Dynamics Surveys for the corresponding years.

Occupational information is available in PALMS up to the four-digit level and is based on the South African Standard Classification of Occupations (SASCO) from 2003 (Statistics South Africa 2003). SASCO 2003 is based on the International Standard Classification of Occupations (ISCO) from 1988 (ISCO-88).[1]

6.3 Inequality and its drivers in South Africa

Today, South Africa has amongst the highest levels of income inequality in the world, with the Gini coefficient between 2012–16 at 0.63 (World Bank 2020). Inequality in labour market income accounts for over 80 per cent of the country's aggregate income inequality (Hundenborn et al. 2018). This influence is partly because labour market income overwhelmingly constitutes the dominant share of household income in the country, compromising the welfare of people and house-holds without access to a wage. Earnings inequality in South Africa has worsened over the period 2000–15, reaching astonishing levels by global standards from an already-high base (Bhorat et al. 2020). The share accruing to the top decile has generally increased over time, from 27 per cent in 2000/04 to more than half of total earnings in 2013/15.

A key explanation for earnings inequality is that it is reproducing inequality in the schooling market (Branson et al. 2012; Finn and Leibbrandt 2018). Only a small share of the employed have post-secondary education, including certifi-cates or diplomas (with or without a high school graduation) as well as higher degrees. In the United States (US), the rate of earnings growth increases mono-tonically with education level, meaning earnings for the most highly educated increased far more quickly than those for the least well-educated (Autor 2019). South Africa departs from this pattern in that the rate of earnings growth has been U-shaped across education level (Bhorat et al. 2020). Earnings growth for the most and least well-educated have roughly kept apace of each other and improved steadily over time, with a noticeable depression in the growth of earnings for those with any level of high school education. Whilst education is key for understand-ing changing wage premia, changes in the sectoral composition of the economy are crucial for understanding employment shifts (Bhorat et al. 2018). South Africa has followed a pattern of 'premature de-industrialization' in which the manufac-turing sector never rose to prominence as an engine of the economy after the decline of agriculture (Bhorat et al. 2020). Protectionism in the late apartheid era

---

[1] See Bhorat et al. (2020) for more information about the data used.

undermined the efficiency of the manufacturing industry resulting in the sector yielding rapidly to more competitive trading partners when South Africa opened its borders to world trade in the mid-1990s (Edwards and Lawrence 2008). As a consequence of this transformation, the employment share of the tertiary sector increased extensively. Financial and community, social, and personal services accounted for almost 80 per cent of the increase in employment between 2001 and 2014 (Bhorat et al. 2018).

The extent to which routine-biased technical change is behind South African inequality has not received as much attention as other explanations so far. The role of routine-biased technical change in explaining rising inequality in industrialized economies is the subject of an extensive and growing literature (Autor et al. 2003; Autor and Dorn 2009; Acemoglu and Autor 2011; Firpo et al. 2011; Autor 2014, 2019; Goos et al. 2014). The twin phenomena of job and wage 'polarization' have been documented in many developed countries in which employment share and earnings grow more quickly for high- and low-skilled jobs, relative to mid-skilled (Goos et al. 2014). This pattern has been linked to the types of tasks people are performing in their jobs as opposed to their education, that is, the skill-biased technical change hypothesis. Routine tasks are considered most prone to labour-replacing automation by machines or computer technology, thus undermining demand and earnings for routine jobs. Many jobs that are high in routine-task content are clustered in the middle of the (industrialized-country) wage distribution, like manufacturing operators and assemblers, but also white-collar office jobs, such as clerks and bookkeepers (Autor 2019). As computer technology increasingly replaces these routine tasks, these occupations grow more slowly than the comparatively less-routine jobs at the poles of the wage distribution, in a pattern called 'job polarization'. Accordingly, job polarization is often accompanied by 'wage polarization', a pattern whereby the wages of these mid-skill routine occupations are eroded relative to those that are either lower- or higher-skilled ones (Autor and Dorn 2009).

A much smaller literature examines whether job polarization exists in developing countries (Crankshaw 2017; Maloney and Molina 2016) and investigations of wage polarization are even rarer (Bhorat et al. 2020). Whilst there is consensus that job polarization is pervasive in industrialized economies (Goos et al. 2014), the developing-country literature has reached less certain conclusions. This is most likely due to key structural differences not only between developed and developing country labour markets, but to extensive diversity within developing markets. It is by no means obvious that polarization patterns of either type should emerge in developing economies or, even if they do, that the drivers of such patterns will be the same as those in developed labour markets. In Section 6.4 we closely inspect to what degree changes in earnings and employment in South Africa can be described as polarized.

6.4 Earnings and employment change and gender in South Africa

The average annual growth rate (AAGR) of earnings over 2000–15 displays a U-shaped pattern across the percentiles (Bhorat et al. 2020). Wages have grown at the bottom and top of the wage distribution but have shrunk in real terms in the middle. This pattern could be described as polarizing and has already been noted by researchers closely studying the South African labour market (Wittenberg 2017a, b). However, there appears to be no corresponding job polarization. Changes in employment share are 'professionalizing', or 'skills-biased': only high-skilled occupations can be described as growing in a robust sense. Mid-skilled occupations do appear to be shrinking more quickly than low-skilled, but low-skilled occupations can hardly be described as growing. Usually, job and wage polarization accompany each other, since declining job market demand and declining wage growth for highly routine occupations are two outcomes of the same underlying explanation of technology replacing routine tasks. The mismatch between the wage and employment changes is likely related to the sectoral minimum wages over the period of study. Key constituencies at the bottom of the income distribution are farm workers and domestic workers, with both of these groups covered by a minimum wage in 2002.

When disaggregating by gender it is notable that women exhibit wage polarization, but not employment polarization, and the opposite is true for men (Bhorat et al. 2020). This divergence by gender points to gender being an important dimension for explaining wage patterns and inequality in South Africa. This is well within expectations given the findings of an extensive local and international literature on the topic of gender in the South African labour market (Mosomi 2019; Casale and Posel 2011). In terms of occupation, women are highly concentrated in three main occupations: domestic work, personal care, and clerks—with these three occupations together making up 47.2 per cent of female employment in 2013–15. By contrast, men are more evenly distributed across different occupations, with concentration in elementary labourer work, drivers and mobile plant operators, trades work and protective services—these four occupations make up about 49.7 per cent of male employment in 2013–15 (Bhorat et al. 2020). Wage growth at the bottom end of the female wage distribution is very likely the result of growth in the domestic worker minimum wage, since as many as 16 per cent of women were domestic workers in 2013/15. Over time, however, the domestic work share of female employment has been shrinking as women shift into services-based industries. By contrast, men continue to be employed in elementary labourer occupations but have lost ground in traditional mid-skilled occupations like machine operators and assemblers and trades work. In addition, non-minimum-wage-covered job growth exceeded minimum-wage-covered for men, which may explain negative wage change at the lower end of the distribution (Bhorat et al. 2020).

Another way to view employment and earnings change by occupation is across the 'skill percentile', which ranks occupations according to their (employment-weighted) mean log wage and is a common analytic tool for researchers studying job polarization (Autor and Dorn 2009; Acemoglu and Autor 2011). In the literature from the US, wage polarization across the skill percentiles mirrors employment polarization across the skill percentiles. In contrast, in South Africa at low skill percentiles, wages are growing for precisely the occupations where employment share contracted. There is little indication of employment polarization for either men or women when using this more detailed way to classify occupations by skill (Bhorat et al. 2020). In fact, women are arguably displaying an inverted polarization pattern: Moving out of low-skilled occupations (almost exclusively domestic work) and dispersing into mid-skilled ones, particularly those around the 30th to 70th percentiles (e.g. cashiers, service clerks, personal care). The task explanation therefore appears to play only a weak role in explaining wage change at this point in the distribution.

In sum, very different wage growth patterns by gender are reconciled when looking at wage growth across occupations in the skill percentile. This suggests that an occupational framework is relevant to wage change in South Africa, and specifically for white-collar office jobs, like clerks. This may be because minimum wage policies have de-linked employment and earnings patterns specifically at the bottom end of the distribution. Next, we explore whether tasks are an important explanation in this regard by introducing a task variable and describing its distribution in South Africa.

6.5 Investigating occupational routine-task content

To investigate the role of routine work in explaining wage and employment changes, we run two sets of regressions and a decomposition. The first of these is a series of simple regressions following the specification of Sebastian (2018) in investigating job polarization in Spain. As expected, the author found a negative linear relationship meaning that the employment share of the most routine jobs grew the least. We run the following specification by gender:

$$\Delta E_j = \beta_0 + \beta_1 log\left(RTI_{j,t-1}\right) \tag{1}$$

$$\Delta logY_j = \beta_0 + \beta_1 log\left(RTI_{j,t-1}\right) \tag{2}$$

where ΔE_j is the percentage change in employment share of two-digit-level occupation j between time period $t-1$ and t; $\Delta logY_j$ is the change in log earnings for the two-digit occupation j between time period $t-1$ and t; $RTI_{j,t-1}$ is the O*NET-based index of routine-task intensity for occupation j in time period $t-1$. We weight all regressions by employment share in period $t-1$. For completeness, we run the same specification for the country-specific RTI but report it in the appendix.

6.5.1 Regression results

The results of our simple regressions are in Table 6.1 with graphical depictions of the full period result in Figure 6.1. The numbers on the bubbles in Figure 6.1 correspond to the two-digit occupational codes in Table 6.2, as does the change reported on the y-axis for employment. The sample size is small at only 27

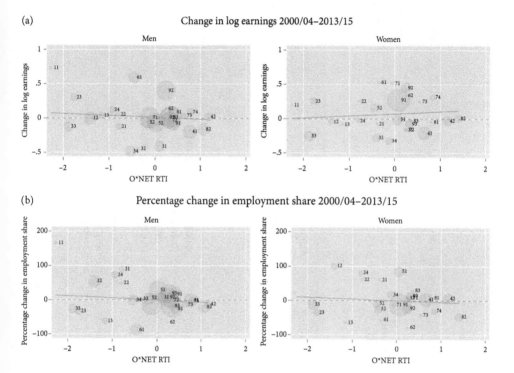

Figure 6.1 Employment weighted scatter plot of change in earnings and employment against O*NET routine-task intensity index at the two-digit occupational level, 2000/04–2013/15

Note: Sample restricted to employees. Bubble size corresponds to size of employment in 2000/04. Bubble number correspond to two-digit occupational codes, as follows: 11 Legislators and senior officials; 12 Corporate managers; 13 Managers of small enterprises; 21 Physical, mathematical and engineering science professionals; 22 Life science and health professionals; 23 Teaching professionals; 24 Other professionals; 31 Physical and engineering science associate professionals; 32 Life science and health associate professionals; 33 Teaching associate professionals; 34 Other associate professionals; 41 Office clerks; 42 Customer services clerks; 51 Personal and protective services worker; 52 Models, salespersons and demonstrators; 61 Skilled agricultural and fishery workers; 62 Subsistence agricultural and fishery workers; 71 Extraction and building trades workers; 72 Metal, machinery and related trades workers; 73 Precision, handicraft, craft printing and related trades workers; 74 Other craft and related trades workers; 81 Stationary plant and related operators; 82 Machine operators and assemblers; 83 Drivers and mobile plant operators; 91 Sales and services elementary occupations (excl. Domestic Workers); 92 Agricultural, fishery and related labourers; 93 Labourers in mining, construction, manufacturing and transport; and 10 Domestic workers.
Source: Authors' calculations using version 3.2 of the Post-Apartheid Labour Market Series adjusted using sampling weights.

Table 6.1 Regression output for employment and earnings changes for two-digit occupations and O*NET-measured routine-task intensity in South Africa, 2000–2015

	Change in log earnings				Percentage change in employment share			
	2005/7–2000/4	2010/2–2005/7	2013/5–2010/2	2013/5–2000/4	2005/7–2000/4	2010/2–2005/7	2013/5–2010/2	2013/5–2000/4
Women								
O*NET RTI	0.0211	0.0189	0.0149	**0.0392**	-3.838	-4.094	3.553	**-10.07**
	(0.0323)	(0.0290)	(0.0281)	**(0.0581)**	(4.704)	(5.702)	(3.560)	**(10.66)**
cons	0.112***	0.0177	-0.0677**	**0.0502**	0.0656	-0.0779	0.0632	**11.70**
	(0.0256)	(0.0232)	(0.0221)	**(0.0441)**	(3.727)	(4.575)	(2.806)	**(8.094)**
N	27	27	27	27	27	27	27	27
Men								
O*NET RTI	0.0172	-0.00997	-0.0273	**-0.00883**	-0.104	-8.378	2.852	**-18.23***
	(0.0450)	(0.0349)	(0.0269)	**(0.0632)**	(6.377)	(6.398)	(3.385)	**(8.294)**
cons	0.115***	-0.00897	-0.0907***	**-0.000997**	0.00496	0.226	0.00106	**8.866**
	(0.0289)	(0.0215)	(0.0174)	**(0.0396)**	(4.085)	(3.950)	(2.194)	**(5.195)**
N	27	27	27	27	27	27	27	27

Note: Sample restricted to employees. Standard errors in parentheses. $^*p<0.05$, $^{**}p<0.01$, $^{***}p<0.001$.
Source: Authors' calculations using version 3.2 of the Post-Apartheid Labour Market Series adjusted using sampling weights.

Table 6.2 Decomposition of the wage Gini coefficient by occupation and gender

	Actual				Shares constant				Means constant			
	2000–2004	2005–2007	2010–2012	2013–2015	2000–2004	2005–2007	2010–2012	2013–2015	2000–2004	2005–2007	2010–2012	2013–2015
Overall Gini	0.56	0.55	0.56	0.66	0.56	0.55	0.56	0.64	0.56	0.56	0.59	0.65
Shapley decomposition:												
Between-occupation	0.28	0.27	0.25	0.28	0.28	0.26	0.24	0.27	0.28	0.28	0.29	0.28
%	0.51	0.48	0.44	0.43	0.51	0.48	0.43	0.42	0.51	0.50	0.49	0.42
Within-occupation	0.27	0.28	0.31	0.38	0.27	0.28	0.32	0.37	0.27	0.28	0.30	0.38
%	0.49	0.52	0.56	0.57	0.49	0.52	0.57	0.58	0.49	0.50	0.51	0.58
Gini between occupations	0.41	0.39	0.38	0.43	0.41	0.39	0.37	0.41	0.41	0.41	0.43	0.43
Concentration index:												
O*NET RTI	0.18	0.19	0.22	0.27	0.18	0.15	0.17	0.22	0.18	0.19	0.26	0.24
%	0.44	0.47	0.57	0.63	0.44	0.38	0.46	0.53	0.44	0.46	0.61	0.56
CS RTI	0.40	0.38	0.37	0.43	0.40	0.37	0.36	0.41	0.40	0.40	0.42	0.42
%	0.97	0.96	0.98	0.98	0.97	0.96	0.97	0.98	0.97	0.97	0.98	0.98

Note: Sample restricted to employees.
Source: Authors' calculations using version 3.2 of the Post-Apartheid Labour Market Series adjusted using sampling weights.

two-digit occupations meaning significance was difficult to achieve. Nonetheless, we interpret the direction and size of the coefficients.

There does not appear to be a very strong relationship between RTI and earnings change; coefficients are close to zero. This conclusion is confirmed in the earnings results in Figure 6.1. Note the strong wage change for agricultural labourers for men (bubble 92) and essential sales and services (bubble 91, dominated by domestic workers) for women. This aligns with increases in minimum wages for these groups and the role these types of interventions have played in potentially de-linking wage change from a routine-tasks explanation. Such interventions could explain the positive association between RTI and wage change for women in Table 6.1: a standard deviation increase in RTI increased women's wages by 3.9 per cent over the whole period.

Results for employment are stronger and in particular for men. A one standard deviation increase in the routine intensity of an occupation led to a statistically significant reduction of 18.23 percentage points in that occupation's employment share. Men have moved largely out of routine work such as machine operation and assembly (bubble 82) and into non-routine work such as protective services (bubble 51), corporate management (bubble 12), and elementary labourer work (bubble 93). Although elementary labourer work is still relatively routine, it is less routine than machine operation and assembly. As such, the pattern of changing male employment has followed the logic of routine-biased technical change more consistently than that for women. The negative correlation between female employment change and routine work is diluted by counter-theoretical changes at the poles of the RTI. Figure 6.1 shows women moving out of highly non-routine teaching (bubbles 23 and 33) and into highly routine clerking (bubble 42).

6.6 Routine work and other explanations for inequality

Even if routine-biased technical change is mildly associated with employment change, how does it compare to other prominent explanations for wage inequality? To answer this question, we run a fuller specification for wage change. We consider the role of explanations such as skill-biased technical change (controlling for education and occupation); structural transformation (controlling for industrial composition); labour market institutions (controlling for trade unions and public sector employment); and, finally routine-biased technical change (with the RTI).

We run a RIF regression, also known as an unconditional quantile regression, developed by (Firpo et al. 2009). This regression makes use of the recentred influence function (RIF) of the outcome variable instead of the outcome itself, and allows us to estimate the relative importance of different variables at different points of the wage distribution. A RIF regression is run for the base period 2000–04 and an end period 2013–15. The specification is as follows for each sex separately and each time period (t):

$$RIF(logearnings)_t = \beta_0 + \beta_1 AGE_t + \beta_2 Age_t^2 + \beta_3 YRSEDUC_t + \beta_4 POPGROUP_t$$
$$+ \beta_5 IND_t + \beta_6 OCC_t + \beta_7 UNION_t + \beta_8 PUBLIC_t + \beta_9 RTI_{t\in}$$
$$(3)$$

where AGE and AGE^2 are age in years and age in years squared; $Y RSEDUC$ is the years of education variable provided in the PALMS data; $POPGROUP$ are three race group dummies with the omitted (base) category being Africans; IND are nine main industry dummies with the omitted (base) category being agriculture; OCC are also nine main occupation dummies with the omitted (base) category being senior managers; $UNION$ is a dummy for union membership; $PUBLIC$ is a dummy for employment in the public sector; and lastly RTI is either the O*NET RTI or country-specific RTI. The RIF regressions are weighted using the 'bracketweight' in PALMS.

Following this, we use an Oaxaca–Blinder decomposition to understand at which points of the wage distribution changes in the wage structure or composition of the employed have been more influential. The Oaxaca–Blinder decomposition decomposes the change in mean wages between two periods into effects owed to changes in the wage structure (coefficient effect), the composition of employment (endowment effect), and their interaction. The endowment effect is defined as the expected change in mean wages for employees in 2000/04, had they had the predictor levels (i.e. characteristics) of those in 2013/15. The coefficient effect is defined as the expected change in mean wages for employees in 2000/04, had they had the regression coefficients (i.e. wage structure) of those in 2013/15 (Jann 2008). We then run a detailed decomposition for each covariate.

6.6.1 RIF regression results

The total change in mean wages between the base and end periods, as well as the division into coefficient, endowment, and interaction effects are plotted in Figure 6.2.[2] The overall changes for men and women mirror the gender differences initially described: wage change is U-shaped for women, but negative for men at the bottom of the distribution. Important roles are played by both changes in the wage structure (coefficient effect) and composition of the employed (endowment effect). For both men and women, the coefficient effect lies above the endowment effect for most wage quantiles. This means that changes in the wage structure have served to increase wages between the early 2000s and mid 2010s; but this has been

---

[2] See Bhorat et al. (2020) for detailed RIF regression output for men and women.

offset to some extent by changes in the composition of employment. For men at the bottom end, it is compositional changes that undermined wage change; whereas for women at the top end, compositional changes supported wage change.

For women, changes in endowments in Figure 6.2 especially seemed to undermine wages between the 60th and 80th wage quantiles. Bhorat et al. (2020) notes that an important change at this point of the wage distribution for women was the decline in teachers, and to a lesser extent nurses. Teachers in particular have strong unions protecting wages for those who remain employed (Mahlangu and Pitsoe 2011; Msila 2014) so fewer teachers would likely affect wage change.

By contrast, descriptive statistics show the growth of residual business occupation categories of 'other professionals' and 'other associate professionals' which often capture business and administrative work (e.g. bookkeeping) (Bhorat et al. 2020). This trend could indicate women moving into less protected temporary employment work which could undermine wages. Temporary employment services are not directly identified in South African labour market data. Researchers have reached some consensus that the industry code 'Business Not Elsewhere Classified' may be capturing the spread of temporary work (Budlender 2013; Bhorat et al. 2016b). The share of both of these residual categories in female

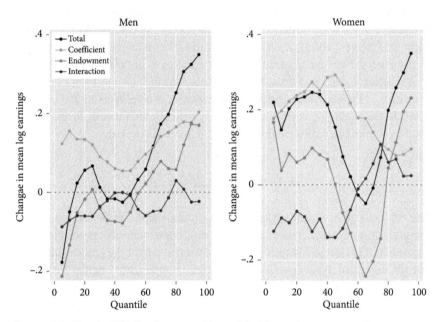

Figure 6.2 Oaxaca–Blinder decomposition of the change in wages across wage quantiles into the coefficient, endowment, and interaction effect for South Africa, 2000/04–2013/15

Note: Sample restricted to employees.
Source: Authors' calculations using version 3.2 of the Post-Apartheid Labour Market Series adjusted using sampling weights.

Business Not Elsewhere Classified increased over time. This could be an indication of the increased casualization of women's work, but it could also be a real increase in residual business categories. For men, the endowment effect undermined wages at the bottom end. We have previously discussed the continuing importance of low-skilled elementary labourer work for men. Here, men are also potentially becoming more 'casualized' since non-minimum-wage-covered labourers grew faster than farm workers, but a thorough test of the increase of casualization for either men or women is beyond the scope of this chapter.

Figure 6.3 summarizes the results of each set of variables, besides the constant term. The figure shows that the O*NET RTI is not very important in any regard for explaining the change in wages between these two periods when we control for other explanations. The RTI is barely visible in all plots. Instead, we see that changes in returns to years of education are crucial for explaining changes in the wage structure. This effect dwindles slightly as we move up the wage distribution for women, but the opposite is the case for men. The endowment effect on the other hand, is driven by age, which could also be proxying for experience which Finn and Leibbrandt (2018) found to be important. Changes in industry and occupation are important for both the coefficient and endowment effect. Industry accounts for wage structure effects at the bottom end, whilst occupation

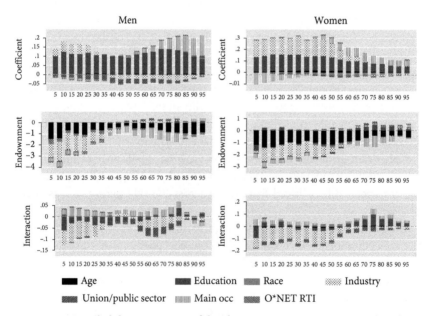

Figure 6.3 Detailed decomposition of the change in wages across wage quantiles, 2000/04–2013/15

Note: Sample restricted to employees.
Source: Authors' calculations using version 3.2 of the Post-Apartheid Labour Market Series adjusted using sampling weights.

(arguably proxying for skill) becomes more important at the top end. This aligns with the notion that minimum wages which intersect closely with low-income industries such as agriculture and domestic work, play an important role at the bottom end. For men, changes in unions and public sector employment also undermined wage growth.

6.7 Decomposing the Gini

A final decomposition investigates the contribution of tasks and occupations to the wage Gini. In Table 6.2 we calculate the wage Gini coefficient in different time periods and undertake various decompositions to understand the contribution of occupations and task content to wage inequality. Two counterfactual decompositions are also estimated: one holding occupational employment shares constant but allowing wages to change over time ('Shares constant' column); and the second holding occupational mean wages constant and allowing occupational employment shares to fluctuate over time ('Means constant').

As discussed in Bhorat et al. (2020), earnings inequality is trending upwards over time and the jump in the last period may reflect data quality issues. Comparing the two counterfactual scenarios allows us to ascertain to what degree changes in the Gini were driven by changes in employment composition versus earnings. The Gini increased very similarly in both counterfactuals suggesting it has been both employment and earnings changes that explain earnings inequality. However, if we ignore the last period, changes in occupational composition look narrowly more important.

The Shapley decomposition reveals that inequality between and within occupations equally contribute to overall inequality in the first period; but, over time, the within-occupation contribution becomes gradually more important. This conclusion also applies across both counterfactual scenarios and once again, there is a large step-up in the last period. The growing significance of the contribution of within-occupation inequality explains why wage growth patterns across the wage percentiles differed from those across the skill percentiles, as already discussed.

Inequality between occupations is high, existing in a range between 0.38–0.43. The concentration index estimates the Gini coefficient sorting occupations by the (inversely ordered) RTI. The between-occupation Gini and the concentration index are equal when average earnings by occupation and average earnings sorted by RTI are perfectly correlated, that is, the concentration index measures how closely RTI is associated with the between-occupation Gini. The O*NET RTI accounts for an increasing share of between-occupation wage inequality. The counterfactual analysis suggests this is owed to both changes in the wage structure and the composition of the employed, with the latter being marginally more important. This result coheres with previous discussions about the rising importance of services which are generally non-routine.

6.8 Discussion and conclusion

Between 2000 and 2015, the South African labour market underwent a process of wage polarization, but employment can better be described as skills-biased rather than polarizing. In spite of this, the routine-biased technical change hypothesis is more relevant for explaining employment than wage changes in South Africa. Across the skill percentile, South African wage change resembles a backwards J-shape, or hockey stick, more than the U-shape classically associated with wage polarization, due to the greater prevalence of low-skilled work in South Africa. Wage growth for low-income earners is more likely driven by the onset and maintenance of minimum wage legislation, especially for domestic workers for women and farm workers for men, than routine-biased technical change. The occupations found in the trough of the J are those typically found in the middle of industrialized country wage distributions: nurses, teachers, administrative workers, and various white-collar office clerks. Routine-biased technical change is likely an important factor for the decline in office clerk wages. However, other factors were at play for the overall fortunes of occupation in the trough of the J: earnings for these occupations shrank severely in real terms following the 2008 Global Financial Crisis, suggesting that the recession played a role. The share of (highly non-routine) teaching jobs declined, the wages for which are well-protected by strong trade unions (Mahlangu and Pitsoe 2011; Msila 2014); and, in their place other office and business administration occupation categories grew (often without corresponding wage growth) which are possibly associated with the casualization of the South African labour market. Therefore, whilst computer and other technology is very likely undermining the wages for office clerks occupying the upper middle of the South African wage distribution, the Global Financial Crisis, minimum wages, and casualization are also important for explaining the overall pattern of polarization.

Due to women clustering in a few care, cleaning, and clerk-based occupations, the routine-biased technical change hypothesis is more relevant for men who are more evenly distributed across occupations in the economy. Even so, routine-biased technical change is more relevant for male employment than wage changes: occupational routine intensity significantly predicted negative employment change for men between 2000 and 2015. This may be because routine intensity has interacted with the rapid structural transformation of the South African economy whereby the primary and secondary sectors have declined and services, business, and finance have risen to prominence. It is tempting to ratio-nalize this change by pointing out that agriculture, mining, and manufacturing are relatively routine, whilst services are non-routine. However, there are instead complex historical and context-specific reasons behind the contraction of mining and agriculture in South Africa (Bhorat et al. 2022). The manufacturing sector has collapsed mainly in the face of global competition. When South Africa opened its borders to international trade at the end of apartheid, the manufacturing sec-tor was unable to compete internationally after years of apartheid isolation had rendered the sector much less efficient than other trading partners (Edwards and Lawrence 2008). In this more global sense, perhaps South African manufacturing has been influenced by the adoption of more advanced machine and computer technologies in its trading partners. However, although mining, manufacturing, and agriculture are amongst the most routine sectors of the economy, it is not clear that routine-biased technical change played a decisive role in their decline from a local viewpoint.

Even if routine-biased technical change is less important for explaining why South Africa's primary and secondary sectors have declined, it likely is of impor-tance for explaining why the tertiary sector has grown. Firpo et al. (2011) describe how certain job task qualities can 'protect' work from being offshored: the need for work to be done on-site, for example, can 'protect' the existence of that job (e.g. a security worker, or personal care worker). These two qualities—being non-routine and requiring physical presence on-site—have probably contributed towards the flourishing of the personal and protective services sector in South Africa as a low-skilled alternative to increasingly scarce manufacturing jobs. These jobs are not necessarily well-paid (most personal care workers earn less than the median wage) and are associated with the growth of temporary employment services, suggesting these jobs are unprotected in important ways (Bhorat et al. 2016b).

At the other end of the wage distribution, jobs in services are growing for dif-ferent reasons. The GDP contribution of the financial and business services sector grew at about 4.8 per cent per year between 2000 and 2015 (Bhorat et al. 2020), making it the fastest growing sector only after construction. In other words, job growth here is stoked by South Africa's comparative advantage in financial ser-vices; however, we also expect service jobs to be growing due to South Africa's status as a destination for offshored service jobs. The documented rise in call cen-tres in Cape Town is testament to this (Benner 2006). The need for jobs to be performed on-site is less important at this point in the distribution and perhaps flexibility in this regard has contributed to job growth here.

This variation within the services sector should be monitored and examined in order to understand how the process of tertiarization will challenge or, more likely, reinforce existing earnings inequality. For example, what factors, along with non-routine intensity, are behind the growth of low-skilled personal and pro-tective services? What are the implications for gender and inequality given that women are mainly sorting into personal care services and men into protective services? And, how will the wage structure adjust to jobs that are growing because they cannot be offshored versus jobs that are growing because they are actively contributing to economic growth? These are some of the important questions illuminated by this analysis. Routine-biased technical change may therefore play a more important role in the future for South Africa and, importantly, a quite different role to the one played in industrialized countries.

References

Acemoglu, D., and D.H. Autor (2011). 'Skills, Tasks and Technologies: Implications for Employment and Earnings'. In In O.C. Ashenfelter and D. Card (eds), *Handbook of Labor Economics*, Vol. 4, pp. 1043–171. Amsterdam: Elsevier. https://doi.org/10.1016/S0169-7218(11)02410-5

Autor, D.H. (2014). 'Polanyi's Paradox and the Shape of Employment Growth' NBER Working Paper 20485. Cambridge, MA: National Bureau of Economic Research. https://doi.org/10.3386/w20485

Autor, D.H. (2019). 'Work of the Past, Work of the Future'. NBER Working Paper 25588. Cambridge, MA: National Bureau of Economic Research. https://doi.org/10.3386/w25588

Autor, D.H., and D. Dorn (2009). 'Inequality and Specialization: The Growth of Low-Skill Service Jobs in the United States'. NBER Working Paper 15150. Cambridge, MA: National Bureau of Economic Research. https://doi.org/10.3386/w15150

Autor, D.H., F. Levy, and R.J. Murnane (2003). 'The Skill Content of Recent Technological Change: An Empirical Exploration'. *The Quarterly Journal of Economics*, 118(4): 1279–333. https://doi.org/10.1162/003355303322552801

Benner, C. (2006). '"South Africa On-call": Information Technology and Labour Market Restructuring in South African Call Centres'. *Regional Studies*, 40(9): 1025–40. https://doi.org/10.1080/00343400600928293

Bhorat, H., T. Caetano, B. Jourdan, R. Kanbur, C. Rooney, B. Stanwix, and I. Woolard (2016a). 'Investigating the Feasibility of a National Minimum Wage for South Africa'. DPRU Working Paper 201601. Cape Town: Development Policy Research Unit, School of Economics, University of Cape Town.

Bhorat, H., A. Cassim, and D. Yu (2016b). 'Temporary employment services in south africa: Assessing the industry's economic contribution', Labour market intelligence project pset report no. 28, Department of Higher Education and Training of the South African Government. Available at: http://www.psetresearchrepository.dhet.gov.za/document/temporary-employment-servicessouth-africa-assessing-industry%E2%80%99s-economic-contribution.

Bhorat, H., C. Rooney, and F. Steenkamp (2018). 'Understanding and Characterizing the Services Sector in South Africa: An Overview'. In R. Newfarmer, J. Page, and F. Tarp (eds), *Industries without Smokestacks: Industrialization in Africa Reconsidered*, p. 275. Oxford: Oxford University Press. https://doi.org/10.1093/oso/9780198821885.003.0014

Bhorat, H., K. Lilenstein, M. Oosthuizen, and A. Thornton (2020). 'Wage Polarization in a High Inequality Emerging Economy: The Case of South Africa'. WIDER

Working Paper 2020/55. Helsinki: UNU-WIDER. https://doi.org/10.35188/UNU-WIDER/2020/812-2

Bhorat, H., K. Lilenstein, M. Oosthuizen, F. Steenkamp, and A. Thornton (2022). 'Economic Growth, Rising Inequality, and Deindustrialization: South Africa's Kuznetsian Tension'. In A.S. Alisjahbana, K. Sen, A. Sumner, and A.A. Yusuf (eds), *The Developer's Dilemma: Structural Transformation, Inequality Dynamics, and Inclusive Growth*. WIDER Studies in Development Economics. Oxford: Oxford University Press.

Branson, N., J. Garlick, D. Lam, and M. Leibbrandt (2012). 'Education and Inequality: The South African Case'. SALDRU Working Papers 75. Cape Town: Southern Africa Labour and Development Research Unit, University of Cape Town.

Budlender, D. (2013). 'Private Employment Agencies in South Africa'. SECTOR Working Paper 291. Geneva: International Labour Office (ILO). Available at: https://www.ilo.org/wcmsp5/groups/public/—ed_dialogue/—sector/documents/publication/wcms_231438.pdf (accessed April 2022).

Casale, D., and D. Posel (2011). 'Unions and the Gender Wage Gap in South Africa', *Journal of African Economies*, 20(1): 27–59. https://doi.org/10.1093/jae/ejq029

Crankshaw, O. (2017). 'Social Polarization in Global Cities: Measuring Changes in Earnings and Occupational Inequality'. *Regional Studies*, 51(11): 1612–21. https://doi.org/10.1080/00343404.2016.1222072

Edwards, L., and R. Lawrence (2008). 'South African Trade Policy Matters Trade Performance and Trade Policy'. *Economics of Transition*, 16(4): 585–608. https://doi.org/10.1111/j.1468-0351.2008.00338.x

Finn, A., and M. Leibbrandt (2018). 'The Evolution and Determination of Earnings Inequality in Post-Apartheid South Africa'. WIDER Working Paper 2018/83. Helsinki: UNU-WIDER. https://doi.org/10.35188/UNU-WIDER/2018/525-1

Firpo, S., N.M. Fortin, and T. Lemieux (2009). 'Unconditional Quantile Regressions'. *Econometrica*, 77(3): 953–73. https://doi.org/10.3982/ECTA6822

Firpo, S., N.M. Fortin, and T. Lemieux (2011). 'Occupational Tasks and Changes in the Wage Structure'. IZA Discussion Paper 5542. Bonn: Institute of Labor Economics. https://doi.org/10.2139/ssrn.1778886

Goos, M., A. Manning, and A. Salomons (2014). 'Explaining Job Polarization: Routine-biased Technological Change and Offshoring'. *American Economic Review*, 104(8): 2509–26. https://doi.org/10.1257/aer.104.8.2509

Hundenborn, J., M. Leibbrandt, and I. Woolard (2018). 'Drivers of Inequality in South Africa'. WIDER Working Paper 2018/162. Helsinki: UNU-WIDER. https://doi.org/10.35188/UNU-WIDER/2018/604-3

Jann, B. (2008). 'The Blinder–Oaxaca Decomposition for Linear Regression Models'. *The Stata Journal*, 8(4): 453–79. https://doi.org/10.1177/1536867X0800800401

Kerr, A., and M. Wittenberg (2017). 'Public Sector Wages and Employment in South Africa'. SALDRU Working Paper 214. Cape Town: Southern Africa Labour and Development Research Unit, University of Cape Town.

Kerr, A., D. Lam, and M. Wittenberg (2017). *Post-Apartheid Labour Market Series: 1993–2017* dataset, University of Cape Town: DataFirst [producer and distributor]. Version 3.2.

Mahlangu, V.P., and V.J. Pitsoe (2011). 'Power Struggle between Government and the Teacher Unions in South Africa'. *Journal of Emerging Trends in Educational Research and Policy Studies*, 2(5): 365–71.

Maloney, W.F., and C. Molina (2016). 'Are Automation and Trade Polarizing Developing Country Labor Markets, too?' Policy Research Working Paper 7922. Washington, DC: World Bank. https://doi.org/10.1596/1813-9450-7922

Mosomi, J. (2019). 'An Empirical Analysis of Trends in Female Labour Force Participation and the Gender Wage Gap in South Africa'. *Agenda*, 33(4): 29–43. https://doi.org/10.1080/10130950.2019.1656090

Msila, V. (2014). 'Teacher Unionism and School Management: A Study of (Eastern Cape) Schools in South Africa'. *Educational Management Administration & Leadership*, 42(2): 259–74. https://doi.org/10.1177/1741143213499265

Sebastian, R. (2018). 'Explaining Job Polarisation in Spain from a Task Perspective'. *SERIEs*, 9(2): 215–48. https://doi.org/10.1007/s13209-018-0177-1

Statistics South Africa (2003). *South African Standard Classification of Occupations (SASCO)*, Technical release October.

Wittenberg, M. (2017a). 'Wages and Wage Inequality in South Africa 1994–2011: Part 1–Wage Measurement and Trends'. *South African Journal of Economics*, 85(2): 279–97. https://doi.org/10.1111/saje.12148

Wittenberg, M. (2017b). 'Wages and Wage Inequality in South Africa 1994–2011: Part 2–Inequality Measurement and Trends'. *South African Journal of Economics*, 85(2): 298–318. https://doi.org/10.1111/saje.12147

World Bank (2020). *Gini Index (World Bank Estimate)*. Available at: https://data.worldbank.org/indicator/SI.POV.GINI

7

Tunisia

Employment and Inequality Trends

Minh-Phuong Le, Mohamed Ali Marouani, and Michelle Marshalian

7.1 Introduction

Tunisia is a lower middle-income country structurally characterized by high unemployment rates despite a sustained average growth rate of 5 per cent from the mid-1990s to the global financial crisis. In the last 20 years, youth employment has been severe, particularly for graduates. Coupled with a widely shared sentiment of political discontent and rising cronyism among the population (Rijkers et al. 2017), the labour market outcomes fuelled the Revolution of 2011, with a long-lasting impact for the whole Middle East and North Africa (MENA) region. Tunisia and MENA are, however, not exceptions. In many places in the world, the combination of a youth bulge and low demand for skills have induced unemployment, overeducation, frustration, and rebellion (Nordås and Davenport 2013).

Our objective in this study is to analyse the dynamics of the jobs and earnings distributions in the decades preceding and following the Revolution and their determinants, with a focus on the evolution of the nature of jobs according to their task content. More precisely, we aim to identify regularities explained by structural factors such as demography, education, or computerization.

Much of the academic literature on employment and wage distribution focuses on levels of education, suggesting that the increasing gap between two distinct skill groups is the strongest determinant of earnings inequality. However, an influential and growing literature (Autor et al. 2003; Acemoglu and Autor 2011; Autor and Dorn 2013) has shown that a significant share of inequality in developed countries is also explained by inequality within skill groups, namely due to occupational change and the tasks associated with occupations. Routine tasks are mainly concentrated in average-wage occupations, while low-wage and high-wage occupations are characterized respectively by high intensity of non-routine manual and non-routine cognitive tasks. The 'routine-biased technical change' (RBTC) claims that the substitution of routine tasks and the complementation of non-routine cognitive tasks with technology are the reason behind the growing disappearance of the middle class in the US. While this work was ground-breaking, it remains biased

Minh-Phuong Le, Mohamed Ali Marouani, and Michelle Marshalian, *Tunisia: Employment and Inequality Trends*.
In: *Tasks, Skills, and Institutions*. Edited by Carlos Gradín, Piotr Lewandowski, Simone Schotte, and Kunal Sen, Oxford University Press © UNU-WIDER (2023). DOI: 10.1093/oso/9700192872241.003.0007

towards the task-based structure of occupations in the most developed countries. Indeed, as shown by Lewandowski et al. (2020), occupations in developing countries are more intensive in routine tasks than similar occupations in developed countries. Studying the case of Portugal, a country with slow adoption of automation, Fonseca et al. (2018) show that the decline of routine manual task jobs is the main determinant of job and wage polarization, while routine cognitive task jobs do not witness a similar outcome. Maloney and Molina (2019) investigate polarization and automation links in developing countries, including the impact of developed countries' automation and offshore strategies, and find either latent polarization forces or insignificant effects of robots' penetration. Using Chinese data, Fleisher et al. (2018) highlight a redistribution of jobs from middle-income skills to low-income categories, but they do not find any evidence of polarization at the upper end of the skill spectrum, despite the development of routine tasks.

Bárány and Siegel (2018) propose an alternative explanation of job polarization, driven by structural change. Their main argument is that polarization started in the 1950s in the US, long before the revolution in information and communication technologies (ICT). Their analysis is based on the complementarity between consumption goods in manufacturing (intensive in medium-skilled workers) and low-skill and high-skill services, and the increase of relative labour productivity in manufacturing, which pushes labour in the two other sectors. This is in line with the work of Kupets (2016), who shows that job polarization in Ukraine is due to a structural change biased towards subsistence agriculture and low value-added services, rather than routine-based technological change.

In this chapter, we first analyse the evolution of employment and earnings distributions and test for the polarization hypothesis before and after the Tunisian Revolution. We then dig deeper into distributional changes across occupations by moving to a fine-grained analysis based on occupations and their task compositions. A recentred influence function (RIF) decomposition is performed to decompose the change in earnings in wage structure and composition effects and to assess the role played by various determinants of inequality. This allows us to check the Tunisian results against previous work and to focus on the specificity of the Tunisian context, including changes that occurred after the 2011 Revolution.

Our main result highlights a wage polarization in Tunisia's labour market, but unlike in developed countries, Tunisian polarization seems to have been mainly led by increases in the lowest wages, similar to the phenomenon observed in China by Fleisher et al. (2018). The RIF decomposition of earnings inequality changes shows that the decrease in the public–private wage gap and in sector wage gaps, and the decreasing education premia were the main determinants of inequality decline. The routine-task intensity (RTI) made a small and negative contribution to inequality change before the Revolution and a positive contribution afterwards. In other words, there is little evidence of the impact of computerization on wage inequality in Tunisia's labour market.

The rest of the chapter is organized as follows. Section 7.2 briefly presents the database and the routine task indices used. Section 7.3 illustrates the changes in jobs and earnings distribution of the labour market over the last two decades. We then focus on the role of the task nature in Section 7.4. A RIF decomposition is implemented in Section 7.5 to disentangle the contribution of underlying factors to changes in earnings inequality. Finally, Section 7.6 draws our conclusions.

7.2 Data and routine task indices

The data used for this chapter are cross-sectional data from the National Population and Employment Survey (Enquête Nationale sur la Population et l'Emploi—ENPE), conducted by the Tunisian National Statistics Institute (INS). Using three waves of data on labour market and household conditions from 2000, 2010, and 2017, we are able to examine the occupational and distributive changes in the decades before and after the Revolution.

The annual ENPE survey was first conducted in 2000 to provide information on the labour market, household composition, and employment policy. For these purposes, the survey is divided into two main modules. The first module provides demographic information on all members of the household, including gender, age, relationship with the householder, marital position, education, working status, and employment sector. The second module describes the working conditions and, exceptionally for paid workers, the remuneration (including net salary, assurance, allowance, and other benefits). Therefore, our analysis will only use the data set of employees, which contains 19,642 observations in the 2000 wave, 92,612 observations in the 2010 wave, and 60,152 observations in the 2017 wave.

We apply two alternative measures of routine-task content. The first one is proposed by Autor et al. (2003), based on the US Department of Labor's DOT, and its successor, O*NET. This RTI index is aggregated from five sub-indices measuring the intensity of five different types of tasks: non-routine cognitive, non-routine interactive, non-routine manual, routine cognitive, and routine manual. The use of O*NET to quantify the RTI in developing countries, however, is contentious due to large differences in technological progress, globalization, structural change, and skill supply (Lewandowski et al. 2019).

Our second routine-task content measure is predicted through a regression-based methodology developed by Lewandowski et al. (2020). It uses job-task information collected from individual-level surveys in 46 countries around the world. This country-specific RTI measure does not only enable capture of the variance of task content of occupations across countries, but also gives more insight into the within-occupation heterogeneity.

7.3 Changes in general job distribution and earnings inequality

7.3.1 A decrease in inequality over the two decades

Labour income inequality in Tunisia has decreased significantly over the past two decades, from 0.353 in 2000 to 0.294 in 2017. The trends in earnings inequality reflect two episodes: before and after the Revolution. The first period witnesses a rapid fall in earnings inequality, with the Gini index dropping by 4 percentage points over 10 years (Table 7.1). While the reduction is clear at the aggregate level, there is also evidence to suggest that the reduction in inequality did not affect all workers in the same way. On a macro level, we see that the variance in earnings may have fallen considerably from 2000 to 2010, but this improvement was followed by an increase in 2017 as compared to 2010. In fact, the difference between earnings in the bottom 50th (median) to 10th percentiles decreased more than those in the top 90th to 50th percentile. The earnings gap between the 90th and 50th percentiles narrowed mostly during the post-Revolution period, whereas the earnings gap between the 50th and 10th percentiles contracted more in the pre-Revolution period. As we will argue in later sections, this decrease of inequality mainly came from the improvement of wages for low-wage workers and, to a lower extent, medium-wage workers.

Examining the earnings growth by percentile (Figure 7.1), we see high growth in low wages from 2000 to 2010 (the lowest decile), but a net loss of earnings in low-wage jobs in the 2010–17 period. We also see the opposite pattern for high-income earners, confirming that for the period prior to the Revolution there was a reduction in the growth of inequality, while after the Revolution some increasing variability of job growth across the earnings distribution was observed. For the rest of the working population, growth was relatively flat in the pre-Revolution period, but increasing in the post-Revolution period. As such, some of the polarization we would expect to observe in the second period is hampered by growth in middle-wage occupations.

Table 7.1 Summary inequality indices and inter-quantile ratios

	Summary indices				Inter-quantile ratios		
	2000	2010	2017		2000	2010	2017
Var	0.645	0.384	0.429	log(p90/p10)	1.636	1.422	1.283
Gini (log)	0.098	0.074	0.069	log(p90/p50)	0.847	0.832	0.772
Gini	0.355	0.315	0.295	log(p50/p10)	0.788	0.590	0.511

Source: Authors' calculations based on ENPE data.

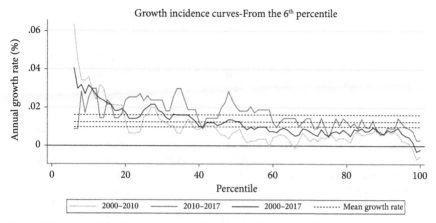

Figure 7.1 Growth incidence curves of the wage distribution (from the 6th percentile)

Source: Authors' illustration based on ENPE data.

7.3.2 An occupational perspective

The trends in earnings inequality show some underlying heterogeneity. One of the reasons for these changes is the evolving share and earnings associated with occupations. When we look at the three skill group levels (Figure 7.2), we find some stable results over the whole period of investigation and some that vary

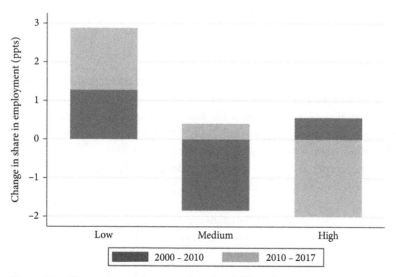

Figure 7.2 Change in employment share by skill level

Source: Authors' illustration based on ENPE data.

Table 7.2 Change in employment and earnings by occupational group

Panel A: Employment share (%)

	Level			Percentage change	
	2000	2010	2017	2000–10	2010–17
1 Managers	3.53	3.39	3.20	−0.14	−0.19
2 Professionals	10.74	11.22	10.94	0.48	−0.28
3 Technicians	6.68	6.90	5.36	0.22	−1.54
4 Clerks	9.79	7.51	5.38	−2.28	−2.13
5 Services	10.12	10.91	14.35	0.80	3.44
6 Skilled agricultural	3.88	3.11	4.74	−0.76	1.63
7 Trades workers	14.85	13.79	13.92	−1.05	0.13
8 Machine operators	15.28	15.97	14.93	0.69	−1.04
9 Elementary	25.15	27.19	27.16	2.04	−0.03

Panel B: Mean weekly earnings (constant 2010 prices)

	Level			Annual growth rate [*]	
	2000	2010	2017	2000–10	2010–17
1 Managers	193.53	202.43	164.60	0.45	−2.91
2 Professionals	161.61	173.44	179.65	0.71	0.50
3 Technicians	121.80	122.64	138.53	0.07	1.76
4 Clerks	102.09	101.58	109.58	−0.05	1.09
5 Services	83.97	80.34	91.76	−0.44	1.92
6 Skilled agricultural	44.71	50.96	61.25	1.32	2.66
7 Trades workers	69.68	81.18	91.52	1.54	1.73
8 Machine operators	69.62	74.16	82.63	0.63	1.56
9 Elementary	51.54	59.13	75.32	1.38	3.52

Note: (*) compound annual growth rate.
Source: Authors' calculations based on ENPE data.

with the sub-period.[1] The share of low-skilled workers increased between 2000 and 2017, with an acceleration after 2010. For medium- and high-skilled workers, we have an inversion of trends: while high-skill workers were progressing at the expense of medium-skilled workers before 2010, high-skilled jobs were reduced and medium-skilled jobs increased afterwards.

Digging deeper at the one-digit occupational level (Table 7.2), we find a significant decrease of high routine-intensive jobs, including clerks and machine operators. Clerks were the biggest losers in terms of jobs. Not only workers in high routine-intensive jobs, but technicians and associated professionals whose share was slightly increasing in the first sub-period were also characterized by a significant decrease after 2010. While these dynamics are in line with sluggish structural

---

[1] The classification of broad skill levels is adapted from the ILO's classification. Groups 1–3 are labelled as high-skilled level; groups 4, 5, 7, and 8 as medium-skilled; and groups 6 and 9 as low-skilled.

change throughout the last two decades and shrinking activity in the transport and telecom sectors after the Revolution (Marouani and Mouelhi 2016), they also suggest that the RTBC might be at work.

On the other side, skilled agricultural, elementary workers and services employees were the main beneficiaries in terms of employment creation during the whole period. For category 5 (service workers), the number of security-related workers almost doubled between 2010 and 2017,[2] while it decreased slightly between 2000 and 2010. This increase after the Revolution was due to the significant increase in the hiring of security forces (police, national guard, etc.). Shop salespersons also increased significantly, as well as housekeepers and restaurant service workers.

The evolution of occupational earnings shown in panel B of Table 7.2 is consistent with our observation of the decline in inequality. The lowest-paid jobs (elementary and skilled agricultural workers) witnessed a remarkable increase in weekly earnings over the whole examined period. As mentioned above, the increasing demand for labour in agriculture while the manufacturing sector stagnated is an important driving force for earnings growth in these groups. It was further promoted by the pro-poor public wage policy under the post-revolution pressures (Amara et al. 2017). The demand side factors are, however, not sufficient to explain the earnings patterns of the labour market. In the next subsection, we will detail the role of skill supply and the trend of the education premium.

7.3.3 The fall of the education premium

Tunisia experienced a high pace of education expansion over the pre-revolution period. The gross tertiary enrolment ratio of Tunisia increased on average 1.4 percentage points per year from 2000 to 2011, whereas the average of the world and the MENA region was about 1.1 percentage points. While the supply of highly educated workers was and remained high, the demand for jobs in more productive and high-earning sectors stagnated (Marouani and Mouelhi 2016).

The unemployment rate of Tunisian graduates soared from 10.4 per cent in 2001 to 22.9 per cent in 2010 (Adel 2013) and 30 per cent in 2017 (Kthiri 2019). As a result, the education premium associated with high-earning jobs decreased for men and women (Figure 7.3). In 2000, men and women educated at tertiary levels gained, respectively, a premium of 30 and 20 percentage points above those who had a secondary level of education. This difference had reduced to 10 percentage points by 2017.

Although the education premium has been decreasing very sharply since 2000 (Figure 7.3), this movement slowed down for men and reversed for women. Prior

---

[2] Authors' calculations based on ENPE data.

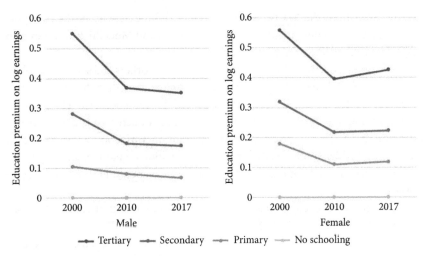

Figure 7.3 Change in the education premium on log earnings by gender
Source: Authors' illustration based on ENPE data.

to the Revolution, the education premium was higher for women than for men at any level of education. In line with the literature on gender and earnings, this suggests that education levels were a more important predictor of earnings for women than for men. For Tunisian wage earners, the Revolution levelled gender-related differences due to the returns to education. The reduction in the education premium finding suggests that not only were workers with different levels of education converging in terms of wages but that this was also the case between males and females.

7.3.4 Polarization tests

The above preliminary description suggests a potential polarized evolution in Tunisia's labour market. From 2000 to 2017, the labour market in Tunisia witnessed a large decrease of some middle-income jobs such as clerical roles, craft and related trade jobs, and manufacturing jobs. In the meantime, the average weekly earnings of low-skilled jobs such as service workers and elementary occupations increased significantly (Table 7.2). To detect the presence of polarization, we adopt a job polarization test proposed by Goos and Manning (2007). The intuition is simple: the relative decrease of middle-income jobs leads to a U-shaped pattern of employment evolution conditional on the initial wage level. More precisely, the specification is as follows:

$$\Delta EmploymentShare_i = \beta_0 + \beta_1\,Earnings_{i,t-1} + \beta_2\,Earnings^2_{i,t-1}$$

Table 7.3 Job and earnings polarization tests

Dependent variable:	Change in employment share			Change in mean log earnings		
	2000–2010	2010–2017	2000–2017	2000–2010	2010–2017	2000–2017
Initial mean log earnings	−2.233	−1.391	−5.579	−1.659***	−1.062*	−1.936***
Sq. initial mean log earnings	0.199	0.149	0.565	0.173***	0.096	0.184**
Constant	5.955	3.049	13.381	4.009***	2.940**	5.121***
Observations	103	102	101	103	102	101

Note: Robust standard errors in parentheses. ***p<0.01, **p<0.05, *p<0.1.
Source: Authors' calculations based on ENPE data.

If there exists a polarization pattern, the coefficient of the linear term should be found to be significantly negative, while the coefficient of the quadratic term is significantly positive.

The decrease in the demand for middle-skilled jobs should result in a decrease in wages at the middle of the distribution relative to the bottom and the top. In other words, if a polarization of jobs exists, changes in wages should also follow the same U-shaped pattern as changes in employment share. Hence, Sebastian (2018) extended this specification to the relationship between wage growth and the initial wage level:

$$\Delta Earnings_i = \beta_0 + \beta_1 Earnings_{i,t-1} + \beta_2 Earnings_{i,t-1}^2$$

Table 7.3 presents our quadratic regressions of changes in employment share and log mean earnings on the initial level of log mean earnings. Although no significant evidence of employment polarization is found in Tunisia, the regression of log earnings growth on the initial log mean earnings provides support for the earnings polarization in the first period. Despite the significant regression estimates, the plot of the changes in log earnings over skill percentiles (Figure 7.4b) show an L-shaped pattern with the increase of earnings at the lower end of the distribution and the stagnancy of earnings at the upper end of the distribution.

7.4 Task-based analysis

Although we observed an earnings polarization in Tunisia's labour market during the 2000–10 sub-period, it is not straightforward to claim a preeminent role for the routinization hypothesis. Other patterns of occupational evolution are also found,

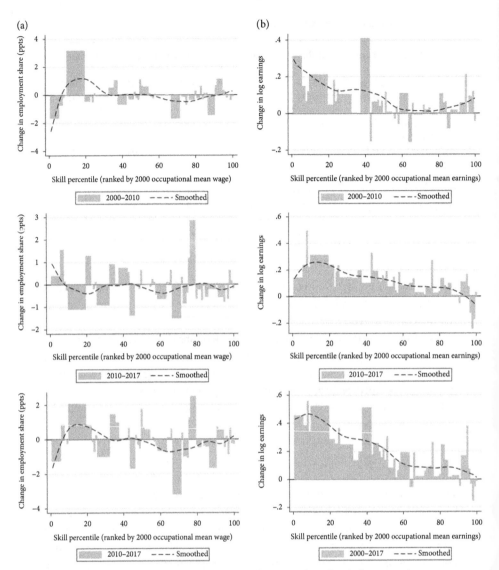

Figure 7.4 Change in log earnings and employment share by skill percentiles
Source: Authors' illustration based on ENPE data.

for example, the decreasing number of technical jobs, the contrasting employment share changes of the agricultural group over the pre- and post-Revolution periods, or the earnings degradation of managers after the Revolution. We further investigate the routinization hypothesis using two direct measures of routine-task intensity, the O*NET RTI and the country-specific RTI. The indices range from

−4.35 to 2.92 and from −0.77 to 0.95 respectively, where higher values correspond to a higher intensity of routine tasks. Before looking for any relationship between RTI and the evolution of jobs and earnings, we need to answer an elemental question: where are the high-RTI jobs located in the earnings distribution? In other words, are the high-RTI jobs low-, medium-, or high-paid jobs? To answer this question, we plot the average three-digit-occupation RTI against the rank of 2000 occupational mean log earnings in Figure 7.5. As we can see, the highest O*NET RTI jobs are the lower-middle jobs while the lowest-RTI jobs are situated at the upper end of the earnings distribution. This is consistent with the observations of Autor and Dorn (2013), Acemoglu and Autor (2011), Goos and Manning (2007), and many other authors using the O*NET RTI. In contrast, the highest country-specific RTI jobs are the worst paid.

The narrative further departs from the previous studies when it comes to the evolution of RTI overtime. Indeed, we found a contrasting trend with the evolution of RTI observed in advanced countries. During the 2000–10 period, the average O*NET RTI increased significantly from 0.529 to 0.602, then slightly decreased over the second sub-period, but until 2017 it had not come back to the 2000 level. The increase in the average country-specific RTI is less remarkable, from 0.401 in 2000 to 0.441 in 2017, but consistent throughout the two decades.[3]

To understand the increasing trend of Tunisia's RTI, we disaggregate the overall change in average RTI into the effect of the change of the occupational structure within each one-digit occupation (within effect) and the effect of changes in

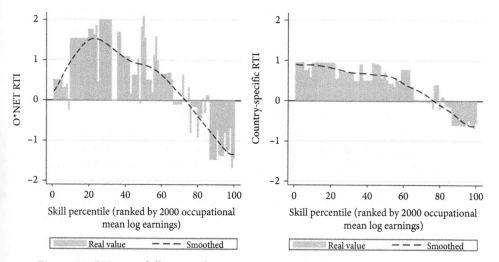

Figure 7.5 RTI over skill percentile
Source: Authors' illustration based on ENPE data.

[3] Authors' calculations based on ENPE data.

the share of each occupation at the one-digit level (between effect). This analysis is repeated for sectors. The decomposition is expressed as follows, where the subscript i represents alternatively one-digit occupations or sectors:

$$\Delta RTI = \sum \overline{RTI}_{i1} * w_{i1} - \sum \overline{RTI}_{i0} * w_{i0}$$
$$= \sum \overline{RTI}_{i1} * w_{i1} - \sum \overline{RTI}_{i0} * w_{i1} + \sum \overline{RTI}_{i0} * w_{i1} - \sum \overline{RTI}_{i0} * w_{i0}$$
$$= \underbrace{\sum \left(\overline{RTI}_{i1} - \overline{RTI}_{i0}\right) * w_{i1}}_{Within} + \underbrace{\sum \overline{RTI}_{i1} * \left(w_{i1} - w_{i0}\right)}_{Between}$$

The decomposition shows that both RTIs increased mostly due to the increase of elementary jobs—labourers in construction and manufacturing—in the first period.[4] However, the contribution of elementary occupations to changes in average country-specific RTI is due to the 'between effect', while the contribution of elementary occupations to changes in average O*NET RTI is due to the 'within effect'. This results from the differences of the two RTIs in the agriculture sector and elementary occupations. Occupations in agriculture are considered to have high RTI using the country-specific RTI: skilled agricultural workers (group 61) have an RTI of 0.76 and agricultural labourers (group 92) have an RTI of 0.95. Measured by the O*NET RTI, the two scores shrink to 0.29 and 0.52, respectively (weighted average using the 2000 employment share). Labourers in construction, mining, and manufacturing (group 93) have high RTI when calculated by O*NET RTI (1.55), but much lower RTI when measured by country-specific RTI (0.95).

Although the average country-specific RTI kept increasing in the aftermath of the Revolution, the drivers at the one-digit occupational level were not the same. After 2010, the manufacturing industry and construction—the main drivers of RTI before the Revolution—now negatively contributed to the average RTI due to a decrease in the share of plant and machine operators. Nevertheless, the higher demand for skilled agricultural workers and protective service workers more than compensated for the former, and aggregate country-specific RTI increased between 2010 and 2017. On the opposite side, we observed a declining trend of the O*NET RTI in the second period because of the occupational group trade workers, which has an O*NET RTI of 1.3 and a country-specific RTI of 0.84.

In the next step, we apply the same specification as in the polarization tests to study the correlation between RTI and the dynamics of employment and earnings in Tunisia. The independent variables are replaced by the RTI and its quadratic term. The insignificant point estimate of $RTI_{i,t-1}$ and $RTI_{i,t-1}^2$ for the employment share change comes as no surprise since we did not find any evidence of job polarization in the previous section. Therefore, we only present the result for log earnings change (Table 7.4). Accordingly, all linear terms are positively significant

---

[4] For the detailed results, please refer to our working paper.

Table 7.4 OLS regression of change in log earnings on the initial level of RTI

	2000–10	2010–17	2000–17	2000–10	2010–17	2000–17
Country-specific RTI	0.076**	0.130***	0.197***	0.021	0.096***	0.113**
Sq. country-specific RTI				0.141	0.088*	0.218*
Constant	0.064**	0.085***	0.147***	0.024	0.059***	0.084*
O*NET RTI	0.031*	0.059***	0.084***	0.029	0.054***	0.080***
Sq. O*NET RTI				0.004	0.007	0.007
Constant	0.078***	0.104***	0.182***	0.074*	0.096***	0.174***
Observations	26	26	26	26	26	26

Note: *** <0.01, **p<0.05, *p<0.1.
Source: Authors' calculations based on ENPE data.

in both periods. This implies that the higher-RTI occupations tended to have larger increases in earnings over time, which is at odds with the routinization hypothesis. These results confirm the absence of job polarization and the L-shaped evolution of earnings conditional on the initial earnings that we observed in Section 4.3.

7.5 Determinants of changes in earnings inequality

How much did the changing nature of jobs contribute to inequality change, in comparison to other factors? To answer this question, we use the recentred influence function RIF decomposition method developed by Firpo et al. (2011). Generalized from the conventional Oaxaca–Blinder decomposition, the RIF decomposition can be applied to any distributional statistics besides the mean, such as median, variance, the Gini index, or interdecile ratios. The key idea is to replace the outcome variable Y by the RIF of the distributional statistic of interest. The recentred influence function $RIF(y; v; F)$ of a distributional statistic $v(F)$ tells us how much an individual observation affects that distributional statistic (Firpo et al. 2009).

Our covariates include RTI, age, sex, education, public sector, region, and industry. All covariates but the RTI are categorical. As noted by Firpo et al. (2011), the total contribution of a categorical variable to the total earnings structure effect varies according to the choice of the omitted based category. The difference will be transferred into the intercept (unobserved characteristics). Although some methods have been proposed to make the earnings structure effects of a categorical variable invariant, they are still somewhat arbitrary or make it difficult to interpret the size of the effects. Since earnings inequality in Tunisia declined, we choose to omit the most favoured category, so that any increase in its returns,

Table 7.5 RIF decomposition of changes in the Gini index

| | Gini | | | |
| | Country-specific RTI | | ONET RTI | |
	2000–10	2020–17	2000–10	2010–17
Total change (F-I)	−0.041 ***	−0.02 ***	−0.041***	−0.02***
Total compostion (C-I)	0.003**	0.005 ***	0.004*	0.008***
RTI	−0.001**	−0.003 ***	−0.002***	0.002***
Age	0.000	0.000	0.000	0.000
Male=0	0.000 ***	0.000 ***	0.001***	0.001***
Public=0	0.003 ***	0.001 ***	0.003***	0.000***
Coast=0	0.001 ***	0.001 ***	0.001**	0.001***
Education	0.009 ***	0.001 ***	0.009***	0.001***
Industry	−0.008 ***	0.005 ***	−0.006***	0.003***
Total earnings structure (F-C)	−0.044 ***	−0.025 ***	−0.044***	−0.028***
RTI	−0.016 ***	0.003	−0.017***	0.005***
Age	−0.018	−0.022 ***	−0.014	−0.018***
Male=0	0.003	0.003 **	0.004*	0.003**
Public=0	−0.046 ***	−0.001	−0.052***	−0.002
Coast=0	−0.005 **	−0.009 ***	−0.004*	−0.008***
Education	−0.019 ***	−0.012 ***	−0.021***	−0.013***
Industry	−0.036 ***	−0.015 **	−0.028**	−0.011*
Intercept	0.093 ***	0.027 **	0.089***	0.017

Note: Bootstrapped standard errors in parentheses. ***$p<0.01$, **$p<0.05$, *$p<0.1$.
Source: Authors' calculations based on ENPE data.

which increases earnings inequality, is interpreted as the result of the individual's unobserved characteristics. More precisely, we take male, public, coastal region, and Hotels-Restaurant as base category. In the case of education, we take the secondary level as the base category according to the common practice in the literature.

The results of the RIF decomposition of changes in Gini index are presented in Table 7.5. In general, the total composition effect contributed to increases in Gini coefficient during the first sub-period. However, the disequalizing composition effect was entirely counteracted by the equalizing wage structure effect. The two effects also had opposite trends: the total composition effect tended to rise while the wage structure effect tended to fall overtime.

The composition effects were mostly induced by the change in the education composition of the labour force. The increase in education attainment had a disequalizing effect (positive coefficient). During the first sub-period, the increase of the private sector's share in the labour market also positively contributed to the overall inequality since wages were more equally distributed in the public sector.

Moving to the detailed wage structure effects, we find that the most important factors are two demand-side factors: the public–private wage gap and the sector wage gap. The reduction in the wage gap between public and private high-skilled workers was the largest contributor to the decline in earnings inequality over the last two decades. Most of the change in the public–private wage gap took place in the first sub-period. No significant change is observed in the second sub-period. The change in the sector premium, mainly before 2011, was the second contributor to the reduction of the overall earnings inequality. The return-to-education decline, despite not being the most important, still contributed largely to the decrease of the Gini index. The smaller contribution of education to the decreases in the Gini index after the Revolution corresponds to the smaller slope of the education premium during this period. Among the covariates, only RTI (measured by the O*NET RTI) had the opposite contributions over the two sub-periods. During the 2000–10 period, the increase in marginal returns to low-wage but relatively high-RTI jobs (the L-shaped pattern of log earnings evolution) enhanced the equality. Despite enhancing equality, the appreciation of low-skilled and highly repetitive jobs is a reversal of the technological progress of the country. Technological changes, however, started by having a small increasing-inequality effect in the second period.

The decomposition of changes in the Gini index provides a good picture of the total contribution of each factor to the total change of the distribution. However, it is silent about how these factors affected the earnings distribution, for example, which factor levelled up the lower end of the distribution, which factor pulled down the upper end of the distribution, etc. Therefore, we also look at the impact of each factor at the percentile level. The results for the O*NET RTI are shown in Figure 7.6. Accordingly, the reduction in the wage gap between the private and public sectors was mostly driven by a reduction in the upper half of the distribution. Meanwhile, the structural changes reduced the overall inequality by upgrading the industrial premium of the low-skilled jobs during the first sub-period and the industrial premium of the middle-skilled jobs during the second sub-period. Technological changes, of which some effects are observed only after the Revolution, disequalized the earnings distribution by improving the earnings of the upper-middle income class.

7.6 Conclusion

In this chapter we investigated the links between inequality and the changing nature of jobs in the context of a revolution. We also study the determinants

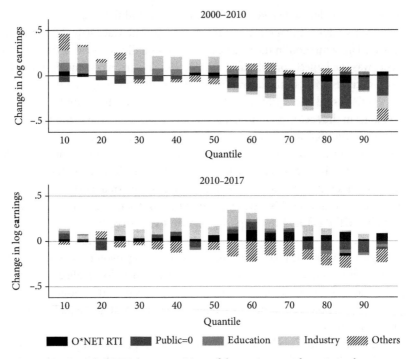

Figure 7.6 Detailed RIF decomposition of determinants of earnings changes
Source: Authors' illustration based on ENPE data.

of inequality variation including the Tunisian Revolution and, in particular, its impact on public hiring and wage policies.

Earnings inequality decreased significantly during the period of investigation in Tunisia due mainly to decreasing education premia. This evolution of education premia is similar in all MENA countries as they are characterized by an excess supply of tertiary-educated job seekers due to a pattern of specialization based on low- and medium-skilled labour. The employment and wage policies in the public sector since the revolution also played a role in reducing inequality. Moreover, wage polarization is highlighted, but unlike developed countries, Tunisian polarization seems to have been mainly led by an increase in the lowest wages similar to what has been observed in China.

In terms of jobs, the share of low-skilled workers increased between 2000 and 2017 at the expense of the share of high- and medium-skilled workers. The main explanation lies in the increase of the share of agriculture and the share of unskilled government workers under pressure following the Revolution.

Despite a significant reduction in clerical positions, the aggregate routine task index increased over the whole examined period, which was probably due to the expanding demand for labourers and machine operators in manufacturing and construction in the first period, and the public recruitment policy together with the increase in agricultural demand in the second period.

While the L-shaped wage polarization and the reduction in clerical positions point to routine-biased technical changes, the positive linear correlation between earnings and RTI put a question mark over its role. Furthermore, we observed strong declining trends of sector premia and the public–private wage gap, which are congruent with the change in overall earnings inequality. Our RIF decomposition of earnings inequality changes confirms that the most important factors are the public–private wage gap and the sector wage gap on the demand side and the education premium on the supply side. The RTI made a small and negative contribution to inequality change before the Revolution and a positive contribution afterwards. In other words, it first enhanced equality by increasing the marginal returns to low-wage jobs, but then had a small disequalizing effect. In conclusion, despite the L-shaped wage evolution, there is little evidence of the impact of computerization on wage inequality in Tunisia's labour market.

References

Acemoglu, D., and D. Autor (2011). 'Skills, Tasks and Technologies: Implications for Employment and Earnings'. In O. Ashenfelter and D. Card (eds) *Handbook of Labor Economics*, volume 4, pp. 1043–171. Amsterdam: Elsevier. https://doi.org/10.1016/S0169-7218(11)02410-5

Adel, B. (2013). *Le chômage en Tunisie: les principales caractéristiques*. Paris: Edition L'Harmattan.

Amara, M., W. Khallouli, and F. Zidi (2017). 'Public–private Wage Differentials in Tunisia: Consistency and Decomposition'. In *Economic Research Forum, Working Paper* (Vol. 1156, pp. 1–28). https://erf.org.eg/app/uploads/2017/11/1156.pdf

Autor, D., and D. Dorn (2013). 'The Growth of Low-Skill Service Jobs and the Polarization of the US Labor Market'. *American Economic Review*, 103(5): 1553–97. https://doi.org/10.1257/aer.103.5.1553

Autor, D., F. Levy, and R.J. Murnane (2003). 'The Skill Content of Recent Technological Change: An Empirical Exploration'. *Quarterly Journal of Economics*, 118(4): 1279–333. https://doi.org/10.1162/003355303322552801

Bárány, Z.L. and C. Siegel (2018). 'Job Polarization and Structural Change'. *American Economic Journal: Macroeconomics*, 10(1): 57–89. https://doi.org/10.1257/mac.20150258

Firpo, S., N.M. Fortin, and T. Lemieux (2009). 'Unconditional Quantile Regressions'. *Econometrica*, 77(3): 953–73. https://doi.org/10.3982/ECTA6822

Firpo, S., N.M. Fortin, and T. Lemieux (2011). 'Occupational Tasks and Changes in the Wage Structure'. IZA Discussion Paper 5542. Bonn: IZA. https://doi.org/10.2139/ssrn.1778886

Fleisher, B.M., W. McGuire, Y. Su, and M.Q. Zhao (2018). 'Innovation, Wages, and Polarization in China'. IZA Discussion Paper 11569. Bonn: IZA. https://doi.org/10.2139/ssrn.3193323

Fonseca, T., F. Lima, and S.C. Pereira (2018). 'Job Polarization, Technological Change and Routinization: Evidence for Portugal'. *Labour Economics*, 51: 317–39. https://doi.org/10.1016/j.labeco.2018.02.003

Goos, M., and A. Manning (2007). 'Lousy and Lovely Jobs: The Rising Polarization of Work in Britain'. *Review of Economics and Statistics*, 89(1): 118–33. https://doi.org/10.1162/rest.89.1.118

Kthiri, W. (2019). 'Inadéquation des qualifications en Tunisie: quels sont les déterminants du sous-emploi?'. Working Paper 01-2019. Tunis: ITCEQ.

Kupets, O. (2016). 'Education–Job Mismatch in Ukraine: Too Many People with Tertiary Education or Too Many Jobs for Low-Skilled?' *Journal of Comparative Economics*, 44(1): 125–47. https://doi.org/10.1016/j.jce.2015.10.005

Lewandowski, P., A. Park, W. Hardy, and Y. Du (2019). 'Technology, Skills, and Globalization: Explaining International Differences in Routine and Nonroutine Work Using Survey Data'. *HKUST IEMS Working Paper 2019-60*. Hong Kong: HKUST IEMS. https://doi.org/10.2139/ssrn.3415008

Lewandowski, P., A. Park, and S. Schotte (2020). 'The Global Distribution of Routine and Non-Routine Work'. WIDER Working Paper 2020/75. Helsinki: UNU-WIDER. https://doi.org/10.35188/UNU-WIDER/2020/832-0

Maloney, W.F., and C. Molina (2019). 'Is Automation Labor-Displacing in the Developing Countries, too? Robots, Polarization, and Jobs'. Working Paper. Washington, DC: World Bank. https://doi.org/10.1596/33301

Marouani, M.A., and R. Mouelhi (2016). 'Contribution of Structural Change to Productivity Growth: Evidence from Tunisia'. *Journal of African Economies*, 25(1): 110–32.

Marouani, M. Ali, Le Minh, P. & Marshalian, M. (2020) Jobs, earnings, and routine-task occupational change in times of revolution: The Tunisian perspective. WIDER Working Paper 2020/171. Helsinki: UNU-WIDER. https://doi.org/10.35188/UNU-WIDER/2020/928-0

Nordås, R., and C. Davenport (2013). 'Fight the Youth: Youth Bulges and State Repression'. *American Journal of Political Science*, 57(4): 926–40. https://doi.org/10.1111/ajps.12025

Rijkers, B., C. Freund, and A. Nucifora (2017). 'All in the Family: State Capture in Tunisia'. *Journal of Development Economics*, 124: 41–59. https://doi.org/10.1016/j.jdeveco.2016.08.002

Sebastian, R. (2018). 'Explaining Job Polarisation in Spain from a Task Perspective'. *SERIEs*, 9(2): 215–48. https://doi.org/10.1007/s13209-018-0177-1

8

Bangladesh

Employment and Inequality Trends

Sayema Haque Bidisha, Tanveer Mahmood, and Mahir A. Rahman

8.1 Introduction and background

There is a growing body of literature on the issue of structural changes in production coupled with technological progress, which has led to a significant shift
in modes of production as well as in patterns of employment. With changed
employment status, the earnings of individual workers with differing skill levels
are expected to change as well, resulting in changes in income distribution across
different skill groups. In addition, with globalized markets and increased international trade, certain types of production and related tasks are being shifted from
developed to developing countries. As Autor et al. (2015) argue, the effect of trade
and technology on the labour market and earnings should be understood together.
Based on such an argument, over time and as a result of several factors such as
structural transformation, international trade, technology-induced change in the
production process, and changing demand, the task content of jobs is expected to
change. This change is likely to differ across countries, based on their pattern of
structural change as well as the skill content of jobs. In the context of developing
countries like Bangladesh, the nexus between labour market variables and income
inequality can be more complex due to an imperfect labour market, the absence
of trade unions, a large agriculture sector in the economy, the flow of remittances,
transfer to the poor, etc.

Against this backdrop, this chapter attempts to understand the effect of the
changing nature of jobs on the labour market of Bangladesh. In particular, it aims
to explore changes in the task content of jobs over time and the resulting impact of
such changes on the earnings distribution of workers with differing skill levels. The
analysis uses different rounds of Labour Force Survey (LFS) data of Bangladesh
and combines it with US Occupational Information Network (O*NET) data as
well as a country-specific O*NET dataset for tracing the returns to different tasks
over time. In the context of Bangladesh, to the best of our knowledge, no study has
attempted to understand the polarization of employment and earnings.

The chapter is organized as follows: Section 8.2 provides a brief overview of relevant literature. Section 8.3 outlines the sources of data and methodological issues.

Sayema Haque Bidisha, Tanveer Mahmood, and Mahir A. Rahman, *Bangladesh: Employment and Inequality Trends*. In:
Tasks, Skills, and Institutions. Edited by Carlos Gradín, Piotr Lewandowski, Simone Schotte, and Kunal Sen, Oxford
University Press. © UNU-WIDER (2023). DOI: 10.1093/oso/9780192872241.003.0008

Section 8.4 discusses the empirical findings of the research. Finally, Section 8.5 summarizes and concludes.

8.2 Literature review

Despite its success in accelerating GDP growth, one important point to note is that, income inequality in both rural and urban areas of Bangladesh has risen, with urban areas having experienced a sharp rise in recent years (Osmani 2017, 2018). Besides, in contrast to rising income inequality, consumption inequality has remained almost stable, especially in recent years (2010–16). As argued by Osmani (2017), this difference between inequality in income and consumption can be due to a number of factors, especially the relatively higher marginal propensity to consume of those at the lower end of the distribution. In addition, the expansion of microcredit programmes has arguably been an important factor in relaxing the binding in liquidity for lower-income rural households (Osmani 2017). Factors such as transfer income and external remittances have also contributed significantly towards poverty reduction in rural areas (Osmani and Sen 2011). Therefore, the interplay among changes in task component, structural transformation along with other economy-specific factors like microcredit operations, and transfer income along with remittances can have interesting implications on overall inequality.

In their discussion of structural transformation, Raihan and Khan (2020) emphasized a very low level of complexity in the manufacturing sector and a lack of diversification as key challenges for tackling inequality and attaining inclusive growth for Bangladesh. On the other hand, Osmani (2015a, b) pointed out that along with a distributional income shift away from labour, it is lower growth in real wages rather than in productivity of labour that has resulted in the acceleration of growth in Bangladesh. Osmani (2015a, b) also emphasized the role of foreign remittance flow in the case of both high growth and increasing inequality in Bangladesh.

In the context of inequality, the Gini decomposition result of Osmani and Sen (2011) of Bangladesh has reflected that transfer income has primarily been responsible for the rising trend in rural inequality during the 2000s. In particular, through a detailed decomposition analysis, the researchers found foreign remittances accounting for as much as 70 per cent of the rise in rural inequality during the 2000s, with self-employment in non-agriculture being another important factor for the rising trend in rural Gini. Both salary and other income in the non-agriculture sector had an equalizing effect during that time period. Khan and Sen (2001) found that during the 1990s, rural wages had an equalizing effect on income distribution in Bangladesh with income from the subsistence component of farming having an equalizing effect, while other sources of rural income (e.g. transfer, property income, and miscellaneous income) have a dis-equalizing effect. In terms of urban income, the authors have found that wage and entrepreneurial farming income have an equalizing effect, whereas wages from non-farm employment tend to have a dis-equalizing effect.

8.3 Data and methodology

8.3.1 Sources of data

In our analysis, we have utilized three rounds of cross-sectional LFS data: 2005/06 (hereafter 2005), 2010, and 2016/17. These three rounds contain the basic information of socio-demographic characteristics of individuals, level of education, status in the labour market, earnings from employment, as well as ISCO occupational classification at the four-digit level. Although the three separate datasets are not of the same ISCO classification, we converted data of all three waves to ISCO-88 classification. Here, 2005 and 2010 data are cross-sectional data whereas 2016/17 data are quarterly data that have been converted to annual data while using annual weights.[1]

In terms of our sample of individuals, we considered those within the age range of 15–64 years and confined the sample to only those who worked for at least 1 hour for pay or profit of households in the 7 days before the survey. The occupational categorization was done based on the primary work of the individual. For earnings data, we included the weekly earnings of the workers and converted the earnings data from monthly to weekly for the last wave of LFS (i.e. QLFS 2016/17).[2] We have considered weekly earnings of only the wage employed and, for the sake of comparability, we adjusted earnings data for inflation (wage changes have been considered with respect to 2010).[3]

8.3.2 Regression of changes in employment and earnings on the level of RTI

To investigate the relationship between changes in employment and earnings and the changes in the task composition of occupations for sub-periods 2005–10 and

---

[1] We should keep in mind that although the 2016/17 data is a rotating panel with one individual repeated twice, the standard errors could be higher.
[2] To ensure consistency across datasets, for 2005 we have cleaned the dataset. For details please check Bidisha et al. (2021).
[3] We have used the consumer price index to adjust for inflation.

2010–16/17 and the entire period 2005–16/17, we applied several econometric methods. Detailed description of these methods can be found in Bidisha et al. 2021.

8.4 Empirical analysis

In Section 8.4.1, we first examine the distribution of workers in terms of basic education and occupational categories as well as of patterns and trends in a skills-biased occupational classification. Next, we apply several regression-based techniques to better understand changes in the task composition of occupations over time and to test the polarization of employment and earnings over time as discussed in Sections 8.4.2 and 8.4.3, respectively. In Section 8.4.4, we link employment and education with earnings and attempt to understand the pattern of education premium. In Section 8.4.5, we attempt to explain earnings inequality over time utilizing several methods used in literature. Finally, in Section 8.4.6, decomposition analysis of inequality is used to analyse the factors behind changes in inequality over time.

8.4.1 Distribution of workers by education and skill levels

As shown in Table 8.1, education-based labour market profiles of workers reflect a low representation of both men and women in tertiary education. On the other hand, although the situation has improved over time, there is an overwhelming proportion of the labour force without any schooling: in 2016/17. Over time, there is also a steady increase of those with secondary education.

In terms of basic skill level (high, medium, low), the highest and increasing proportion of workers were found in mid-skilled occupations over the years;

Table 8.1 Distribution of workers by gender and level of education (%)

Highest level of education completed	Male			Female			Total		
	2005	2010	2016/17	2005	2010	2016/17	2005	2010	2016/17
No schooling	36.98	39.75	28.22	51.64	40.79	35.68	40.4	40.07	29.98
Primary	24.50	23.29	27.35	23.35	23.07	23.44	24.23	23.22	26.43
Secondary	32.94	32.20	37.05	21.89	33.98	35.14	30.36	32.75	36.60
Tertiary	5.58	4.76	7.39	3.13	2.15	5.74	5.01	3.96	7.00

Source: Authors' calculation using various rounds (2005, 2010, 2016/17) of Labour Force Survey (LFS).

Table 8.2 Distribution of workers by gender and occupation (%)

Skill level	Male			Female			Total		
	2005	2010	2016/17	2005	2010	2016/17	2005	2010	2016/17
High	5.48	6.56	8.46	4.86	3.77	10.37	5.33	5.70	8.91
Medium	40.88	39.85	50.79	19.76	23.32	36.78	35.95	34.77	47.49
Low	53.64	53.59	40.75	75.38	72.91	52.85	58.72	59.53	43.60

Source: Authors' calculation using various rounds (2005, 2010, 2016/17) of LFS.

the proportion of low-skilled workers, on the contrary, has decreased by a large margin. As for the two separate time periods (i.e. 2005–10 and 2010–16/17), we observe a fall in the proportion of those in mid-skilled occupations with a corresponding rise in the high- and low-skilled groups, indicating a polarization of jobs at two extremes of the skill distribution at least in the first period (see Section 8.4.3 for job polarization). This trend has almost reversed in the second period (Table 8.2). The increase in mid-skilled workers are driven by occupations within craft and related trades as well as plant and machine operators. Focusing particularly on paid employees, however, paints a different picture. Further discussions on the structure of the skill component and its relationship with attained education can be found in Bidisha et al. (2021).

8.4.2 Distributional changes and task composition

Changes in the task content of occupations

Changes in the occupational structure and a shift of workers from low-skilled occupations to mid- and high-skilled occupations suggest a shift towards less routine-intensive occupations over time. We have found that average RTI has indeed fallen regardless of whether we measured average RTI using O*NET or a country-specific measure. (Table 8.3).

In this section, following Autor and Dorn (2013) and Firpo et al. (2011) distributions based on O*NET RTI index, survey RTI index, and country-specific

Table 8.3 Average routine-task intensity (RTI), 2005–2016/17

RTI measure	All workers			Paid employees		
	2005	2010	2016/17	2005	2010	2016/17
Country-specific	0.85	0.86	0.67	0.36	0.42	0.31
O*NET	0.28	0.43	0.29	0.18	0.33	0.11

Source: Authors' calculation using various rounds (2005, 2010, 2016/17) of LFS.

RTI index across skill percentiles (ranked by 2005 occupational mean wage) have been utilized (details are available in Bidisha et al. 2021). Although not confirmative, the graphical analysis indicates—especially for paid employees—a decline in the share of routine manual tasks with an almost unchanged pattern of routine cognitive tasks. As expected, there is an overall increase in non-routine cognitive tasks and non-routine cognitive interpersonal tasks (Figure 8.1). We also found a negative relationship between RTI and skill percentiles, implying that high-skilled workers are engaged in less routine-intensive tasks (Figure 8.2), with the pattern

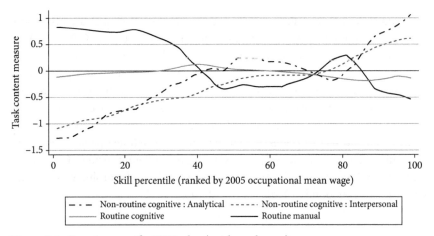

Figure 8.1 Country-specific RTI index (paid employees)

Source: Authors' calculation using various rounds (2005, 2010, 2016/17) of Labour Force Survey (LFS).

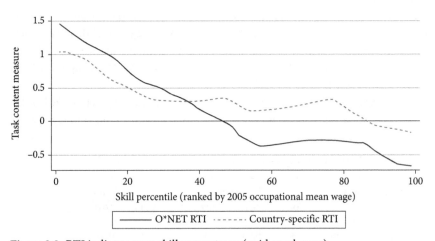

Figure 8.2 RTI indices across skill percentages (paid employees)

Source: Authors' calculation using various rounds (2005, 2010, 2016/17) of LFS.

becoming stronger when measured with O*NET RTI rather than country-specific RTI. Therefore, for the country-specific case, it takes more skill to have negative task content measures. In this context, the experience of Bangladesh has closely mirrored that of India (Vashisht and Dubey 2018) but is in contrast with that of the US (Autor and Dorn 2009).

Regression analysis of changes in employment and earnings on the level of RTI

Our ordinary least square estimates reflect no statistically significant evidence of a systematic relationship between employment share and RTI over the entire period; we found similar results for both O*NET RTI and country-specific RTI measures (Table 8.4). However, in estimation results focusing on changes in earnings, we found that earnings decline for occupations with higher routine-task content. The results become significant when the country-specific RTI measure is applied. Our results, therefore, are indicative of greater returns for more skilled and less routine-intensive works.

8.4.3 Changes in occupation structure and polarization of employment and earnings

Following Goos and Manning (2007), we applied a regression-based test of job and earnings polarization. As shown in Table 8.5, the results indicate a U-shaped pattern of job polarization in Bangladesh only in the first period of our analysis (and only in the case of all workers), and over time we observe almost an opposite scenario of job polarization. Given the low (initial) skill base of the economy, it is quite plausible that, although in the first period of our analysis there is a shift of workers towards opposite ends of the distribution, over time with a greater accumulation of skills and/or due to the effect of off-shoring jobs from developed countries, the proportion of mid-skilled workers increases (see Section 8.4.1). The trend is likely to continue in the near future because the overall skill base of workers is still at a low level, with high-skilled workers making up less than one-tenth (8.91 per cent in 2016/17) of the workforce.

When considering the log change in mean wage as the dependent variable, we found strong evidence of a U-shaped relationship. This result was consistently negative and significant in both of the periods, which is indicative of earnings polarization (further discussed in Section 8.4.4). Our regression-based polarization tests, therefore, confirm earnings polarization in Bangladesh but not job polarization.

Table 8.4 Correlation between O*NET RTI and country-specific RTI measures and changes in employment and earnings, 2005–2016/17 (all)

Variables	Log change in employment share			Change in log (mean) earnings		
	2005–10	2010–16/17	2005–16/17	2005–10	2010–16/17	2005–16/17
ONET*RTI variables						
ONET*RTI	0.909*	0.095	0.122	0.089**	0.005	0.128
	(0.466)	(0.183)	(0.109)	(0.041)	(0.045)	(0.082)
Square ONET*RTI	-0.112	0.029	-0.014	-0.042**	0.011	-0.029
	(0.151)	(0.094)	(0.050)	(0.018)	(0.012)	(0.025)
Constant	-0.848**	-0.711*	-0.341***	0.188***	0.100**	0.218**
	(0.417)	(0.403)	(0.122)	(0.063)	(0.040)	(0.090)
Observations	108	106	106	107	102	103
Adjusted R-squared	0.289	-0.00870	-0.00421	0.127	-0.00701	0.138
Country-specific RTI variables						
Country-specific*RTI	0.645	-0.546	0.344	0.013	-0.678***	-0.463
	(1.106)	(1.063)	(0.651)	(0.170)	(0.184)	(0.299)
Square country-specific *RTI	-1.142	0.007	-0.494	0.189	0.374**	0.317
	(1.475)	(1.117)	(0.537)	(0.207)	(0.159)	(0.334)
Constant	-0.215	-0.174	-0.164	-0.015	0.365***	0.342***
	(0.192)	(0.243)	(0.225)	(0.045)	(0.051)	(0.049)
Observations	108	106	106	107	102	103
Adjusted R-squared	0.0473	0.0191	0.00741	0.170	0.378	0.0285

Note: Robust standard errors in parentheses, *** $p<0.01$, ** $p<0.05$, * $p<0.1$.
Source: Authors' calculation using various rounds (2005, 2010, 2016/17) of LFS.

Table 8.5 Correlation coefficients between change in log employment share and change in log of labour earnings (paid)

Variables	Log change in employment share			Change in log (mean) earnings		
	2005–10	2010–16/17	2005–16/17	2005–10	2010–16/17	2005–16/17
All employment						
(Log) mean weekly earnings (t–1)	-50.423**	68.937**	9.835	-4.341**	-9.571**	-12.373***
	(24.492)	(27.764)	(8.569)	(1.820)	(3.915)	(2.985)
Square (log) mean weekly earnings (t–1)	3.469**	-4.595**	-0.678	0.269**	0.664**	0.844***
	(1.700)	(1.874)	(0.602)	(0.129)	(0.266)	(0.209)
Constant	181.820**	-258.256**	-35.858	17.362***	34.591**	45.393***
	(87.631)	(102.524)	(30.414)	(6.416)	(14.371)	(10.591)
Observations	107	105	106	107	102	103
Adjusted R-squared	0.268	0.232	0.00961	0.716	0.101	0.592
Paid employment						
(Log) mean weekly earnings (t–1)	-23.191*	10.845	-10.685	-13.874***	-13.506**	-8.600**
	(11.833)	(22.479)	(9.226)	(4.612)	(6.356)	(4.328)
Square (log) mean weekly earnings (t–1)	1.513*	-0.741	0.679	0.900***	0.884**	0.596**
	(0.793)	(1.459)	(0.622)	(0.307)	(0.413)	(0.290)
Constant	88.383**	-40.399	41.135	53.327***	51.587**	31.037*
	(44.087)	(86.497)	(34.111)	(17.364)	(24.396)	(16.150)
Observations	99	96	102	99	96	102
Adjusted R-squared	0.0218	-0.00778	-0.00476	0.172	0.0749	0.0678

Note: Robust standard errors in parentheses, *** $p<0.01$, ** $p<0.05$, * $p<0.1$.
Source: Authors' calculation using various rounds (2005, 2010, 2016/17) of LFS.

8.4.4 Distribution of earnings of workers by education and skill levels

However, in order to get better insights into the linkages between education and earnings and the trend of the education premium, we utilized a parametric method (details in Bidisha et al. 2021). In the third set of graphs (Figure 8.3)—which are probably the most comprehensive ones incorporating the effects of other relevant covariates—we find a significant effect of gender on returns to education. Considering these, it can be inferred that (i) for those holding a degree in tertiary education, the education premium was the highest and increased consistently for both sexes; (ii) for those with secondary education, although there is a consistent increment for women, for men the education premium only registered an increase in the second half of our analysis; and (iii) for those with primary education, for both genders, the education premium declined in the first half but registered an increase in the second half.

In terms of returns to skill of workers, comparing the three waves of inflation-adjusted mean weekly earnings for one-digit ISCO-88 occupation groups, we get a clear indication of earnings polarization and we find that the largest increase is registered for high-skilled workers, followed by low-skilled workers. Mid-skilled workers experienced a comparatively moderate increase in earnings (Table 8.6). For paid employees, a number of mid-skilled- and low-skilled workers (e.g. service and sales workers, craft and trade workers, skilled agriculture workers, and those in elementary occupations) experienced a small decline in their real earnings over time.[4]

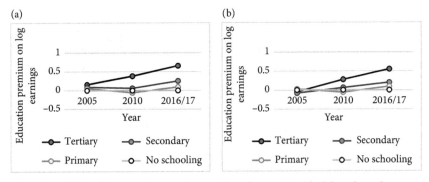

Figure 8.3 Education premium on log earnings (regression 3): (a) male and (b) female

Source: Authors' calculation using various rounds (2005, 2010, 2016/17) of LFS.

---

[4] Due to coding differences across the three waves of LFS, we could not separately calculate earnings for RMG workers. It is unlikely that RMG workers' wages have declined over time, particularly with increases in the minimum wage over time.

Table 8.6 Real mean weekly earnings by gender and skill level (in BDT)

Skill	Male			Female			Total		
	2005	2010	2016/17	2005	2010	2016/17	2005	2010	2016/17
High	2,399	2,843	4,035	2,265	2,065	3,372	2,366	2,701	3,841
Medium	1,643	1,793	1,861	1,232	1,498	1,655	1,572	1,753	1,814
Low	910	1,258	1,324	823	1,214	1,143	901	1,254	1,284
Total	1,342	1,611	1,981	1,276	1,468	1,821	1,332	1,594	1,943

Source: Authors' calculation using various rounds (2005, 2010, 2016/17) of LFS.

8.4.5 Distribution of earnings and task content

Assessing RTI based on earnings percentile revealed that, with certain exceptions at the top percentiles, the country-specific RTI measure is negatively correlated with earnings percentiles. However, across all waves the concentration of routine tasks is still higher at the bottom percentiles and declines sharply at the top. Furthermore, movements in the share of income for the bottom to mid-deciles and for the top deciles can be utilized to explain why inequality as measured by the Gini index remained almost constant during the first sub-period and a decrease in inequality during this period. (Details in Bidisha et al. 2021.)

Based on Gini indices, between 2005 and 2010, we do not observe much change in earnings inequality; however, comparing 2010 and 2016/17 indices, we can see a decline in the Gini for earnings (Table 8.7). A similar trend of declining inequality between 2010 and 2016/17 can be seen in the variance of log earnings as well (Table 8.8).

From the growth incidence curve bar graphs, we observe that, during the first sub-period, workers in the middle of the distribution had almost no fluctuation in earnings. However, with the exception of the topmost percentiles, those at the upper percentiles fell below average. Although one would expect a larger decline in income inequality during the first sub-period based on the inter-quantile ratios (Table 8.8), this polarizing trend of above-average income at the

Table 8.7 Commonly used inequality indices (all workers)

	2005	2010	2016/17
Variance	0.512	0.397	0.309
Gini ln	0.057	0.049	0.039
Gini	0.368	0.370	0.320

Source: Authors' calculation using various rounds (2005, 2010, 2016/17) of LFS.

Table 8.8 Inter-quantile ratios (all workers)

	2005	2010	2016/17
ln(q90)–(q10)	1.83	1.54	1.20
ln(q90)–(q50)	0.98	0.85	0.80
ln(q50)–(q10)	0.85	0.69	0.41

Source: Authors' calculation using various rounds
(2005, 2010, 2016/17) of LFS.

bottom and, to a lesser extent, the topmost percentiles, is likely to explain the
rather slight increase in inequality observed in the first sub-period. The lower
tail started from higher than the average and then fell below average. For the second sub-period (2010–16/17), there is a clear pro-poor growth pattern, resulting
in inequality declining strongly in 2016/17. For the entire period (2005–16/17),
a pro-poor growth pattern is visible and reflects the fall in inequality observed
(Figure 8.4).

8.4.6 Decomposition analysis

In addition to knowing the pattern of inequality over time, we apply appropriate decomposition techniques to identify the factors that have been acting as key
drivers of inequality. We decompose the earnings inequality as measured by the
Gini index between the two sub-periods: 2005–10 and 2010–16/17 using Shapley
decomposition and RIF decomposition.

Shapley decomposition
From Table 8.9 we can infer that differences in average earnings across occupations (i.e. between-occupation differences) could explain a sizeable portion
of overall earnings inequality in 2005. However, over time this share has fallen
significantly, with within-occupation differences accounting for almost three-
quarters of the overall earnings inequality in 2010. Keeping in mind the changes
in employment shares of different skill groups, we can infer that factors other than
earnings and job characteristics must have driven the trend in inequality during the first sub-period. During the second sub-period of our study, inequality
fell significantly and the between-occupation effect became important once again,
explaining more than half of the total earnings inequality (51 per cent). During
2010–16/17, the share of employment in mid-skilled occupations increased significantly, with a strong decline in the share of low-skilled jobs and a moderate
increase in high-skilled jobs. In terms of earnings, during this period, high-skilled

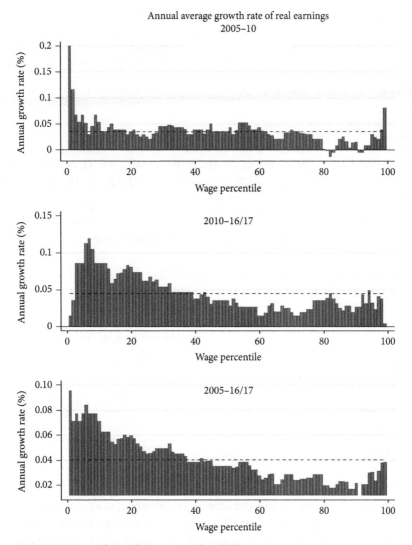

Figure 8.4 Growth incidence curves bar (all)

Source: Authors' calculation using various rounds (2005, 2010, 2016/17) of LFS.

workers experienced the highest increase in average earnings. In this context, as the share of high-skilled workers is quite low (around 8 per cent), the trend in inequality is most likely to be driven by changes in mid-skilled occupations. Other factors such as education and information asymmetry between workers and employers might have also played an important role in increasing friction in the labour market.

Table 8.9 Gini index decomposed into between- and within-occupation inequality

	Actual			Shares constant			Means constant		
	2005	2010	2016/17	2005	2010	2016/17	2005	2010	2016/17
Overall Gini	0.3677	0.3698	0.3198	0.3677	0.3571	0.3092	0.3677	0.3915	0.3004
Shapley decomposition									
Between-occupation	0.1491	0.0975	0.1615	0.1491	0.0999	0.15200	0.1491	0.1343	0.1373
% Ratio	41	26	51	41	28	49	41	34	46
Within-occupation	0.2186	0.2723	0.1583	0.2186	0.2572	0.1572	0.2186	0.2572	0.1631
% Ratio	59	74	49	59	72	51	59	66	54

Source: Authors' calculation using various rounds (2005, 2010, 2016/17) of LFS.

Table 8.10 Change in the Gini index decomposed into the contribution of changes in employment shares and in mean earnings (Shapley decomposition based on Table 8.9), 2005–2016/17

	2005–10	2010–16/17	2005–16/17
Change in employment shares (mean earnings constant)	−0.009	0.025	0.016
Change in mean earnings (employment shares constant)	−0.043	0.039	−0.004
Total change	−0.052	0.064	0.012

Source: Authors' calculation using various rounds (2005, 2010, 2016/17) of LFS.

Moreover, following Gradín and Schotte (2020), we separate the direct role of changes in the composition of employment by occupation from the role of changes in mean earnings by occupations in order to more specifically identify the drivers behind the fall in inequality between occupations. In one specification we hold occupation shares constant, whereas in the other we hold mean earnings constant. The Shapley decomposition results are reported in Table 8.10.

Our findings show that, in the first sub-period, the tightening of the gap in average earnings across occupations is mostly responsible for the fall in between-occupation inequality. As a result, we observe an equality-enhancing effect associated with changes in the reward of job characteristics, such as skills and tasks on the labour market. Furthermore, changes in employment shares across occupations also help to explain the decline in between-occupation inequality. Therefore, shifts in the structure of employment across occupations helped to decrease

Table 8.11 Concentration index, 2005–2016/17

	Actual			Shares constant			Means constant		
	2005	2010	2016/17	2005	2010	2016/17	2005	2010	2016/17
Gini between occupations Concentration index	0.2215	0.1584	0.2239	0.2215	0.1612	0.2117	0.2215	0.2103	0.1949
RTI (country-specific)	0.1959	0.114	0.2004	0.1959	0.1253	0.1928	0.1959	0.1758	0.1713
% Ratio	88	72	90	88	78	91	88	84	88
RTI (O*NET)	0.1072	0.1128	0.1611	0.1072	0.1085	0.1413	0.1072	0.0999	0.1048
% Ratio	48	71	72	48	67	67	48	48	54

Source: Authors' calculation using various rounds (2005, 2010, 2016/17) of LFS.

inequality (Table 8.10). On the other hand, in the second sub-period, both changes in average earnings and changes in employment shares across occupations have an inequality-enhancing effect and help to explain the rise in between-occupation inequality. If we consider the overall survey period, Table 8.11 further suggests that changes in employment shares had a dis-equalizing effect whereas changes in mean earnings across occupations had a slightly equalizing effect, resulting in an overall increase in between-occupation inequality.

In Table 8.11, the results of isolating the effect of RTI have been shown using a concentration index. This index measures the extent to which the average earnings of occupations tend to systematically increase in jobs with less routine-intensive tasks (Gradín and Schotte 2020). As reflected in Table 8.12, the roles of RTI and average earnings of occupations in explaining inequality are quite similar, accounting for about 72–90 per cent of between-occupation inequality. This finding is even more pronounced in the first and third survey waves of the analysis. The somewhat weaker relationship in 2010 can perhaps be explained by the possibility of average earnings being less relevant in explaining inequality in that year.

Furthermore, comparing the corresponding figures of country-specific RTI with those of O*NET RTI, we observe that significant differences across occupation rankings exist in the first wave (2005) based on corresponding concentration ratios (varies between 88 per cent using the country-specific measure and 48 per cent using O*NET). The country-specific measure suggests that the relationship between RTI and average earnings in explaining between-occupation inequality grew weaker over the first sub-period, although there was an increase in rank correlation between earnings and the O*NET RTI measure. However, during the second sub-period as well as the entire period, the correlation increased based on both measures (to a ratio of 90 and 72 per cent, respectively), suggesting that the relationship between the RTI of occupations and average earnings strengthened over time.

RIF decomposition

Our RIF decomposition analysis shows that the changes in demographic characteristics such as age, gender, level of education, or the change in the composition of routine-task content of occupations do not explain the trend in earnings inequality in Bangladesh. This has been witnessed during both the sub-periods of 2005–10 and 2010–16/17, where the composition effect of educational attainment was found to be dis-equalizing whereas the effect of RTI (i.e. the structure of employment) was equalizing at the first sub-period. According to our analysis, it is the earnings structure effect that explains the trend in inequality during both of the sub-periods. An earnings structure effect of education was found to be equalizing for the first sub-period and dis-equalizing for the second sub-period in both the country-specific and O*NET RTI measures. Both O*NET and country-specific RTI measures show the earnings structure effect of RTI having an equalizing effect in the first sub-period but a dis-equalizing effect in the second period (Table 8.12). If we use the O*NET measure, then the effects are equalizing in both cases. For both of the sub-periods, the growth of the education premium was inequality reducing. For changes in routine versus non-routine tasks, if measured by O*NET, it was inequality reducing; if measured by the country-specific measures, it was instead inequality inducing during the first sub-period but inequality reducing for the second.

In this analysis, RIF decomposition has been applied to decompose changes in earnings over time across different quantiles. The results reflect that the earnings structure effect primarily dominates the total change in earnings in both of the sub-periods across the entire distribution (see Figure 8.5). We deduce that for the first sub-period (2005–10) the detailed decomposition of earnings structure effect (country-specific measure) suggest a pro-rich profile of the change in RTI whereas the effect of education is not entirely pro-rich for the first sub-period as the effects are found to be negative for the uppermost percentiles of the distribution (see Figure 8.6). For the second sub-period, we observe a pro-poor feature of the RTI. During this period, education accounts for decreasing inequality for most of the upper tail of the distribution. So, during the second sub-period we witness a combined effect of returns to education and RTI on the decline in inequality.

Table 8.12 RIF regression decomposition (earnings)

	RTI (country-specific)			RTI O*NET		
	2005–10	2010–16/17	2005–16/17	2005–10	2010–16/17	2005–16/17
Distribution						
Final *F*	0.403	0.354	0.354	0.403	0.354	0.354
	(0.002)	(0.001)	(0.002)	(0.002)	(0.001)	(0.002)
Initial *I*	0.359	0.403	0.359	0.359	0.403	0.359
	(0.015)	(0.008)	(0.002)	(0.015)	(0.008)	(0.002)
Total change (*F–I*)	0.044	-0.049	-0.005	0.044	-0.049	-0.005
	(0.017)	(0.008)	(0.005)	(0.017)	(0.008)	(0.005)
Reweighting decomposition						
Counterfactual *C*	0.362	0.406	0.358	0.364	0.405	0.356
	(0.011)	(0.008)	(0.006)	(0.011)	(0.009)	(0.005)
Total composition *C–I*	0.002	0.002	-0.001	0.005	0.002	-0.004
	(0.004)	(0.000)	(0.004)	(0.004)	(0.002)	(0.002)
Total earnings structure *F–C*	0.041	-0.051	-0.004	0.039	-0.051	-0.002
	(0.013)	(0.008)	(0.008)	(0.013)	(0.010)	(0.007)
RIF composition						
Age	0.000	0.000	0.000	0.000	0.000	0.000
	(0.001)	(0.001)	(0.000)	(0.001)	(0.001)	(0.000)
Sex	0.003	-0.001	0.005	0.003	-0.001	0.004
	(0.002)	(0.000)	(0.004)	(0.002)	(0.000)	(0.004)
Education	0.001	0.008	-0.002	0.002	0.010	-0.003
	(0.002)	(0.003)	(0.000)	(0.003)	(0.002)	(0.000)
Religion	0.001	0.002	0.000	0.001	0.002	0.000
	(0.000)	(0.002)	(0.001)	(0.000)	(0.002)	(0.001)

Continued

Table 8.12 *Continued*

	RTI (country-specific)			RTI O*NET		
	2005–10	2010–16/17	2005–16/17	2005–10	2010–16/17	2005–16/17
RTI	-0.002	0.000	-0.002	0.001	-0.003	-0.002
	(0.002)	(0.002)	(0.001)	(0.001)	(0.001)	(0.000)
Explained	0.003	0.008	0.001	0.006	0.007	-0.001
	(0.005)	(0.001)	(0.002)	(0.005)	(0.003)	(0.002)
RIF earnings structure						
Age	0.011	0.001	0.014	0.010	0.000	0.017
	(0.011)	(0.007)	(0.000)	(0.009)	(0.009)	(0.001)
Sex	-0.012	0.016	-0.002	-0.010	0.014	0.001
	(0.005)	(0.004)	(0.010)	(0.003)	(0.004)	(0.007)
Education	-0.040	0.023	-0.018	-0.045	0.028	-0.007
	(0.013)	(0.006)	(0.006)	(0.010)	(0.002)	(0.007)
Religion	-0.005	0.001	-0.001	-0.006	0.002	-0.002
	(0.004)	(0.000)	(0.004)	(0.005)	(0.001)	(0.004)
RTI	0.021	-0.056	-0.037	-0.026	0.007	-0.016
	(0.023)	(0.009)	(0.004)	(0.001)	(0.000)	(0.001)
Constant	0.066	-0.036	0.041	0.115	-0.098	0.006
	(0.012)	(0.001)	(0.004)	(0.008)	(0.007)	(0.011)
Unexplained	0.041	-0.051	-0.003	0.039	-0.048	-0.002
	(0.013)	(0.007)	(0.008)	(0.013)	(0.009)	(0.008)

Note: Bootstrap standard errors in parentheses; number of replications: 100.
Source: Authors' calculation using various rounds (2005, 2010, 2016/17) of LFS.

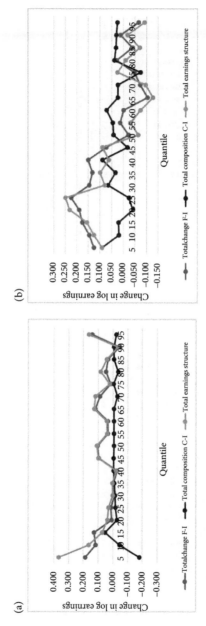

Figure 8.5 RIF decomposition (country-specific): (a) 2005–10; (b) 2010–16/17

Source: Authors' calculation using various rounds (2005, 2010, 2016/17) of LFS.

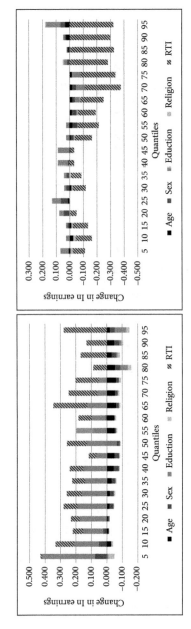

Figure 8.6 Detailed RIF decomposition of earnings structure: (a) 2005–10; (b) 2010–16/17

Source: Authors' calculation using various rounds (2005, 2010, 2016/17) of LFS.

8.5 Summary of results and recommendations

Summing up the results, we can deduce that, in terms of the skill content of the workers, there has been a shift towards educated and better skilled workers with a gradual movement towards jobs with less routine-intensive tasks. We also observe that, although there has been increase in real labour earnings for all education and broad skill levels with an increase in returns to education, this has not been translated into growing inequality as we have observed a decline in earnings inequality in recent years.

Against the backdrop of our analysis, we suggest a number of policies. First, given the high education premium, investing in education should be the highest priority. The need to reorient education programmes catering to the necessities of the labour market is even more pertinent in light of the results of our detailed RIF decomposition analysis, which indicates the exhaustion of the pro-poor effect of education in the later part of our analysis. Our analysis also reflects that the share of workers with tertiary education is quite low so, despite those with tertiary education enjoying the highest earnings premium, we have not been able to reap the benefits of this premium.

Second, with the declining importance of routine-intensive tasks, a greater emphasis is needed on skills-biased training programmes, particularly those involving cognitive skill. With the pro-poor effect of RTI in recent years, training related to jobs with less routine-intensive tasks will be equality-inducing as well.

Third, we should not be complacent about the falling trend of earnings inequality in the country, as our findings reveal that this can be linked primarily to a number of factors apparently outside of the labour market. Our Shapley decomposition also suggests that inequality is mostly explained by institutional factors that are not directly related to mean earnings across occupations. The striking differences in the trend of income and consumption Gini also suggest interpreting inequality with caution. Therefore, earnings inequality should be explained and analysed while considering the broader picture of the economy.

Fourth, the role of structural change in transforming the occupational as well as earnings structure of the country is quite apparent. However, given the shift towards less routine-intensive tasks, low-skilled jobs, particularly those in agriculture, still constitute a significant part of the labour force. The fruits of structural transformation, therefore, have not quite benefited the labour market that necessitates, on the one hand, the creation of jobs in the non-agriculture sector targeting the mid-skilled and, on the other hand, investment in upskilling the low-skilled.

Fifth, as Bangladesh continues its journey towards becoming a developed country backed by a structural shift towards less routine-intensive tasks and a skilled workforce, it would be pertinent to bring more sectors under the umbrella of the minimum wage law and to establish trade unions in order to ensure that benefits emanating from such a structural change are distributed evenly across all worker groups.

Finally, we have found that despite a relatively moderate increase in earnings in mid-skilled jobs compared with high-skilled roles, employment in mid-skilled jobs has significantly increased. This indicates the presence of a skill mismatch/skill gap that needs to be addressed through effective policy interventions. Our findings of regression analysis with regard to job polarization also emphasize this mismatch, as earnings have increased for less routine-intensive tasks but this has not resulted in a proportional increase in the employment share of less routine-intensive tasks.

Acknowledgement

The chapter's findings were presented at the 2020 Online Jobs and Development Conference, organized by the World Bank, the Institute of Labor Economics, and UNU-WIDER. The authors are thankful to the participants of the conference for their useful comments. Usual disclaimer applies.

References

Autor, D.H., and D. Dorn (2009). 'Inequality and Specialization: The Growth of Low-Skill Service Jobs in the United States'. NBER Working Paper 15150. Cambridge, MA: National Bureau of Economic Research (NBER).

Autor, D., and D. Dorn (2013). 'The Growth of Low-Skill Service Jobs and the Polarization of the US Labor Market'. *American Economic Review*, 103(5): 1553–97. https://doi.org/10.1257/aer.103.5.1553

Autor, D.H., D. Dorn, and G.H. Hanson (2015). 'Untangling Trade and Technology: Evidence from Local Labour Markets'. *The Economic Journal*, 125(584): 621–46. https://doi.org/10.1111/ecoj.12245

BBS (2018). Labour Force Survey. Dhaka: Bangladesh Bureau of Statistics (BBS). Available at: https://www.ilo.org/surveyLib/index.php/catalog/2214 (accessed December 2020).

BBS (2019). Household Income and Expenditure Survey, 2016–2017. Dhaka: Bangladesh Bureau of Statistics (BBS). Available at: https://catalog.ihsn.org/index.php/catalog/7399 (accessed December 2020).

Berman, E., and S. Machin (2000). 'Skill-Biased Technology Transfer around the World'. *Oxford Review of Economic Policy*, 16(3): 12–22. https://doi.org/10.1093/oxrep/16.3.12

Bidisha, S. H., Mahmood, T., and Rahman, M. A. (2021). 'Earnings Inequality and the Changing Nature of Work: Evidence from Labour Force Survey Data of Bangladesh'. WIDER Working Paper 2021/7. Helsinki: UNU-WIDER. https://doi.org/10.35188/UNU-WIDER/2021/941-9

Chantreuil, F., and A. Trannoy (1997). 'Inequality Decomposition Values'. Mimeo. France: Université de Cergy-Pointoise.

Du, Y., and A. Park (2018). 'Changing Demand for Tasks and Skills in China'. Background Report for the World Bank Group (WBG)–Development Research Center under the State Council (DRC) Report on New Drivers of Growth in China. Washington, DC: The World Bank. Available at: http://hdl.handle.net/10986/32351 (accessed December 2020).

Eden, M., and P. Gaggl (2020). 'Do Poor Countries Really Need More IT?'. *The World Bank Economic Review*, 34(1): 48–62. https://doi.org/10.1093/wber/lhy022

Export Promotion Bureau (2020). Export Promotion Bureau, Bangladesh. Available at: http://www.epb.gov.bd (accessed 20 August 2020).

Firpo, S., N.M. Fortin, and T. Lemieux (2011). 'Occupational Tasks and Changes in the Wage Structure', IZA Discussion Paper 5542. Bonn: Institute of Labor Economics. Available at: http://ftp.iza.org/dp5542.pdf (accessed December 2020).

Goos, M., and A. Manning (2007). 'Lousy and Lovely Jobs: The Rising Polarization of Work in Britain'. *The Review of Economics and Statistics*, 89(1): 118–33. https://doi.org/10.1162/rest.89.1.118

Gradín, C., and S. Schotte (2020). 'Implications of the Changing Nature of Work for Employment and Inequality in Ghana'. WIDER Working Paper 2020/119. Helsinki: UNU-WIDER. https://doi.org/10.35188/UNU-WIDER/2020/876-4

Khan, A.R., and B. Sen (2001). 'Inequality and Its Sources in Bangladesh, 1991/92 to 1995/96: An Analysis Based on Household Expenditure Surveys'. *The Bangladesh Development Studies*, 27(1): 1–49. Available at: https://www.jstor.org/stable/40795620 (accessed December 2020).

Ministry of Finance (2019). *Bangladesh Economic Review* (Chapter 3). Dhaka: Finance Division, Ministry of Finance, Government of the People's Republic of Bangladesh. Available at: https://mof.gov.bd/site/page/44e399b3-d378-41aa-86ff-8c4277eb0990/Bangladesh-Economic-Review (accessed December 2020).

Osmani, S.R. (2015a). 'Linking Equity and Growth in Bangladesh'. Background paper prepared for the Seventh Five Year Plan of the Government of Bangladesh. Dhaka: Bangladesh Planning Commission, Government of the People's Republic of Bangladesh.

Osmani, S.R. (2015b). The Growth–Equity Nexus in Bangladesh: An Analysis of Recent Experience. *Bangladesh Development Studies*, 38(2): 1–59. Available at: https://pure.ulster.ac.uk/ws/portalfiles/portal/11545786/Growth-Equity+Nexus+in+Bangladesh.pdf (accessed December 2020).

Osmani, S.R. (2017). 'Eradicating Poverty and Minimizing Inequality for Ensuring Shared Prosperity in Bangladesh'. A background paper prepared for the Perspective Plan, 2021–2041. Dhaka: General Economics Division, Planning Commission, Government of the People's Republic of Bangladesh.

Osmani, S.R. (2018). 'Aspects of the Poverty Scenario in Bangladesh during 2010–2016'. *Bangladesh Development Studies*, 41(3): 1–31.

Osmani, S.R., and B. Sen (2011). 'Inequality in Rural Bangladesh in the 2000s: Trends and Causes'. *The Bangladesh Development Studies*, 34(4): 1–36. Available at: https://www.jstor.org/stable/23342752 (accessed December 2020).

Raihan, S., and S.S. Khan (2020). 'Structural Transformation, Inequality Dynamics, and Inclusive Growth in Bangladesh' WIDER Working Paper 2020/44. Helsinki: UNU-WIDER. https://doi.org/10.35188/UNU-WIDER/2020/801-6

Vashisht, P., and J.D. Dubey (2018). 'Changing Task Contents of Jobs in India: Implications and Way Forward'. ICRIER Working Paper 355. New Delhi: Indian Council for Research on International Economic Relations (ICRIER). Available at: https://icrier.org/pdf/Working_Paper_355.pdf (accessed December 2020).

9

China

Employment and Inequality Trends

Chunbing Xing

9.1 Introduction

China's labour market conditions have changed significantly in recent years. Due to waning rural-to-urban migration and population aging, China's total employment has increased more slowly in the past than in previous decades and even declined after 2018. But the human capital level has increased. With Chinese households enthusiastically investing in human capital, the younger cohorts have become much more highly educated than older cohorts.[1] At the same time, technological change and globalization are redefining industries and occupations. For example, China invested heavily in industrial robot development, and it has become one of the most active industrial robot markets. According to Cheng et al. (2019), in 2016, robot sales in China accounted for nearly 30 per cent of global sales of 294,000 units, rising from less than 1 per cent in 2000. Another example of the influence of technology comes from the rise of the platform economy: DiDi (a Chinese version of Uber) drivers have had a major impact on the taxi driver profession. Technological change has also made working from home (WFH) a feasible practice in some firms' working arrangements (Bloom et al. 2015). These changes also have a significant impact on inequality.

In this chapter, we document the evolution of China's occupational structure over the last two decades and link it to the changes in earnings inequality. In the whole period of 1990–2015, China's agricultural occupations declined significantly from over 70 per cent to 31 per cent, and most of the changes happened in the first decade of the twenty-first century. Employment in service and manufacturing jobs increased significantly between 2000 and 2010. In the most recent period of 2010–15, however, manufacturing occupations began to decline and service jobs continued rising. When occupational structure changed, so did workers' tasks. Routine manual and non-routine physical manual tasks that are typical in agricultural jobs declined; non-routine cognitive tasks, both analytical and

---

[1] In 2015, while 34 per cent of those aged 20 to 29 had tertiary degrees, only 10 per cent of those aged 40 to 49 had tertiary degrees (NBS 2016: Table 4–1).

Chunbing Xing, *China: Employment and Inequality Trends*. In: *Tasks, Skills, and Institutions*. Edited by Carlos Gradín, Piotr Lewandowski, Simone Schotte, and Kunal Sen, Oxford University Press. © UNU-WIDER (2023). DOI: 10.1093/oso/9780192872241.003.0009

interpersonal, kept rising. Routine cognitive tasks typical in manufacturing and clerical jobs first increased and then declined in the most recent period of 2010–15.

We do not find an occupational polarization as observed in developed economies. When China transformed from an agricultural to industrial economy, the burgeoning manufacturing and service jobs are characteristic of routine tasks. We observe an increase rather than decline in jobs in the middle skill range. Although routine tasks began to decrease in the most recent period of 2010–15, a U-shaped relationship between employment growth and occupational wages is yet readily observed.

China's wage inequality has continued to rise over the last two decades. The wage premium for educated workers rose sharply in the 1990s and remained high thereafter, and education has become the largest contributor to China's wage inequality. But the relationship between job tasks (and related skills) and earnings inequality is more complicated.

As emphasized in a burgeoning literature, tasks performed in different jobs play an important role in shaping the wage distribution. This literature emphasizes the distinction between different types of tasks: routine cognitive, non-routine cognitive, routine manual, non-routine manual, and non-routine interpersonal tasks. It is the routine tasks that are readily influenced by technological change characterized by the widespread use of computers and automated machineries. We find that the routine-task intensity (RTI) has become increasingly negatively correlated with wages. As occupation-specific task content is coded using the US occupational dictionary, we also use a corrected RTI to consider the difference in the economic development levels between the USA and China (Lewandowski et al. 2019, 2020). We find that RTI plays an even more prominent role when using the country-specific measure. This finding is important and suggests that the labour market penalizes occupations characterized by routine tasks that are easily performed by robots or computers.

The results of this chapter are of great importance for China's educational development. Following its significant expansion of the education system, the pattern of secondary and tertiary education development has become an urgent policy issue. For example, with nearly 90 per cent of middle school graduates enrolling in higher level education, the government is guiding roughly an equal number of them to academic and vocational high schools. Whether this policy is justified depends on the returns to a different type of skill. In particular, the negative association between RTI and wages suggests that heavy investment in vocational training that emphasizes specific skills (which are easily routinized) may be unwise.

This study is also crucial for understanding the income inequality trend. For several reasons (such as stimulating domestic consumption and combating high levels of inequality), the Chinese government has emphasized enlarging the middle-income group in recent years. Our results suggest that the force of technological change has made this objective particularly challenging.

This chapter is organized as follows. Section 9.2 summarizes the related literature to China's wage or earnings inequalities. Section 9.3 introduces the data used
for this study. Section 9.4 describes in detail how the sectoral and occupational
structures have changed since the 1990s, with an emphasis on the decades after
2000. Section 9.5 examines the evolution of wage inequality in China. Section 9.6
explores the relationship between occupational structure and wage inequality
and investigates the changes in wage inequality using the decomposition method.
Section 9.7 concludes.

9.2   Literature and background

Income inequality has become an crucial issue in China as it reached a high level in
the 1990s and 2000s. While some scholars suggest that China's income inequality
is heading downwards, as predicted by an inverted-U-shape hypothesis (Kanbur
et al. 2021), others argue that it will likely remain high (Luo et al. 2020). Wages
have become increasingly important in shaping overall income inequality. During
the planning economy era, region and seniority played an important role. With
market reform, the wage gaps between different areas, industries, types of ownership, and demographic groups evolved and widened significantly (Knight and
Song 2003; Xing 2008, 2012). Of these factors, education has played an increasingly important role. A considerable amount of effort has been taken to estimate
the returns to education, which increased considerably in the late 1990s and early
2000s and remained high thereafter (despite the sharp increase in education levels). The findings show that the returns to education (or skill prices) for urban
China have increased continuously since the late 1980s (Zhang et al. 2005).

Several studies have quantified the influence of different factors to wage inequality and have found that the contribution of education has been ever-increasing to
the point that it has become the largest contributor. The importance of other factors, such as seniority (experience) and region, has declined. While, in the past,
regional disparity was the most critical contributor to wage inequality, it has been
surpassed by other factors, particularly education.

There are several reasons for the increased returns to education and wage
inequality. First, market-oriented reform (such as ownership restructuring or pri-
vatization in the late 1990s) is closely associated with an increased return to
skills. Even within state-owned enterprises, workers increasingly work in a competitive environment for wages that are determined by performance or supply-
and-demand forces. Second, China's deeper integration into the world economy
has increased the demand for skilled workers. Third, technological change has
fundamentally changed the nature of jobs. As a developing country, China has
embraced technological change enthusiastically. The declining price of computers has induced the widespread use of personal computers and the internet, which

can replace routine cognitive tasks in jobs and therefore influence the occupational structure.

Although several studies have noted the occupational (task-based) approach to understanding China's labour market, there has been little examination of the changing occupational structure. There has been even less effort taken to measure the changing number of different tasks performed and their link to wages. Ge et al. (2021) is one of the few exceptions that studied the dynamics of China's occupational structure, but Ge and colleagues did not examine the relationship between occupational structure and wage inequality. Job structure can influence wage levels and wage inequality even after controlling for general skill levels. It is not an uncommon practice in research to control for occupation, industry, and ownership when examining wage determination. These characteristics are primarily auxiliary control variables, and how these characteristics affect wages is seldom reported.

9.3 Data

We use census or mini-census data and a household survey to explore the changing nature of work and inequality in China. First, we use the Chinese population census data for 1990, 2000, 2010, and the 1 per cent population survey (or the mini census) data for 2015 to examine industrial and occupational structural changes.[2] We use random samples of these census data, which cover all (31) provinces of mainland China and contain detailed industry and occupation information for a large number of individuals each year. The three-digit occupation codes, in particular, allow us to reclassify the data following the International Standard Classifications of Occupation (1988 version, or ISCO-88). We then link the occupation data to the occupational task content information to examine the changing trends in different tasks. The census data also collect detailed information such as location of residence, age, gender, and education. However, they do not have income information.

Several household surveys in China contain income and occupation information. In this chapter, we mainly use the China General Social Survey (CGSS).[3] It collects detailed (three-digit) occupation information according to the ISCO system, which allows us to assign task measures to individuals with different occupations at a more disaggregated (three-digit) level. The CGSS covers all mainland provinces, but unlike some other surveys, it only collects income information for the respondent and their spouse within a household.

---

[2] We accessed the census and mini census data from the National Bureau of Statistics of China but these are not yet publicly available.
[3] This CGSS survey was conducted by the National Survey Research Center at Renmin University of China (NSRC). See NSRC (n.d.). To complement the CGSS data, we also use the China Household Income Project Survey (CHIP), which has high-quality income information but is short of detailed occupational data. See Xing (2021) for related results.

To focus on the labour market consequences of the changing nature of work, we examine workers' wages in both rural and urban China. The outcome variable of interest is annual earnings, which is deflated using the national consumer price index.

9.4 Changes in occupational structure

Table 9.1 reports the employment shares by one-digit occupation from 1982 to 2015. As the industrial structural transformation suggests, employment continuously shifted out of agriculture to manufacturing and service jobs. In 1990, three-quarters of the workforce had agricultural jobs, declining to 31 per cent by 2015. In contrast, service workers and market sales workers accounted for 4 per cent in 1990, increasing to 24 per cent in 2015. Manufacturing jobs (craft workers and machine operators) also accounted for 24 per cent of the workforce in 2015, compared to 11 per cent in 1990. Professional jobs (including technicians and associate professionals) increased from around 7 per cent in 1990 to 16 per cent in 2015.

The pace of transformation in the occupational structure varied in different periods and the most significant changes happened between 2000 and 2010. In this decade, the share of agriculture-related jobs declined by 30 percentage points, accounting for three-quarters of the decline between 1990 and 2015. Accordingly, employment increased for non-agricultural jobs, especially manufacturing and service jobs. These significant changes were due to China's entry

Table 9.1 Occupational structure in China, 1982–2015

	1982	1990	2000	2010	2015
By one-digit occupation category					
Legislators, senior officials, and managers	0.46	1.20	1.76	2.34	1.78
Professionals	1.36	2.16	5.55	8.38	7.90
Technicians and associate professionals	4.09	4.86	3.99	6.40	7.68
Clerks	1.76	2.45	0.87	1.55	1.09
Service workers and market sales workers	2.37	4.16	8.47	20.00	24.48
Skilled agricultural and fishery workers	74.57	72.31	62.44	32.46	31.27
Craft and related trades workers	8.33	6.96	6.39	12.31	13.46
Plant and machine operators and assemblers	4.93	3.87	8.62	13.08	10.70
Elementary occupations	2.11	2.07	1.93	3.51	1.59
By low, mid, high skill					
Low skill (agricultural, elementary)	76.68	74.38	64.37	35.97	32.86
Mid skill (clerical, sales, production)	17.39	17.44	24.35	46.94	49.73
High skill (managerial, professional, technical)	5.91	8.22	11.3	17.12	17.36

Source: Author's calculations based on census or mini census for various years.

into the World Trade Organization (WTO), massive rural–urban migration, and rapid urbanization. Between 2010 and 2015, however, the pace and nature of occupational change seems to be different from the previous decade. First, manufacturing jobs declined slightly (rather than increased). Second, service and professional jobs kept increasing, but the change was slower. The new direction of occupational change may partly reflect the penetration of technological change into the Chinese labour market.

In Table 9.2, we consider the occupational structure between 1990 and 2010 in rural and urban areas separately.[4] Even in urban areas, agricultural jobs accounted for one-third of employment in 1990, followed by craft workers and those in related trades (16 per cent), technicians (13 per cent), and plant workers (9.6 per cent). By 2010, the share of agricultural and fishery workers declined to 11 per cent; meanwhile, the percentages of service and market sales workers increased to 27 per cent and plant workers to 15 per cent. Unlike for the whole sample, occupational change within urban areas between 1990 and 2000 (which was a consequence of enterprise ownership restructuring) seems more substantial

Table 9.2 One-digit occupation between 1990 and 2010, by rural and urban

	Urban			Rural		
	1990	2000	2010	1990	2000	2010
By one-digit occupation category						
Legislators, senior officials, and managers	2.80	4.07	3.63	0.55	0.57	0.61
Professionals	5.67	12.35	12.86	0.72	2.09	2.39
Technicians and associate professionals	12.50	10.06	10.07	2.54	0.90	1.42
Clerks	6.34	2.19	2.33	0.90	0.19	0.46
Service workers and market sales workers	9.09	19.65	27.37	2.12	2.80	10.05
Skilled agricultural and fishery workers	33.08	19.47	11.48	86.04	84.20	60.70
Craft and related trades workers	15.82	11.99	13.14	3.65	3.54	11.16
Plant and machine operators and assemblers	9.61	16.24	14.72	1.97	4.79	10.88
Elementary occupations	5.09	3.98	4.38	0.84	0.89	2.33
By low, mid, high skill						
Low skill (agricultural, elementary)	38.17	23.45	15.86	86.88	85.09	63.03
Mid skill (clerical, sales, production)	40.86	50.07	57.56	8.64	11.32	32.55
High skill (managerial, professional, technical)	20.97	26.48	26.56	3.81	3.56	4.42

Source: Author's calculations based on census or mini census for various years.

[4] The mini census of 2015 is not used because the rural–urban divide is not consistent with former years.

than that for the following decade. In contrast, the change in rural occupational structure was more significant in the 2000–10 period than in the previous decade. Within rural areas, agricultural and fishery workers decreased by 23 percentage points between 2000 and 2010. Accordingly, service and manufacturing jobs increased dramatically. It is worth mentioning that there was massive rural–urban migration during this time, with the number of rural migrants increasing from 60 million in 2000 to 240 million in 2010 (Li and Xing 2020). Most migrants held occupations in the service and manufacturing sectors.

In Tables 9.1 and 9.2, we also aggregate the occupations into three groups, namely low-skilled (agricultural and elementary workers), mid-skilled (clerical, sales, and production workers), and high-skilled (managerial, professional, and technical workers). Our findings are different to those for developed countries. In the last two decades, especially in the ten years following China's entry into the WTO, low-skilled jobs decreased dramatically, but this trend slowed down in the most recent period.

Occupational structural change indicates that the number of tasks performed by the workforce changed. To investigate this, we merge the task contents from O*NET with the occupational structure to calculate an average score for each task, weighted by the employment share of all occupations each year. This practice relies on two assumptions: (1) that the tasks of the same occupation across countries are comparable; and (2) that the task contents within occupations do not change over time. Keeping these caveats in mind, we examine the changes to several types of tasks in Figure 9.1. Non-routine cognitive analytical (nr_cog_anal) and interpersonal (nr_cog_pers) tasks, routine cognitive tasks (r_cog), and non-routine interpersonal manual tasks increased between 1990 and 2010. However, routine manual tasks (r_man) and non-routine physical manual tasks (nr_man_phys) decreased from 1990 to 2015. These changes are consistent with our previous description of the occupational structural change. We observe that the increase in non-routine cognitive tasks continued, while routine cognitive tasks decreased slightly between 2010 and 2015.

Meanwhile, offshorable tasks increased significantly from 1990 to 2010. As a result of China's integration into the world economy following its entry into the WTO, the increase was particularly substantial between 2000 and 2010. However, offshorable tasks decreased between 2010 and 2015 because of the global financial crisis and domestic consumption growth.

Between 1990 and 2000, there was a substantial increase in RTI, but a decline in the most recent period from 2010 to 2015. As China's economic structure is different from that of the US, the task contents will not be identical between these two countries. The last panel of Figure 9.1 shows the changing pattern of RTI, taking account of this difference. The results suggest only a slight increase between 2000 and 2010 and stagnation in the following five years.

How have the share of occupations of different characteristics changed? Figure 9.2 shows the change in employment share against various occupational

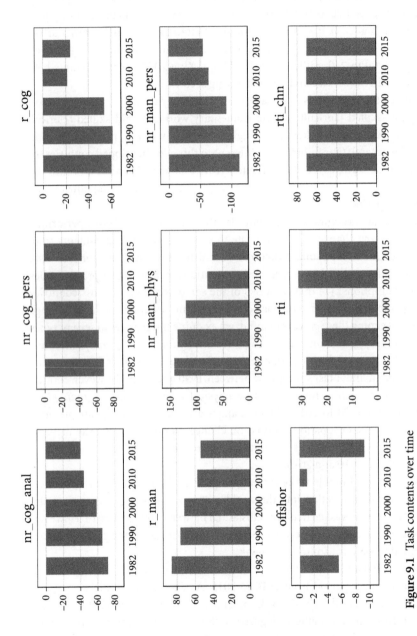

Figure 9.1 Task contents over time

Note: We merged the task contents with the census occupation at the three-digit level and calculated the average task contents based on the occupational structure.

Source: Author's calculations based on census and mini census data for 1982, 1990, 2000, 2010, and 2015.

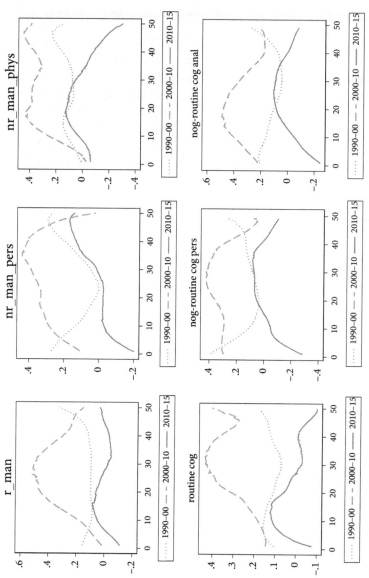

Figure 9.2 Changes in logarithm occupation share against task quantiles

Note: The horizontal line is for (50) quantiles of the three-digit occupations ranked by the level of different tasks; the vertical line is the log change in employment share.

Source: Author's calculation of the employment share change using census data for 1990, 2000, 2010, and 2015.

tasks and RTI measures. The y-axis is the log change in employment share, and the x-axis is the quantiles of the three-digit occupations ranked by the level of different tasks. As the occupational employment share differs considerably, the change in employment share may not reflect the growth trend. For example, a five-percentage-point change means different growth rates for occupations whose initial shares are different. Thus, we examine the logarithm change in employment share by skill quantiles. We split the whole 1990–2015 period into three sub-periods and estimate the lowest curve between the change in employment shares and quantiles of tasks. Between 1990 and 2000, the relationship is roughly U-shaped. Occupations at the middle range of specific tasks experienced the lowest growth. In the following two periods, an inverted U-shape relationship between employment change and task quantile became apparent. The 2000–10 period witnessed the highest employment growth in non agricultural occupations. It was at the middle range of various task contents that occupations grew the most. The most recent period, from 2010 to 2015, exhibits a notable change. The employment shares of occupations with high non-routine manual tasks and routine cognitive tasks decreased. Correspondingly, those with low non-routine cognitive tasks also decreased.

In Figure 9.3, we examine the relationship between changes to occupational employment shares and RTIs. Again, we find a U-shaped relationship over the 1990–2000 period, and the shape is asymmetric. The increase in high-RTI occupations is more prominent than those with low RTI. In later periods, however, the

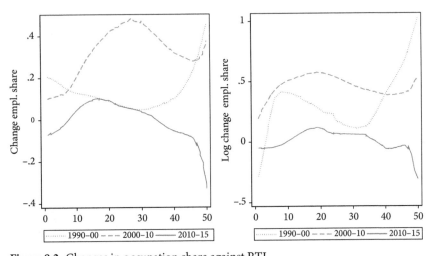

Figure 9.3 Changes in occupation share against RTI

Note: The horizontal line is for (50) quantiles of the three-digit occupations ranked by the level of tasks; the vertical line is the (log) change in employment share at the three-digit occupation level.
Source: Author's calculation of the employment share using census data for 1990, 2000, 2010, and 2015.

relationships have an inverted U-shape. The decline in the employment share for high-RTI occupations is sharper in the 2010–15 period. Examining log changes produces similar results.

The labour force composition of a given occupation changes over time, as do the wage levels of different occupations. Table 9.3 reports wages (in log) and years of schooling for different occupations (at the one-digit level) for different years. Wage levels differ considerably across occupations. Professionals, technicians, and managers earned the highest wages followed by service and manufacturing

Table 9.3 Wage levels and years of schooling by occupation

	Log annual wage			
	2005	2012/13	2015/17	2005–2015/17
Legislators, senior officials, and managers	9.22	10.38	10.50	1.29
Professionals	9.54	10.22	10.61	1.07
Technicians and associate professionals	9.55	10.27	10.51	0.97
Clerks	9.31	10.09	10.45	1.15
Service workers and market sales workers	9.09	9.75	10.02	0.93
Skilled agricultural and fishery workers	7.76	8.54	8.83	1.06
Craft and related trades workers	8.90	9.68	9.94	1.04
Plant and machine operators and assemblers	9.11	9.89	10.00	0.89
Elementary occupations	8.62	9.46	9.64	1.02
	Years of schooling			
Legislators, senior officials, and managers	9.79	12.30	11.54	1.75
Professionals	14.04	14.83	15.08	1.05
Technicians and associate professionals	12.79	13.61	13.71	0.92
Clerks	11.91	13.25	13.64	1.73
Service workers and market sales workers	10.21	10.35	10.32	0.11
Skilled agricultural and fishery workers	5.56	6.49	6.77	1.21
Craft and related trades workers	9.36	9.00	9.11	−0.25
Plant and machine operators and assemblers	9.88	9.96	9.86	−0.02
Elementary occupations	8.37	9.17	8.42	0.05

Source: Author's calculations based on CGSS 2005, 2012, 2013, 2015, and 2017 (NSRC n.d.).

workers, and wages for agricultural and elementary occupations were the lowest. The growth rates also vary across occupations. Managerial jobs had the highest growth, while those of plant operators grew the least. Education levels also differ considerably across occupations. Professionals were the most educated, and agricultural workers were the least educated. It is worth emphasizing that although average education levels increased, those of plant workers, trades workers, and service and sales workers stagnated or even declined.

We also use the occupation log wage in the CGSS to measure the skill levels of occupations (at the two-digit occupational level). The relationship between employment change and skill level is depicted in Figure 9.4. The most noticeable feature is the high growth in medium- to low-wage occupations in 1990–2010. The growth in high-wage occupations is also apparent. In 2010–15, low-wage occupations declined, mid-wage occupations increased, and high-wage occupations remained constant.

In Figure 9.5, we further examine how occupational wage changes are associated with wage levels. With the y-axis depicting the average occupational log wage change and the x-axis being the quantile of mean log wage, a U-shaped relationship is readily observed. The low- and high-wage occupations experienced higher wage growth in rural and urban areas. These results are consistent with the

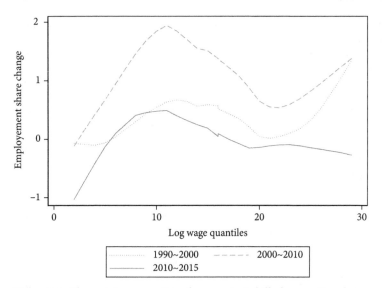

Figure 9.4 Changes in occupation share against skills (occupational wage)

Note: The horizontal line is for (30) quantiles of the two-digit occupation ranked by the level of mean occupational wages; the vertical line is the change in employment share at the two-digit occupation level.

Source: Author's calculation of mean wages using CGSS data for 2012/13 (NSRC n.d.) and employment share using census data for 1990, 2000, 2010, and 2015.

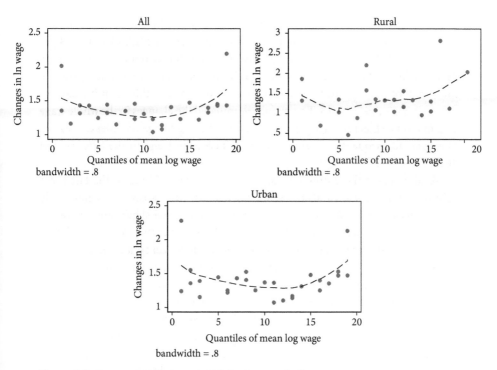

Figure 9.5 Occupational wage growth by wage quintiles
Note: The occupation is at two-digit level.
Source: Author's calculation based on CGSS (NSRC n.d.).

patterns in Figure 9.2, where we find a decline in occupations with high-routine and low-non-routine tasks. They are also consistent with the apparent decline in high-RTI occupations in recent years shown in Figure 9.3. As medium-level wage occupations typically require high-routine tasks, a decline in their employment share and sluggish wage growth reflect the substitution effect of technological changes.

9.5 Earnings inequality

We use the CGSS data to examine earnings inequalities between 2005 and 2017. Table 9.4 reports the wage levels and wage inequalities in several alternative measures. Annual wages increased dramatically, by nearly four times, between 2005 and 2017. In 2005, the mean annual wage was 12,800 Yuan and, by 2017, it had reached 60,000 Yuan. We also report the means and various percentiles of the earnings distributions. All statistics significantly increased during the 2005–17 period.

Meanwhile, wage inequality increased slightly. The Gini coefficient of annual wages increased from 43 per cent in 2005 to 44 per cent in 2012/13 and to 48 per cent in 2015/17. The variance of log wages shows a similar trend. The inequality between different percentiles shows a slightly different pattern. The wage gap at the lower half of the wage distribution (P50–P10) declined (rather than increasing) between 2005 and 2012/13. This change dominated the changes in the whole wage distribution so that the wage gap between the 10th and 90th percentiles decreased. However, all inequality measures show an increasing trend in the latter period 2012/13 to 2015/17.

We also report the corresponding statistics for rural China in the last three columns of Table 9.4. In all the years considered, rural areas had significantly lower wages than urban areas, but rural wages increased significantly between 2005 and 2017 as well. Inequality, however, did not increase monotonically. In 2005, inequality was high in the Gini coefficient (50 per cent); it declined slightly between 2005 and 2012/13 and increased again thereafter. The other inequality measures show a similar trend: the percentile gap inequalities (P90–P10) and the variance of log wages kept increasing between 2005 and 2017.

As China's urbanization proceeds, the continuous increase in wage inequality has a significant implication for overall inequality in China. Many believe that China will enter the downward trajectory of the Kuznetsian curve after several decades of rapid growth. However, recent trends in rural and urban inequalities cast serious doubt on that hypothesis.

Existing research shows that the educational wage gap has become a significant factor in influencing wage inequality. Table 9.5 shows the average wages of different education groups, namely middle school graduates, high school

Table 9.4 Wages and wage inequality in urban and rural China, CGSS

	Urban			Rural		
	2005	2012/13	2015/17	2005	2012/13	2015/17
Annual wage (RMB)	12,816	36,477	60,297	4,398	14,622	21,429
Gini	0.4309	0.4445	0.4848	0.5000	0.4909	0.5117
Ln(Annual wage)						
Mean	9.089	9.891	10.218	7.935	8.878	9.156
Median	9.210	9.992	10.279	8.006	8.987	9.298
p10	8.006	8.946	8.928	6.908	7.378	7.689
p90	10.127	10.933	11.231	9.210	10.086	10.502
P50–10	1.204	1.045	1.351	1.099	1.609	1.609
P90–50	0.916	0.942	0.952	1.204	1.099	1.204
P90–10	2.120	1.987	2.303	2.303	2.708	2.813
Variance	0.824	0.837	0.920	0.921	1.106	1.249
Gini	0.055	0.050	0.051	0.068	0.067	0.068

Source: Author's calculations based on CGSS 2005, 2012, 2013, 2015, and 2017 (NSRC n.d.).

Table 9.5 Annual wages (in log) by education, gender, and region

	Urban				Rural			
	2005	2012/13	2015/17	Change (2005–15/17)	2005	2012/13	2015/17	Change (2005–15/17)
Female								
Primary and below	8.264	8.917	9.311	1.047	7.543	8.245	8.482	0.939
Middle school	8.747	9.356	9.696	0.949	7.866	8.743	9.041	1.176
High school	9.077	9.757	10.002	0.925	8.091	9.023	9.220	1.129
Professional coll.	9.517	10.100	10.363	0.846	8.793	9.655	9.870	1.078
College	9.987	10.405	10.778	0.791	9.903	9.946	10.055	0.152
Male								
Primary and below	8.617	9.480	9.692	1.075	7.905	8.921	9.060	1.155
Middle school	9.051	9.781	10.103	1.052	8.402	9.309	9.507	1.105
High school	9.319	10.041	10.295	0.975	8.614	9.402	9.729	1.115
Professional coll.	9.755	10.372	10.681	0.926	9.236	9.799	10.182	0.945
College	9.906	10.644	10.992	1.086	.	10.102	10.272	

Source: Author's calculations based on CGSS 2005, 2012, 2013, 2015, and 2017 (NSRC n.d.).

graduates, professional college graduates, and college/university graduates. The first three columns are for urban areas and the last three for rural areas. The wage gaps between different educational levels are significant for both genders in rural and urban areas. The gap between college and non-college graduates is the largest, and the gap between middle and high school graduates is relatively small.

Table 9.5 also shows significant wage gaps between workers of different genders. Women earn significantly less than men, and the gender gap is more prominent in rural than in urban areas. There are also significant wage gaps across age groups, regions, and individuals with the same observable but different unobservable characteristics. We do not present them to save space.

9.6 Education, occupational tasks, and wage determination

Many studies have estimated Mincerian wage equations for rural and urban China. We also estimate an augmented Mincerian equation to explore the role of education and RTI (as well as gender, experience, experience squared, and region dummies) in determining individual wages. The regression results suggest that educated workers earn significantly more than less-educated workers in rural and urban China. In 2015/17, college graduates earned 0.56 log points more than high school graduates in urban areas. The college premium was significant in rural areas but lower than in urban areas. In 2015/17, college graduates earned 0.47 log points more than high school graduates in rural China. When we use years of schooling as an independent variable, one more year of schooling is associated with a 7–9 per cent wage increase in urban areas. The schooling year coefficient is significantly lower in rural areas, around 2–4 per cent in recent years. In rural and urban China, the education gap does not show a declining trend over time despite a sharp increase in the education levels of rural and urban residents.

Our estimation procedure controls for province dummies and RTIs. As work location and occupation are correlated with education, the results indicate only a lower bound of the returns to education. They also suggest that education and occupational tasks are not perfectly correlated.

We obtain significantly negative RTI coefficients in most cases. A one-unit increase in RTI is associated with an 8–10 per cent wage decrease in urban areas, suggesting that the urban labour markets are favourable to those who perform non-routine tasks. In contrast, the situation for those who perform routine tasks is disadvantageous. For the rural sample, the RTI coefficients are negative but smaller in magnitude than for urban areas. In 2015/17, a unit increase in RTI is associated with a 3 per cent wage decrease.

We also consider the robustness of our results by replacing the RTI measure with a China-specific one. The results suggest that RTI has a significantly negative effect on wages, larger in magnitude than its counterparts when the RTI is uncorrected. For example, for urban areas, in 2005 a one-unit increase in RTI (which is about the difference between production workers and professionals) was associated with a 20 per cent wage decrease; this association increased to over 25 per cent in 2015/17. The RTI coefficient for rural observations also increased in absolute values but was half of the magnitudes in urban areas.

In summary, our results suggest that the rewards for different tasks in the Chinese labour markets differ significantly. The labour markets provide higher returns to non-routine cognitive tasks but punish routine tasks, as the latter are more easily replaced by automated machines.

How does occupational change help to shape wage inequality? We apply the methods developed by Firpo et al. (2011, 2018) to decompose the changes in the Gini coefficients of wages. The basic idea is as follows. The wage distribution is determined by the distribution of individuals' characteristics (education, experience, gender, and job tasks) and the wage differentials between groups. The traditional Oaxaca decomposition method can divide the average wage gap into two: the gap caused by the difference in personal characteristics and the gap caused by the difference in wages (or the returns to personal traits). In a similar vein, the recentred influence function (RIF) base decomposition developed by Firpo et al. (2011, 2018) can decompose the changes in wage inequality into explained and unexplained parts. This method can also determine the contribution of each factor in shaping wage inequality.

First, we consider the results for urban areas. The Gini coefficient increased from 0.431 in 2005 to 0.485 in 2017. Around 70 per cent (0.0384/0.0539) of the Gini increase is due to unexplained factors or the gap between individuals of different characteristics. The returns to experience and education are the two significant factors in the rise in the Gini coefficients. The exercise that considers the two sub-periods 2005–12/13 and 2013–2015/17 suggests that the returns to education played a more substantial role in the former period than in the latter. The results are consistent with the literature which shows that increased skill prices were the major contributor to wage inequality (Li et al. 2007; Knight and Song 2008; Liu et al. 2010; Meng et al. 2010). In both periods, RTI played a minor role in shaping wage inequality. While changes in RTI distribution tended to increase wage inequality, changes in RTI prices tended to reduce it as RTI coefficients declined slightly. In the last three columns, we replace the RTI with the country-specific RTI, which played a more significant role in wage determination. Its role in changing wage inequality, however, is still minor.

We also decompose the changes in wage inequality in rural areas between 2005 and 2017. Similar to urban areas, the increase in wage inequality in rural China is mainly attributable to unexplained factors and RTIs played a minor role in changing wage inequality.

9.7 Conclusion

China's economy has experienced record growth and significant structural change in the past four decades. Under the influence of its economic transition, integration into the world economy, and technological change, economic activities have continuously shifted out of the agricultural sector towards manufacturing and service sectors. As the number and composition of products and services produced evolved, so too did the workforce's skills and tasks. These changes are associated with a significant rise in wage inequality.

In this chapter, we first documented the evolution of the occupational structure using census data. We reclassified the occupation information in the census according to ISCO-88, which allowed us to link task contents to the census data. We showed that cognitive and manual routine tasks have declined and analytical and interpersonal non-routine cognitive tasks have increased since the 1990s. We also observed an inverted U-shaped relationship between the growth of employment shares and RTIs.

We then linked the task contents to the CGSS data, which contain earnings and detailed occupation information. We showed that: (1) wage inequality increased significantly by the early 2000s and, after a period of stagnation, it increased again between 2013 and 2018; (2) education is a significant factor in wage determination; and (3) RTI is negatively correlated with wages, and the correlation has recently become more robust in both rural and urban areas. These results suggest that occupational structure is an essential channel through which technological change influences wage inequality. The RIF decomposition exercise confirmed that the wage gap between individuals with different RTIs played a significant role in increasing wage inequality in rural and urban China.

Acknowledgement

I acknowledge the constructive suggestions from Kunal Sen, Carlos Gradín, Piotr Lewandowski, and Simone Schotte and constructive comments from the workshop on 'The changing nature of work and inequality'. All errors are my own.

References

Bloom, N., J. Liang, J. Roberts, and Z. J. Ying (2015). 'Does working from home work? Evidence from a Chinese Experiment', Quarterly Journal of Economics, 130(1): 165–218.

Cheng, H., R. Jia, D. Li, and H. Li (2019). 'The Rise of Robots in China'. Journal of Economic Perspectives, 33(2): 71–88. https://doi.org/10.1257/jep.33.2.71

China Institute for Income Distribution (n.d.). 'CHIP Dataset Homepage'. [Online]. Available at: http://ciidbnu.org/chip/index.asp (accessed June 2021).

Firpo, S., N.M. Fortin, and T. Lemieux (2011). 'Occupational Tasks and Changes in the Wage Structure'. IZA Discussion Paper 5542. Bonn: IZA.

Firpo, S., N.M. Fortin, and T. Lemieux (2018). 'Decomposing Wage Distributions Using Recentered Influence Function Regressions'. Econometrics, 6(2): 28. https://doi.org/10.3390/econometrics6020028

Ge, P., W. Sun, and Z. Zhao, (2021). 'Employment Structures in China from 1990 to 2015: Demographic and Technological Change'. Journal of Economic Behavior and Organization, 185: 168–90. https://doi.org/10.1016/j.jebo.2021.02.022

Kanbur, R., Y. Wang, X. Zhang, (2021). 'The great Chinese inequality turnaround'. Journal of Comparative Economics, 49(2): 467–482.

Knight, J., and L. Song (2003). 'Increasing Urban Wage Inequality in China: Extent, Elements and Evaluation'. Economics of Transition, 11(4): 597–619. https://doi.org/10.1111/j.0967-0750.2003.00168.x

Knight, J., and L. Song (2008). 'China's Emerging Urban Wage Structure, 1995–2002'. In B. Gustafsson, S. Li, and T. Sicular (eds), Inequality and Public Policy in China, pp. 221–242. Cambridge: Cambridge University Press.

Lewandowski, P., A. Park, W. Hardy, and Y. Du (2019). 'Technology, Skills, and Globalization: Explaining International Differences in Routine and Nonroutine Work Using Survey Data'. IZA DP 12339. Bonn: IZA.

Lewandowski, P., A. Park, and S. Schotte (2020). 'The Global Distribution of Routine and Non-routine Work'. WIDER Working Paper 2020/75. Helsinki: UNU-WIDER. https://doi.org/10.35188/UNU-WIDER/2020/832-0

Li, X., Y. Zhao, and L. Lu (2007). 'Effects of Education on Wage Inequality in Urban China, 1988–2003'. The 6th PEP Research Network General Meeting. Lima: Partnership for Economic Policy.

Li, Y., and C. Xing (2020). 'Structural Transformation, Inequality, and Inclusive Growth in China'. WIDER Working Paper 2020/33. Helsinki: UNU-WIDER. https://doi.org/10.35188/UNU-WIDER/2020/790-3

Liu, X., P. Albert, and Y. Zhao (2010). 'Explaining Rising Returns to Education in Urban China in the 1990s'. IZA Discussion Paper 4872. Bonn: IZA.

Luo, Chuliang, S. Li, and T Sicular (2020). 'The Long-term Evolution of National Income Inequality and Rural Poverty in China'. *China Economic Review*, 62: 101465.

Meng, X., K. Shen, and X. Sen (2010). 'Economic Reform, Education Expansion, and Earnings Inequality for Urban Males in China, 1988–2007'. IZA Discussion Paper 4919. Bonn: IZA.

NBS (National Bureau of Statistics) (2016). *Tabulation on the National 1% Population Survey 2015*. Beijing: China Statistical Press.

NSRC (National Survey Research Center at Renmin University of China) (n.d.). 'CGSS Dataset Homepage'. [Online]. Available at: cgss.ruc.edu.cn (accessed June 2021).

O*NET (n.d.). 'O*NET Website'. [Online]. Available at: https://www.onetonline.org/ (accessed June 2021).

Xing, C. (2008). 'Human Capital and Wage Determination in Different Ownerships, 1989–97'. In G. Wan (ed.), *Understanding Inequality and Poverty in China: Methods and Applications*, pp 117–136. London: Palgrave Macmillan.

Xing, C. (2012). 'Residual Wage Inequality in Urban China, 1995–2007'. *China Economic Review*, 23(2): 205–22. https://doi.org/10.1016/j.chieco.2011.10.003

Xing, C. (2021). 'The Changing Nature of Work and Earnings Inequality in China'. WIDER Working Paper 2021/105. Helsinki: UNU-WIDER. https://doi.org/10.35188/UNU-WIDER/2021/045-0

Zhang, J., Y. Zhao, A. Park, and X. Song (2005). 'Economic Returns to Schooling in Urban China, 1988 to 2001'. *Journal of Comparative Economics*, 33: 730–52. https://doi.org/10.1016/j.jce.2005.05.008

10

India

Employment and Inequality Trends

Saloni Khurana and Kanika Mahajan

10.1 Introduction

In this chapter, we look at changes in earnings inequality and the skill content of jobs for India. The evolution of earnings inequality in India has been examined by Kijima (2006) and Chamarbagwala (2006), and later by Azam (2012). A study by Sarkar (2019) looks at changes in earnings inequality under the lens of a changing occupational structure in India up to 2011. She concludes that earnings inequality has been increasing in India and, to some extent, this can be explained by employment and wage polarization in the country. However, none of these studies examine changes in wage earnings inequality and its determinants post-2011 for India. Specifically, this chapter contributes to the literature in two ways. First, it extends the existing analyses on wage inequality in India to the most recently available data for 2017, which enables us to examine how earnings inequality has changed post-2011.[1] Second, we also extend this work methodologically by decomposing the changes in inequality using semi-parametric methods. This allows us to delineate the role of changing occupational structure, or changing returns to occupations in shaping the observed trends in wage inequality.[2] A simultaneous examination of the two over the last 35 years in India throws up interesting patterns. Contrary to the existing literature that finds a rise in wage inequality in India up to 2004, our analyses show that wage inequality was stable during 2004–11 and showed a distinct decline post-2011 in India. This pattern holds for overall earnings as well as within rural and urban areas. To determine the factors behind the observed evolution in earnings inequality, we then undertake a detailed analysis of the changing occupational structure in the urban non-agriculture sector and its implications for the trends in wage inequality.

---

[1] We closely follow the methodology of Gradín and Schotte (2020), which examines similar questions for Ghana.

[2] There are various ways of measuring inequality: earning, wealth, or labour plus non-labour incomes. In this chapter, partly because of data availability over time, we focus on changes in earnings inequality (labour incomes in paid jobs).

Saloni Khurana and Kanika Mahajan, *India: Employment and Inequality Trends.* In: *Tasks, Skills, and Institutions.* Edited by Carlos Gradín, Piotr Lewandowski, Simone Schotte and Kunal Sen, Oxford University Press. © UNU-WIDER (2023). DOI: 10.1093/oso/9780192872241.003.0010

We find that a polarization of jobs occurred in urban India post-2004, and increased in pace during 2011–17. However, we do not find evidence for earnings polarization during this period. At the same time, we find that the share of employment in occupations with larger routine-task requirements has also fallen in non-agriculture sectors of urban India, with the largest declines during 2004–17. However, we do not find a commensurate decrease in real wages in occupations with larger RTI. In fact, we find that occupations with higher routine-task involvement have witnessed a larger increase in mean wages, a finding that underscores the conclusion in this study that changing returns to RTI in India have had an equalizing effect on wage earnings. These findings are at odds with increased demand at the upper end of the skill distribution, resulting in increased earnings for high-skilled workers. This is also in contrast to the findings of existing studies for the US, where job polarization has been accompanied by earnings polarization. A possible factor that can explain these patterns for India is change in the supply of skilled workers outstripping the change in the demand for skilled workers, resulting in increased employment growth but a decline in earnings growth at the upper end of the skill distribution. At the lower end of the skill distribution, institutional factors such as increasing minimum wages may have played an important role.

Lastly, we undertake a decomposition analysis to isolate the effect of changing occupational structure, controlling for other competing factors. The results show that changing demographic workforce structure (age, gender, education, caste, and religion) and RTI in occupations (i.e. the shift of workers towards less routine occupations) has contributed little to the changing patterns of wage earnings inequality in India. In fact, we find that earnings inequality increased during 1983–2004 and then fell during 2011–17, largely due to changing returns to education and RTI over time. While changes in returns to education had a dis-equalizing effect on wage earnings, changes in returns to the routine-task content of an occupation had an equalizing effect on wage earnings. However, despite the contribution of changing returns to education and RTI, a large part of the earnings structure remains unassigned to any factor, perhaps due to changes in demand and supply of labour and institutional factors such as changes in minimum wage regulations.

The rest of the chapter is organized as follows. Section 10.2 elucidates the data used in the analyses. Section 10.3 gives a brief overview of the changes in employment and earnings structure in India, and the results from the Shapley decomposition. The results from the decomposition methods based on recentred influence functions (RIF) are discussed in Section 10.4. Conclusions are gathered in Section 10.5.

10.2 Data and variable construction

10.2.1 Data

We use data from the nationally representative employment survey waves in India. These surveys capture the age, gender, educational qualifications, and employment status of the sampled individuals, with details about occupation and industry of employment. There have been nine major employment surveys in India since the 1980s: 1983–84, 1987–88, 1993–94, 1999–2000, 2004–05, 2007–08, 2009–10, 2011–12 (called the National Sample Surveys (NSS)) and 2017–18 (Periodic Labour Force Survey (PLFS)). To cover broad time periods, before and after liberalization in India, we choose the following years for our analyses (we refer to each round by the first year throughout the paper): 1983, 1993, 2004, 2011, and 2017. The NSS surveys are comparable to the PLFS surveys in methodology, design, and the variables on which data are collected.[3] We use data for working-age adults who were 15–64 years of age at the time of the survey who worked either as paid employees (salaried/casual labourer) or self-employed (employer or unpaid family helper) for the majority of the time in the last year (at least six months), and use the primary activity or occupation of work. The weekly earnings schedule records the earnings in the last reference week for paid workers (casual/salaried) and is taken as our main earnings variable.[4]

Earnings for self-employed workers are not captured in any survey apart from the PLFS 2017. Thus, we focus on trends in earnings for paid workers at the overall level but check the robustness of our main findings to imputed earnings for self-employed urban workers for rounds before 2017, based on the methodology discussed in the working paper's appendix.[5] Additionally, in 2017–18 the earnings of salaried workers were captured by asking them about their earnings in the last month. These were converted to weekly earnings by dividing the monthly earnings by 4.3. As mentioned, since earnings for the self-employed are not captured in four out of five data rounds, we focus on the paid employees for earnings results. All earnings data are deflated and reflect real values in 2017 INR. For urban India we use the Consumer Price Index for Industrial Workers (CPIIW) and for rural

---

[3] One departure point is the stratification methodology, which changed to give adequate representation to all education groups in 2017. But this has no bearing on population estimates since all estimates are weighted by sampling weights provided in each round.

[4] Since we use the earnings of persons primarily employed in the labour market, the results do not differ if daily earnings are calculated by dividing weekly earnings by days worked in the last week.

[5] Appendix available at https://www.wider.unu.edu/publication/evolution-wage-inequality-india-1983%E2%80%932017. We do not impute the earnings for rural self-employed workers because a large proportion of these work in the agriculture sector and therefore the imputation is likely to be unreliable.

workers we use the Consumer Price Index for Agricultural Laborers (CPIAL) at the all-India level to generate real earnings. All analyses are weighted using survey weights.[6]

10.2.2 Construction of variables

Matching occupational classifications across surveys

The National Classification of Occupations 1968 (NCO-68), which is a variant of the International Standard Classification of Occupations (ISCO), is used in employment data collected in 1983, 1993, and 2004 for recording the occupational classification of each employed person. In the years 2011 and 2017, NCO-04 was used. A concordance was generated across NCO-68 and NCO-04 at the three-digit level. While NCO-68 recorded 458 occupations at the three-digit level, NCO-04 recorded 113 occupations at the same level. Thus, multiple 1968 codes can be matched to a single NCO-04 code. The concordance between NCO-04 in India and ISCO-88 was then undertaken.[7]

Mapping task content to occupations

We use two alternative data sources to measure the task content of each occupation. We first match each occupation (which is now at the ISCO-88 three-digit occupation level) to the task measures derived using the O*NET 2003 database (the methodology is based on Acemoglu and Autor 2011). We also use an India-specific measure for the task content of occupations, constructed by Lewandowski et al. (2020), and refer to this as a country-specific measure of RTI. The country-specific task measure for India is constructed at the two-digit occupational classification level and matched to the Indian employment data. We also rescale the two-digit country-specific RTI measures using the three-digit level variation from the O*NET RTI measures to check the robustness of our results.

We use the above two mappings of occupations to tasks (O*NET and the country-specific measure) and construct a measure of RTI using the methodology in Autor and Dorn (2009) and Goos et al. (2014).

10.3 Background: trends in earnings inequality and employment

10.3.1 Economic context

India's GDP has seen significant growth since the 1980s. After the liberalization reforms of 1991, the country recorded a GDP growth rate of more than 6 per cent

---

[6] The outliers at the lower end of the earnings distribution were capped at the first percentile (Rs.99.4) for paid employees.

[7] The concordances generated at each level are available in the Technical Appendix to the working paper of this chapter (Khurana and Mahajan 2020).

for most years. The Indian growth experience has been different from other Asian countries that saw export-led growth. Its growth is based on the services sector boom in the country. The momentum of spectacular GDP growth continued for most of the 2000s at around 6–8 per cent per annum but has slowed down since 2011.

Economic growth has been accompanied by structural transformation in sectoral income shares, poverty reduction and mixed trends in inequality. The share of agriculture and allied activities dropped from 35.69 per cent in 1980 to 14.39 per cent in 2018, while the share of services increased from 37.65 per cent in 1980 to 54.15 per cent in 2018. However, the decline in agriculture's share in income has not been commensurate with the decline in its share of employment. Around 40 per cent of rural Indian employment (which covers about 70 per cent of the Indian population) is still based on agricultural activities. In urban areas, agriculture plays a minimal role while employment in construction (at the low end of the skill spectrum) has increased. Workers moving out of agriculture but not having the education or training for high-skilled occupations are moving into construction sector jobs, since manufacturing (which is located in the middle of the earnings distribution in India) has seen a fall in urban employment share over time. There has also been an increase in the workforce in wholesale and retail trade in urban areas. However, rising education levels with little growth in employment has resulted in swelling numbers of educated-unemployed youth in 2017–18.

There has been a steady decline in the proportion of Indians living in poverty over the last three decades. During 1983–93, the percentage of poor declined by 9 percentage points. The proportion of poor further reduced from 45.9 per cent in 1993 to 38.2 per cent in 2004 and 21.2 per cent in 2011. The trends in inequality, however, depend on the measures used—consumption or total income (salaried/casual earnings plus self-employed earnings). The consumption-based inequality measure saw a large increase between 1993 and 2004 (by almost four points). Thereafter, there has been some increase up to 2011, but only very moderately so, by one point.[8] The income-based Gini index derived using the Indian Human Development Survey (IHDS) shows a modest increase during 2004–11, from 0.53 to 0.55, an increase of two points (Himanshu, 2018). On average, despite the trends, the level of inequality in India is large. In the next section we discuss the trends in earnings-based inequality for paid workers.

---

[8] These estimates are based on the authors' compilation of World Bank data (including Gini) and national estimates of poverty from the Reserve Bank of India. The poverty rates are calculated using US$1.90 a day as the poverty line.

10.3.2 Trends in earnings inequality and occupational structure in India

Changes in aggregate earnings inequality
We document the changes in weekly wage earnings inequality in India for paid workers over the last three decades. Table 10.1 shows the Gini coefficient, variance of earnings, and inter-quantile ratios for all areas, and separately for urban and rural areas. There is pro-rich growth during 1983–2004, with an increase in the overall Gini from 0.52 to 0.56, but this reversed during 2004–17 and fell from 0.56 to 0.51 and further to 0.45. Hence, we see an overall decline in paid earnings inequality during 1983–2017, but the trends differ by the sub-period under consideration. Also, there are differences by location in changes in earnings inequality at the lower (50th to 10th percentile) and higher ends (90th to 50th percentile) of the distribution. For rural areas, inequality has declined over the entire period at both the ends; in urban areas, inequality has declined at the lower end and increased at the upper end. However, there is a perceptible decline since 2004 in urban areas at the upper end of the earnings distribution as well. The patterns for inequality changes in urban areas, excluding agriculture, mimic the overall patterns well. Therefore, we now examine wage earnings inequality patterns in detail for urban areas.

We also plot the growth incidence curves for weekly earnings by percentile for urban areas. These figures in the working paper (Khurana and Mahajan 2020) show that during 1983–2004 (a period of lower economic growth), higher growth in wage earnings was observed at the top of the wage earnings distribution. This pattern reversed during 2004–17 and lower growth in wage earnings occurred at the top of the earning distribution and higher wage earnings growth was seen at the bottom of the earnings distribution. We observe similar patterns in rural and urban areas, but it is more pronounced for urban workers. The main take-away from the above analysis is that following an increase in paid earnings inequality up to 2004, there has been a clear reduction in earnings inequality in India post-2004. This pattern in wage earnings inequality change holds for both men and women.

The above findings may appear to be at odds with the consumption inequality estimates (Dang and Lanjouw 201; Chancel and Piketty 2019).[9] There are no comparable consumption data for years post-2011 to verify what happened to consumption inequality post-2011. Notably, the growth in consumption inequality slowed drastically during 2004–11 compared to the previous decade, a trend that also holds for paid earnings inequality. There are, however, a few differences between our inequality measure and those used in the literature. First, both

---

[9] Chancel and Piketty (2019) show that the top 1 per cent of earners captured less than 21 per cent of total income in the late 1930s; this reduced to 6 per cent in the early 1980s, but rose to 22 per cent in the recent period between 1980 and 2015.

Table 10.1 Inter-quantile ratios and summary inequality indices

	1983	1993	2004	2011	2017
Panel A: all areas					
ln(q90)–ln(q10)	2.516	2.533	2.565	2.234	2.100
ln(q90)–ln(q50)	1.445	1.503	1.600	1.337	1.180
ln(q50)–ln(q10)	1.070	1.030	0.965	0.896	0.920
Var(log earn)	0.853	0.919	0.936	0.743	0.648
Gini(log earn)	0.084	0.082	0.078	0.064	0.059
Gini(earn)	0.520	0.524	0.558	0.505	0.452
Panel B: urban					
ln(q90)–ln(q10)	2.100	2.339	2.547	2.314	2.120
ln(q90)–ln(q50)	0.868	1.066	1.449	1.397	1.253
ln(q50)–ln(q10)	1.232	1.273	1.099	0.916	0.868
Var(log earn)	0.712	0.871	0.945	0.856	0.663
Gini(log earn)	0.068	0.071	0.073	0.067	0.058
Gini(earn)	0.419	0.443	0.512	0.507	0.447
Panel C: rural					
ln(q90)–ln(q10)	1.966	1.983	1.946	1.609	1.666
ln(q90)–ln(q50)	1.050	1.063	1.030	0.790	0.819
ln(q50)–ln(q10)	0.916	0.920	0.916	0.820	0.847
Var(log earn)	0.562	0.609	0.648	0.503	0.513
Gini(log earn)	0.071	0.069	0.067	0.054	0.054
Gini(earn)	0.450	0.438	0.479	0.404	0.397
Panel D: urban (non-agriculture sector)					
ln(q90)–ln(q10)	2.079	2.197	2.447	2.335	2.097
ln(q90)–ln(q50)	0.856	1.019	1.386	1.419	1.253
ln(q50)–ln(q10)	1.224	1.179	1.061	0.916	0.844
Var(log earn)	0.656	0.830	0.911	0.844	0.652
Gini(log earn)	0.064	0.068	0.071	0.066	0.057
Gini(earn)	0.404	0.429	0.504	0.503	0.444

Note: The sample includes paid workers.
Source: Authors' calculations based on NSS 1983, 1993, 2004, and 2011, and PLFS 2017.

consumption and income data are measured at the household level, while paid earnings are measured at an individual level, for those who are working. Therefore, our inequality estimates are not directly comparable to either consumption or income inequality measures at the household level. Falling earnings inequality could still create higher consumption inequality at the household level because of rising assortative mating and women's decisions to work in the labour market as their level of education increases. Second, the measure of income inequality using IHDS data or National Accounts Statistics includes capital earnings and wealth measures, which are not included in the paid worker earnings in our measure of inequality.

We henceforth concentrate on urban paid workers for our analyses since rural employment in India is still predominantly agricultural. Also, within urban paid workers we look at only those who are employed in the non-agriculture sector for two reasons: (1) in urban areas the agriculture workforce forms a small proportion of the total workforce; and (2) measuring RTI for the agricultural workforce seems to be more error prone, as discussed in the working paper.

Changes in educated workers and education earnings premium
Over the years the Indian workforce has become more educated. The gradient of increase is sharper for women than for men. The proportion of illiterate women in the urban workforce has fallen from 60 per cent in 1983 to 22 per cent in 2017. The proportion of women with tertiary education has increased from 3 per cent in 1983 to 30 per cent in 2017. For men, the reduction in illiterate workers in urban areas has been made up by an increase in the proportion of men in tertiary education. These trends show that the supply of workers with secondary and tertiary education has risen in India over the last three decades.

Given the increasing supply of educated workers, it is instructive to look at the changing education premium over time. We calculate the returns to different education levels for each year and how they are changing over time for men and women in urban areas after controlling for sociodemographic characteristics such as age, religion, caste, and Indian state of residence. Occupational structure is added as a control at the two-digit level. Urban areas show an increase in the education premium for those having secondary and tertiary education up to 2004, and thereafter the premium declines with respect to the illiterate category during 2004–11. These findings are evidence of the supply of educated workers outstripping demand, or a worsening quality in the higher-educated workforce, or institutional factors like minimum wages increasing the earnings of illiterate workers. If anything, women have borne a larger brunt of the declining premiums.

However, the earnings premium across individuals having some education (i.e. between middle/secondary–tertiary education categories) shows differential trends. For instance, urban non-agriculture workers (both men and women) witness an increase in the premium between tertiary–secondary and tertiary–middle during 1983–2017. Largely during 2011-17, the education premium across tertiary–middle/secondary education categories has remained stable. The detailed figures for changing education distribution and premiums are provided in the working paper.

Changes in the occupational structure of the workforce

Table 10.2 shows the occupation-level changes in employment and earnings at the one-digit level of the occupational classification for urban paid workers in non-agricultural sectors.[10] It can be seen that over time there has been an increase in employment share by managers and professionals at the upper end and in services at the mid-level (retail, tourism-related mostly), while clerical jobs at the mid-level and machine operators at the low-skill level have fallen. Elementary workers, especially the share of construction workers, has increased post-2004. There was a rise in the *Trades* workforce share during 1983–2017, but this fell during 2004–17 along with a decline in the rate of increase for services. These trends clearly point to a reduction in the workforce in sectors more amenable to automation. On the other hand, movement in wages differs across the sub-periods. During 1993–2004 the rise in weekly earnings was the highest for managers, professionals, and technicians, but during 2004–11 the growth in wages in these occupations fell relative to those in elementary or mid-skill occupations. In fact, during 2011–17 the real earnings for managers and professionals fell by 6.3 and 4.1 per cent per annum, respectively. Notably, wage earnings growth is determined by both demand for and supply of skills. While the demand for high-skilled jobs has increased over time, an increase in the supply of high-skilled workers exceeding the increase in demand can lead to a decline in wage earnings for the skilled sector.

Changes in average RTI over time

The above changes in occupational structure show that over time there has been a clear increase in high-skill jobs such as managers and professionals with some increase in retail and tourism service-related jobs and construction jobs. This shift implies a larger increase in non-routine jobs over time. Therefore, we next calculate the RTI of jobs and examine how the average RTI changed over the last three decades in India. We find that the average RTI has decreased over time in India for both O*NET and country-specific RTI measures. On average, the O*NET measure (from 0.55 to 0.43) shows a larger decline in RTI than the country-specific measure (from 0.46 to 0.40).

Changes in minimum wage and other institutional factors in India

Two types of workers have seen an increased employment share in urban India since 2004. One is construction labourers at the lower end of the skill spectrum; the other is managers and professionals. However, real earnings for managers and professionals have fallen post-2011, while they had slowed in growth during 2004–11, whereas those of construction labourers have risen consistently. These patterns point to a demand–supply skills gap in India or institutional factors playing a role in the evolution of earnings across occupations. The earnings for construction

---

[10] The non-agriculture workforce is kept on the basis of industrial classification. However, we still find that a few report themselves under the skilled agriculture occupation even after we drop those employed in the agricultural industry.

Table 10.2 Changes in employment and earnings: main occupational groups (urban non-agriculture, paid)

		Levels					Percentage growth (annual)			
		1983	1993	2004	2011	2017	1983–93	1993–2004	2004–11	2011–17
				Panel A: employment share (%)						
1	Managers	2.3	3.3	3.6	4.7	5.9	3.7	0.4	3.7	3.9
2	Professionals	6.7	7.6	7.3	11.0	12.4	1.3	-0.2	6.0	2.0
3	Technicians	9.7	10.5	9.4	9.3	9.6	0.8	-0.5	-0.1	0.4
4	Clerks	11.9	11.0	9.1	8.8	7.1	-0.7	-0.9	-0.4	-3.6
5	Services	11.9	11.6	15.4	13.6	15.2	-0.3	1.4	-1.7	1.8
7	Trades workers	23.6	23.6	27.4	21.0	19.0	0.0	0.7	-3.7	-1.7
8	Machine operators	13.4	12.8	11.1	12.2	10.7	-0.5	-0.7	1.3	-2.2
6	Skilled agricultural	0.4	0.4	0.3	0.3	0.2	0.4	-2.2	0.0	-2.3
9	Elementary	20.1	19.2	16.5	19.1	20.0	-0.5	-0.7	2.2	0.8
				Panel B: mean weekly earnings (INR, constant 2017 prices)						
1	Managers	3,758.9	6,026.6	9,979.1	11,743.7	7,922.9	4.8	2.4	2.4	-6.3
2	Professionals	3,091.8	4,591.1	7,110.3	8,377.5	6,505.2	4.0	2.1	2.4	-4.1
3	Technicians	2,190.4	3,442.1	4,968.4	5,484.8	5,368.4	4.6	1.8	1.4	-0.4
4	Clerks	2,039.6	3,237.5	4,407.5	4,820.0	4,568.6	4.7	1.5	1.3	-0.9
5	Services	1,144.5	1,711.6	2,095.3	2,741.4	2,539.0	4.1	1.0	3.9	-1.3
7	Trades workers	1,163.9	1,711.5	1,813.1	2,325.9	2,331.4	3.9	0.3	3.6	0.0
8	Machine operators	1,585.5	2,151.4	2,486.0	2,907.4	2,849.2	3.1	0.7	2.3	-0.3
6	Skilled agricultural	1,320.0	2,443.5	2,376.1	2,223.8	2,575.4	6.4	-0.1	-0.9	2.5
9	Elementary	1,011.7	1,291.3	1,449.8	1,779.8	1,912.3	2.5	0.6	3.0	1.2

Note: The sample includes urban non-agricultural paid workers.
Source: Authors' calculations based on NSS 1983, 1993, 2004, and 2011, and PLFS 2017.

workers are linked to minimum wages for agricultural workers, which are 10 times higher in 2017 as compared to 2004.

10.3.3 Is earnings inequality affected by the changing nature of occupations and skills?

Regression-based evidence: job polarization

We conduct a regression-based test for job polarization in India (Goos and Manning 2007) for urban paid workers in the non-agriculture sector using a quadratic specification in initial log mean weekly earnings.

Table 10.3 Polarization in employment and earnings: paid, non-agriculture, urban

	(1) 1983–93	(2) 1993–2004	(3) 2004–11	(4) 2011–17	(5) 1983–2017
Dependent variable →	Panel A: change in log(employment share)				
ln wage $(t-1)$	−0.146	−0.754	−1.060	−3.310***	−8.038**
	(1.854)	(1.383)	(2.338)	(1.143)	(3.813)
Sq (ln wage $(t-1)$)	0.020	0.040	0.077	0.208***	0.563**
	(0.126)	(0.090)	(0.146)	(0.071)	(0.261)
Constant	−0.018	3.316	3.342	13.029***	28.240**
	(6.779)	(5.309)	(9.336)	(4.611)	(13.878)
Observations	101	101	101	106	101
R-squared	0.079	0.061	0.020	0.069	0.057
Adj. R-squared	0.0607	0.0418	−8.47e−05	0.0504	0.0382
F-test	0.0470	0.276	0.351	0.0114	0.0450
Dependent variable →	Panel B: change in log(mean wage)				
ln wage $(t-1)$	1.021**	−3.021***	−1.590	1.347***	−1.486*
	(0.445)	(0.725)	(1.042)	(0.395)	(0.876)
Sq (ln wage $(t-1)$)	−0.068**	0.215***	0.089	−0.097***	0.095
	(0.032)	(0.049)	(0.066)	(0.025)	(0.061)
Constant	−3.451**	10.737***	7.100*	−4.577***	6.509**
	(1.555)	(2.693)	(4.094)	(1.581)	(3.144)
Observations	101	101	101	106	101
R-squared	0.083	0.364	0.265	0.639	0.128
Adj. R-squared	0.0640	0.351	0.250	0.632	0.110
F-test	0.000578	1.68e−07	0.00142	0	0.0103

Note: The sample includes urban non-agricultural paid workers.
Source: Authors' calculations based on NSS 1983, 1993, 2004, and 2011, and PLFS 2017.

Estimates for polarization in employment are reported in Table 10.3. The results show evidence of job polarization during 2004–17. Workforce shares decrease with initial earnings and then rise (negative coefficient on log initial wage and positive coefficient on square of log initial wage).[11] Earnings polarization also occurred during 1993–2011, but the time period of earnings polarization does not coincide with job polarization. Hence, the period 2011–17 shows conflicting evidence—job polarization without earnings polarization—unlike the findings for the US, where earnings polarization has accompanied job polarization.

10.3.4 Regression-based evidence: changes in employment by RTI measures

Next, we look at change in employment and earnings by the routine-task content of jobs. We conduct a regression-based test using a quadratic specification in RTI calculated at the three-digit occupational classification using O*NET and at the two-digit level using the country-specific RTI values.

The changes in employment shares and mean wage based on RTI of the occupation using both O*NET RTI and country-specific measures are shown in Table 10.4. The results show that there has been a decline in employment share for occupations that have a higher routine-task content and that these results are stronger for country-specific RTI measures at the two-digit level. On the other hand, earnings have increased in occupations with the largest RTI during 2004–17.

10. 3.5 Shapley decomposition

As a next step, we examine whether changes in the task content of jobs over time can explain the trends in inequality. We decompose the change in earnings inequality during every sub-period from 1983/84 to 2017/18 in our analyses, as well as over the entire time period, using Shapley decomposition.

Table 10.5 shows the Shapley decomposition for urban, paid, non-agriculture workers. The measure of inequality used in this decomposition is the mean log deviation in earnings (Chakravarty, 2009). On average, contribution of within-occupation factors towards earnings inequality is greater. Between-occupation inequality explained 36.41 per cent of income inequality in 1983. This increased to 46 per cent in 2004, remained stable during 2004–11, and declined during 2011–17 to reach 43 per cent. Therefore, overall inequality among urban workers increased from 1983 to 2004 largely due to a rise in between-occupation inequality (0.15 in 1983 to 0.24 in 2011) rather than the rise in within-occupation inequality (0.26 in 1983 to 0.27 in 2011). Overall inequality has contracted in 2017 compared to

---

[11] Working paper's Appendix Figure B1 also plots the changes in employment and earnings by skill percentiles captured through wages.

Table 10.4 Change in employment and earnings by RTI: paid, non-agriculture, urban

	(1) 1983–93	(2) 1993–2004	(3) 2004–11	(4) 2011–17	(5) 1983–2017
Dependent variable →	Change in log(employment share)				
Panel A: O*NET RTI (three-digit)					
O*NET RTI	−0.057*	−0.026	0.012	−0.090**	−0.098
	(0.030)	(0.034)	(0.067)	(0.036)	(0.080)
Sq (O*NET RTI)	−0.005	−0.007	0.066	0.038	0.065
	(0.016)	(0.023)	(0.042)	(0.024)	(0.056)
Constant	0.008	−0.034	−0.322***	−0.071	−0.350***
	(0.035)	(0.064)	(0.118)	(0.048)	(0.131)
Observations	101	101	101	106	101
Adj. R-squared	0.0517	−0.00882	0.0140	0.0820	0.0130
F-test	0.116	0.726	0.161	0.0334	0.287
Panel B: country-specific RTI (two-digit)					
CS RTI	−0.266**	0.220	−0.593**	−0.251**	−0.955***
	(0.123)	(0.161)	(0.262)	(0.092)	(0.291)
Sq (CS RTI)	0.179	−0.300	0.735**	0.314*	1.038***
	(0.150)	(0.265)	(0.290)	(0.164)	(0.321)
Constant	0.039	−0.013	−0.069	−0.041	−0.070
	(0.046)	(0.074)	(0.078)	(0.049)	(0.130)
Observations	26	26	26	26	26
Adj. R-squared	0.0799	−0.0127	0.174	0.0509	0.203
F-test	0.0391	0.401	0.0586	0.0384	0.00882
Dependent variable →	Change in log(mean wage)				
Panel C: O*NET RTI (three-digit)					
O*NET RTI	−0.022**	−0.103***	0.065**	0.073***	0.007
	(0.010)	(0.018)	(0.028)	(0.017)	(0.025)
Sq (O*NET RTI)	−0.007	0.003	−0.005	−0.004	−0.005
	(0.004)	(0.009)	(0.015)	(0.007)	(0.012)
Constant	0.359***	0.235***	0.193***	−0.022	0.758***
	(0.013)	(0.024)	(0.046)	(0.021)	(0.032)
Observations	101	101	101	106	101
Adj. R-squared	0.0630	0.293	0.0568	0.244	−0.0178
F-test	0.0197	4.42e–07	0.0656	1.12e–06	0.895

Continued

Table 10.4 *Continued*

	(1) 1983–93	(2) 1993–2004	(3) 2004–11	(4) 2011–17	(5) 1983–2017
		Panel D: country-specific RTI (two-digit)			
CS RTI	0.030	-0.425***	0.182**	0.364***	0.158**
	(0.050)	(0.089)	(0.075)	(0.067)	(0.071)
Sq (CS RTI)	-0.134**	0.234**	-0.069	-0.211***	-0.167**
	(0.057)	(0.097)	(0.113)	(0.072)	(0.074)
Constant	0.376***	0.274***	0.147***	-0.068**	0.726***
	(0.013)	(0.035)	(0.033)	(0.025)	(0.022)
Observations	26	26	26	26	26
Adj. R-squared	0.377	0.548	0.196	0.612	0.0654
F-test	0.00602	4.07e–05	0.00981	1.05e–05	0.0915

Note: The sample includes urban, non-agricultural, paid workers. Country-specific RTI at the two-digit level and O*NET RTI at the three-digit level is used.
Source: Authors' calculations based on NSS 1983, 1993, 2004, and 2011, and PLFS 2017.

2011, again mostly due to a decline in between-occupation inequality (0.24 in 2011 to 0.19 in 2017). Although the bulk share is dominated by the presence of within-occupation inequality, trends are more sensitive to between-occupation inequality.

We further decompose the inequality in earnings between occupations into the contribution of differences in mean earnings across occupations (holding occupation shares constant in Panel B) and differences in occupation shares (holding mean earnings constant in Panel C). The results show that the period of rising between-occupation inequality (1983–2011) is explained largely by a change in the structure of earnings rather than occupational shares changing—that is, due to an increasing gap in average earnings across occupations. On the other hand, results for the period of inequality decline (2011–17) show that inequality would have been lower if occupational shares were held constant (0.18 vs 0.20 actual between-occupation inequality). One of the major take-aways is that income inequality has increased due to the changes in earnings structure from 1983 to 2011 and declined due to changes in employment structure from 2011 to 2017.

Overall, the above results throw up a question about whether there is any role of the tasks performed by workers and in the returns to these tasks that could explain the observed trends in between-occupation inequality. To ascertain the effect of RTI (i.e. whether the extent of manual task content of occupations is associated with changes in earnings inequality between occupations), we look at the changes in the concentration index. We infer the extent to which the decrease in the routine intensity of occupations is associated with this initial increase in

Table 10.5 Gini index decomposed into inequality between and within occupations: paid, non-agriculture, urban

	1983	1993	2004	2011	2017
			Panel A: actual		
1 Overall Gini	0.404	0.429	0.504	0.503	0.444
2 Between-occupation	0.147	0.174	0.233	0.235	0.193
Percentage ratio	36.41	40.68	46.16	46.77	43.53
3 Within-occupation	0.257	0.254	0.271	0.268	0.251
Percentage ratio	63.59	59.32	53.84	53.23	56.47
			Panel B: shares constant		
1 Overall Gini	0.404	0.429	0.504	0.503	0.428
2 Between-occupation	0.147	0.174	0.233	0.235	0.172
Percentage ratio	36.41	40.68	46.16	46.77	40.18
3 Within-occupation	0.257	0.254	0.271	0.268	0.256
Percentage ratio	63.59	59.32	53.84	53.23	59.82
			Panel C: means constant		
1 Overall Gini	0.404	0.413	0.450	0.465	0.449
2 Between-occupation	0.147	0.152	0.155	0.184	0.202
Percentage ratio	36.41	36.86	34.53	39.61	44.94
3 Within-occupation	0.257	0.261	0.295	0.281	0.247
Percentage ratio	63.59	63.14	65.47	60.39	55.06

Note: The sample includes urban, non-agricultural, paid workers.
Source: Authors' calculations based on NSS 1983, 1993, 2004, and 2011, and PLFS 2017.

earnings inequality between occupations (1983–2011) and then a decline in earnings inequality (2011–17).[12] With an increase in between-occupation inequality from 1983 to 2011, there is an increase in rank correlations between earnings and both measures of RTI from 0.16 in 1983 to 0.29 in 2011 for O*NET, and 0.18 in 1983 to 0.31 in 2011 for the country-specific RTI measure. With a decline in between-occupation inequality, both country-specific RTI and O*NET RTI declined. Overall, an increase in correlation using both RTI measures indicates that the relationship between the routine intensity of occupations and average earnings has become stronger for the period as a whole, but there are important sub-period trends: the relation between RTI and average earnings was stronger during 1983–2011 but has declined during the most recent period of 2011–17.

---

[12] The detailed table is provided in the working paper.

10.4   RIF-based decomposition: what drives the change in inequality?

Next, we use a RIF regression-based decomposition (Firpo et al. 2018) to further probe the role played by RTI of occupations in shaping inequality, while controlling for other competing explanations. This enables us to decompose the effect into changes in the composition of employment by occupation and other characteristics (composition effect) or in the changes in returns to characteristics (earnings structure effect).

The covariates include age group, gender, education categories, religion categories, caste categories, and a quadratic in country-specific two-digit RTI.[13] The RIF decomposition analyses show that changes in the demographic characteristics (i.e. age, gender, religion, caste) and education levels of the workforce, or in the structure of employment (i.e. shift of workers towards less routine occupations), do not seem to explain the trends in inequality. The change in the structure of earnings across occupations explains the inequality trends observed: increase between 1983 and 2004 and a subsequent decline during 2011–17. The decomposition effects are plotted for each quantile for each sub-period in Figure 10.1. The contribution of each type of effect does not vary much by quantile and sub-period, and the earnings structure effect dominates. This warrants a detailed look at what factors contribute towards the change in the structure of earnings.

Figure 10.2 plots the component of the earnings structure that can be explained by the factors included in the regression analyses. The detailed effects are plotted for each quantile to see how much of the change in earnings for that quantile is explained by the changing structure of earnings over time for each explanatory variable. The results for the entire period 1983–2017 show that changes in returns to education and changes in returns to RTI have contributed the most to the change in earnings structure across all quantiles. The direction for the two is, however, opposite. While changes in the returns to education contribute positively to the increased earnings at the upper quantiles, they result in decreased earnings at the lower quantiles. This shows that a change in returns to education have had a dis-equalizing effect on earnings in India. This is in line with the findings that between 1983 and 2017, education premiums have increased in India. On the other hand, changes in the return to RTI have resulted in lower earnings at the upper end and higher earnings in the lower quantiles. This shows that the change in returns to RTI have had an equalizing effect on earnings in India. Therefore, controlling

---

[13] We also check the robustness of the results using O*NET-based RTI measures and find that they do not differ much. A detailed look at the RIF decompositions shows that while the reweighting error is small across specifications, the specification errors can be large in some specifications, especially for the whole period 1983–2017. The RIF decomposition for the entire period is provided in the working paper.

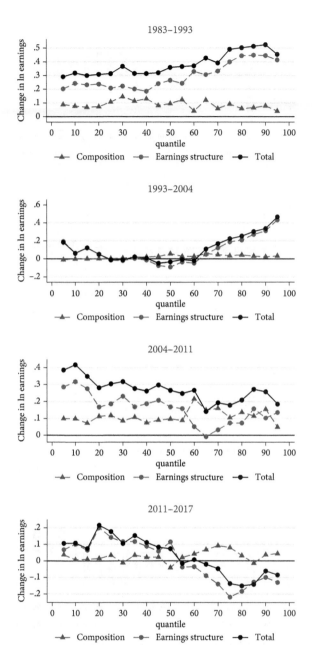

Figure 10.1 Decomposition of the change in Gini by quantile
(by sub-period)

Note: The sample includes urban, non-agricultural, paid workers.
Country-specific RTI at the two-digit level is used to control for RTI of an
occupation.
Source: Authors' calculations based on NSS 1983, 1993, 2004, and 2011,
and PLFS 2017.

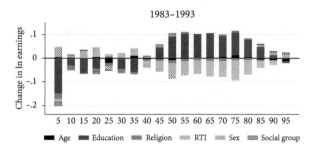

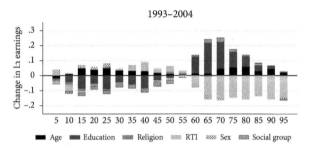

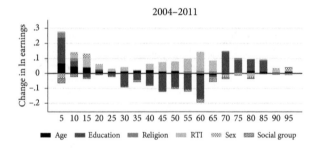

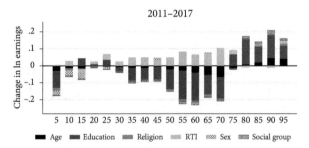

Figure 10.2 Detailed decomposition of the change in
Gini by quantile for earnings structure (by sub-period)

Note: The sample includes urban, non-agricultural, paid workers.
Country-specific RTI at the two-digit level is used to control for RTI
of an occupation.
Source: Authors' calculations based on NSS 1983, 1993, 2004, and
2011, and PLFS 2017.

for other factors, changes in returns to routine tasks in jobs would have led to a decline in inequality in India.

In line with our previous findings, the sub-period graphs also show that changes in returns to education have a dis-equalizing effect in each sub-period which is stronger during 1983–2004. Post-2004, returns to education contribute positively to the earnings of the bottom quartile, resulting in an equalizing effect at the lower end of the earnings distribution and in a dis-equalizing effect at the upper end of the earnings distribution. The only notable difference in the effect of education on wage inequality is during 2004–17. This is in line with falling education premiums but largely with respect to the illiterate category of workers. The overall rising/stable education premiums across other categories of workers reflect the effect of education earnings structure in the upper-middle part of the distribution. Changes in returns to RTI increase the wages in the middle part of the distribution and therefore continue to have an equalizing effect.

10.5 Conclusion

We use data on employment and unemployment rounds for the last three decades to examine the trends in wage earnings inequality for paid urban workers in non-agriculture sectors. We find that there was an increase in earnings inequality in India during 1983–2004, and thereafter a strong decline in earnings inequality during 2011–17, a finding hitherto unexplored for India. Can the trends in inequality be explained by the changing occupational structure in India? We find evidence for job polarization in urban India post-2004 driven by the rise in employment share of managerial and professional jobs at the upper end, and of construction and services such as retail at the lower end. There is, however, little evidence for earnings polarization, unlike the developed countries, and if anything there is an increase in earnings at the lower end and a decline in real earnings at the upper end of the wage distribution post-2011. In general, wage earnings are determined by both demand and supply factors. In developing countries, such as India, it is possible that the increase in supply of an educated workforce at the upper end outstripped the increase in demand for these workers, resulting in lower wage growth at the upper end. On the other hand, higher earnings growth in occupations with lower initial wages could also be due to domestic policies of rising minimum wages, especially post-2004 and rural public employment guarantee programmes (with spillover effects on urban wages) which picked up pace after 2006.

We also evaluate the role of the changing RTI of occupations in contributing towards the inequality changes. There is an inverted U-shape relation between earnings and RTI after 2011 which shows the changing structure of earnings post-2011 that may have been equalizing for wages. The decomposition analyses confirm these findings while controlling for other factors. The results show that the trends in inequality can be attributed to a changing earnings structure rather than changes in the composition of the workforce (age, gender, education, and RTI). Within the earnings structure, changes in returns to education had a dis-equalizing effect, while changes in returns to RTI had an equalizing effect on earnings inequality. Notably, a large part of the change in earnings inequality remains unexplained in the model, which shows that the changes in RTI and returns to education have had a modest overall impact in shaping it. Domestic policies on minimum wages and a possible mismatch of demand and supply in skills may be more important in the Indian context.

References

Accmoglu, D., and D. Autor (2011). 'Skills, Tasks and Technologies: Implications for Employment and Earnings'. In O. Ashenfelter and D. Card (eds), *Handbook of Labor Economics*, vol.4, pp. 1043–171. Amsterdam: Elsevier. https://doi.org/10.1016/S0169-7218(11)02410-5

Autor, D., and D. Dorn (2009). 'This Job Is "Getting Old": Measuring Changes in Job Opportunities Using Occupational Age Structure'. *American Economic Review*, 99(2): 45–51. https://doi.org/10.1257/aer.99.2.45

Azam, M. (2012). 'Changes in Wage Structure in Urban India, 1983–2004: A Quantile Regression Decomposition'. *World Development*, 40(6): 1135–50. https://doi.org/10.1016/j.worlddev.2012.02.002

Chakravarty, S.R. (2009). *Inequality, Polarization and Poverty: Advances in Distributional Analysis*. New York: Springer. https://doi.org/10.1007/978-0-387-79253-8

Chamarbagwala, R. (2006). 'Economic Liberalization and Wage Inequality in India'. *World Development*, 34(12): 1997–2015. https://doi.org/10.1016/j.worlddev.2006.02.010

Chancel, L., and T. Piketty (2019). 'Indian Income Inequality, 1922–2015: From British Raj to Billionaire Raj?' *Review of Income and Wealth*, 65: S33–S62. https://doi.org/10.1111/roiw.12439

Dang, H.-A., and P. Lanjouw (2018). 'Inequality Trends and Dynamics in India'. Working Paper 2018/189. Helsinki: UNU-WIDER. https://doi.org/10.35188/UNU-WIDER/2018/631-9

Firpo, S.P., N.M. Fortin, and T. Lemieux (2018). 'Decomposing Wage Distributions Using Recentered Influence Function Regressions'. *Econometrics*, 6(2): 28. https://doi.org/10.3390/econometrics6020028

Goos, M., and A. Manning (2007). 'Lousy and Lovely Jobs: The Rising Polarization of Work in Britain'. *Review of Economics and Statistics*, 89(1): 118–33. https://doi.org/10.1162/rest.89.1.118

Goos, M., A. Manning, and A. Salomons (2014). 'Explaining Job Polarization: Routine-Biased Technological Change and Offshoring'. *American Economic Review*, 104(8): 2509–26. https://doi.org/10.1257/aer.104.8.2509

Gradín, C., and S. Schotte (2020). 'Implications of the Changing Nature of Work for Employment and Inequality in Ghana'. WIDER Working Paper 2020/119. Helsinki: UNU-WIDER. https://doi.org/10.35188/UNU-WIDER/2020/876-4

Himanshu (2018). *India Inequality Report 2018: Widening Gaps.* New Delhi: Oxfam India.

Kakwani, N.C. (1980). *Income Inequality and Poverty.* New York: World Bank.

Khurana, S., and K. Mahajan (2020). 'Evolution of Wage Inequality in India (1983–2017): The Role of Occupational Task Content'. WIDER Working Paper 2020/167. Helsinki: UNU-WIDER. https://doi.org/10.35188/UNU-WIDER/2020/924-2

Kijima, Y. (2006). 'Why Did Wage Inequality Increase? Evidence from Urban India 1983–99'. *Journal of Development Economics*, 81(1): 97–117. https://doi.org/10.1016/j.jdeveco.2005.04.008

Lewandowski, P., A. Park, W. Hardy, and Y. Du (2019). 'Technology, Skills, and Globalization: Explaining International Differences in Routine and Nonroutine Work Using Survey Data'. IZA Discussion Paper 12339. Bonn: IZA. https://doi.org/10.2139/ssrn.3415008

Lewandowski, P., A. Park, and S. Schotte (2020). 'The Global Distribution of Routine and Non-Routine Work'. Working Paper 2020/75. Helsinki: UNU-WIDER. https://doi.org/10.35188/UNU-WIDER/2020/832-0

Medina, C., and C. Posso (2010). 'Technical Change and Polarization of the Labor Market: Evidence for Brazil, Colombia and Mexico'. Working Paper 614. Bogotá: Banco de la República.

Papola, T., and P.P. Sahu (2012). 'Growth and Structure of Employment in India'. Research Study. New Delhi: Institute for Studies in Industrial Development.

Sarkar, S. (2019). 'Employment Change in Occupations in Urban India: Implications for Wage Inequality'. *Development and Change*, 50(5): 1398–429. https://doi.org/10.1111/dech.12461

Vashisht, P., and J. Dubey (2019). 'Changing Task Content of Jobs in India: Implications and the Way Forward'. *Economic and Political Weekly*, 54(3).

11

Indonesia

Employment and Inequality Trends

Arief Anshory Yusuf and Putri Riswani Halim

11.1 Introduction

Structural transformation or the transition of an economy from lower- to higher-productivity activities has been the key to achieving higher economic growth. For Indonesia, a country that aspires to become a high-income economy before its 100 years' anniversary of independence (1945–2045), that high and sustained economic growth, higher than the country has experienced for the last two decades, is the key. For a country that experienced quite successful industrialization during the 1980s and 1990s, a new structural transformation that can enable it to jump-start the stalled industrialization of the last two decades can be considered as the only solution.

Economic growth is not Indonesia's only problem. Despite its success in lowering the incidence of poverty, the country's population is still economically vulnerable. Data from the World Bank World Development Indicator suggests that 53 per cent of the Indonesian population (in 2018) either lives in extreme and moderate poverty or is economically vulnerable (see World Bank 2020). In contrast, Malaysia, its closest neighbour, has an insecure population (i.e. those who live below 2018 PPP \$5.5 per person per day) of only 3.7 per cent. The other neighbouring country, Thailand, has an economically vulnerable population of 8.4 per cent.

The vulnerability and insecurity of the economy has proven to be a serious problem during the COVID-19 pandemic. In September 2020, the worst month of the COVID-19 pandemic, the Indonesian poverty incidence (by national poverty line) increased to the level it was 3 years earlier (BPS 2021). This is despite the massive amount of social assistance given to the poor and vulnerable population (Sparrow et al. 2020).

One may argue (Yusuf et al. 2014; Yusuf and Sumner 2015) that the high vulnerability of the Indonesian population, despite moderate economic growth, is due to economic growth not being considered inclusive. The period from 2000 to 2012 was one of unprecedented rising inequality. This was also the period when

Arief Anshory Yusuf and Putri Riswani Halim, *Indonesia: Employment and Inequality Trends*. In: *Tasks, Skills, and Institutions*. Edited by Carlos Gradín, Piotr Lewandowski, Simone Schotte, and Kunal Sen, Oxford University Press. © UNU-WIDER (2023). DOI: 10.1093/oso/9780192872241.003.0011

structural transformation had a different character compared with the period before the Asian financial crisis (AFC) of 1997–98. The period before the AFC was one of inclusive growth, when economic growth stood consistently at around 7 per cent with poverty declining and inequality remaining stable. This was a period of rapid industrialization. However, during the 2000s, industrialization stalled and agriculture continued to shrink in terms of both value added and employment. What happened was an increasing tertiarization of employment. The tertiary sectors holding all of these new incoming workers are sectors that are not modern, have low productivity, and are often informal.

The link between structural transformation and inequality has been continuously at the centre of debates in development economics since Kuznets (1955, 1973). In the context of rising inequality in Indonesia, which happened during a remarkably short period of time, the an explanation based in structural transformation is more appealing than other hypotheses. Other factors, such as a commodity boom and fiscal policies, have been discussed. Yet, a commodity boom is often temporary and government presence (in terms of fiscal policies and its power to affect income distribution) in the Indonesian economy is still low. Therefore, examining structural transformation during the period of rising inequality in Indonesia can help a better understanding of the nature and cause of the rising inequality.

To find the cause of rising inequality in advanced economies during the 1980s and 1990s, economists turned to the skill-biased technical change hypothesis (Johnson 1997; Berman et al. 1998; Card and DiNardo 2002). Highly skilled workers benefited more from new information and communication technology (ICT), and this new technology displaced low-skilled jobs. The new ICTs increased returns from skills (Katz and Autor 1999).

An alternative hypothesis, routine-biased technical change (RBTC), referring to a shift away from manual and routine cognitive work towards non-routine cognitive work was put forward by economists (Autor et al. 2003; Goos and Manning 2007; Acemoglu and Autor 2011; Goos et al. 2014; Harrigan et al. 2016). In the context of advanced economies, RBTC vis-à-vis labour market polarization has been sufficiently established. RBTC can explain the rising inequality, at least in advanced economies.

This chapter's objective is to explore the extent to which labour market dynamics, including the changing nature of work (job polarization, routinization), can be a factor for the rising inequality in Indonesia. The chapter starts by revisiting the development of inequality in Indonesia from 1960 to 2020. It then describes the structural transformation in Indonesia in the era before and after the AFC. The rest of the chapter includes analyses using labour force survey data to explore different dimensions of labour market dynamics and links them in the context of rising inequality in Indonesia.

11.2 Development of inequality in Indonesia

When inequality in Indonesia is discussed in a typical academic discussion or even political discourse, it normally refers to inequality in consumption per capita. Consumption per capita is also used to calculate official poverty incidence. In this section, we discuss the development of consumption inequality in Indonesia from 1964 to 2020.[1] Later in Section 11.4, we discuss inequality in formal labour earnings in Indonesia. We also show that inequality in formal labour earnings tends to be highly correlated with inequality in consumption per capita. This strengthens the relevance of the rest of this chapter.

As Figure 11.1 shows, from early 1960s to the end of the 1970s, inequality in Indonesia increased. One explanation is that during the same period an increase in urban workers' skills premium because of import substitution policies aimed at developing capital-intensive sectors (e.g., see Leigh and Van der Eng 2009).

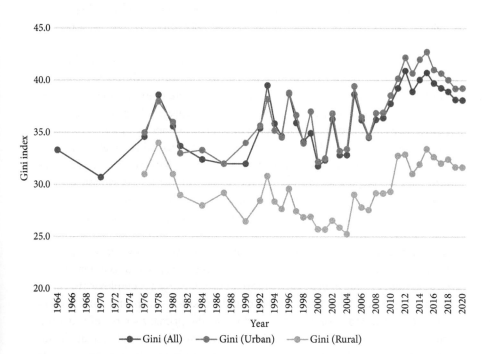

Figure 11.1 Gini index of consumption, 1964–2020
Source: Author's calculation based on BPS (2021).

---

[1] This is generally an update of Yusuf et al. (2014) and extending the work of Kim et al. (2020). Yusuf et al. (2014) cover the years from 1993 to 2013 and Kim et al. (2020) cover only up to 2017.

From 1980 to the end of the 1990s, before the AFC, the Gini coefficient was stable, if not slightly decreasing. However, after the AFC the Gini coefficient had a strong upward trend, evident in both urban and rural areas. The Gini coefficient after the AFC was 0.31 in 2001 but rose to 0.41 in 2013 (an increase of 0.1 or 33 per cent) in urban areas. The rate of change in rural areas is rather similar, where in 2001 the Gini coefficient was 0.24 and in 2013 it rose to 0.32 (an increase of 34 per cent). After its peak in 2012, the Gini coefficient started to show a slowly declining trend until 2019. In 2020, the Gini coefficient started to slightly rise again, most likely due to the economic crises from the COVID-19 pandemic.

The causes of recent changes in inequality in Indonesia are complex but it is possible to identify a set of specific factors with sufficient empirical evidence that would be worthy of future exploration. The first factor is related to trade. Indonesia has experienced a commodity boom in coal and palm oil, and this has had an impact on inequality: Yusuf (2014) used a computable general equilibrium model to show that the changes in inequality are due to the world prices of mining commodities rather than estate crops. Relatedly, the commodity boom hypothesis could be advanced to explain the widening gap between poor and rich groups in rural areas.

During more or less the same period, there has been a trend towards an increase in the price of commodities, particularly those that are traditional Indonesian export commodities such as estate crops. Those estate crops are mainly located in rural areas and are owned by landowners in rural areas. The richer households in rural areas benefit disproportionately from this commodity boom.

A second factor is the domestic price of rice. One inequality spike occurred in 2003–05. There are various possible reasons for this sharp rise, but one may be that the domestic price of rice increased by almost 20 per cent during this period after being stable for a long period. This could have hurt the poor.

A third factor is related to changes in labour market policy in Indonesia. Yusuf et al. (2014) argue that changes in the formal labour market, including interrelated changes in labour market regulation—an increase in severance payments, the strengthening of labour unions, rising minimum wages, reduced demand for unskilled labour, and an increase in informality in lower-wage employment—have had an impact on inequality in skilled and unskilled urban and rural sectors. Before the AFC, the manufacturing sector was the primary source of economic growth in Indonesia. Almost a decade after the crisis, the role of the manufacturing sector in generating employment seems to have halted. Its economic growth for the period 2000–08 was almost the same as the national average (4.7 per cent), but its employment growth was only 0.9 per cent. Employment opportunities in the formal manufacturing sector, historically, have been a haven for people in rural areas seeking better paying livelihoods. When such opportunities are limited, there is an excess supply of unskilled labour in rural areas. As the labour market in rural areas is more flexible, overall rural real wages are pushed down as a consequence of increasing inequality in rural areas.

A fourth and last, but not the least, factor that may be related to changing inequality in Indonesia is structural transformation. This is, perhaps, one of the most plausible explanations, given that inequality is slow to change over time. The changing inequality in Indonesia is relatively fast by historical standards and thus structural transformation may just be the big driver that is behind this. From 1990 to 2018, industrialization (the rising share of manufacturing value added) occurred from 1990 until 1997, before the AFC (Yusuf and Halim 2021). The share of manufacturing value added changed from 19.3 per cent in 1990 to 22.5 per cent in 1997. Its employment share also increased from 10.3 to 13.2 per cent (Yusuf and Halim 2021). Employment in non-business service sectors also rose from 30 to 38 per cent in 1997, yet the value added by non-business sectors did not change much. It seems that employment in the agricultural sector moved to almost all non-agricultural sectors, including manufacturing and services. In this period, the change in inequality was not significant. Kim et al. (2020) named this period as benign or weak Kuznetsian tension: a period of strong growth-enhancing structural transformation, yet stable or declining inequality.

After the AFC, however, the rising trend of the manufacturing sector's value added seems to have halted. The share of the manufacturing sector's value added in 2018 (21.4 per cent) was still lower than the share in 1997 (22.5 per cent). The share of its employment also stayed the same. As employment in agriculture continued to fall, service sectors absorbed most of the labour from agriculture. During the 2000s, Indonesia experienced stalled industrialization and tertiarization.

The period of stalled industrialization was accompanied by unprecedented rising inequality. Kim et al. (2020) have described what happened in Indonesia during this period as the period of adverse Kuznetsian tension; that is, a period of weak growth-enhancing structural transformation accompanied by increasing inequality.

Yusuf and Halim (2021) conducted a decomposition of inequality by economic sector using the Atkinson index of inequality that additionally helps to explain what happened to within- and between-sector inequality in the context of structural transformation, particularly during the period of 2001 to 2020. They found that the largest contributor to rising inequality in Indonesia overall is the change in inequality within sectors, and certainly not inequality between sectors.

11.3 Labour market dynamics and earnings inequality

In this section, we use the National Labour Force Survey (*Survey Angkatan Kerja Nasional*, SAKERNAS), a nationally representative survey of the labour force in

Indonesia to explore the extent to which labour market dynamics, including the changing nature of work (job polarization, routinization), can be a factor in rising inequality in Indonesia. For this study, we have SAKERNAS data from 1994 to 2017. However, workers' occupation type has only been recorded since 2001. Moreover, the standard coding for occupations varies from year to year and is presented here. The International Standard Classification of Occupations (ISCO) code of most SAKERNAS data (2001–07 and 2012–15) is based on ISCO-68. We only have the data for 2008–10 (3 years) with occupation data based on ISCO-88. Based on the above constraint, while maximizing the duration for the analysis, we chose four different years for the analysis: 2001, 2005, 2010, and 2015.

11.3.1 Earnings inequality

Our first analysis is to check how inequality in earnings changes over time. Table 11.1 shows inter-quantile ratios and inequality indices for 2001–15. The Gini coefficient of real earnings increased from 0.38 in 2001 to 0.48 in 2015, a rise of over 25 per cent in just 14 years. Between 2001 and 2015, the rise was almost 30 per cent (29.7 per cent). However, when we look at the inter-quantile ratio, particularly the ratio between the 10th decile and the 1st decile, the rise in inequality during the same number of intervening years is larger.

As discussed earlier in this chapter, despite formal labour earnings constituting only some part of the headline consumption inequality in Indonesia, the trend of the inequality in labour earnings turns out to be consistent with the trend of consumption inequality. This consistency is presents an opportunity to further explore the notion that the increase in consumption inequality in Indonesia, to a large extent, may be due to labour market dynamics, particularly the rise in formal labour earnings inequality.

We confirm the rising inequality of earnings by showing the growth incidence curve of labour earnings for various years to understand what is behind the changing inequality between time periods (see Yusuf and Halim 2021: Figure 7).

Table 11.1 Inter-quantile ratios and inequality indices

	Inter-quantile ratios					Inequality indices			
	2001	2005	2010	2015		2001	2005	2010	2015
ln(q90)–ln(q10)	1.83	1.70	1.95	2.44	Var (log earn)	0.55	0.49	0.61	0.92
ln(q90)–ln(q50)	0.91	0.76	1.03	0.98	Gini (log earn)	0.03	0.03	0.03	0.04
ln(q50)–ln(q10)	0.92	0.93	0.92	1.46	Gini (earn)	0.38	0.37	0.42	0.48

Source: Authors' calculation.

The following subsections explore other dimensions of labour market dynamics that may be some of the factors behind these remarkable increases in inequality.

11.3.2 Education

Next, we look at the educational attainment of these workers and explore trends that can potentially be related to the rising earnings inequality. Figure 11.2 shows the distribution of workers by education level for all workers (on the left) and for only salaried workers (on the right). Both categories show the declining share of workers with primary education and below and the increasing share of workers with secondary and tertiary education.

The dynamics are slightly different among salaried workers. The share of workers with primary education or below declines in a similar manner. Between 2001 and 2015, the share of workers with primary education fell by 10 percentage points, almost the same as for all workers (10.7 per cent). However, the increase in the share of workers with secondary education only rose by 2.7 percentage points, in contrast to an increase of 11 per cent among all workers. The most notable difference is the increase in the share of workers with tertiary education among salaried workers. This rose from 13.9 per cent in 2001 to 24.2 per cent in 2015, an increase of 10.3 percentage points. Yusuf and Halim (2021: Figure 9) estimate the education premium by gender and education level for 2001, 2005, 2010, and

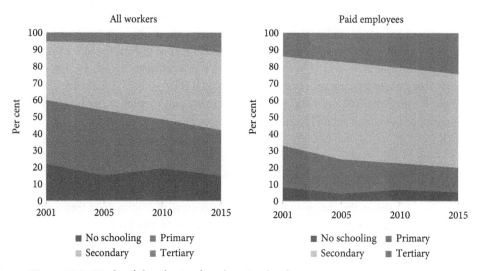

Figure 11.2 Workers' distribution by education level
Source: Authors' calculation.

2015 and find that for men, for example, the return to tertiary education (1.18) was more than twice the return to secondary education (0.48) in 2015. They also found that, the return to education (in 2015) was highest for female workers with tertiary education (see Yusuf and Halim 2021: Figure 9).

In summary, we establish two important facts that may help to identify factors behind the rising earnings inequality. First and foremost, we observe a disproportionate increase in the returns to tertiary education. This naturally has a tendency towards increasing inequality. Second, the increasing share of workers with tertiary education may also be accompanied by rising inequality. We explore this further in Section 11.4.

11.3.3 Employment status composition

Changing employment status, particularly from unpaid (informal) to paid/salaried (formal) employment is relevant, particularly when we want to establish a good connection between earnings inequality and headline consumption inequality. The more labour becomes formal, the more formal earnings inequality becomes relevant.

Looking at the years 2001, 2005, 2010, and 2015, the share of salaried workers increased from 30.25 per cent in 2001 to 40.15 per cent in 2015 (see Table 11.2). A similar increase is also observed for both male and female workers. Except for the share of casual employees, which shows an increase or remains stable during the same period, it seems that the declining share of all other less informal workers contributes to an increase in the share of salaried workers.

The increasing trend of the share of salaried workers not only heightens the relevance of rising earnings inequality in the context of overall (headline) consumption inequality in Indonesia; when combined with other trends such as the rising share of tertiary education within formal worker groups, it also may have direct consequences on overall earnings inequality and to some extent on overall consumption inequality. Of course, this needs further empirical analysis.

11.3.4 Occupational structure

Table 11.3 shows the changing occupational structure of employment from 2001 to 2015. Over this period, we note several long-term (14-year) trends.

We observe the increasing share of high-skilled employment (most notably professionals, services and sales workers, technicians and associate professionals) as well as the increasing share of elementary occupations. This is a sign of job polarization. We also observe the declining share of craft and related trades workers, skilled agriculture, fisheries and forestry, and managers. We find a relatively

Table 11.2 Distribution of workers by employment status (per cent)

	2001	2005	2010	2015
All workers				
Paid employees	30.25	28.73	31.12	40.15
Self-employed without employees	19.21	18.59	19.11	16.42
Self-employed with temporary/unpaid worker	21.41	21.12	18.5	14.55
Self-employed with permanent worker	3.01	2.89	2.92	3.38
Casual employee in agriculture	4.01	5.83	5.46	4.43
Casual employee not in agriculture	2.75	4.75	5.01	6.77
Unpaid worker	19.37	18.08	17.89	14.3
Male workers				
Paid employees	26.04	26.93	29.35	37.36
Self-employed without employees	16.65	15.01	16.84	16.47
Self-employed with temporary/unpaid worker	12.34	11.98	11.58	9.78
Self-employed with permanent worker	1.03	1.15	1.27	1.74
Casual employee in agriculture	4.43	5.57	4.95	3.82
Casual employee not in agriculture	1.15	2.17	1.98	2.49
Unpaid worker	38.36	37.19	34.03	28.34
Female workers				
Paid employees	32.71	29.69	32.2	41.8
Self-employed without employees	20.72	20.5	20.49	16.39
Self-employed with temporary/unpaid worker	26.71	25.99	22.71	17.4
Self-employed with permanent worker	4.17	3.82	3.92	4.36
Casual employee in agriculture	3.77	5.98	5.76	4.8
Casual employee not in agriculture	3.69	6.12	6.84	9.32
Unpaid worker	8.25	7.91	8.08	5.93

Source: Authors' calculation.

constant share of plant and machine operators and assemblers and clerical support workers. In other words, the decline in the share of certain occupations occurs, generally, around the middle-skill level, for example clerical support workers (a decline from 13.6 per cent in 2001 to 10.8 per cent in 2015) and plant and machine operators and assemblers (a decline from 15.7 per cent in 2001 to 10.6 per cent in 2015).

We also observe a disproportionate increase in the mean earning of workers that belong to certain occupational or skill groups that possibly contribute to the rising inequality of earnings. The mean salary of managers and technicians and associate professionals, for example, increased by 4.1 and 3.5 per cent annually, respectively. Moreover, for the period 2005–15, managers and technicians and associate professionals experienced the highest earnings growth, whereas plant and machine operators only increased by 1.0 per cent annually. With this we may expect that inequality in earnings in the industrial sector or in manufacturing may tend to increase.

Table 11.3 Employment share and mean weekly earning by main occupational groups

	Paid employees								
	Level				Percentage growth (annual)				
	2001	2005	2010	2015	2001–05	2005–10	2010–15	2001–15	2005–15
Panel A: Share of employment (%)									
1 Managers	1.35	1.48	2.78	2.56	2.3	13.4	-1.6	4.7	5.6
2 Professionals	10.12	11.04	14.26	13.02	2.2	5.3	-1.8	1.8	1.7
3 Technicians and associate professionals	4.83	5.55	5.83	8.69	3.5	1.0	8.3	4.3	4.6
4 Clerical support workers	13.58	12.34	13.90	10.83	-2.4	2.4	-4.9	-1.6	-1.3
5 Services and sales workers	9.02	11.93	14.33	12.81	7.2	3.7	-2.2	2.5	0.7
6 Skilled agriculture, forestry, and fishery	1.44	0.99	0.78	1.52	-8.9	-4.7	14.3	0.4	4.4
7 Craft and related trades workers	23.88	24.06	12.90	13.74	0.2	-11.7	1.3	-3.9	-5.4
8 Plant and machine operators and assemblers	15.67	15.39	10.58	11.88	-0.4	-7.2	2.3	-2.0	-2.6
9 Elementary occupations	20.12	17.22	24.63	24.94	-3.8	7.4	0.3	1.5	3.8
Panel B: Mean weekly earnings (constant 2010 prices)									
1 Managers	1,073,359	952,189	1,215,762	1,421,598	-3.0	5.0	3.2	2.0	4.1
2 Professionals	618,222	569,668	622,153	681,310	-2.0	1.8	1.8	0.7	1.8
3 Technicians and associate professionals	602,147	617,884	730,983	873,998	0.6	3.4	3.6	2.7	3.5
4 Clerical support workers	541,256	539,114	590,770	642,021	-0.1	1.8	1.7	1.2	1.8
5 Services and sales workers	363,798	363,351	381,087	403,862	0.0	1.0	1.2	0.7	1.1
6 Skilled agriculture, forestry, and fishery	300,052	278,641	291,266	272,254	-1.8	0.9	-1.3	-0.7	-0.2
7 Craft and related trades workers	322,347	336,756	321,385	420,641	1.1	-0.9	5.5	1.9	2.2
8 Plant and machine operators and assemblers	349,374	362,758	438,672	400,295	0.9	3.9	-1.8	1.0	1.0
9 Elementary occupations	234,875	261,916	290,705	343,789	2.8	2.1	3.4	2.8	2.8

Source: Authors' calculation.

Yusuf and Halim (2021) analysed to what extent between- and within-occupation inequality contributes to inequality in earnings using a Shapley decomposition. As occupation category is typically ordered by skill level, between-occupation inequality tells us whether the earnings gap between high- and low-wage workers plays a big role. On the other hand, if within-occupation inequality contributes to a large part of the overall inequality, it can mean two things: (a) the gap between low- and high-wage workers is big in most occupation types; (b) occupation category does not necessarily reflect the monotonically increasing mean earning. See Yusuf and Halim (2021) for detailed explanation of the decomposition.

From a counterfactual analysis of the Shapley decomposition, it was found that the slowly increasing between-occupation inequality (4 per cent) is due to the widening gap of between-occupation earnings (37 per cent), not because of the changing composition of occupations. In fact, the composition has a narrowing effect so large that it almost negates the effect of the earnings gap. This finding indicates that inequality in returns to occupation may play an important role in the rising overall earnings inequality, which will be discussed further analytically in Section 11.4.

11.3.5 Testing job polarization

To statistically test job polarization, we regress both the log change in employment share of different types of occupation against the initial log (mean) wage (earning) and its square (Goos and Manning 2007; Sebastian 2018). See Yusuf and Halim (2021) for further explanation about the regression.[2]

Job polarization is observed when the coefficient of initial mean wage is negative and statistically significant, and the coefficient of its square is positive and statistically significant (see Table 11.4). We used five different periods: 2001–05, 2005–10, 2010–15, 2001–15, and 2005–15. The results of the regression are shown in Yusuf and Halim (2021: Tables 10 and 11).

We found an indication of job polarization during the period of 2005–10 and 2005–15. For those two periods, we found that the initial wage was negative and statistically significant, and its square was positive and statistically significant for the regression, with both the dependent variable change in employment share and change in earnings. All the coefficients were statistically significant at the 1 per cent level.

---

[2] We also use the change in mean-wage as an alternative specification but cannot find a sign of polarization.

Table 11.4 Polarization regression in employment

Variables	Log change in employment share				
	2001–05	2005–10	2010–15	2001–15	2005–15
(Log) mean weekly wage $(t-1)$	7.930	−34.937**	−3.780	−16.435	−29.197**
	(4.810)	(16.039)	(7.213)	(12.802)	(12.104)
Square (log) mean weekly wage $(t-1)$	−0.307	1.381**	0.142	0.666	1.159**
	(0.189)	(0.634)	(0.279)	(0.506)	(0.476)
Constant	−51.151	220.647**	25.077	101.036	183.607**
	(30.595)	(101.370)	(46.602)	(80.957)	(76.819)
Observations	25	25	25	25	25
R-squared	0.220	0.134	0.025	0.131	0.143
Adjusted R-squared	0.1490	0.05570	−0.0638	0.0516	0.0649
F-test	0.1440	0.1170	0.6940	0.0708	0.0329

Note: Robust standard errors in parentheses; ***$p<0.01$, **$p<0.05$, *$p<0.1$.
Source: Authors' calculation.

11.3.6 Testing routinization

Table 11.5 shows how RTI changes over time from 2001 to 2015. O*NET RTI clearly shows that the intensity of routine tasks declined from 0.40 in 2001 to 0.34 in 2015 for all workers. However, country-specific RTI shows that the decline only happened for paid employees.

Earlier analysis does not necessarily reflect the changing nature of work for lowering the intensity of routine jobs (routinization). To test routinization, we regress the changes in employment share with the initial routine intensity as well as using the changes in mean (log) earnings as the dependent variables. As can be seen from Table 11.6, the initial O*NET RTI is negative and statistically significant in all the regressions where the dependent variable is the change in (log) employment share for all periods except 2010–15. This negative relationship between the initial RTI and the change in employment share suggests that certain occupations that have an advantage in routine tasks at the beginning of each period will experience a

Table 11.5 Average routine-task intensity (RTI) over time

RTI measure	All workers				Paid employees			
	2001	2005	2010	2015	2001	2005	2010	2015
Country-specific	0.80	0.81	0.88	0.87	0.73	0.71	0.70	0.70
O*NET	0.40	0.40	0.31	0.34	0.43	0.36	0.23	0.30

Source: Authors' calculation.

Table 11.6 Change in employment by O*NET RTI

	Log change in employment share				
	2001–05	2005–10	2010–15	2001–15	2005–15
O*NET RTI (t–1)	–0.068**	–0.177*	0.049	–0.242**	–0.190**
	(0.029)	(0.086)	(0.065)	(0.098)	(0.077)
Squared O*NET RTI (t–1)	0.030	–0.010	0.066	0.118	0.069
	(0.034)	(0.120)	(0.040)	(0.129)	(0.118)
Constant	–0.020	–0.098	–0.159*	–0.207	–0.171
	(0.066)	(0.166)	(0.077)	(0.145)	(0.136)
Observations	25	25	25	25	25
Adjusted R-squared	0.1270	0.0566	0.0293	0.2030	0.1180

Note: Robust standard errors in parentheses; ***$p<0.01$, **$p<0.05$, *$p<0.1$.
Source: Authors' calculation.

decline in the share of employment in a future period. The squared O*NET RTI is not significant, suggesting that the negative relationship dies out. This is a sign of routinization.

However, when using country-specific RTI (Yusuf and Halim 2021: Table 14), the square of the coefficient is positive and significant. This means that the negative relationship is U-shaped, or valid only until a certain point. For the long-term periods of 2005–15 and 2001–15, the RTI turning point is calculated as 0.632 and 0.702, respectively. The value is quite close to the mean of the RTI. In summary, using country-specific RTI (as developed by Lewandowski et al. 2019) gives rather mixed results in the Indonesian case. We also check whether change in earnings is associated with RTI and found no significant association between a change in earnings and RTI.

Despite the insignificant relationship between changing labour earning and RTI, we observed[3] that RTI tends to be lower in a higher-skill decile and higher in a lower-skill decile. The relationship is more obvious if we use O*NET RTI but less obvious if we use country-specific RTI.

11.4 Determinants of rising earnings inequality: the role of routinization

To analyse the determinant of rising earnings inequality, Yusuf and Halim (2021) use RIF regression method developed by Firpo et al. (2007, 2009).[4] They show that

---

[3] See Yusuf and Halim (2021: Figure 10).
[4] See Yusuf and Halim (2021) for more explanation.

in all the periods where the Gini of earnings was rising, it was the changing earnings structure, not the composition of workers, that contributed to the increase. For example, if the focus is on the longer timespan, the changing earnings structure contributed almost entirely (99.1 per cent) to the 0.093-point change in earnings inequality between 2005 and 2015. Moreover, when the period 2001–15 recorded a higher increase in inequality (0.111), the contribution of the composition effect is negative. The role of explaining the rising inequality is left to the changing earnings structure in the labour market. The supremacy of the earnings structure is generally similar in the proportion of its contribution throughout all the periods.

The decomposition effect plotted for each quintile can highlight the story more clearly. The plots for the periods 2005–15 and 2001–15 show the positively sloped curve of total change in log earnings, suggesting a notable rise in inequality. The changing composition component, however, is rather flat, suggesting that it does not contribute much to the rise in earnings inequality. The pattern of changing earnings structure across quantiles appears to follow quite closely the pattern of change in total earnings across quintiles. It can be concluded that the returns to the endowment of labour must be behind the rising earnings inequality in Indonesia during the years 2001–15.

Detailed analysis done in Yusuf and Halim (2021) further found that education actually contributes the most to the changing earnings structure. This is consistent with the earlier discussion about the returns to education, particularly the observation that the higher the education premium, the higher the level of education. An earlier study by Akita and Miyata (2008) confirmed this finding. They found that the urban sector's higher educational group contributed significantly to overall inequality. This, together with educational expansion, led to a conspicuous rise in urban inequality.

11.5 Conclusions

Unlike the 1980s and 1990s, when Indonesia experienced a strong growth-enhancing structural transformation yet stable or declining inequality, after the AFC of 1997–98, Indonesia experienced a stalled industrialization accompanied by unprecedented rising inequality. The question of what factors are behind the rise in inequality during these periods remains unanswered. This chapter explored the possibility of labour market dynamics including the changing nature of work contributing to rising inequality. Using various analyses with labour force survey data from 2001 to 2015, we highlight some important findings.

We observed a disproportionate increase in the returns to tertiary education. This naturally has a tendency towards increasing inequality. We also recorded an increasing share of workers with tertiary education. We found increasing shares of highly skilled as well as elementary workers, a sign of job polarization. However, we also found that mainly within-occupation inequality, not between-occupation inequality, contributes to earnings inequality in Indonesia. More importantly, we found that between-occupation inequality of earnings is mostly due to the widening gap of between-occupation earnings, not to the changing nature of occupations. This indicates that inequality in returns to occupation may play an important role in the rising overall earnings inequality.

We statistically tested the evidence of job polarization and found an indication of job polarization during 2005–10 and 2005–15. We also found that certain occupations that have an advantage in terms of routine tasks (i.e. has higher RTI) at the beginning of a period experience a decline in the share of employment in a future period. However, this result is not robust to different measurements of RTI.

Finally, RIF regressions as done in Yusuf and Halim (2021), found that in all the periods where the Gini of earnings was rising, the changing earnings structure, not the composition of workers, contributed to most of the rise. Therefore, we conclude that the returns to the endowment of labour must be behind the rising earnings inequality in Indonesia during the years 2001–15. The contribution of returns to task content, however, is mixed.

References

Acemoglu, D., and D. Autor (2011). 'Skills, Tasks and Technologies: Implications for Employment and Earnings'. In O. Ashenfelter and D. Card (eds), *Handbook of Labor Economics*, Vol. 4, pp. 1043–171. Amsterdam: Elsevier. https://doi.org/10.1016/S0169-7218(11)02410-5

Akita, T., and S. Miyata (2008). 'Urbanization, Educational Expansion, and Expenditure Inequality in Indonesia in 1996, 1999, and 2002'. *Journal of the Asia Pacific Economy*, 13(2): 147–67. https://doi.org/10.1080/13547860801923558

Autor, D.H., F. Levy, and R.J. Murnane. (2003). 'The Skill Content of Recent Technological Change: An Empirical Exploration'. *The Quarterly Journal of Economics*, 118(4): 1279–333. https://doi.org/10.1162/003355303322552801

Berman, E., J. Bound, and S. Machin (1998). 'Implications of Skill-Biased Technological Change: International Evidence'. *The Quarterly Journal of Economics*, 113(4): 1245–79. https://doi.org/10.1162/003355398555892

Card, D., and J.E. DiNardo (2002). 'Skill-Biased Technological Change and Rising Wage Inequality: Some Problems and Puzzles'. *Journal of Labor Economics*, 20(4): 733–83. https://doi.org/10.1086/342055

Firpo, S., N.M. Fortin, and T. Lemieux (2007). Decomposing Wage Distributions Using Recentered Influence Function Regressions. University of British Columbia (June).

Firpo, S., N.M. Fortin, and T. Lemieux (2009). 'Unconditional Quantile Regressions'. *Econometrica*, 77(3): 953–73. https://doi.org/10.3982/ECTA6822

Goos, M., and A. Manning (2007). 'Lousy and Lovely Jobs: The Rising Polarization of Work in Britain'. *The Review of Economics and Statistics*, 89(1): 118–33. https://doi.org/10.1162/rest.89.1.118

Goos, M., A. Manning, and A. Salomons (2014). 'Explaining Job Polarization: Routine-Biased Technological Change and Offshoring'. *American Economic Review*, 104(8): 2509–26. https://doi.org/10.1257/aer.104.8.2509

Harrigan, J., A. Reshef, and F. Toubal (2016). 'The March of the Techies: Technology, Trade, and Job Polarization in France, 1994–2007'. NBER Working Paper 22110. Cambridge, MA: National Bureau of Economic Research (NBER). https://doi.org/10.3386/w22110

Johnson, G.E. (1997). 'Changes in Earnings Inequality: The Role of Demand Shifts'. *Journal of Economic Perspectives*, 11(2): 41–54. https://doi.org/10.1257/jep.11.2.41

Katz, L., and D. Autor (1999). 'Changes in the Wage Structure and Earnings Inequality'. In O. Ashenfelter and D. Card (eds), *Handbook of Labor Economics*, Vol. 3A, pp. 1463–555. Amsterdam: Elsevier. https://doi.org/10.1016/S1573-4463(99)03007-2

Kim, K., A. Mungsunti, A. Sumner, and A. Yusuf (2020). 'Structural Transformation and Inclusive Growth'. WIDER Working Paper 2020/31. Helsinki: UNU-WIDER. https://doi.org/10.35188/UNU-WIDER/2020/788-0

Kuznets, S. (1955). 'Economic Growth and Income Inequality'. *The American Economic Review*, 45(1): 1–28.

Kuznets, S. (1973). 'Modern Economic Growth: Findings and Reflections'. *The American Economic Review*, 63(3): 247–58.

Leigh, A., and P. Van der Eng (2009). 'Inequality in Indonesia: What Can We Learn from Top Incomes?' *Journal of Public Economics*, 93(1–2): 209–12. https://doi.org/10.1016/j.jpubeco.2008.09.005

Lewandowski, P., A. Park, W. Hardy, and Y. Du (2019). 'Technology, Skills, and Globalization: Explaining International Differences in Routine and Nonroutine Work Using Survey Data'. IBS Working Paper 04/2019. Warsaw: IBS.

Sebastian, R. (2018). 'Explaining Job Polarisation in Spain from a Task Perspective'. *SERIEs*, 9(2): 215–48. https://doi.org/10.1007/s13209-018-0177-1

Sparrow, R., T. Dartanto, and R. Hartwig (2020). 'Indonesia under the New Normal: Challenges and the Way Ahead'. *Bulletin of Indonesian Economic Studies*, 56(3): 269–99. https://doi.org/10.1080/00074918.2020.1854079

Yusuf, A.A. (2014). 'International Commodity Prices and Inequality in Indonesia'. Working Papers in Economics and Development Studies (WoPEDS) 201409. Bandung, Indonesia: Department of Economics, Padjadjaran University. Available at: https://ideas.repec.org/p/unp/wpaper/201409.html (accessed April 2021).

Yusuf, A.A., and P.R. Halim (2021). 'Inequality and Structural Transformation in the Changing Nature of Work: The Case of Indonesia'. WIDER Working Paper 2021/81. Helsinki: UNU-WIDER. https://doi.org/10.35188/UNU-WIDER/2021/019-1

Yusuf, A.A., and A. Sumner (2015). 'Growth, Poverty, and Inequality under Jokowi'. *Bulletin of Indonesian Economic Studies*, 51(3): 323–48. https://doi.org/10.1080/00074918.2015.1110685

Yusuf, A.A., A. Sumner, and I.A. Rum (2014). 'Twenty Years of Expenditure Inequality in Indonesia, 1993–2013'. *Bulletin of Indonesian Economic Studies*, 50(2): 243–54. https://doi.org/10.1080/00074918.2014.939937

12

Argentina

Employment and Inequality Trends

Roxana Maurizio and Ana Paula Monsalvo

12.1 Introduction

There is an intense debate worldwide on the impact of the ongoing technological change and task automation on the present and future nature of work. The discussion, however, is not novel. During the 1990s there was consensus on skill-biased technological change, especially in developed countries. This was the canonical explanation regarding the expanding demand of high-skilled workers over low-skilled. This skill upgrading process was, in turn, a contributing factor to the rise in earnings inequality.

Recently, a new phenomenon has spread among high-income countries: middle-skilled jobs have seen a decline over high- and low-skilled/low-wage occupations. This job polarization phenomenon has mainly been found in the US (Wright and Dwyer 2003; Autor et al. 2006; Autor and Dorn 2013) and in some European countries (Goos et al. 2014; Sebastian 2018).

Job polarization, however, does not always entail earnings polarization. While Autor et al. (2006) have found that these two phenomena go hand in hand in the US, Goos and Manning (2007) have accounted for job but not wage polarization in the UK.

Despite the increasing importance of these topics, the empirical literature for less developed countries—including Argentina—is scarce.[1] Additionally, given that the composition of employment, the speed and type of technological adoption, the position of countries in global value chains, and the macroeconomic and productive conditions are very different across the globe, the results obtained for the developed world are not necessarily the same for developing or emerging countries.

The main aim of this chapter is to evaluate the scope and patterns of the structural transformation as evidenced by changes in the composition of jobs and tasks in Argentina, and its impact on earnings and distribution.

---

[1] Among them, Maloney and Molina (2016), Messina et al. (2016), Apella and Zunino (2017, 2021), Brambilla and Tortarolo (2018).

Roxana Maurizio and Ana Paula Monsalvo, *Argentina: Employment and Inequality Trends*. In: *Tasks, Skills, and Institutions.* Edited by Carlos Gradín, Piotr Lewandowski, Simone Schotte, and Kunal Sen, Oxford University Press. © UNU-WIDER (2023). DOI: 10.1093/oso/9780192872241.003.0012

This study makes three contributions to a better understanding of the evolution of employment and inequality in Argentina. First, it thoroughly examines the changes in the composition of employment based on country-specific information on job task content. Therefore, unlike previous analyses on this topic in Argentina, this study does not assume that the task composition of jobs is the same as in developed countries.

Second, this study discusses the extent to which changes in occupations and job task content result in a polarizing pattern, taking into account the specific characteristics of the Argentine labour market.

Third, the chapter evaluates the role of occupation and its content changes in shaping the evolution of earnings distribution. In this way, it contributes to the existing Argentine literature on inequality by adding a novel dimension.

The chapter is organized as follows. Section 12.2 details the source of information. Section 12.3 presents an overview of the evolution of labour market and income distribution in Argentina. Section 12.4 analyses changes in the composition of employment and evaluates the hypothesis of job polarization. Section 12.5 studies trends in real earnings and assesses the hypothesis of earnings polarization. Section 12.6 evaluates the role of changes in job task content in shaping the evolution of earning inequality. Section 12.7 discusses all previous results in an integrated manner and concludes.

12.2 Data

The microdata used in this chapter come from the *Encuesta Permanente de Hogares* (EPH), a survey carried out by Argentina's National Institute of Statistics and Censuses (INDEC). This survey collects detailed information on jobs, income, and socio-demographic characteristics of the population. The survey is carried out on a quarterly basis and covers 31 urban centres. As it does not cover rural areas, agricultural workers were left out of the analysis.

Argentina has its own national occupational classification (CNO-01). Therefore, it was necessary to adapt the CNO-01 to make it compatible with the International Standard Classification of Occupations (ISCO). To that end, we matched the five-digit CNO-01 with the two-digit ISCO-08, using the crosswalk built by INDEC (2018). Then, we matched ISCO-08 to ISCO-88 (both at the two-digit level) using the crosswalk made by the International Labour Organization.[2]

In order to study patterns and trends of job task content we use a routine-task intensity (RTI) measure based on previous literature (Autor and Dorn 2013; Goos et al. 2014).[3] Previous empirical studies on job task content have relied on the

---

[2] We map ISCO-08 to ISCO-88 for comparability with other country studies included in this book.
[3] For methodological details see Chapter 2 of this book.

O*NET survey, since data on this have only recently become available for a larger group of countries. However, the task composition of occupations in Argentina, and in general in developing countries, might differ significantly from those in developed countries.

For this reason, the present study is based on an estimation of the country-specific RTI (CS-RTI) by occupation built by Lewandowski et al. (2019, 2020). Then, Argentina's estimated RTIs are merged at the two-digit ISCO-88 to the EPH data. Therefore, unlike in previous analyses of job polarization in Argentina, this study does not assume that the task composition of jobs is the same as in developed countries.

The period studied is between 2003 and 2019, in particular, the fourth quarters of each year in order to avoid potential seasonality problems. This is a period characterized by economic growth and inequality reduction but, at the same time, by marked business cycles and significant changes in labour market institutions. Therefore, the selected time period makes it possible to assess to what extent these trends may have affected the adoption of technology and the composition of employment.

12.3 An overview of the erratic evolution of the Argentine labour market and income distribution over the 2000s

Argentina is characterized by high records of macroeconomic instability, which not only slows the process of adopting technology and automation but also can generate significant disruption to the productive structure and labour market composition.

The economic dynamism during the first years after the collapse of the Convertibility Plan in 2001 led to a rapid expansion of aggregate employment (at a pace that even surpassed output growth), to an improvement in the quality of the new occupations, and to an increase in real mean wages. In particular, the positive performance of labour market variables took place mainly between 2003 and 2008–10 when the unemployment rate declined from 20 per cent to 8 per cent, and labour informality among paid employees fell by 10 percentage points (pp). After that point, however, all these labour improvements slowed down, stagnated, or began to reverse.

During these years, Argentina also witnessed a process of reducing inequality, breaking the upward trend witnessed during the 1990s. However, in parallel to macroeconomic and labour market changes, earnings distribution showed strong movements over the 2000s. In particular, it is possible to identify two different phases among both paid employees and all workers: (i) 2003–12, when inequality fell (Gini index fell by about 6 pp); (ii) 2012–19, when earnings distribution worsened, after a subperiod of relative distributive stability between 2012 and 2015.

Table 12.1 Inequality indicators

	2003	2006	2009	2012	2015	2019
All workers						
Var (log earn)	0.84	0.78	0.73	0.63	0.65	0.74
Gini (log earn)	0.063	0.059	0.055	0.051	0.053	0.057
Gini (earn)	0.41	0.40	0.37	0.35	0.35	0.367
Paid workers	2003	2006	2009	2012	2015	2019
Var (log earn)	0.70	0.69	0.63	0.58	0.58	0.62
Gini (log earn)	0.06	0.05	0.05	0.05	0.05	0.05
Gini (earn)	0.39	0.37	0.35	0.33	0.33	0.34

Source: Authors' elaboration based on EPH.

However, since the first process was not fully reversed by the distributive worsening of the second phase, in 2019 the Gini coefficient was approximately 4–5 pp lower than in 2003 (Table 12.1).

12.4 Changes in employment composition and job polarization hypothesis

12.4.1 Employment growth by education level and type of occupation

Despite the erratic Argentine macroeconomic and labour market performance, some long-term trends were observed during the almost 20 years under study. In particular, following a long-standing trend, the Argentine workforce became more skilled: there was an increase in the proportion of workers with secondary and university education (+14 pp) and a fall in workers with no schooling or primary education.

In 2019, almost all workers had completed primary education (only 4 per cent had no education). However, for about 40 per cent of men and 26 per cent of women this was the only level of schooling achieved in Argentina. At the other extreme, a third of women and about 20 per cent of men have a university degree.

Changes in the composition of employment by type of occupation were also significant during the period analysed. Elementary occupations—biggest share in total employment at the beginning of the period—experienced the greatest reduction over time (–6 pp) (Figure 12.1). This was the most outstanding change in the occupation composition between 2003 and 2019. This fall meant that it stopped being the main source of employment to become the second at the end of the period. The increase in the proportion of the three most important groups of occupations located in the centre of the ranking—clerks, sales and services workers, and machine operators—is also evident. Additionally, there is partial compensation

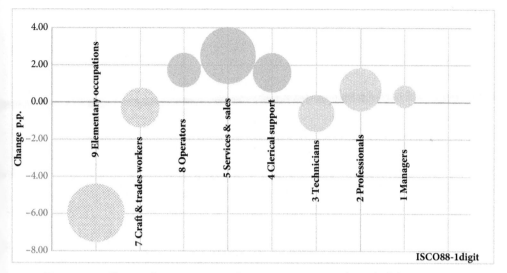

Figure 12.1 Changes between 2003 and 2019 in occupation share (pp) (ISCO-88, one-digit)

Note: pp, percentage point. Bubble size indicates the initial relative importance of each occupation in total urban employment. Colour groups are organized as follows: red for low-skilled (low-paying) manual occupations, blue for middle-skilled (white and blue collar) occupations, and green for non-manual cognitive high-skilled jobs.
Source: Authors' elaboration based on EPH.

among the highest-educated groups, with a drop in technicians and a rise in professionals.

The increase in operators, assemblers, clerical, and sales and services workers compared with the reduction of elementary occupations over the 2000s clearly contrasts with the trends of high-income countries and, consequently, questions the appropriateness of the job polarization hypothesis in Argentina. On the contrary, the relocation from low- and—to a lesser extent—from high- to middle-skilled occupations seem to be more consistent with an inverted U-shaped profile.

Figure 12.2 displays the percentage point change in the employment share as measured by ISCO-88 two-digit occupations and ranked by the initial log mean of weekly earnings for each job. First, the ranking is similar to that observed previously. In particular, those occupations included in groups 7 and 9 are mostly located at the bottom tail while those pertaining to groups 1, 2, or 3 are top-paid jobs. Second, the pattern of changes in the employment shares over time are also similar to those observed previously: worker relocation from low-paying to middle-paying jobs (with some exceptions). This is more evident in the case of paid employees. High-paying occupations exhibit a slight increase along the whole period.

These trends, however, were not homogeneous over the 2000s. During 2003–12, a shrinking in top-paid jobs was additional to the decline in the bottom-paid

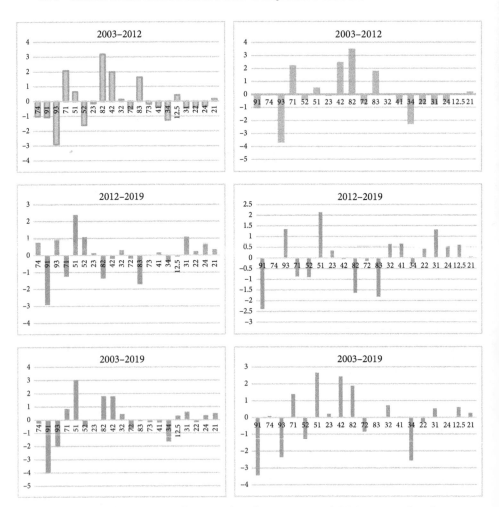

Figure 12.2 Changes in employment share by occupation (ISCO-88, two-digits)
Source: Authors' elaboration based on EPH.

occupations, especially among employees. In particular, the two (low-skilled) elementary occupations (located at the bottom part of the distribution) lost relative importance between 2003 and 2012. Additionally, almost all groups of workers classified as managers, professionals, or technicians (located mostly at the top tail of the distribution) also reduced their share in total employment or remained relatively unchanging. The joint consequence of these movements is an enlargement of the central part of the distribution. In particular, the categories of operators and clerks increased their relative importance.

These findings seem to be in line with those shown by Maloney and Molina (2016) for other Latin American countries, where they did not find a fall in operators and assemblers, but they did find a decline in elementary occupations and positive employment growth among high-skilled occupations.

In a context of low economic dynamism and increasing labour market difficulties, the trend for the period 2012–19 is less clear. Several occupation groups show the opposite tendency to that observed during the first period. In particular, most of the two-digit jobs pertaining to the three highest skilled occupations saw slight growth, while some middle-paying occupations diminished. At the other end of the earnings distribution, after the sharp fall in construction, manufacturing, and transport occupations during the first subperiod, these workers partially recovered their share in total and salaried employment. However, sales and services elementary occupations—where half are domestic helpers and cleaners—recorded a continued decline, even more marked than that of the first period.

The overall result of all these changes is slight growth in the share of non-routine cognitive occupations located at the upper end of the distribution and a sharp fall in elementary occupations. Changes in the middle are more heterogeneous.

A quadratic model is used to evaluate, econometrically, the statistical significance of those trends (Goos and Manning 2007; Sebastian 2018). A polarization pattern involves a negative first (linear) coefficient followed by a positive quadratic coefficient. Table 12.2 summarizes the results.

Table 12.2 OLS regressions for job polarization

| | Log change in employment share | | | | | |
| | All workers | | | Paid employees | | |
Covariates	2003–12	2012–19	2003–19	2003–12	2012–19	2003–19
(Log) mean hourly wage (t–1)	5.360	2.313	5.483	5.386	–1.499	4.681
	(3.896)	(4.758)	(3.206)	(3.386)	(3.823)	(3.043)
Square (log) mean hourly wage (t–1)	–0.332	–0.134	–0.429***	–0.339	0.099	–0.284
	(0.243)	(0.285)	(0.049)	(0.214)	(0.231)	(0.194)
Constant	–21.625	–9.970	–22.460*	–21.395	5.587	–19.287
	(15.552)	(19.780)	(12.586)	(13.304)	(15.734)	(11.882)
Observations	20	20	20	19	19	19
R-squared	0.057	0.046	0.126	0.073	0.092	0.098
Adjusted R-squared	–0.0540	–0.0670	0.0240	–0.0426	–0.0214	–0.0149
F-test	0.3830	0.7070	0.0290	0.2960	0.2560	0.0384

Note: Standard errors in parentheses; ***$p<0.01$, **$p<0.05$, *$p<0.1$.
Source: Authors' elaboration based on EPH.

As expected considering the previous analysis, we did not find a job polarization profile in Argentina over the 2000s. On the contrary, the sign of the coefficients for the whole period, and especially for the first subperiod, is consistent with an inverted U-shaped growth; however, the results were non-significant. This means that the relocation from bottom-paid and, to a lesser extent, from high-paid workers to middle-paid workers does not seem large enough to be reflected in the econometric results. In the second subperiod, the signs are even different among the total workers and employees. Only in the latter case they are consistent with a polarizing pattern. However, in neither group were the coefficients statistically significant.[4]

12.4.2 Employment composition by job task content

Figure 12.3 shows the changes in employment share by ranking occupations according to CS-RTI instead of mean earnings. The patterns are again different for the two periods under analysis. During 2003–12, there was a reduction in the employment share at the lowest end of the distribution, showing a diminished share of occupations with a high intensity of manual routine tasks, and a less marked drop (and a somewhat slight increase) among jobs placed at the other end of the distribution. During 2012–19, the contrast between the extremes is more evident: a decline in the relative importance of jobs located at the bottom tail of the distribution and an increase of those occupations at the top.

To further evaluate the patterns of changes in occupations, based on a task perspective, we again perform a quadratic regression—at the two-digit occupational level—of the log change in employment share on the level of routine intensity, using the CS-RTI measure. Even when the sign of the coefficients for the whole period is consistent with this inverted U-shape, these changes were once more not strong enough to throw statistically significant results.[5] Therefore, the routine-task content of occupations does not account for any definite pattern in employment changes at the occupational level.

12.5 The evolution of real earnings over time

As mentioned in Section 12.3, we can draw two marked cycles along the whole period. In particular, an upward trend is observed for the period 2003–13, followed by a strong decline from 2013 to 2019. The increasing macroeconomic

---

[4] Given the availability of data in Argentina, we can run regression analyses at the two-digit level using only 20 observations. This limitation may partly explain the non-significant results.
[5] For econometric results, see Maurizio and Monsalvo (2021).

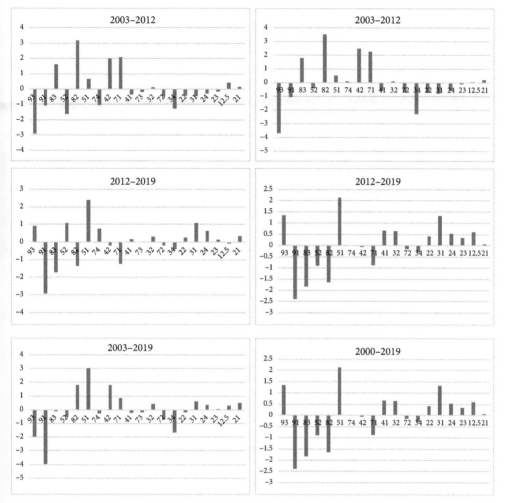

Figure 12.3 Changes in employment share by country-specific RTI
Source: Authors' elaboration based on EPH.

difficulties, in general, and the acceleration of inflation, in particular, are responsible for this result. Between both ends of the period, however, there was a rise in
average real earnings of around 10 per cent, both for paid employees and for all
workers.

The two subperiods also show highly contrasting wage behaviour across occupations (Figure 12.4). In particular, during 2003–12 the groups of jobs initially
located in the first half of the distribution experienced a greater increase than
those in the upper tail. However, there seems to be no linear trend between them,
but rather an inverted U-shaped pattern. It is more evident for all workers than
for specifically paid employees. During the second phase almost all occupations

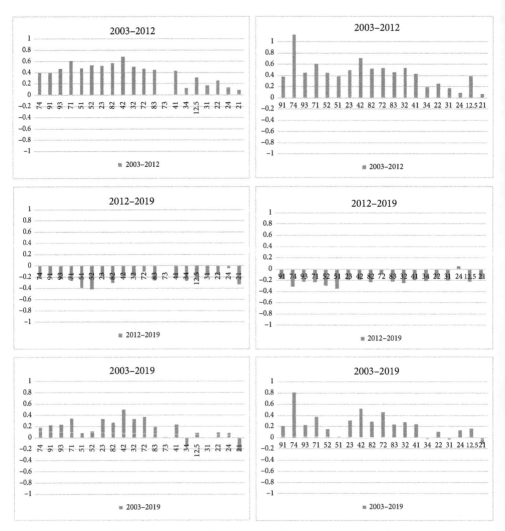

Figure 12.4 Changes in earnings by occupation (ISCO-88, two-digits)
Source: Authors' elaboration based on EPH.

suffered a reduction in real earnings, being somewhat stronger for low-paying and middle-paying occupations. Over the 2000s, real earnings growth was observed in almost all occupations but, consequently, lower than that of the first period.

In order to evaluate whether these changes are consistent with a polarizing pattern, we fit a quadratic model, but with the dependent variable being the change in the (log) mean earnings over time. The results are presented in Table 12.3.

Unlike what happens with employment, here all the coefficients are significant. For both groups of workers, inverted U-shaped growth is found in the first period, showing that, in the subperiod characterized by a decreasing trend in

Table 12.3 OLS regressions for earnings polarization

| | Change in (log) mean wage | | | | | |
| | All workers | | | Paid employees | | |
	2003–12	2012–19	2003–19	2003–12	2012–19	2003–19
(Log) mean hourly wage (t–1)	6.703***	–5.773**	3.668**	5.489***	–3.603*	2.928*
	(0.765)	(2.263)	(1.675)	(1.043)	(1.752)	(1.604)
Square (log) mean hourly wage (t–1)	–0.429***	0.349**	–0.237**	–0.348***	0.217*	–0.188*
	(0.049)	(0.138)	(0.106)	(0.066)	(0.106)	(0.101)
Constant	–25.666***	23.553**	–13.941**	–21.145***	14.686*	–11.186*
	(2.962)	(9.265)	(6.574)	(4.092)	(7.187)	(6.349)
Observations	20	20	20	19	19	19
R-squared	0.750	0.362	0.314	0.611	0.284	0.217
Adjusted R-squared	0.721	0.287	0.234	0.562	0.194	0.119
F-test	0.000000	0.036000	0.043000	0.000324	0.070400	0.069200

Note: Standard errors in parentheses; ***$p<0.01$, **$p<0.05$, *$p<0.1$.
Source: Authors' elaboration based on EPH.

inequality, real earnings growth was more intense in the middle part of the distribution. On the contrary, an earnings polarization pattern is found between 2012 and 2019. In the context of a generalized fall of real earnings and rising inequality, the greatest reductions were observed among middle-paid jobs. The results for the whole period reflect what happened in the first subperiod, although less strongly.

Two important points arise from these results. First, the international literature finds statistically significant changes either in occupations and earnings or only in occupations. As mentioned, for the US, Autor and Dorn (2013) find that the changes in jobs followed the same pattern as those in earnings. In contrast, Goos and Manning (2007) for the UK and Sebastian (2018) for Spain account for job but not wage polarization. For Argentina, however, we find a third outcome: non-significant results in occupations but significant changes in earnings.

Second, earnings grew in low-paying occupations (elementary occupations) while, as mentioned before, employment shares fell for these jobs. This finding implies that forces other than labour demand and technology may also have had a significant impact on recent wage dynamics and inequality in Argentina. In particular, the influence of labour institutions, such as the minimum wage or collective bargaining, which strengthened in Argentina especially during the first subperiod, can also account for wage rises and reducing inequality (Keifman and Maurizio 2012; Casanova and Alejo 2015; Maurizio and Vázquez 2016).[6]

12.6 The role of changes in job task content in shaping the evolution of earnings inequality

Finally, to further assess the role played by the routine-task content of occupations in shaping inequality over time, we use a RIF-regression decomposition approach to estimate the relative importance of this factor controlling for other personal or job attributes.[7]

Table 12.4 presents the results of the Gini coefficient decomposition for the whole period and for each subperiod. The first step of the decomposition shows that the changes in returns to the variables considered was the main driver of distributive shifts over time. In particular, the return effect explains 75 per cent or more of the Gini coefficient variation. The aggregate composition effect, however, also contributed to the fall in inequality during the first subperiod and over the whole of the period. Interestingly, the distributive worsening during the second phase is only explained by the unequalizing behaviour of the aggregate return effect.

Looking inside the composition effect, with the exception of age, changes in the demographic characteristics (sex, education, and ethnicity) do not seem to explain the trend in inequality. Consistent with previous empirical studies (ECLAC-ILO, 2014; Beccaria et al., 2015; Maurizio, 2015), a reduction of labour informality has been one of the most relevant contributing factors to inequality decline, especially during the period 2003–12.

However, we are here particularly interested in identifying the impact of changes in the employment composition according to the job task content on income distribution. In the US, the consensus is that occupation polarization has contributed to a deepened economic inequality (Autor et al. 2006; Firpo et al. 2018). In Argentina, as detailed earlier, there was a movement from low-paying occupations—routine intense—to middle-paying occupations, especially during the period 2003–12 characterized by high job creation and decreasing unemployment and inequality. Consequently, we could expect most of these changes to reflect a transition of workers towards better paying occupations. If that was the case, occupational mobility patterns may have contributed to a better distribution over these years. In fact, as shown in Table 12.4, the shift of workers towards less routine-intensive occupations was equalizing, especially for paid employees.

---

[6] For further discussion about the impact of labour institutions on wages and inequality, see Maurizio and Monsalvo (2021).
[7] For methodological details, see Chapter 2.

Table 12.4 RIF-regression decomposition of Gini

	All workers						Paid employees					
	2003–12		2012–19		2003–19		2003–12		2012–19		2003–19	
	Coef.	SE	Coef.	SE	Coef.	SE	Coef.	SE	Coef.	SE	Coef.	SE
Distribution												
Final F	0.368	0.004***	0.389	0.003***	0.389	0.003***	0.351	0.004***	0.357	0.003***	0.357	0.003***
Initial I	0.465	0.004***	0.368	0.003***	0.465	0.004***	0.431	0.005***	0.351	0.004***	0.431	0.005***
Total change F–I	-0.097	0.006***	0.021	0.005***	-0.076	0.005***	-0.079	0.006***	0.006	0.005	-0.074	0.006***
RIF aggregate decomposition												
RIF composition	-0.019	0.002***	-0.001	0.002	-0.018	0.003***	-0.020	0.003***	-0.004	0.002*	-0.022	0.003***
RIF specification error	0.001	0.001	0.000	0.001	0.000	0.001	0.001	0.001	0.000	0.001	0.001	0.001
RIF earnings structure	-0.078	0.005***	0.022	0.004***	-0.057	0.005***	-0.060	0.006***	0.011	0.004**	-0.052	0.005***
RIF reweighting error	-0.001	0.000*	0.000	0.000	0.000	0.001	-0.001	0.000	0.000	0.000	-0.001	0.000
RIF detailed decomposition												
RIF composition												
Age	-0.002	0.001***	-0.001	0.001	-0.003	0.001***	-0.001	0.001**	-0.001	0.001	-0.002	0.001**
Sex	0.000	0.000	0.001	0.001**	0.001	0.000*	0.000	0.000	0.001	0.001	0.000	0.000
Education	0.000	0.001	0.001	0.001	0.001	0.002	0.000	0.001	0.000	0.001	0.001	0.002
Ethnicity	0.000	0.000	0.000	0.000	0.000	0.000	0.000	0.000	0.000	0.000	0.000	0.000
Region	0.002	0.000***	0.001	0.000***	0.002	0.000***	0.001	0.000***	0.001	0.000***	0.002	0.000***
Formality	-0.017	0.002***	-0.001	0.002	-0.018	0.002***	-0.015	0.002***	-0.005	0.002***	-0.020	0.002***
CS-RTI	-0.002	0.001**	-0.002	0.001**	-0.002	0.001*	-0.004	0.001***	0.000	0.001	-0.003	0.001**
Total explained	-0.019	0.002***	-0.001	0.002	-0.018	0.003***	-0.020	0.003***	-0.004	0.002*	-0.022	0.003***

Continued

Table 12.4 *Continued*

	All workers						Paid employees					
	2003–12		2012–19		2003–19		2003–12		2012–19		2003–19	
	Coef.	SE	Coef.	SE	Coef.	SE	Coef.	SE	Coef.	SE	Coef.	SE
RIF earnings structure												
Age	-0.005	0.005	-0.002	0.004	-0.007	0.004*	-0.005	0.006	-0.001	0.004	-0.005	0.005
Sex	0.018	0.005***	0.002	0.004	0.018	0.004***	0.025	0.006***	0.002	0.005	0.025	0.005***
Education	-0.003	0.007	0.001	0.007	0.001	0.007	-0.007	0.007	0.003	0.007	-0.002	0.008
Ethnicity	0.019	0.026	-0.011	0.019	-0.004	0.025	-0.001	0.033	-0.007	0.023	-0.013	0.029
Region	-0.009	0.004**	-0.012	0.004***	-0.020	0.005***	-0.012	0.005**	-0.004	0.004	-0.014	0.004***
Formality	-0.015	0.005***	0.012	0.004***	0.000	0.005	-0.003	0.005	0.004	0.004	0.005	0.004
CS-RTI	0.021	0.006***	-0.007	0.005	0.010	0.005**	0.020	0.006***	-0.003	0.006	0.014	0.006**
Intercept	-0.102	0.032***	0.040	0.022*	-0.055	0.028*	-0.077	0.040*	0.016	0.027	-0.061	0.032*
Total unexplained	-0.078	0.005***	0.022	0.004***	-0.057	0.005***	-0.060	0.006***	0.011	0.004**	-0.052	0.005***

Note: RIF, recentred influence function; Coef. Coefficient; SE, standard error. Standard errors were estimated applying bootstrapping process with 200 replications; p-values were estimated assuming normal distribution;*** $p<0.01$, ** $p<0.05$, * $p<0.1$.
Source: Authors' elaboration based on EPH.

To better understand these results, it is useful to disentangle the impact of the different effects along the whole earnings distribution. Figure 12.5 displays the contribution of each variable to changes in quantiles across the distribution.[8]

The figure highlights the pro-poor profile associated with the increase in formality, in particular for the 2003–12 period. Occupational changes towards lower average levels of RTI during these years entailed a wage increase in the lowest quantiles, while the opposite effect is observed in the highest quantiles, thus rendering an equalizing effect. During the second period, the earnings increase associated with these changes was generalized but more intense in the lower end of the distribution.

Interestingly, the detailed decomposition of the earnings structure clearly shows a 'pro-rich' pattern of shifts in the returns to routine versus non-routine tasks in the first period, with a sort of upgrading effect (associated with an earnings reduction below the median and an increase above that).[9] Although, during the second subperiod, returns to RTI seemingly had the opposite effect, particularly at the lower end of distribution, the net effect on Gini is not significant. Therefore, the net impact of this factor over the whole period was unequalizing.

12.7 Discussion and final remarks

This study has analysed the scope and characteristics of the structural transformation resulting from changes in the task content of jobs, and their impact on employment, earnings, and income distribution in Argentina during the new millennium.

We observed the existence of a relocation from low-paying and, to a lesser extent, high-paying jobs to middle-paying jobs. This is not consistent with the job polarization pattern registered in some high-income countries. However, econometric results also reject the inverted U-shaped profile, implying that these changes were not strong enough—at least to date—to throw statistically significant results. On the contrary, in the case of earnings, we found an inverted U-shaped growth in the first period. During the second period, however, an earnings polarizing pattern appeared in the context of a widespread fall in real earnings and weakening of labour institutions.

Therefore, as in some other countries, the trends in jobs did not follow the same patterns as the trends in earnings. However, unlike them, in Argentina we found a third outcome: non-significant changes in employment but significant changes in earnings. Furthermore, earnings grew in low-paying occupations while employment shares fell for these jobs.

---

[8] Appendix A2 in Maurizio and Monsalvo (2021) shows the full results of these decompositions.
[9] See Appendix A1 in Maurizio and Monsalvo (2021).

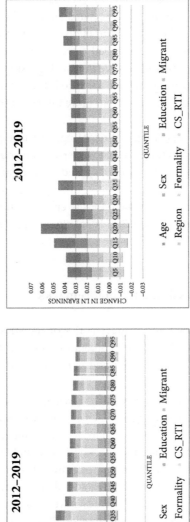
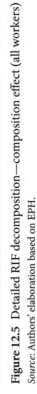

Figure 12.5 Detailed RIF decomposition—composition effect (all workers)

Source: Authors' elaboration based on EPH.

The changes in the occupations towards lower average levels of RTI had, in turn, an equalizing effect, mostly in the first period, characterized by strong job creation and falling inequality. However, during the later years, this positive trend stagnated hand in hand with the weakening or reversion of other forces that also made the distributive improvements possible during the first years of the new millennium.

All results considered, we now deem it relevant to discuss two aspects: first, the extent to which we should expect the trends in the composition of employment by occupation and its drivers in high-income countries to be replicated in less developed countries; second, the distributive consequences of this process, which could also differ across countries.

In relation to the first, Maloney and Molina (2016) state several reasons why we may not observe the same trends registered in the advanced world. In their view, the scope and speed of automation depends on the initial occupational composition (where, in some developing countries, there is a lower proportion of middle-income workers engaged in codifiable tasks), the technology absorptive capacity, the skill level of the workforce, and in some countries, the net result between being an offshoring destination and increased robotization.

To these arguments, we could add others for Argentina's particular case. This country registers the highest macroeconomic instability in the region (Rapetti 2019), which not only slows the process of adopting technology and automation but can also cause significant disruption in the production structure, leading in turn to changes in employment composition. The high real exchange rate during the first years after the collapse of the Convertibility Plan led to growth in activity and employment levels in the tradable sectors, especially in manufacturing industries. This, in part, explains the initial relative increase of one key job category—plant and machine operators and assemblers—which partially reverted when job creation diminished in those industries, something that went hand in hand with growing currency appreciation.

The contrasting changes in job composition observed between the first and second subperiods also open the question as to whether these are a reflection of strong macroeconomic fluctuations or rather a structural change that is closer to that in the advanced world, a full realization of which calls for a longer period of time. Consequently, as they are ongoing processes, monitoring must continue.

As to the second aspect, the distributive impacts of the changing nature of work, in most advanced countries, the combination of routine-biased technological change and offshoring led to the displacement of middle-paid workers in routine occupations towards the extremes: less-educated workers moved towards bottom occupations, while higher-educated workers shifted towards highly paid non-routine occupations. These occupational changes are, in turn, the drivers of earnings polarization and unequalizing changes. However, again, we would not necessarily expect to see the same pattern across the globe. Moreover, the absence of polarization does not imply that those processes do not hold.

Whether or not technological change and offshoring result in a polarizing pattern depends on several factors: (i) whether the jobs with the highest RTI are located at the bottom, middle, or top of the earnings distribution; (ii) the speed and type of technology adoption in the country; (iii) the position of the country in global value chains, in particular, whether it is a sender or receiver of offshored labour; and (iv) the existence of other domestic factors (e.g. labour institutions, education premium, formality).

Overall, the results seem to suggest that macroeconomic conditions, the production structure, and domestic labour market institutions shape the impact of technology on job demand, on its composition, and on earnings distribution in a specific country.

Acknowledgement

The authors are grateful for valuable feedback and comments on previous versions of this chapter from the internal and external research team of UNU-WIDER collaborating under the project component 'The changing nature of work and inequality'. A previous version of this chapter was presented at the 3rd Annual IZA/World Bank/NJD/UNU-WIDER Jobs and Development Conference: Better Jobs for Development, 1–4 September 2020, held online.

References

Apella, I., and G. Zunino (2017). 'Cambio tecnológico y el mercado de trabajo en Argentina y Uruguay. Un análisis desde el enfoque de tareas' ['Technological Change and the Labour Market in Argentina and Uruguay. A Task Content Analysis']. Serie de informes técnicos del Banco Mundial en Argentina, Paraguay y Uruguay No. 11. Buenos Aires: Banco Mundial. Available at: http://documents1.worldbank.org/curated/en/940501496692186828/pdf/115685-NWP-SPANISH-P161571-ApellaZuninoCambiotecnologico.pdf (accessed December 2020).

Apella, I., and G. Zunino (2021). 'Technological Change and Labour Market Trends in Latin America and the Caribbean: A Task Content Approach'. CEPAL Review, 136: 63–85.

Autor, D., and D. Dorn (2013). 'The Growth of Low-Skill Service Jobs and the Polarization of the US Labor Market'. American Economic Review, 103(5): 1553–97. https://doi.org/10.1257/aer.103.5.1553

Autor, D.H., L.F. Katz, and M.S. Kearney (2006). 'The Polarization of the US Labor Market'. American Economic Review, 96: 189–94. https://doi.org/10.1257/000282806777212620

Beccaria, L., R. Maurizio, and G. Vázquez (2015). 'Recent Decline in Wage Inequality and Formalization of the Labour Market in Argentina'. International Review of Applied Economics, 29(5): 677–700. https://doi.org/10.1080/02692171.2015.1054369

Brambilla, I., and D. Tortarolo (2018). 'Investment in ICT, Productivity, and Labor Demand: The Case of Argentina'. Policy Research Working Paper 8325. Washington, DC: The World Bank. https://doi.org/10.1596/1813-9450-8325

Casanova, L., and J. Alejo (2015). 'El efecto de la negociación colectiva sobre la distribución de los ingresos laborales Evidencia empírica para Argentina en los años dos mil' ['The Effect of the Collective Bargaining on the Labour Income Distribution. Empirical Evidence for Argentina in the 2000s']. Serie de Documento No. 8. Argentina: Organización Internacional del Trabajo. Available at: https://www.ilo.org/wcmsp5/groups/public/—americas/—ro-lima/—ilo-buenos_aires/documents/publication/wcms_353539.pdf (accessed December 2020).

ECLAC-ILO (2014). 'Formalización del empleo y distribución de los ingresos laborales' ['Labour Formalization and Labour Income Distribution']. Coyuntura laboral en América Latina y el Caribe, # 11,CEPAL/OIT. Available at: https://repositorio.cepal.org/bitstream/handle/11362/37119/1/S1420500_es.pdf (accessed December 2020).

Firpo, S., N.Fortin, T.Lemieux (2018) 'Decomposing wage distributions using recentered influence function regressions'. Econometrics, 6(2): 28. https://doi.org/10.3390/econometrics6020028

Goos, M., and A. Manning (2007). 'Lousy and Lovely Jobs: The Rising Polarization of Work in Britain'. Review of Economics and Statistics, 89(1): 118–33. https://doi.org/10.1162/rest.89.1.118

Goos, M., A. Manning, and A. Salomons (2014). 'Explaining Job Polarization: Routine-Biased Technological Change and Offshoring'. American Economic Review, 104(8): 2509–26. https://doi.org/10.1257/aer.104.8.2509

INDEC (2018). Correspondencias entre el CNO-17 y la CIUO-08 ['Correspondences between CNO-17 and ISCO-08']. Buenos Aires: Instituto Nacional de Estadística y Censos (INDEC). Available at: https://www.indec.gob.ar/ftp/cuadros/menusuperior/clasificadores/correspondencias_cno2017_ciuo2008.pdf (accessed December 2020).

Keifman, S., and R. Maurizio (2012). 'Changes in Labour Market Conditions and Policies: Their Impact on Wage Inequality during the Last Decade'. WIDER Working Paper 2012/14. Helsinki: UNU-WIDER. Available at: https://www.wider.unu.edu/publication/changes-labour-market-conditions-and-policies (accessed December 2020).

Lewandowski, P., A. Park, W. Hardy, and Y. Du (2019). 'Technology, Skills, and Globalization: Explaining International Differences in Routine and Nonroutine Work Using Survey Data'. IBS Working Paper 04/2019. Warsaw: Institute for Structural Research (IBS). https://doi.org/10.2139/ssrn.3415008

Lewandowski, P., A. Park, and S. Schotte (2020). 'The Global Distribution of Routine and Non-Routine Work'. WIDER Working Paper 2020/75. Helsinki: UNU-WIDER. https://doi.org/10.35188/UNU-WIDER/2020/832-0

Maloney, W., and C. Molina (2016). 'Are Automation and Trade Polarizing Developing Country Labor Markets, too?'. Policy Research Working Paper 7922. Washington, DC: The World Bank. https://doi.org/10.1596/1813-9450-7922

Maurizio, R. (2015). 'Transitions to Formality and Declining Inequality: Argentina and Brazil in the 2000s'. Journal of Development and Change, 46(5): 1047–79. https://doi.org/10.1111/dech.12195

Maurizio, R., and A.P. Monsalvo (2021). 'Changes in Occupations and Their Task Content: Implications for Employment and Inequality in Argentina, 2003–19'. WIDER

Working Paper 2021/15. Helsinki: UNU-WIDER. https://doi.org/10.35188/UNU-WIDER/2021/949-5

Maurizio, R., and G. Vázquez (2016). 'Distribution Effects of the Minimum Wage in Four Latin American Countries: Argentina, Brazil, Chile and Uruguay'. *International Labour Review*, 155(1): 97–131. https://doi.org/10.1111/ilr.12007

Messina, J., G. Pica, and A. Oviedo (2016). 'Job Polarization in Latin America' [Unpublished]. Washington, DC: The World Bank. Available at: http://www.jsmessina.com (accessed December 2020).

Rapetti, M. (2019). 'Conflicto distributivo y crecimiento en Argentina' ['Distributive Conflict and Economic Growth in Argentina']. *Boletín Informativo Techint*, 357, Buenos Aires. Available at: http://iosapp.boletintechint.com/Utils/Document PDF.ashx?Codigo=eaf7e7d6-a778-4530-b503-af5f738f5572&IdType=2 (accessed December 2020).

Sebastian, R. (2018). 'Explaining Job Polarisation in Spain from a Task Perspective'. *SERIEs*, 9: 215–48. https://doi.org/10.1007/s13209-018-0177-1

Wright E., and R. Dwyer (2003). 'The Patterns of Job Expansions in the USA: A Comparison of the 1960s and 1990s'. *Socioeconomic Review*, 1(3): 289–325. https://doi.org/10.1093/soceco/1.3.289

13

Brazil

Employment and Inequality Trends

Sergio Firpo, Alysson Portella, Flavio Riva, and Giovanna Úbida

13.1 Introduction

In recent years, researchers in labour economics have advocated for the empirical and theoretical fruitfulness of a distinction between 'skills' (worker capabilities, whether innate or acquired by training) and 'tasks' (units of work activity that directly participate in production) (see, for instance, Acemoglu and Autor 2011; Fortin et al. 2011). It has been argued that models that overemphasize the role of skills in the determination of labour earnings and composition end up missing important features of recent labour market trends, at least in developed countries. Therefore, 'task approaches' (Autor 2013) are now extensively used to describe, in a more nuanced way, how the most recent technological revolutions, openness to trade, and offshoring altered the structure of labour demand and, thereby, the employment structure and labour earnings distribution. In this framework, occupations assume a prominent role, since the task content of work is typically determined at the occupational level.

Despite the agreement on the contribution that 'task approaches' have made to a better understanding of the job market trends in advanced economies (Acemoglu and Autor 2011; Autor and Dorn 2013; Goos et al. 2014; Sebastian 2018), there are still few applications to developing and under-developed economies. This chapter contributes to our understanding of the joint roles of 'skills' and 'tasks' in shaping the evolution of employment and earnings distribution, using Brazil as a case study.

Brazil is a particularly interesting country for a couple of reasons. It has historically been characterized by high levels of inequality, even by Latin American standards. Starting in the mid-1990s, Brazil went through two decades of continuous reductions in inequality, with respect to both labour and non-labour income. This decline has been extensively studied,[1] and it provides an important background to assess the importance of occupations and their task content in developing countries, in contrast to other factors that also affect labour markets.

---

[1] See, for instance, Firpo and Portella (2019) and Neri (2021).

Sergio Firpo et al., *Brazil: Employment and Inequality Trends*. In: *Tasks, Skills, and Institutions*. Edited by Carlos Gradín, Piotr Lewandowski, Simone Schotte, and Kunal Sen, Oxford University Press. © UNU-WIDER (2023).
DOI: 10.1093/oso/9780192872241.003.0013

This long period of declining inequality has recently come to an end, with inequality in Brazil rising since 2015. Our analysis, which spans the years 2003–19, covers both the inequality-decreasing and inequality-increasing time intervals.

Our objective in this chapter is twofold. First, we document shifts in the employment structure in Brazil, highlighting the role of occupations and their task content, and how they have evolved over time. In particular, we use measures of job task content that rely on country-specific information and contrast this to results obtained using measures based on US data, therefore departing from the assumption of uniformity with respect to job content (Lewandowski et al. 2019). Second, we evaluate how occupations and their task content are associated with changes in polarization and inequality in Brazil. We evaluate the hypothesis of polarization in employment and earnings in Brazil, with respect to both initial earnings and routine-task content. We also assess the importance of occupations and their routine-task content in explaining inequality and the changes observed in the period. In particular, we test whether routine-task content has any relation to changes in earnings inequality after we account for changes in skills and other factors.

Our results show a considerable association between occupations' average earnings and their task content. Jobs that are more intensive in terms of routine tasks in Brazil are the ones with the lowest earnings. Between-jobs inequality accounts for nearly half of overall inequality, although its relevance has declined over time. Earnings inequality between occupations is similar to concentration indices that order individuals by the routine-task content of their occupations instead of earnings, highlighting the importance of job task content in Brazil.

Despite the fact that the Brazilian economy has not changed dramatically in the last two decades, we find a declining intensity of routine tasks across the whole economy, a precondition for polarization as found in developed countries. We find some evidence of earnings polarization, but not with respect to employment. However, the patterns resemble much more those of pro-poor or pro-rich growth rather than polarization itself, as we find no evidence of hollowing out in the middle of the distribution.

When we look at changes in overall inequality, we find that the reduction in the Gini coefficient in the first period is mostly explained by changes in the structure of returns, while the rise in the second period is mostly determined by changes in the composition of workers. The supply of skilled labour and changes in its return are the main factors driving these results. Our results, thus reinforce previous conclusions with respect to the dual role of education in affecting inequality, in what has been called the 'paradox of progress' (Bourguignon et al. 2005). With respect to the routine-task intensity (RTI) of occupations, we observe an inequality-reducing composition effect in the first period, but an inequality-enhancing effect in the second. Returns to RTI contribute to reducing inequality in the whole period, but its effect is small, not always significant, and measures based on country-specific or O*NET information vary. Finally, when we include

RTI into our inequality decomposition, we see that the part explained by educational levels—both composition and structure—reduce in magnitude, although both remain significant.

The remainder of the chapter is structured as follows. Section 13.2 presents our survey data and the aggregate measures of job task content. Section 13.3 discusses the methodology employed in our analysis. We conduct a descriptive analysis of the Brazilian economy in Section 13.4, examining the main factors associated with labour market outcomes, as well as changes in the occupational structure. The results of our main analyses are presented in Section 13.5, including a discussion of polarization, inequality, and the role of occupations in accounting for them. Section 13.6 concludes.

13.2 Data

13.2.1 Demographics, employment, and earnings

Our main sources of data are the Brazilian National Household Sample Survey (PNAD) and the Continuous Brazilian National Household Sample Survey (PNADC), both conducted by the Brazilian Institute of Geography and Statistics. In 2015, the PNAD was replaced by the PNADC, which is a rotating-panel version of the former. Thus, the PNAD covers the years 2003–09 and 2011–15, while the PNADC covers the years 2016–19. Both surveys are nationally representative.

We use effective earnings from the main work activity, converted to 2012 real weekly values.[2] Workers are divided between formal employees, those with legal labour contracts (a signed 'labour' booklet or *com carteira*); informal employees, those without legal labour contracts; and self-employed workers. Self-employed workers are further divided into those who contribute to social security (INSS) and those who do not. When specifically stated as such, self-employed workers who contributed to INSS are put together with formal employees in a wider formality definition. We restrict our analysis to individuals between 15 and 64 years old, dividing them into three categories (15–24, 25–44, 45–64). Our racial variable has five categories: White, Black, Brown (*Pardo*), Indigenous, and Asian descendent. We also have information on gender and geography (27 Brazilian states and rural residency). We use the second version of the Brazilian Classification of Economic Activities (CNAE 2.0) to classify workers according to their sector of activity. We use ISCO-88 (the International Standard Classification of Occupations) at the three-digit level to classify workers' occupations. Both PNAD and PNADC use Brazilian classification systems that differ between themselves and with respect to ISCO-88. The matching between both classifications is described

---

[2] We use the *Índice Nacional de Preços ao Consumidor Restrito*.

232 BRAZIL: EMPLOYMENT AND INEQUALITY TRENDS

in detail in Appendix B of the working paper version of this chapter (Firpo et al. 2021).

Our analysis relies not only on the harmonized classification of occupations over time, but also on their task content, especially their RTI. We use measures on task content based on O*NET (2003) and on country-specific factors (Lewandowski et al. 2019, 2020). The latter are relevant to account for differences in technology adoption, labour productivity, and skill supply across countries, which might impact how tasks are distributed across occupations. The RTI measures the intensity of routine tasks. Therefore, higher values of this variable means that a certain occupation is composed of tasks that are more repetitive and require less cognitive efforts (Autor et al. 2003). For details on how we construct our RTI variables, see Firpo et al. (2021) and Lewandowski et al. (2019, 2020).

13.3 Methodology

We conduct three main exercises in our empirical analysis: an evaluation of polarization based on employment shares and weekly earnings; an evaluation of the importance of occupation in overall inequality; and a decomposition of inequality on structure and composition effects. We only provide a short summary on the methodology here, and refer readers to Gradín and Schotte (2020) and Firpo et al. (2021) for further details.

The first analysis aims to evaluate job polarization at the occupational level in Brazil, both in terms of employment and earnings. To do so, we aggregate individuals at the three-digit level of ISCO-88 and regress changes in log employment shares and log mean weekly earnings on initial log mean weekly earnings and its square (Goos and Manning 2007; Sebastian 2018):

$$\Delta \log \left(y_{j,t}\right) = \varphi_0 + \varphi_1 \log \left(x_{j,t-1}\right) + \varphi_2 \log \left(x_{j,t-1}\right)^2 + \varepsilon_{j,t} \qquad (1)$$

where $\Delta \log \left(y_{j,t}\right)$ represents either changes in log employment share or changes in log mean earnings in occupation j between periods $t-1$ and t. The independent variable, $\log \left(x_{j,t-1}\right)$, and its square refer to the log of mean earnings in occupation j in the initial period, $t-1$. Occupations are weighted by their initial share in total employment. In a similar manner, we replace the explanatory variables— log of mean earnings and its square—with the initial level of RTI and its square (Sebastian 2018) to evaluate polarization based on task content.

In our second analysis we evaluate the importance of occupations in explaining trends in overall inequality. To do so, we perform Shapley decompositions (Shorrocks 2013) of the Gini index using occupations to group individuals. That is, we measure how much of the Gini index is determined within and between occupations, following the approach proposed by Gradín and Schotte (2020):

$$G = G_B + G_W \tag{2}$$

where G is the overall Gini index, G_B is the Gini index between occupations, and G_W is the Gini index within occupations. Those two are defined by:

$$G_B = \frac{1}{2}\left[G(y_b) + G - G(y_w)\right]$$

$$G_W = \frac{1}{2}\left[G(y_w) + G - G(y_b)\right] \tag{3}$$

The vector y_b is a vector in which earnings of all workers are replaced by the average earnings of their respective occupation j, while y_w is the vector of earnings re-scaled, so that all occupations have the same average earnings.[3] Hence, $G(y_w)$ and $G(y_b)$ are simply the Gini index computed based on these alternative vectors of earnings, instead of $G = G(y)$, the actual Gini index computed using the actual vector of earnings, y.[4]

In a related exercise, we also compute the RTI concentration index for the distribution of average earnings by occupation. While in the conventional Gini between occupations, $G(y_b)$, occupations are sorted by their average earnings, in the RTI concentration index they are sorted by their (inverted) routine-task intensity. This provides evidence on the extent to which between-occupations inequality is linked with RTI or with other factors associated with occupations.

Finally, we apply the recentred influence function (RIF) methodology (Firpo et al. 2009, 2011; Fortin et al. 2011; Firpo et al. 2018) to decompose changes in the Gini coefficient across time. This approach can be used to attribute changes in inequality (Δ_o^v) to workers' characteristics (composition effects, Δ_X^v) and the returns to these characteristics (structure effects, Δ_S^v).

The aggregated decomposition of the Gini coefficient, or any functional $v(F_y)$ of the earnings distribution, can be written as

$$\begin{aligned}\Delta_o^v &= v\left(F_{y_1|t=1}\right) - v\left(F_{y_0|t=0}\right)\\ &= \left[v\left(F_{y_1|t=1}\right) - v\left(F_{y_0|t=1}\right)\right] + \left[v\left(F_{y_0|t=1}\right) - v\left(F_{y_0|t=0}\right)\right]\\ &= \Delta_S^v + \Delta_X^v\end{aligned} \tag{4}$$

Here, $F_{y_s|t}$ is the earnings distribution when workers in period t are remunerated under the earnings structure prevailing at period s. $F_{y_0|t=0}$ and $F_{y_1|t=1}$ are observed,

[3] See the methodological appendix of Gradín and Schotte (2020) for further details.
[4] In the working paper, we also decompose change in between-occupations inequality. See Gradín and Schotte (2020) and Firpo et al. (2021) for details. We refrain from doing so here for lack of space.

as well as their functionals $v(F_{y_0|t=0})$ and $v(F_{y_1|t=1})$. The counterfactual distribution, $F_{y_0|t=1}$, which gives the distribution of earnings under the structure of $t = 0$ for workers at time $t = 1$, is estimated using reweighting and is consistent under the ignorability and common overlapping assumptions (Firpo et al. 2018).

The detailed decomposition uses the concepts of (recentered) Influence functions to assess the impact of individual covariates on overall changes in inequality, both through composition and structure channels. Assuming linear relationships between the RIF and covariates, we can decompose changes in inequality in four components:

$$
\begin{aligned}
\Delta_o^v &= \Delta_S^v + \Delta_X^v \\
&= (\gamma_1 - \gamma_c) X_{i1} + \gamma_c (X_{i1} - X_{ic}) + \gamma_0 (X_{ic} - X_{i0}) + (\gamma_c - \gamma_0) X_{ic} \\
&= \Delta_{S,p}^v + \Delta_{S,e}^v + \Delta_{X,p}^v + \Delta_{X,e}^v
\end{aligned}
\tag{5}
$$

These four terms are: the pure structure effect, $\Delta_{S,p}^v$; the reweighting error, $\Delta_{S,e}^v$; the pure composition effect, $\Delta_{X,p}^v$; and the specification error, $\Delta_{X,e}^v$. The two error terms provide an evaluation of the quality of the decomposition. The reweighting error, $\gamma_c (X_{i1} - X_{ic})$, arises because the reweighting procedure is unable to perfectly replicate the distribution of workers' characteristics observed in $t = 1$, and should disappear asymptotically. The specification error, $(\gamma_c - \gamma_0) X_{ic}$, arises because of departures of the linearity assumption, and its size reflects how much the estimated RIF coefficients vary after we reweight the distribution of workers' characteristics in $t = 0$ to equal that observed in $t = 1$. Therefore, the specification error reflects a form of composition effect, as it measures the indirect effects of changes in workers' characteristics on the estimated coefficients.

13.4 The Brazilian economy between 2003 and 2019

In the first decade of the twenty-first century, and up to the mid-2010s, Brazil underwent considerable economic expansion that has resulted in increased average wages and lower unemployment rates. However, 2015 marks the beginning of an ongoing recession that increased unemployment rates to more than 12 per cent in a few years, while real average earnings remain at the same level as in 2014.

The Brazilian boom and bust had consequences for inequality as well. Table 13.1 summarizes some inequality measures for three periods: 2003/04, 2011/12, and 2018/19. The first interval comprises the period of rapid economic expansion and inequality reduction. We can see that inter-quantile ratios reduced at both ends of the distribution, as well as the variance of log earnings and the Gini index.

Table 13.1 Inter-quantile ratios and summary inequality indices

	Inter–quantile ratios				Summary indices		
	2003/04	2011/12	2018/19		2003/04	2011/12	2018/19
ln(q90)–ln(q10)	2.46	2.04	2.31	Var (log earn)	0.966	0.769	0.892
ln(q90)–ln(q50)	1.36	1.16	1.18	Gini (log earn)	0.106	0.085	0.089
ln(q50)–ln(q10)	1.10	0.88	1.12	Gini (earn)	0.536	0.485	0.493

Note: This table presents summary statistics on distribution for three time periods (pooled cross-sections for 2003–2004, 2011–2012, and 2018–2019) using data from the PNAD (2003/12) and PNADC (2018/19), deflated to October 2012 prices.
Source: Authors' compilation based on data from the PNAD (2003/12) and PNADC (2018/19).

In the second period, however, inequality increased only with respect to the bottom of the distribution, reflecting the considerable losses that this group suffered. The ratio between the earnings of the 90th and 10th percentiles went from 2.04 in 2011/12 to 2.31 in 2018/19, almost reversing the reduction observed between 2003 and 2012. The ratios between the 90th and the 50th percentiles, however, remained basically the same in both periods. The variance of log earnings increased substantially, while the Gini index (measured using earning or their log) remains basically stable.

The causes of the decrease in labour inequality up to the mid-2010s and its increase thereafter are still under debate. Firpo and Portella (2019) conducted a large survey of the literature and point to several factors that may have contributed to the fall in wage inequality up to 2015. These include changes in the supply of skilled labour, changes in the demand for labour spurred by trade liberalization and the commodities boom, as well as institutional factors associated with formality in the labour market and increases in the minimum wage. An important factor that has been neglected in this literature is the role played by changes in occupational structure and polarization.[5] In the remainder of this section we provide a more detailed picture of the evolution of the Brazilian economy in the 2000s and 2010s, before analysing the particular role of occupation and RTI in the changes in inequality observed in the period.

Brazil has around 90% of all workers employed in non-agriculture activities, and this scenery has increased continuously since 2003/04 (Table 2 in Firpo et al. 2021). Formal workers comprise almost half of the entire workforce. During the period of economic growth, their share in the non-agriculture sector went from 44.5 per cent in 2003/04 to 53.6 per cent in 2011/12. However, in the later period their share dropped to 50.8 per cent. The share of informal workers has

[5] Some assessment of polarization can be found in Maloney and Molina (2016).

decreased continuously since 2003/04, even during the recession. This was in part due to a considerable increase in the share of self-employed workers, which decreased during the boom between 2003/04 and 2011/12, and increased again after.

The occupational structure remained somewhat stable during the period, with no significant change in most of the groups (Table 3 in Firpo et al. 2021). The three upper occupational groups increased their participation from around 19 per cent to 25 per cent between 2003/04 and 2018/19, but the pattern was not the same within subgroups. The share of employment of clerical support workers and services and sales remained more or less stable in both periods, together with skilled workers in agriculture and similar activities. Craft workers and plant and machine operators both incremented their share in total employment. Finally, elementary occupations, the group with the lowest average earnings, observed a considerable reduction in the share of employment.

The trends in industry composition show a continuous fall of employment in agriculture and manufacturing, while construction expanded in the first period and contracted in the second (Table 4 of Firpo et al. 2021). The services sector incremented its share of total employment in both periods. In particular, transport, storage, and communications; accommodation and food; and educational and health services expanded quickly.

Although changes in the occupational and industrial composition of the Brazilian economy in the last decades were not dramatic, they have likely had an impact on the way that production is organized and should be reflected in measures of RTI. Figure 13.1a shows that average RTI decreased in the period under analysis, suggesting a reduction in the supply of jobs that are routine-intensive and traditionally linked to middle-class occupations, a pattern observed in developed countries that has been linked to polarization, as in Firpo et al. (2011). Figure 13.1b shows a negative association between earnings and RTI in all time periods.[6] We can observe a reduction on the average RTI in almost every demi-decile, but the reduction is concentrated among the worst-paying jobs.

Starting in the 1990s, Brazil has gone through a rapid increase in schooling. These changes in the supply of skilled labour have been pointed out as important factors behind the reduction in inequality in Brazil (Barros et al. 2010) through their effect on the educational premium. More recent research, however, highlights the dual role played by the expansion of educational levels. At the same time that a larger supply of skilled labour reduces education premia, higher education levels have an inequality-enhancing effect because of the convexity of returns to education (Fernandez and Messina 2018; Haanwinckel 2018; Ferreira et al. 2021).

---

[6] Figure 6 in Firpo et al. (2021) includes country-specific and O*NET RTI measures.

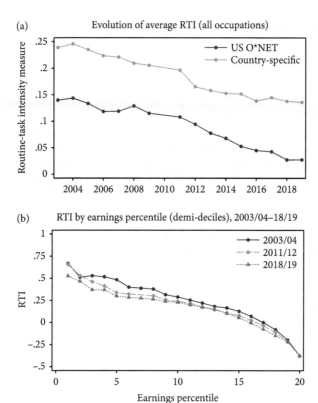

Figure 13.1 Routine-task intensity across periods

Note: In Panel (a), workers are grouped in occupations defined at the two-digit ISCO-88 level. Average RTI levels for each year are computed weighing each occupation by the number of employees. In Panel (b), individuals are ranked based on their average earnings and grouped into 20 demi-deciles.We compute average country-specific RTI for each group using survey weights.
Source: Authors' compilation based on data from the PNAD (2003-15) and the PNADC (2016-19)

The minimum wage (MW) increased in real terms in Brazil during the period under analysis, especially between 2003 and 2012, when its real value more than doubled. Its bite is considerable and has a noticeable impact on the wage distribution of workers in both the formal and informal sectors. Researchers have argued that the increase in MW is an important factor behind the drop in inequality observed in the period. Engbom and Moser (2021) estimate that around one-third of the observed 25.9 log-point reduction in the variance of log earnings inequality in Brazil between 1996 and 2012 can be attributed to MW increases. Therefore, the rises in MW may have contributed to reducing earnings gaps between occupations, everything else constant.

13.5 The role of tasks and skills in changing earnings inequality

13.5.1 Job and earnings polarization

In this section we focus on evaluating employment and earnings polarization in Brazil, applying the methodology proposed by Goos and Manning (2007) and Sebastian (2018). Table 13.2 shows the results of regressions of changes in employment and mean earnings on lagged earnings and its square at the occupation level, following Equation 1. The results provide mixed support for the polarization hypothesis in terms of employment, but confirm this phenomenon with respect to earnings.

In the first period, we observe the opposite of polarization in the share of employment, since the coefficients suggest larger growth in the middle of the distribution. In the second period, however, we find evidence of polarization, as the square of initial earnings is positive and significant. The results comparing 2018/19 with 2003/04 are not statistically significant, although the point estimates suggest a small polarization.

All estimated coefficients are significant for the relationship between changes in mean earnings and support the conclusion of polarization. The magnitude of the phenomenon, however, is weaker between 2003 and 2012, being mostly driven by changes in earnings between 2012 and 2019.

In a similar way, Panel C in Table 13.2 shows how changes in employment and average earnings at the occupation level are associated with RTI, thus evaluating the polarization argument with respect to the task content of occupations. Again, we find mixed evidence of polarization with respect to employment, but average earnings display some polarization, especially in the later period.

The estimated coefficients are only significant for changes in employment observed between 2003 and 2012 using the country-specific RTI and suggest the opposite conclusion of polarization, just as in the regression using earnings instead of RTI. The point estimate using the O*NET classification is also negative, but not significant. Using data from other periods, we find no evidence of polarization.

When we consider average earnings, in Columns 4–6, the point estimates all suggest polarization using both measures, although the precision is small. As in Panel (B), polarization seems much stronger in the second period than the first.

13.5.2 Earnings inequality across occupations and its relationship to RTI

To evaluate the importance of occupations in earnings inequality, we first conduct a Shapley decomposition of the Gini index, as in Equation 2. Table 13.3 shows the

Table 13.2 Regression model on the relationship between lagged earnings and RTI with employment and current earnings

	Log change in employment share			Change in log mean earnings		
	(1) 2003/04–2011/12	(2) 2011/12–2018/19	(3) 2003/04–2018/19	(4) 2003/04–2011/12	(5) 2011/12–2018/19	(6) 2003/04–2018/19
Panel A: Lagged earnings						
(Log) mean earnings ($t-1$)	1.069**	-2.722**	-0.909	-0.631***	-2.625***	-2.384***
	(0.407)	(1.344)	(1.054)	(0.117)	(0.735)	(0.512)
Sq. (log) mean earnings ($t-1$)	-0.084**	0.224*	0.086	0.044***	0.207***	0.189***
	(0.039)	(0.117)	(0.099)	(0.011)	(0.062)	(0.046)
Constant	-3.294***	8.074**	2.237	2.409***	8.270***	7.706***
	(1.026)	(3.815)	(2.741)	(0.300)	(2.178)	(1.417)
Observations	78	78	78	78	78	78
Adjusted R^2	0.179	0.059	-0.015	0.647	0.422	0.669
*Panel B: RTI - O*NET measures*						
O*NET RTI	-0.149*	0.034	-0.050	0.153***	0.027	0.180***
	(0.075)	(0.104)	(0.122)	(0.024)	(0.049)	(0.061)
Sq. O*NET RTI	-0.161	0.366	0.067	0.128**	0.277	0.405
	(0.257)	(0.256)	(0.306)	(0.056)	(0.228)	(0.265)
Constant	0.141	-0.229*	-0.122	0.227***	0.038	0.264***
	(0.122)	(0.121)	(0.166)	(0.022)	(0.086)	(0.092)
Observations	78	78	78	78	78	78
Adjusted R^2	0.019	0.045	-0.025	0.540	0.118	0.317
Panel C: RTI country-specific measures						
RTI	-0.161**	-0.028	-0.189	0.168***	0.127	0.296***
	(0.075)	(0.141)	(0.166)	(0.030)	(0.079)	(0.090)

Table 13.2 *Continued*

	Log change in employment share			Change in log mean earnings		
	(1) 2003/04–2011/12	(2) 2011/12–2018/19	(3) 2003/04–2018/19	(4) 2003/04–2011/12	(5) 2011/12–2018/19	(6) 2003/04–2018/19
Sq. RTI	−0.310**	0.110	−0.199	0.080	0.431**	0.510*
	(0.139)	(0.285)	(0.285)	(0.084)	(0.195)	(0.258)
Constant	0.083	−0.096	−0.014	0.273***	0.006	0.278***
	(0.063)	(0.065)	(0.086)	(0.027)	(0.033)	(0.049)
Observations	78	78	78	78	78	78
Adjusted R^2	0.182	−0.024	0.017	0.387	0.282	0.430

Note: This table presents formal estimates on the quadratic fit following Equations 2 and 3. Columns 1–3 (4–6) are for ordinary least squares estimates for the change in the logarithm of employment share (the logarithm of mean hourly earnings (panel A) and its square and on RTI and its square (panels B and C). Regression at the three-digit level ISCO-88 occupations. Occupations are weighted by their initial employment share. Robust standard errors are in parentheses. *** $p <$ 0.01, ** $p < 0.05$, * $p < 0.1$.
Source: Authors' calculations.

results of this decomposition for all three periods under analysis.[7] Nearly half of the Gini index is accounted for by differences in earnings across occupations in 2003/04. This share decreases to around 40 per cent in the later period, meaning that most of inequality is explained by differences in earnings observed between individuals in the same occupations.[8] Occupations play a more important role in accounting for inequality in Brazil than in Argentina or Ghana (Gradín and Schotte 2020; Maurizio and Monsalvo 2021; Chapters 5 and 12 in this book).

When we hold the share of employment of each occupation the same as that observed in the first period, the share of the Gini index resulting from differences between and within occupations remains almost the same. We obtain a similar result when we hold average occupation earnings constant at their 2003/04 levels.

Table 13.3, Panel B, shows the concentration index measuring inequality based on the ranking of occupation using RTI, comparing it with the Gini index between occupations. When the ratios between these two measures are similar it means that the ranking of occupations by earnings and by RTI are alike, suggesting that the intensity of routine tasks is an important component in determining differences in earnings between occupations, rather than other factors such as skills. In Brazil, the concentration index using RTI is around 90 per cent of the Gini between occupations, pointing to the importance of routine tasks in explaining earnings differences between occupations. The conclusion is the same whether we use country-specific measures or O*NET, and reflects the patterns uncovered in Figure 13.1b, where we observe a large negative association between RTI and average earnings across occupations.

13.5.3 Disentangling inequality drivers: the RIF regression decomposition

Here, we use RIF regressions to assess the role of changes in the structure of earnings and workers' characteristics in accounting for observed changes in inequality, and the role of changes in RTI in particular. Table 13.4 shows the results of Gini decomposition using the reweighting approach to decomposition, as in Equation 5. The bulk of changes in the first period (Columns 1 and 4) are accounted for by changes in the structure of earnings, corresponding to a drop of 5 Gini points between 2003/04 and 2011/12. Changes in worker composition would not have affected inequality if there were no change in earnings structure.

---

[7] The results in Table 13.3 change marginally from those published in the working paper version (Firpo et al. 2021, Tables 7 and 9). This is so because we have mistakenly excluded two occupational groups from our previous analysis.

[8] In the working paper version, we further decompose changes in between-occupation inequality into a part attributed to changes in the average occupational wages and changes in the share of employment across these occupations (Table 8 in Firpo et al. 2021).

Table 13.3 Gini index decomposed into inequality between and within occupations

	Actual			Shares constant			Means constant		
	2003/04	2011/12	2018/19	2003/04	2011/12	2018/19	2003/04	2011/12	2018/19
Panel A: Gini index decomposition									
Gini (G)	.537	.485	.493	.537	.490	.497	.537	.508	.507
Between-occupation (B)	.251	.215	.216	.251	.192	.201	.251	.222	.225
% (B/G)	46.8	44.2	43.7	46.8	39.2	40.4	46.8	43.67	44.45
Within-occupation (W)	.286	.271	.278	.286	.298	.256	.286	.286	.282
% (W/G)	53.2	55.8	56.3	53.2	60.8	59.6	53.2	56.3	55.6
Panel B: Concentration index based on RTI and Gini index between occupations									
Gini Between-occupations (B)	.391	.322	.313	.391	.337	.316	.391	.384	.372
Concentration index									
RTI (country-specific) (C)	.362	.294	.278	.362	.313	.277	.362	.334	.321
% (C/B)	92.4	91.4	88.7	92.4	92.8	87.5	92.4	87	86.3
RTI (O*NET) (O)	.357	.287	.288	.357	.305	.298	.357	.330	.317
% (O/B)	91.1	89.4	92.1	91.1	90.5	94.3	91.1	85.9	85.3

Note: The decomposition follows the Shapley methodology explained in Equation 3 and 4, using as reference groups occupations defined at the ISCO-88 two-digit level. 'Shares constant' reweights the sample so the share of employment across occupations is the same as the one observed in 2003/04, while 'means constant' rescales earnings within occupations so average earnings of each occupation are the same as those observed in 2003/04.
The Gini and concentration indices are estimated by replacing individuals' earnings by the average of their occupation, using as reference groups occupations defined at the ISCO-88 two-digit level.
Source: Authors' compilation based on data from the PNAD (2003/04 and 2011/12) and PNADC (2018/19).

Table 13.4 RIF decomposition of Gini (×100)

	Country-specific RTI			O*NET RTI		
	(1)	(2)	(3)	(4)	(5)	(6)
	2003/04–2011/12	2011/12–2018/19	2003/04–2018/19	2003/04–2011/12	2011/12–2018/19	2003/04–2018/19
Overall						
Gini, period 1	44.72*** (0.14)	46.94*** (0.17)	46.94*** (0.17)	44.72*** (0.14)	46.94*** (0.17)	46.94*** (0.17)
Counterfactual	49.78*** (0.12)	47.18*** (0.19)	51.63*** (0.14)	49.67*** (0.12)	47.17*** (0.18)	51.65*** (0.14)
Gini, period 2	49.76*** (0.10)	44.72*** (0.14)	49.76*** (0.10)	49.76*** (0.10)	44.72*** (0.14)	49.76*** (0.10)
Difference	-5.04*** (0.16)	2.22*** (0.23)	-2.82*** (0.21)	-5.04*** (0.16)	2.22*** (0.23)	-2.82*** (0.21)
Total composition	0.02 (0.07)	2.46*** (0.09)	1.87*** (0.10)	-0.08 (0.07)	2.45*** (0.08)	1.89*** (0.10)
Pure composition	1.16*** (0.08)	4.05*** (0.10)	6.74*** (0.15)	1.03*** (0.08)	4.05*** (0.10)	6.70*** (0.15)
Specif. error	-1.14*** (0.05)	-1.59*** (0.05)	-4.86*** (0.10)	-1.11*** (0.05)	-1.60*** (0.05)	-4.80*** (0.10)
Total structure	-5.06*** (0.17)	-0.24 (0.25)	-4.69*** (0.23)	-4.96*** (0.17)	-0.23 (0.24)	-4.71*** (0.23)
Pure structure	-5.08*** (0.17)	-0.18 (0.25)	-4.60*** (0.23)	-4.95*** (0.16)	-0.22 (0.24)	-4.64*** (0.23)
Rwg. error	0.02* (0.01)	-0.06*** (0.01)	-0.09*** (0.02)	-0.00 (0.01)	-0.01 (0.01)	-0.07*** (0.02)
Pure composition						
Education	1.87*** (0.06)	2.88*** (0.08)	6.05*** (0.14)	1.73*** (0.06)	2.64*** (0.08)	5.77*** (0.13)
Age	0.18*** (0.02)	0.28*** (0.02)	0.37*** (0.03)	0.17*** (0.02)	0.27*** (0.02)	0.34*** (0.03)
Gender	-0.05*** (0.01)	-0.09*** (0.01)	-0.12*** (0.01)	-0.04*** (0.01)	-0.09*** (0.01)	-0.12*** (0.01)
Race	0.07*** (0.01)	-0.02*** (0.01)	0.15*** (0.03)	0.08*** (0.01)	-0.01 (0.01)	0.17*** (0.03)
Formality	-0.73*** (0.03)	0.60*** (0.05)	0.01 (0.06)	-0.80*** (0.03)	0.58*** (0.04)	-0.05 (0.06)
RTI	-0.19*** (0.03)	0.41*** (0.03)	0.27*** (0.04)	-0.11*** (0.03)	0.67*** (0.03)	0.59*** (0.04)
Specif. error						
Education	-2.86*** (0.10)	-3.38*** (0.17)	-8.00*** (0.19)	-2.89*** (0.10)	-3.47*** (0.16)	-8.11*** (0.21)
Age	-0.18*** (0.04)	0.02 (0.06)	-0.39*** (0.10)	-0.19*** (0.04)	-0.02 (0.06)	-0.42*** (0.10)
Gender	-0.01 (0.04)	0.41*** (0.07)	0.45*** (0.08)	0.02 (0.04)	0.40*** (0.06)	0.50*** (0.08)
Race	-0.13*** (0.05)	-0.26*** (0.07)	0.15 (0.12)	-0.15*** (0.04)	-0.27*** (0.07)	0.08 (0.12)
Formality	-0.43*** (0.04)	-1.32*** (0.06)	-1.69*** (0.09)	-0.42*** (0.03)	-1.28*** (0.06)	-1.67*** (0.09)
RTI	-0.05 (0.03)	-0.23*** (0.06)	-0.65*** (0.08)	0.33*** (0.04)	0.28*** (0.06)	0.53*** (0.09)
Constant	2.52*** (0.12)	3.18*** (0.19)	5.28*** (0.24)	2.19*** (0.13)	2.77*** (0.19)	4.28*** (0.29)

Continued

Table 13.4 *Continued*

	Country-specific RTI			O*NET RTI		
	(1) 2003/04–2011/12	(2) 2011/12–2018/19	(3) 2003/04–2018/19	(4) 2003/04–2011/12	(5) 2011/12–2018/19	(6) 2003/04–2018/19
Pure structure						
Education	0.06 (0.30)	1.05*** (0.37)	1.63*** (0.31)	-0.04 (0.29)	1.09*** (0.36)	1.43*** (0.32)
Age	0.59*** (0.17)	0.08 (0.25)	0.98*** (0.23)	0.57*** (0.17)	0.16 (0.24)	1.03*** (0.23)
Gender	-0.21 (0.16)	-0.48* (0.26)	-0.75*** (0.23)	-0.12 (0.16)	-0.50** (0.25)	-0.71*** (0.23)
Race	-1.10*** (0.17)	-0.13 (0.21)	-1.85*** (0.24)	-1.03*** (0.17)	-0.13 (0.21)	-1.75*** (0.23)
Formality	0.67*** (0.16)	0.20 (0.26)	0.70*** (0.25)	0.68*** (0.16)	-0.11 (0.26)	0.40 (0.25)
RTI	-0.17 (0.15)	0.17 (0.20)	0.28 (0.18)	-1.44*** (0.12)	0.98*** (0.16)	-0.43*** (0.16)
Constant	-4.93*** (0.49)	-1.07** (0.53)	-5.59*** (0.54)	-3.58*** (0.51)	-1.71*** (0.53)	-4.61*** (0.58)
Rwg. error						
Education	-0.01* (0.00)	-0.04*** (0.00)	-0.10*** (0.01)	-0.01 (0.00)	-0.04*** (0.00)	-0.09*** (0.01)
Age	-0.00** (0.00)	-0.01*** (0.00)	-0.00 (0.00)	-0.00** (0.00)	-0.01*** (0.00)	-0.00 (0.00)
Gender	0.00 (0.00)	-0.00*** (0.00)	-0.01*** (0.00)	0.00** (0.00)	0.00*** (0.00)	-0.00 (0.00)
Race	-0.01*** (0.00)	-0.01*** (0.00)	-0.02** (0.01)	-0.01*** (0.00)	-0.01*** (0.00)	-0.02** (0.01)
Formality	-0.01** (0.00)	-0.02*** (0.00)	-0.05*** (0.01)	-0.01* (0.00)	0.01** (0.00)	-0.03*** (0.01)
RTI	0.04*** (0.00)	0.02*** (0.00)	0.10*** (0.01)	0.02*** (0.00)	0.04*** (0.00)	0.07*** (0.01)
Observations	603128	651485	655261	603128	651485	655261

Note: the years 2003, 2011, and 2018 also include data from 2004, 2012, and 2019, respectively. The table reports full results for RIF decompositions of the Gini, using reweighting. For details of the decomposition, see Equation 11.
Bootstrap standard errors with 100 replications in parentheses. * $p < 0.10$, ** $p < 0.05$, *** $p < 0.01$
Source: Authors' compilation based on data from the PNAD (2003/04 and 2011/12) and PNADC (2018/19).

Between 2011/12 and 2018/19, there was a small rise in inequality driven by composition effects. Across the whole period, between 2003/04 and 2018/09, there was a small decrease in inequality, brought about by a large compressing effect in the structural component partially counteracted by changes in worker composition. The results are the same whether we use O*NET or country-specific RTI.

One limitation of our estimation is due to the large and significant specification errors. All of them work in the direction of reducing inequality, and are particularly large when we consider all time periods. This indicates departures from linearity and are possibly a consequence of large changes in the distribution of covariates or institutional factors, such as the increases in minimum wages.

The detailed decomposition shows that the increase in education drives most of the increase in inequality. Changes in the return to education, captured by pure structure effects, have not affected inequality in the first period, and increased it in the second. This differs from the literature, which points to decreases in the education premium as a major source of inequality reduction (Fernandez and Messina 2018; Ferreira et al. 2021). However, the specification error is driven mostly by a large negative impact of education, which is even larger than the effect of education in the pure composition effect. This highlights the fact that changes in the returns to education are linked to increases in the supply of education, as the pure structure effect is not contaminated by the distribution of covariates. Hence, the specification error must be capturing part of this unexplained change driven by increases in the level of education. Therefore, our findings corroborate those of Ferreira et al. (2021), related to the 'paradox of progress'.

Other factors also play a role, although a minor one. We highlight compositional changes in formality, which decreased inequality in the first period, but increased it in the later. There was also a considerable reduction in racial gaps in the first period, which contributed to decrease overall inequality.

Both RTI measures show a small compression composition effect in the first period and a larger inequality-enhancing effect in the later period. The second effect dominates when we analyse changes in the whole period. The country-specific RTI structural effects are not significant apart from the whole period, when it contributed to a slight increase in inequality. This effect, however, is imprecisely measured. The O*NET measures have much larger impacts on inequality, corresponding to a large decrease in the first period and a large increase in the last period. The net effect between 2003/04 and 2018/19 is a reduction in overall inequality from changes in the return to RTI.

As a robustness check, we replicate the work of Ferreira et al. (2021) for the period between 2002 and 2012.[9] Our estimates are similar to theirs, although not exactly. One major difference is that we do not observe the same compression

---

[9] See Tables A1 and A3 in the working paper version of this chapter (Firpo et al. 2021).

effect of potential experience. This difference is possibly due to their use of potential experience,[10] whereas we use age. Second, we include age as three categories, while they use a quadratic term for potential experience.

Most interesting, however, is that the estimated composition and structural effects in their paper are similar to ours when we include RTI, with composition effects contributing slightly to increasing inequality and structure effects contributing to reducing it, especially using the O*NET definition. When we consider a reweighted approach to decomposition, the results are similar, although the effect of pure structure changes in RTI are much larger and counterbalanced by specification error, especially using country-specific RTI.

We further note that when we apply the reweighting methodology to their specification, we find large positive pure structure effects for both education and potential experience that become negative when we include the specification error. This provides further evidence that changes in the composition of workers are indirectly responsible for changes in the earnings structure in the period, something that has been highlighted by structural estimations by Haanwinckel (2018), among others.

Figure 13.2 shows the results of the aggregate decomposition across several percentiles. In the first period, we see that workers in all positions of the earnings distribution had increases in wages, but the benefits were larger at the bottom. Structure effects benefited mostly the bottom percentiles too, decreasing in size and eventually becoming null for the very top. Composition effects were positive throughout the distribution, but especially at the bottom and top of the distribution.

For the period between 2011/12 and 2018/19, however, the picture is very different. The bottom suffered losses that were driven mostly by changes in structure. The rest of the distribution had small gains. Interestingly, the top 25 per cent observed two conflicting tendencies. On the one hand, composition effects contributed to increased earnings. On the other, structure effects reduced earnings significantly. On net, their gains were similar to the middle of the distribution.

Figure 13.3 shows the results of a detailed decomposition of the pure structural effect using the RIF-regression methodology with reweighting. In panel (a) we observe the changes in log earnings in the first period. In the bottom of the distribution, the formality and education effects dominate, followed by contributions from race and gender gaps. Structure effects are almost null in the 20th and 25th percentiles, the region where the minimum wage is binding. In the 30th to 50th percentiles of the distribution, education has an small negative effect, while formality, gender, race, and RTI contribute to increase earnings. In the top 10 per cent, education again contributes to increases in earnings, while gender and

---

[10] Defined as age minus years of schooling minus 6.

(a)

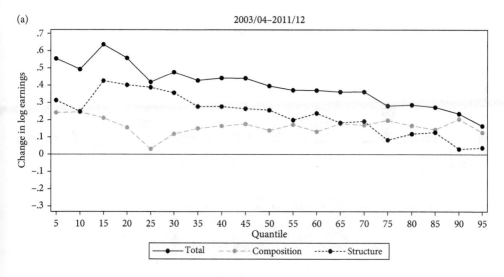

(b)

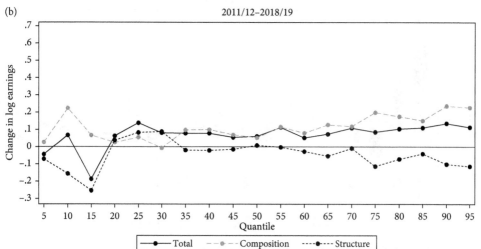

Figure 13.2 Aggregate decomposition by quantile

Note: These figures plot the changes in log earnings observed for the 5th to 95th quantiles, as well as the aggregated composition and structure effects estimated using RIF decompositions with reweighting (see Equation 5).

Source: Authors' compilation based on data from the PNAD (2003/04 and 2011/12) and PNADC (2018/19).

race have negative effects. RTI has negative impacts between the 50th to the 90th percentiles, but a positive impact in the very top.

In the period between 2011/12 and 2018/19 we see much larger, but more varied structural effects. The very bottom percentiles observe gains that are driven mostly

(a)

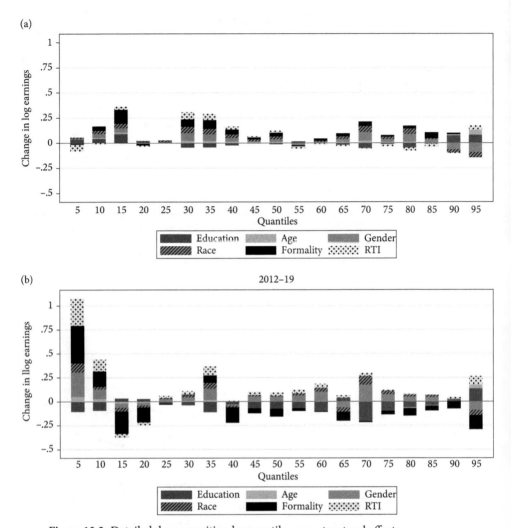

Figure 13.3 Detailed decomposition by quantile, pure structural effects

Note: these figures plot the contribution of each factor to changes in log earnings observed for the 5th to 95th quantiles, based on the detailed decomposition of pure structural effects. The decomposition relies on RIF regressions with reweighting (see Equation 5).

Source: Authors' compilation based on data from the PNAD (2003/04 and 2011/12) and PNADC (2018/19).

by formality and RTI, although the benefits of formality become negative there after. This is possibly related to a reduction in the gap between formal and informal workers. The RTI, however, indicates benefits throughout the wage distribution, with a few exceptions. The positive effects of changes in the return to education are only seen at the top of the distribution.

13.6 Conclusion

This chapter investigates the role that occupations and their task content play in explaining trends in labour market polarization and earnings inequality in Brazil. We use information on country-specific job task content to construct measures of RTI. We show that this measure is highly correlated with average earnings across occupations and that changes in the Brazilian economy led to a decline in average RTI between 2003 and 2019.

We do not find evidence of employment polarization in the period, and polarization in earnings is more associated with considerable pro-poor growth between 2003 and 2012 and pro-rich growth between 2012 and 2019. This was reflected in overall earnings inequality, which declined in the first period but marginally increased in the second.

Decomposition exercises show that the drop in inequality observed in the first period is mainly attributable to changes in the earnings structure, and particularly associated with large declines in the education premium. In the second period, composition effects dominated and resulted in increased inequality. The main driver is again education. The routine-task content of occupations helps to account for part of the change in inequality, although to a much smaller extent. In particular, the reduction in average RTI increased inequality, while changes in its return had mixed effects in the period, decreasing inequality in the first period and reducing it in the second. Moreover, changes in RTI reduce the overall contribution of education to inequality, although this factor remains highly significant after accounting for the occupation's routine-task content.

References

Acemoglu, D., and D. Autor (2011). 'Skills, Tasks and Technologies: Implications for Employment and Earnings'. In O. Ashenfelter and D. Card (eds), *Handbook of Labor Economics*, vol. 4, pp. 1043–171. Amsterdam: Elsevier. https://doi.org/10.1016/S0169-7218(11)02410-5

Autor, D. (2013). 'The Task Approach to Labor Markets: An Overview'. Working Paper 18711. Cambridge, MA: National Bureau of Economic Research. https://doi.org/10.3386/w18711

Autor, D., and D. Dorn (2013). 'The Growth of Low-Skill Service Jobs and the Polarisation of the US Labor Market'. *American Economic Review*, 103(5): 1553–97. https://doi.org/10.1257/aer.103.5.1553

Autor, D.H., F. Levy, and R.J. Murnane (2003). 'The Skill Content of Recent Technological Change: An Empirical Exploration'. *Quarterly Journal of Economics*, 118(4): 1279–333. https://doi.org/10.1162/003355303322552801

Barros, R., M. De Carvalho, S. Franco, and R. Mendonça. (2010). 'Markets, the State, and the Dynamics of Inequality in Brazil'. In L.F. Lopez-Calva and N. Lustig (eds), *Declining Inequality in Latin America: A Decade of Progress*. Washington, DC: Brookings Institution Press.

Bourguignon, F., F. Ferreira, and N. Lustig. 2005. *The Microeconomics of Income Distribution Dynamics in East Asia and Latin America*. Washington, DC: World Bank Publications Oxford University Press.

Engbom, N., and C. Moser (2021). 'Earnings Inequality and the Minimum Wage: Evidence from Brazil'. Working Paper 28831. Cambridge, MA: National Bureau of Economic Research. https://doi.org/10.3386/w28831

Fernández, Manuel and Messina, Julián (2018). 'Skill Premium, Labor Supply, and Changes in the Structure of Wages in Latin America'. *Journal of Development Economics*, 135(1): 555–73.

Ferreira, F.H., S.P. Firpo, and J. Messina (2021). 'Labor Market Experience and Falling Earnings Inequality in Brazil: 1995–2012'. *World Bank Economic Review*. https://doi.org/10.1093/wber/lhab005

Firpo, S., and A. Portella (2019). 'Decline in Wage Inequality in Brazil: A Survey'. World Bank Policy Research Working Paper 9096. Washington, DC: World Bank. https://doi.org/10.1596/1813-9450-9096

Firpo, S., N.M. Fortin, and T. Lemieux (2009). 'Unconditional Quantile Regressions'. *Econometrica*, 77(3): 953–73. https://doi.org/10.3982/ECTA6822

Firpo, S., N.M. Fortin, and T. Lemieux (2011). 'Occupational Tasks and Changes in the Wage Structure'. IZA Discussion Paper 5542. Bonn: IZA.

Firpo, S.P., N.M. Fortin, and T. Lemieux (2018). 'Decomposing Wage Distributions Using Recentered Influence Function Regressions'. *Econometrics*, 6(2): 28. https://doi.org/10.3390/econometrics6020028

Firpo, S., A. Portella, F. Riva, G. Úbida, (2021). 'The Changing Nature of Work and Inequality in Brazil (2003-19): A Descriptive Analysis'. WIDER Working Paper 162/2021. Helsinki: UNU-WIDER. https://doi.org/10.35188/UNU-WIDER/2021/102-0

Fortin, N., T. Lemieux, and S. Firpo (2011). 'Decomposition Methods in Economics'. In O. Ashenfelter and D. Card (eds), *Handbook of Labor Economics*, vol 4. Amsterdam: Elsevier. https://doi.org/10.1016/S0169-7218(11)00407-2

Goos, M., and A. Manning (2007). 'Lousy and Lovely Jobs: The Rising Polarisation of Work in Britain'. *Review of Economics and Statistics*, 89(1): 118–33. https://doi.org/10.1162/rest.89.1.118

Goos, M., A. Manning, and A. Salomons (2014). 'Explaining Job Polarisation: Routine-Biased Technological Change and Offshoring'. *American Economic Review*, 104(8): 2509–26. https://doi.org/10.1257/aer.104.8.2509

Gradín, C., and S. Schotte (2020). 'Implications of the Changing Nature of Work for Employment and Inequality in Ghana'. WIDER Working Paper 119/2020. Helsinki: UNU-WIDER. https://doi.org/10.35188/UNU-WIDER/2020/876-4

Haanwinckel, D. (2018). 'Supply, Demand, Institutions, and Firms: A Theory of Labor Market Sorting and the Wage Distribution'. Mimeo.

Lewandowski, P., A. Park, W. Hardy, and D. Yang (2019). 'Technology, Skills, and Globalization: Explaining International Differences in Routine and Nonroutine Work Using Survey Data'. IBS Working Papers 04/2019. Warsaw: Instytut Badan Strukturalnych.

Lewandowski, P., A. Park, and S. Schotte (2020). 'The Global Distribution of Routine and Non-Routine Work'. IZA Discussion Paper 13384. Bonn: IZA.

Maloney, W.F., and C. Molina (2016). 'Are Automation and Trade Polarizing Developing Country Labor Markets, Too?'. World Bank Policy Research Working Paper 7922. Washington, DC: World Bank. https://doi.org/10.1596/1813-9450-7922

Maurizio, R., and A.P. Monsalvo (2021). 'Changes in Occupations and Their Task Content: Implications for Employment and Inequality in Argentina, 2003–19'. WIDER Working Paper 15/2021. Helsinki: UNU-WIDER. https://doi.org/10.35188/UNU-WIDER/2021/949-5

Neri, M. (2021). 'Changes in the New Millennium?'. In C. Gradín, M. Leibbrandt, and F. Tarp (eds), *Inequality in the Developing World*. Oxford: Oxford University Press.

O*NET (2003). O*NET 5.0 Database. September 2003 release. Washington, DC: US Department of Labor.

Sebastian, R. (2018). 'Explaining Job Polarisation in Spain from a Task Perspective'. *SERIEs*, 9(2): 215–48. https://doi.org/10.1007/s13209-018-0177-1

Shorrocks, A.F. (2013). 'Decomposition Procedures for Distributional Analysis: A Unified Framework Based on the Shapley Value'. *Journal of Economic Inequality*, 11(1): 99. https://doi.org/10.1007/s10888-011-9214-z

14
Chile

Employment and Inequality Trends

Gabriela Zapata-Román

14.1 Introduction

A key issue in development economics has been to understand the effects of technological changes in the labour market, in terms of their impact on both wage inequality and job creation and destruction. The literature of the late 1990s suggested that technological change was skill-biased and would favour high-skill workers and replace routine tasks. Skill-biased technological change (SBTC) increases the marginal productivity of skilled labour in relation to unskilled labour, and consequently its demand and salary premium, which leads to an increase in wage inequality (Berman et al. 1998).

More recent literature has built on Autor et al.'s (2003) hypothesis, which argues that technological change has two effects on labour markets: first, it replaces workers in performing routine cognitive and manual tasks that can be achieved by following explicit rules (which can be automated); second, it complements workers in the performance of non-routine problem solving and complex communications. Therefore, technological change will lead to a lower demand not necessarily for all low-skilled workers, only for those involved in routine tasks that can now be replaced with the use of technology. At the same time, this can lead to a greater demand for workers whose tasks are complementary to computerization, such as people who work in occupations where non-routine cognitive skills are required (Acemoglu and Restrepo 2017), which are generally measured at the occupational level (Firpo et al. 2011).

The relative share of cognitive and manual routine jobs has declined over time in the US and other developed economies (Autor et al. 2003; Goos et al. 2014; Jensen and Kletzer 2010; Michaels et al. 2013), contributing to wage polarization and therefore higher levels of inequality. While this is true for advanced economies, there is evidence suggesting that developing countries and emerging economies are not following the same trends. Surveys in China and some Central and Eastern European countries show that the proportion of people employed in routine-intensive occupations has increased in recent decades (Du and Park 2017; Hardy et al. 2018).

Gabriela Zapata-Román, *Chile: Employment and Inequality Trends*. In: *Tasks, Skills, and Institutions*. Edited by Carlos Gradín, Piotr Lewandowski, Simone Schotte, and Kunal Sen, Oxford University Press. © UNU-WIDER (2023).
DOI: 10.1093/oso/9780192872241.003.0014

Inequality trends also behave differently in developing countries. While most of the developed world has experienced rising inequality since the 2000s, most countries in Latin America have followed the opposite pattern. Messina and Silva (2019) argue that the absence of skill-biased technological change and little evidence of job polarization in Latin America have facilitated the decline of wage inequality in the region. Job polarization occurs when the relative demand for well-paid skilled jobs and low-paid low-skilled jobs increases, diminishing the relative demand in the middle of the distribution. While skilled jobs are characterized by the performance of non-routine cognitive tasks, low-skilled jobs consist mostly of non-routine manual tasks. Middle-skill jobs, on the other hand, commonly involve executing routine manual and cognitive tasks. Messina and Silva (2019) found that wages expanded rapidly in low-paying occupations relative to high-paying occupations, while technological advances that complement skill-intensive occupations predict the opposite.

Building on these important bodies of literature, this chapter investigates the factors behind variations in earnings inequality in Chile between 2000 and 2017, exploring how the nature of work and the structural composition of employment have changed over time, and which factors have contributed to these changes. It analyses the impact of the changes in occupational structure and the routinization of work on earnings dispersion. Finally, it decomposes changes in earnings inequality to understand whether these changes are due to variations in the characteristics of occupations (i.e. gender, age, years of schooling, and the different skills or routine-task intensity contents of occupations) or to changes in rewards depending on these characteristics. The empirical analysis builds on the Chilean household income surveys for 2000, 2006, and 2017 (Encuesta de Caracterización Económica Nacional; CASEN) matched with the skill content of job indicators at the occupational level (ISCO-88) obtained from two different sources: the US estimation of tasks derived from the US Occupation Information Network survey (O*NET 2003); and the country-specific values of standard task measures at the ISCO-88 two-digit level estimated for Chile by Lewandowski et al. (2020), using information on the task content of occupations from PIAAC data, collected by the OECD (2014/15).

The remainder of the chapter is structured as follows: the next section describes the data used. The third section describes the country context, the main changes in inequality in Chile, and the institutional factors that might have had an impact over these trends. The fourth section examines the role of tasks and skills in changing earnings inequality over time and provides evidence to discard the hypothesis of occupational and earnings polarization. The final empirical section analyses the role of occupational changes in shaping the evolution of inequality by performing two inequality decompositions, that is, the Shapley decomposition and the RIF regression decomposition.

14.2 Data

This study draws on the Chilean household survey CASEN in three waves: 2000, 2006, and 2017. This is a cross-sectional household survey that uses a multistage stratified sampling design, representative at the national and regional levels. The CASEN survey holds a wealth of information on the demographics and income sources of all household members aged 14 and above. This analysis focuses on a subsample of the working-age population, this being individuals aged between 15 and 64 years active in the labour market as employees, employers, or self-employed.

The income concept used is labour earnings from the main occupation. This includes earnings from dependent and independent work (cash and in kind), net of direct taxes and social security contributions, while also incorporating income from self-production. This income concept was chosen since the occupational data are associated with the main occupation. The survey provides net monthly earnings in Chilean pesos for each year, which have been transformed into weekly earnings. These have been corrected to observe real earnings at November 2017 prices in purchasing power parity (PPP) to ensure comparability over time and across countries.

We divide the analysis into two subperiods—2000–06, and 2006–17. The selection of these years is based on the trajectory that income inequality has followed in Chile. From 2000 inequality has been on a downward trajectory, with the largest drop between 2000 and 2006. After 2006 a milder drop in inequality has been observed, since it remained almost constant until 2012, then it fell and rose slightly between 2015 and 2017.

14.3 Inequality trends

Chile is commonly described as a successful case of rapid economic growth, sound economic management, macroeconomic stability, export orientation, and bold structural reforms such as trade and foreign investment liberalization. Most of these pro-market reforms were implemented during the military dictatorship in the 1980s, including a bundle of social reforms that privatized education, health, and pensions.

The return to democracy in 1990 was a period of rising private investment, high GDP growth (average growth rates of more than 7 per cent between 1991 and 1998), and job creation that helped to reverse the rises in unemployment and depression of real wages from the dictatorship period in the 1980s (Contreras and Ffrench-Davis 2012). Rapid growth, favoured by high commodity prices, moved Chile from having the third-lowest GDP per capita in South America, US$4,511, in 1990 to taking the lead in the region from 2010, reaching $25,155 in 2019 (World Bank 2020a).

Good economic results came along with a poverty reduction of 30 percentage points during the 1990s (from 68.5 per cent in 1990 to 37.6 per cent in 2000). After the year 2000, the poverty rate reduced further, reaching 8.6 per cent in 2017 (MDS and PNUD 2020). This was accompanied by increased social spending and the creation of a social protection system, which has played a key role in overcoming extreme poverty. In this period there was also a reduction in the level of informality, or the proportion of wage earners and self-employed workers not making contributions to the pension system. From 40.6 per cent in 1990 (Perticará and Celhay 2010) to 32 per cent in 2015 (OECD 2018). Additionally, sustained increases in the real minimum wage—at an average annual rate of 4 per cent during the 1990s and of 3 per cent during the 2000s—have contributed to improving the quality of life of the Chilean population in the last few decades.

Despite these positive developments, Chile still displays persistent inequality of income and wealth. The Gini coefficient for both monetary incomes (adjusting for transfers) and net wealth places Chile as the most unequal country in the OECD, and it ranks 28th among the countries with the highest inequality in the world, preceded only by other countries in Latin America and sub-Saharan Africa (OECD 2020; World Bank 2020b). Inequality in Chile is characterized by high concentration at the top of the income distribution, due to an elite that concentrates most of the national income—60.2 per cent by the top decile and 27.8 per cent by the top 1 per cent—combined with much lower inequality among the rest of the distribution (survey and tax data; WID 2020).

High growth rates experienced by the country in the 1990s slowed down starting in the year 2000, moving to average rates of 4.3 per cent in the 2000s and 3.2 per cent between 2011 and 2017 (World Bank 2020a). This was accompanied by a reduction of inequality, the Gini coefficient of earnings fell from 0.514 in 2000 to 0.443 in 2017,[1] with the largest drop of 0.071 points between 2000 and 2006 (see Table 14.1). The 90–10 interquartile ratio confirms a gain for the bottom decile relative to the wealthiest in the period 2000–17, but more substantially between 2006 and 2017. A similar development is observed between the top decile and the median. Since 2000, the income shares of the wealthiest 10 per cent have shrunk compared to the middle of the distribution. The 50–10 ratio illustrates the gap between the median and the poorest 10 per cent, which, interestingly, increased until 2006 and only declined slightly after 2006—suggesting larger gains for the middle of the distribution between 2000 and 2006 and pro-poor growth only after 2006.

---

[1] Own calculations based on information of the CASEN Survey years 2000, 2006, and 2017 from the subsample of active people aged 15–64.

Table 14.1 Summary inequality indices and inter-quantile ratios

	Summary indices				Inter-quantile ratios		
	2000	2006	2017		2000	2006	2017
Var (log earn)	0.806	0.761	0.658	ln(q90)-ln(q10)	2.157	2.120	1.897
Gini (log earn)	0.098	0.094	0.081	ln(q90)-ln(q50)	1.226	1.165	1.050
Gini (earn)	0.514	0.475	0.443	ln(q50)-ln(q10)	0.931	0.956	0.847

Source: Author's construction based on CASEN (2000, 2006, 2017).

Growth incidence curves, which show income growth rates between two points in time at each percentile of the distribution, confirm above average growth from the 20th percentile to the median of the earnings distribution in the period 2000–06, and negative growth for the top quintile (from the 80th percentile), as well as for the bottom decile (see Figure 8 in Zapata-Román (2021)). This is very different from the growth pattern of the period 2006–17, for which we observe strong growth for the bottom 30 per cent and below-average growth for the top 30 per cent. This last trend at the extremes of the distribution would have been inequality-reducing.

In sum we observe a general reduction in earnings inequality since 2000, which benefited mainly the middle of the distribution in the period 2000–06 and the bottom deciles (pro-poor growth) after 2006.

14.4 Occupational trends

Over recent decades, the Chilean population has become more skilled, due to a large structural expansion in education that has increased school coverage since the 1980s and access to higher education since the 1990s (UNDP 2019). This rise in schooling has been reflected in sectorial changes in the occupational structure, displacing workers from low-skill occupations such as skilled agricultural, craft and trade, and elementary occupations,[2] towards jobs demanding non-routine higher skills, including professionals and technicians. There has also been a significant increase in the share of services and sales workers, who tend to perform routine manual and cognitive tasks. The services sector is the one that has grown the most since the 1990s and currently employs 70 per cent of the country's workforce and 86 per cent of female workers (Solimano and Zapata-Román 2019).

When examining earnings across occupations, we observe significant differences in returns favouring high-skill occupations in Figure 14.1 (top part). This

---

[2] These occupations are those with the lowest average years of education; see Figure A5 in Zapata-Román (2021).

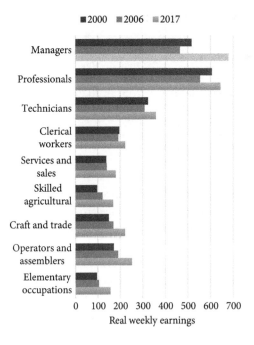

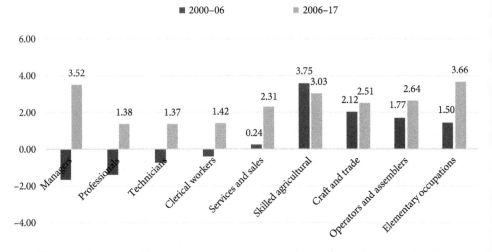

Figure 14.1 Real weekly earnings and average annual growth rate by occupational groups

Source: Author's illustration based on CASEN (2000, 2006, 2017).

translates into earnings ratios of 5.4 and 6.3 times in 2000 between people in managerial and professional positions and those in elementary occupations, respectively. However, these gaps have been gradually shortening over the years to 4.4 and 4.5 times in 2017.

As shown in Figure 14.1 (bottom part), changes in occupational earnings have had a positive equalizing effect, with more substantial gains favouring lower-skill occupations such as skilled agricultural workers, craft and related trade workers, plant and machine operators, and elementary occupations. We also observe this equalizing effect at the top of the skill premium, with the earnings of managers and professionals becoming closer. Despite these positive changes in inequality, there are still substantial differences between the rewards of low- and high-skill occupations that are not necessarily related to formal skills. For example, in 2017, people employed as technicians and clerks—with a similar level of education as managers—had salaries equivalent to half and one-third of those of managers. This suggests that other factors besides education might play a more decisive role in determining the earnings of these well-rewarded occupations.

14.5 The role of tasks and skills in changing earnings inequality over time

14.5.1 The RTI of jobs

Up until now, we have implicitly associated skill levels with ISCO-88 one-digit occupations and educational attainment. In this section we incorporate a formal task-based approach to explore job polarization and changes in earnings inequality in Chile. We compare the results obtained by two different methods of imputing RTI to occupations classified using the ISCO-88 two-digit level: the O*NET standard values and the country- and occupation-specific values of standard task measures predicted for Chile by Lewandowski et al. (2020), using PIAAC data (OECD 2014/15).

Country-specific RTI measures are, in general, lower than O*NET measures. This is more noticeable particularly for occupations at the extremes of the distribution (elementary occupations and professionals and managers). For sales, at the centre of the skill distribution, a higher routine content is predicted using country-specific RTI measures, as shown in Table 14.2.

Figure 14.2 displays RTI by earnings percentile and shows a solid monotonic relationship between RTI and earnings percentiles using both the O*NET and the country-specific measures in 2000, which flattened at the bottom in subsequent years and slightly increased before the middle of the distribution in 2006 and more markedly in 2017. An inverted U shape, with the routine-task-intensive occupations dominating close to the centre of the earnings distribution, is only

Table 14.2 O*NET and country-specific RTI, average by year

	2000		2006		2017	
	O*NET	Country RTI	O*NET	Country RTI	O*NET	Country RTI
Managers	−1.19	−0.42	−1.21	−0.42	−1.20	−0.42
Professionals	−1.20	−0.65	−1.17	−0.66	−1.15	−0.64
Technicians	−0.45	−0.28	−0.46	−0.25	−0.44	−0.23
Clerks	0.16	0.07	0.14	0.10	0.16	0.15
Service & sales	−0.21	0.29	−0.21	0.29	−0.21	0.28
Skilled agricultural	0.46	0.51	0.44	0.51	0.39	0.51
Craft & trade	1.17	0.37	1.16	0.37	1.16	0.36
Operators and assemblers	1.17	0.62	1.15	0.61	1.13	0.66
Elementary occupations	1.15	0.70	1.09	0.70	1.15	0.69
Total	0.31	0.23	0.36	0.27	0.25	0.21

Source: Author's construction based on CASEN (2000, 2006, 2017).

more apparent in 2017 with both measures. However, it is more compressed with country-specific RTI. Overall, average RTI has declined over the whole period, whether measured using O*NET or the country-specific measures, despite an increase in 2006 (see more details of RTI at ISCO-88 two-digit level in Table A3 in Zapata-Román (2021)). As the RTI values are estimated at ISCO-88 two-digit level and do not change over time, this average decline in the RTI of jobs is driven by restructuring the labour force away from more-routine and towards less-routine occupations. Interestingly, we observe this 'reshuffling' at the bottom and the top of the distribution. At the same time, the average RTI of workers in middle-income occupations has remained relatively unchanged, leading to an increasingly hump-shaped pattern (visibly, especially for O*NET).

14.5.2 Job polarization

Simple test for job polarization

The polarization phenomenon predicts an increase in the relative demand for well-paid skilled jobs (consisting of non-routine cognitive tasks), and low-paid low-skill jobs (linked to non-routine manual tasks), diminishing the relative demand in the middle of the distribution, where routine manual and cognitive tasks are commonly executed. Therefore, jobs that would be displaced by technology include routine tasks that require precision, such as manual craft and bookkeeping jobs. Jobs that are complementary to technology, such as skilled professional and managerial jobs, consist of non-routine tasks. Other non-routine

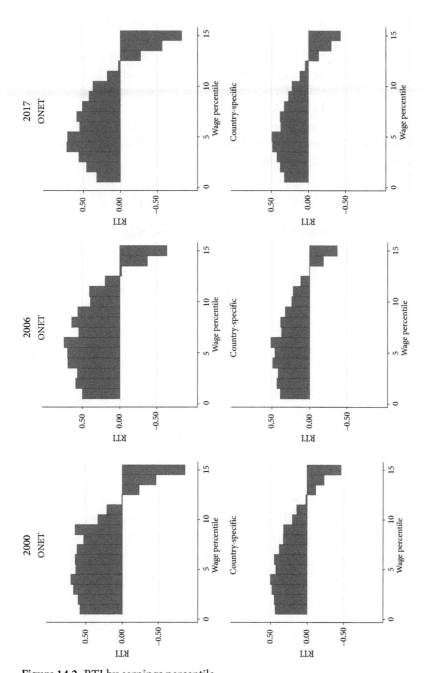

Figure 14.2 RTI by earnings percentile
Source: Author's illustration based on CASEN (2000, 2006, 2017).

manual jobs, such as cleaning, which are not directly affected by technology, might rise due to the effects of technology in other parts of the economy (Autor 2019; Goos and Manning 2007).

To test for job polarization, we regress the log change in employment share (equation 1), and the change in log mean earnings (equation 2) between survey waves, on initial log mean weekly earnings and its square, testing the significance of the parameters following Goos and Manning (2007) and Sebastian (2018). Both equations are estimated by weighting each occupation—at the three-digit level— by its initial employment share to avoid the results being biased by compositional changes in small occupation groups.

$$\Delta \log E_{j,t} = \alpha_0 + \alpha_1 \log \left(y_{j,t-1}\right) + \alpha_2 \log \left(y_{j,t-1}\right)^2 \qquad (1)$$

$$\Delta \log \left(y_{j,t}\right) = \beta_0 + \beta_1 \log \left(y_{j,t-1}\right) + \beta_2 \log \left(y_{j,t-1}\right)^2 \qquad (2)$$

where $\Delta \log E_j$ is the change in the (log) employment share of occupation j between survey wave $t-1$ and t, $\log \left(y_{j,t-1}\right)$ is the logarithm of the mean labour earnings in occupation j in survey wave $t-1$, and $\log \left(y_{j,t-1}\right)^2$ is the square of initial (log) mean labour earnings. The same model is also estimated using (log) change in earnings as the dependent variable $\Delta \log y_j$.

A U-shaped pattern of polarization implies that the first coefficient is significantly negative, with a positive quadratic coefficient, indicating that employment and/or earnings decline in middle-income occupations while increasing at the extremes of the income distribution. We find this pattern in both periods for changes in employment shares, but not for changes in log mean earnings, although none of these findings are statistically significant, as observed in Table 14.3. The opposite (significant) pattern (inverted U-shaped growth) is found for changes in log mean earnings in 2000–06, suggesting that real earnings grew more in the middle of the distribution.

We can also observe these trends when plotting log changes in employment shares and changes in mean log earnings against occupations at ISCO-88 three-digit levels ranked by earnings skill percentile (see Figure 13 in Zapata-Román (2021)). The period (2000–06) shows a small displacement of employment away from high-paid occupations towards middle- and low-income occupations, with even smaller gains in earnings for low- and middle-income occupations and bigger losses at the top (subtle inverted U shape). The final period (2006–17) describes a displacement of employment at the bottom and the median of the skill distribution towards the best-rewarded occupations, and higher gains in earnings before the median and at the top of the skill distribution.

Table 14.3 Regressions for job and earnings polarization

Variables	Log change in employment share		Change in (log) mean wage	
	2000–2006	2006–2017	2000–2006	2006–2017
(log) mean weekly earnings (initial period)	−0.459 (0.727)	−0.076 (1.266)	0.629** (0.272)	−0.015 (0.362)
Sq. (log) mean weekly earnings (initial period)	0.031 (0.069)	0.032 (0.120)	−0.069*** (0.025)	−0.009 (0.034)
Constant	1.466 (1.891)	−0.478 (3.306)	−1.353* (0.726)	0.601 (0.966)
Observations	113	113	113	113
R-squared	0.069	0.127	0.236	0.245
Adj. R-squared	0.052	0.111	0.222	0.231
F test	0.027	0.001	0.000	0.000

Note: Robust standard errors in parentheses; *** $p<0.01$, ** $p<0.05$, * $p<0.1$.
Source: Author's construction based on CASEN (2000, 2006, 2017).

Regression of changes in employment and earnings on the level of routine intensity

Now we test for job polarization by estimating a quadratic regression in which we try to explain the variance of employment and earnings using our measures of the RTI of jobs (equations 3 and 4). Table 14.4 presents the results of the ordinary least squares (OLS) quadratic regressions of changes in employment share and log mean earnings for the periods 2000–06, and 2006–17, along with the initial level of routine intensity of each occupation (using country-specific RTI measures), at the three-digit occupational level. A negative relationship would be expected between the two variables, indicating that higher RTI leads to larger declines in employment and earnings.

$$\Delta \log E_{j,t} = \delta_0 + \delta_1 RTI_j + \delta_2 (RTI_j)^2 \tag{3}$$

$$\Delta \log (y_{j,t}) = \varphi_0 + \varphi_1 RTI_j + \varphi_2 (RTI_j)^2 \tag{4}$$

Comparing the results of the OLS regressions, we obtain the expected negative and significant relationship in employment shares in the period 2006–17, indicating that a positive employment displacement is expected as the routine content of tasks increases. In earnings, we find a positive and significant relationship between changes in mean log wage and the RTI measure in both periods, suggesting that earnings tend to increase more in more-routine occupations, which is not observed in employment in 2006–17. Overall, the routine content of tasks explains an important part of the variability of earnings, and to a lesser extent the variability of employment (higher R-squared in earnings regressions). Therefore,

Table 14.4 OLS regression of changes in employment share and in log mean wage, at the initial level of routine intensity, using country-specific RTI

	Log change in employment share		Change in (log) mean wage	
	2000–2006	2006–2017	2000–2006	2006–2017
Variables				
Country-specific RTI	0.197***	−0.227***	0.093***	0.105***
	(0.067)	(0.067)	(0.034)	(0.021)
Sq. Country-specific RTI	−0.154*	0.156	−0.045	0.036
	(0.092)	(0.101)	(0.051)	(0.033)
Constant	−0.038	−0.056	0.027	0.276***
	(0.045)	(0.052)	(0.018)	(0.014)
Observations	113	113	113	113
R-squared	**0.095**	**0.084**	**0.124**	**0.289**
Adj. R-squared	0.079	0.067	0.108	0.277
F test	0.016	0.004	0.029	0.000

Note: Robust standard errors in parentheses; *** $p<0.01$, ** $p<0.05$, * $p<0.1$.
Source: Author's illustration based on CASEN (2000, 2006, 2017).

in this period of declining earnings inequality (pro-poor growth) the degree of routinization of occupations seems to play a significant role.

14.6 The role of occupational changes in shaping the evolution of inequality

In this section, we use two decomposition methods to investigate the role of occupations in explaining changes in earnings inequality in Chile. We decompose total inequality to understand whether its changes are due to variations in the characteristics of occupations (i.e. average years of schooling, different skills, or RTI contents) or to changes in the reward of occupations. Then, we examine the role played by the RTI of occupations in shaping inequality.

14.6.1 Shapley decomposition

The Shapley decomposition allows us to disaggregate total inequality, measured using the Gini index, into inequality between and within occupations (Shorrocks 2013). As shown in Table 14.5, both components are very similar. Despite the similarity, we observe a dominance of inequality within occupations in 2006 and 2017. This indicates that inequality variations are mostly associated with changes in factors not related to the occupations' characteristics, such as differences in

Table 14.5 Shapley decomposition—Gini between occupations and concentration index

	Actual			Shares constant			Means constant		
Gini	**2000**	**2006**	**2017**	**2000**	**2006**	**2017**	**2000**	**2006**	**2017**
Overall	0.517	0.477	0.444	0.517	0.491	0.439	0.517	0.508	0.503
Shapley decomposition									
Between occupations	0.272	0.222	0.220	0.272	0.232	0.209	0.272	0.261	0.292
Share %	53	46	50	53	47	48	53	51	58
Within occupations	0.245	0.255	0.223	0.245	0.259	0.230	0.245	0.247	0.211
Share %	47	54	50	47	53	52	47	49	42
Gini between occupations	0.383	0.322	0.313	0.383	0.336	0.301	0.383	0.370	0.397
Concentration index									
RTI (country-specific)	0.340	0.280	0.262	0.340	0.291	0.251	0.340	0.331	0.352
% Ratio	89	87	84	89	87	84	89	89	89
RTI (O*NET)	0.309	0.245	0.250	0.309	0.264	0.232	0.309	0.294	0.329
% Ratio	81	76	80	81	79	77	81	80	83

Source: Author's construction based on CASEN (2000, 2006, 2017).

skills, or elements that affect a worker's productivity in performing similar jobs. Higher within-occupation earnings dispersion might also be reinforced by other unknown elements that favour workers unequally, such as family and contact networks or financial and social capital, which are very relevant elements in the Chilean labour market.

We decompose the non-monotonic trajectory of inequality between occupations into variations in mean earnings (holding occupation shares constant) and changes in occupational shares (holding mean earnings constant). When holding occupation shares constant, changes in inequality will be associated with changes in the remuneration of skills, tasks, or other job characteristics (return effect). When holding mean earnings constant, shifts in inequality will be associated with movements of workers to jobs with different skill or RTI content (composition effect). Table 14.5 (top part) presents the results of the decomposition. We observe that holding the occupational shares constant results in a reduction in between-occupations inequality (in levels but in shares). Whereas holding the mean earnings constant has a more noticeable inequality-enhancing effect. Therefore, the decline in inequality between occupations from 2000 to 2017 is driven by changes in average earnings, not in shares—despite all the structural changes in employment the country has experienced, such as increasing average years of education, displacement of workers from low-skill occupations towards jobs demanding non-routine higher skills, reduction of informal jobs, and increasing female participation.

Table 14.5 also presents the results of the concentration index. This index provides a measure of how low (high) average remuneration by occupation is correlated with a high (low) degree of job routinization. The concentration index is equivalent to the Gini index when RTI is perfectly correlated to average earnings. Hence, the ratio between both indexes is a measure of the association between RTI and average earnings. In Chile the concentration index is very high, and it is higher using country-specific RTIs instead of O*NET measures. The estimation shows that average earnings across occupations have become less unequal over time, and the strong monotonic correlation with RTI has been reducing, shown by a lower concentration index when shares are kept constant. When means are kept constant, we observe a slightly higher rank correlation and almost no variation between those years—indicating that the relationship between the routine intensity of occupations and average earnings has not weakened.

14.6.2 RIF regression decomposition

In the final section, following Firpo et al. (2011, 2018), we use the RIF regression approach to decompose inequality differences into a composition effect (changes due to varying worker characteristics, for example age, gender, schooling, formality, and occupations) and a structure effect (changes in the return to those characteristics). This decomposition also allows us to further divide these two components into the contribution of each covariate.

Table 14.6 presents the results of the RIF decomposition of the Gini coefficient. In both periods, we observe falls in overall inequality mainly driven by changes in the earnings structure or return effect. In 2000–06, the return effect explains 60 per cent of the inequality reduction, with a composition effect also contributing to this inequality reduction (negative sign). The bottom part of the table shows the contribution of each covariate to each effect. The covariates used in the RIF regressions are age (in three categories, 15–24, 45–65, and 25–44 omitted), sex (male omitted), education (seven categories of complete education, with primary complete omitted), informality (having a formal job omitted), and RTI (continuous variable), plus all of their interactions. We cannot distinguish the associated characteristics behind the equalizing effect in the wage structure since most of it is in the constant. Education, routinization, and informality contribute to the reduction in inequality in the composition effect. In this period, there is a larger expansion of secondary education, average RTI increases—indicating a displacement of workers towards more-routine occupations—and there is a reduction in informality. In the last period (2006–17), the earnings structure or return effect is more relevant in explaining the fall in earnings inequality, compensating even for

Table 14.6 RIF regression decomposition

	Country-specific RTI				O*NET RTI			
	2000–2006		2006–2017		2000–2006		2006–2017	
	Estimate	SE	Estimate	SE	Estimate	SE	Estimate	SE
Final Gini	0.4766		0.4435		0.4766		0.4435	
Initial Gini	0.5172		0.4766		0.5172		0.4767	
Total change	−0.0406	(0.0100)	−0.0331	(0.0050)	−0.0406	(0.0100)	−0.0332	(0.0050)
Reweighting								
Composition	−0.0163	(0.0033)	0.0121	(0.0017)	−0.0177	(0.0030)	0.0127	(0.0016)
Earning structure	−0.0243	(0.0081)	−0.0451	(0.0048)	−0.0229	(0.0086)	−0.0458	(0.0047)
RIF								
Composition	−0.0117	(0.0034)	0.0290	(0.0022)	−0.0119	(0.0025)	0.0305	(0.0021)
Specification error	−0.0046	(0.0019)	−0.0169	(0.0013)	−0.0058	(0.0018)	−0.0179	(0.0014)
Earnings structure	−0.0236	(0.0081)	−0.0448	(0.0048)	−0.0226	(0.0086)	−0.0454	(0.0047)
Reweighting error	−0.0007	(0.0002)	−0.0004	(0.0001)	−0.0003	(0.0002)	−0.0004	(0.0001)
RIF composition								
Age	0.0032	(0.0011)	0.0037	(0.0005)	0.0030	(0.0011)	0.0038	(0.0006)
Sex	−0.0017	(0.0004)	−0.0015	(0.0003)	−0.0023	(0.0006)	−0.0027	(0.0004)
Education	−0.0030	(0.0014)	0.0221	(0.0020)	−0.0036	(0.0017)	0.0260	(0.0020)
Informality	−0.0033	(0.0006)	−0.0059	(0.0006)	−0.0033	(0.0005)	−0.0059	(0.0005)
RTI	−0.0069	(0.0018)	0.0106	(0.0013)	−0.0057	(0.0007)	0.0094	(0.0009)
Explained	−0.0117	(0.0034)	0.0290	(0.0022)	−0.0119	(0.0025)	0.0305	(0.0021)
RIF earnings structure								
Age	0.0023	(0.0080)	0.0074	(0.0053)	0.0048	(0.0083)	0.0070	(0.0055)
Sex	0.0173	(0.0051)	0.0030	(0.0036)	0.0172	(0.0061)	0.0007	(0.0042)
Education	0.0024	(0.0071)	0.0314	(0.0066)	0.0066	(0.0063)	0.0251	(0.0063)
Informality	0.0051	(0.0034)	0.0047	(0.0023)	0.0054	(0.0032)	0.0033	(0.0024)
RTI	0.0026	(0.0121)	−0.0181	(0.0062)	−0.0040	(0.0039)	0.0141	(0.0039)
Intercept	−0.0533	(0.0145)	−0.0732	(0.0115)	−0.0526	(0.0207)	−0.0956	(0.0112)

Note: Bootstrapped standard errors are in parentheses (100 replications); estimates in grey p>0.1.
Source: Author's calculation based on data from Income Survey CASEN 2000, 2006, and 2017.

the inequality-enhancing role played by the composition effect (the composition effect is positive, while inequality is dropping). In this period, there is an important contribution to the changes associated with the average income per occupation as a function of its RTI. In contrast, there are other effects in the opposite direction (equalizing) associated with the returns to education and, to a lesser extent, informality.

One of the features of the RIF regression decomposition is that it allows us to observe changes in inequality at different points of the earnings distribution, unlike the previous case in which we use the Gini index to summarize distributional changes in the whole earnings distribution. Figure 14.3 (row A) shows the RIF decomposition of changes in (log) quantiles over time. The grey line shows changes in the variability of (log) wages at each percentile of the earnings distribution (composition and structure effects added). We observe that changes in the earnings structure mostly drive the variation in earnings along the distribution in both periods. The composition effect tends to be more relevant at the top and surpasses the return effect only in 2006–17 after the 70th percentile. In general, both effects contribute to a deeper increase in wages as we move down in the income distribution.

Row B in Figure 14.3 shows the disaggregation of the composition effect of different covariates. We observe that occupational changes towards higher levels of the routinization of jobs in 2000–06 (average RTIs increased in that period) reduced wages (negative sign), with a subtle inverted U-shape, but with more intensity at the top of the earnings distribution. Rising levels of schooling slightly increased wages at every percentile but were more noticeable for the bottom quantiles. Also, higher formality rates have positively affected increasing wages, particularly for the poorest quantiles. In the last period, 2006–17, we observe that moving towards lower RTIs increases earnings, particularly after the median, with more significant wins for the top quantiles. Increasing schooling is the most relevant factor in rising wages, particularly for the upper part of the distribution. This coincides with the implementation of a new funding system for higher education, the 'Credit with state guaranty' (CAE for the Spanish acronym), which increased the coverage of tertiary education massively. In the last period, we also observed that changes related to gender, such as more female participation, slightly reduced wages over the whole earnings distribution.

Row C shows the earning structure effect. From the covariates, education dominates the earnings structure effect. With very few exceptions, returns to schooling have an inequality-diminishing effect in all periods, reducing wages mainly above the median in 2000–06 and below the median in 2006–17. Changes associated with informality have led to more erratic behaviour in wages, with increased earnings dispersion around the median in 2000–06, and below the median in 2006–17. Changes in the returns to routine versus non-routine tasks increased earnings in both periods and throughout the entire distribution. In the first period,

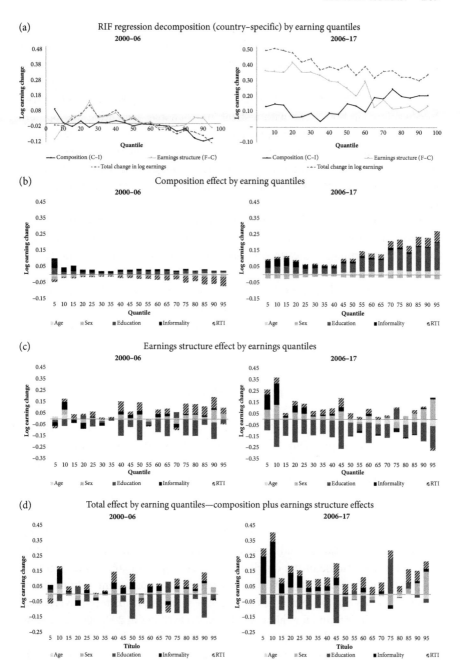

Figure 14.3 RIF regression decomposition (country-specific) by earning quantiles

Source: Author's illustration based on CASEN (2000, 2006, 2017)

the effect is more significant for the top of the distribution. In the last period, the effect is concentrated before the median of the distribution. Changes in the returns associated to gender have a positive effect, increasing female wages more noticeably at the extremes of the distribution. To sum up, we observe an inequality-enhancing impact of changes in returns to RTI and the opposite effect of returns to education—in both cases with a slight 'pro-rich' bias benefiting the top part of the distribution in the first case and reducing wages more for the bottom quantiles in the second case. However, the earnings structure analysis is limited, since we observe that most of the impact is found in the constant, as in the Gini decomposition (see Figure A8 and Tables A4, A5, and A6 in Zapata-Román (2021)).

Finally, the total effect of each covariate (wage structure plus composition effect) is reported in row D of Figure 14.3. RTIs account for an important part of the variability of earnings, indicating that the net movement of workers towards less-routine tasks has contributed to increasing wages in 2006–17. Education is also a relevant covariate, where the total net effect reduces earnings, with more intensity at the top of the distribution in 2000–06 and at the bottom in 2006–17. Changes in formality rates have contributed to improving wages particularly at the bottom of the distribution.

14.7 Conclusions

Using household data from the income survey CASEN, this chapter analyses the trends in earnings inequality in Chile from 2000 to 2017, and the role of tasks and skills in shaping inequality movements. The estimations show that inequality has dropped in Chile since the 2000s, explained by a fall in earnings in the top percentiles of the distribution which has been reallocated most noticeably around the median (2000–06) and the bottom 30 per cent of the distribution (2006–17).

The polarization phenomenon predicts an increase in the relative demand for well-paid high-skilled and low-paid low-skill jobs, diminishing the relative demand in the middle of the distribution, where routine manual and cognitive tasks are commonly executed. We find this pattern for employment—although not significant—but not for earnings. The opposite (significant) pattern (inverted U-shaped growth) is found for changes in log mean earnings in 2000–06, suggesting that in this period real earnings grew more in the middle of the distribution.

We observe an average rise in the routinization of jobs in the period 2000–06 and a strong reduction of the RTI of jobs since 2006. Given that the RTI values are constant, this average decline in routinization in the second period is driven by a restructuring of the labour force away from more-routine towards less-routine occupations. The results of the RIF decomposition by percentiles show that the period of rising average RTI is associated with small net gains at the top of the earnings distribution. In the second period, the movement of workers towards less-routine tasks is associated with increasing earnings, also more noticeable for the upper quantiles, while the changes in the returns of RTIs benefited more the bottom and middle part of the distribution (increasing wages). Nevertheless, when we look at inequality changes using the Gini coefficient, the effect of RTI is weaker, combining a positive composition effect with a negative wage structure effect (2006–17). The robust effect of RTI in explaining changes in inequality at different percentiles is in line with the polarization analysis of Section 14.5.2. We find that the routine content of tasks explains an important part of changes in the variability of earnings, and to a lesser extent the variability of employment. However, the strong monotonic correlation of earnings with RTI has been reducing over time, as shown by the Shapley decomposition. The Shapley decomposition also shows that average earnings across occupations have become less unequal over time, contributing to the overall decline in inequality.

It has been argued that changes in returns to education are the main driver of wage inequality dynamics in Chile (PNUD 2017; Torche 2014). The first part of our research (in Section 3.3 of Zapata-Román 2021) confirms this reduction in the returns to education, particularly higher education. Although, the RIF decomposition analysis indicates different effects depending on the income percentile. Changes in the composition of education, such as the expansion of secondary and higher education, have contributed to increasing earnings throughout the distribution, with a strong bias towards the upper percentiles in the period 2006–17. As an opposite force, changes in the returns to education have reduced earnings. The net effect of education on earnings is mostly negative, particularly after the 40th quantile in 2000–06 and below the median in 2006–17. Therefore, we do not observe an equalizing effect of education, particularly for the lower part of the income distribution.

Changes in the occupational structure confirm a displacement of workers from low-skill occupations towards jobs demanding non-routine higher skills. Changes in occupational earnings have had a positive equalizing effect, with more substantial gains in favour of lower-skill occupations and at the top of the skill premium, with earnings of managers and professionals becoming closer. Despite these positive changes in inequality, we still observe substantial differences between the rewards of low- and high-skill occupations which cannot be explained by the educational premium. As discussed by Messina and Silva (2019), there are several factors related to the drop in earnings inequality which changes in education cannot account for, such as changes in the labour supply due to the experience premium and compression of wages across workers with similar skills.

Another factor that is slightly significant in inequality changes is the reduction of informality. Establishing the link between formalization and inequality is not trivial, since the direction of causality is unclear (Messina and Silva 2019). Job market reforms helped to increase formal work in Chile during the 2000s. The RIF decomposition shows that changes in the distribution of wages associated with this process contributed slightly to reducing inequality, increasing wages particularly at the bottom of distribution.

It is important to acknowledge that the decomposition of changes in inequality due to changes in structure and composition is primarily an analytical exercise, since these are not fully separable effects. A clear example is that changes in the returns to education (structure effect) may be due to a change in the population's overall level of education (composition), which in turn adjusts the educational premium.

Acknowledgement

The author is grateful for valuable feedback on previous versions of this chapter from the internal and external UNU-WIDER research team, collaborating under the project 'The changing nature of work and inequality', and particularly for the comments from Carlos Gradín, Simone Schotte, and Piotr Lewandowski. The author also acknowledges the support of the Chilean Research and Development Agency (ANID), Fondecyt Postdoctorado N° 3210480.

References

Acemoglu, D., and P. Restrepo (2017). *Robots and Jobs: Evidence from US Labor Markets.* SSRN Scholarly Paper 2941263. Rochester, NY: Social Science Research Network (SSRN). https://doi.org/10.2139/ssrn.2940245

Autor, D.H. (2019). 'Work of the Past, Work of the Future'. NBER Working Paper 25588. Cambridge, MA: National Bureau of Economic Research (NBER). https://doi.org/10.3386/w25588

Autor, D.H., F. Levy, and R.J. Murnane (2003). 'The Skill Content of Recent Technological Change: An Empirical Exploration'. *The Quarterly Journal of Economics*, 118(4): 1279–33. https://doi.org/10.1162/003355303322552801

Berman, E., J. Bound, and S. Machin (1998). 'Implications of Skill-Biased Technological Change: International Evidence'. *The Quarterly Journal of Economics*, 113(4): 1245–79. https://doi.org/10.1162/003355398555892

CASEN (2000). 'Encuesta de caracterización socioeconómica nacional'. Santiago: Ministerio de Desarrollo Social y Familia. Gobierno de Chile. Available at: http://observatorio.ministeriodesarrollosocial.gob.cl/encuesta-casen-2000 (accessed 25 April 2020).

CASEN (2006). 'Encuesta de caracterización socioeconómica nacional'. Santiago: Ministerio de Desarrollo Social y Familia. Gobierno de Chile. Available at: http://observatorio.ministeriodesarrollosocial.gob.cl/encuesta-casen-2006 (accessed 25 April 2020).

CASEN (2017). 'Encuesta de caracterización socioeconómica nacional'. Santiago: Ministerio de Desarrollo Social y Familia. Gobierno de Chile. Available at: http://

observatorio.ministeriodesarrollosocial.gob.cl/encuesta-casen-2017 (accessed 25 April 2020).

Contreras, D., and R. Ffrench-Davis (2012). 'Policy Regimes, Inequality, Poverty and Growth: The Chilean Experience, 1973–2010'. WIDER Working Paper 2012/04. Helsinki: UNU-WIDER.

Du, Y., and A. Park (2017). 'Changing Demand for Tasks and Skills in China'. Background report for the World Bank Group (WBG)-Development Research Center under the State Council (DRC) Report on New Drivers of Growth in China. Washington, DC: World Bank.

Firpo, S., N.M. Fortin, and T. Lemieux (2011). 'Occupational Tasks and Changes in the Wage Structure'. SSRN Scholarly Paper 1778886. Rochester, NY: SSRN.

Firpo, S., N.M. Fortin, and T. Lemieux (2018). 'Decomposing Wage Distributions using Recentered Influence Function Regressions'. Econometrics, 6(2): 1–40. https://doi.org/10.3390/econometrics6020028

Goos, M., and A. Manning (2007). 'Lousy and Lovely Jobs: The Rising Polarization of Work in Britain'. The Review of Economics and Statistics, 89(1): 118–33. https://doi.org/10.1162/rest.89.1.118

Goos, M., A. Manning, and A. Salomons (2014). 'Explaining Job Polarization: Routine-Biased Technological Change and Offshoring'. American Economic Review, 104(8): 2509–26. https://doi.org/10.1257/aer.104.8.2509

Hardy, W., R. Keister, and P. Lewandowski (2018). 'Educational Upgrading, Structural Change and the Task Composition of Jobs in Europe'. Economics of Transition and Institutional Change, 26(2): 201–31. https://doi.org/10.1111/ecot.12145

Jensen, J.B., and L.G. Kletzer (2010). 'Measuring Tradable Services and the Task Content of Offshorable Services Jobs'. In K.G. Abraham, J.R. Spletzer, and M. Harper (eds), Labor in the New Economy, pp. 309–335. Chicago: The University of Chicago Press.

Lewandowski, P., A. Park, and S. Schotte (2020). 'The Global Distribution of Routine and Non-Routine Work'. WIDER Working Paper 75/2020. Helsinki: UNU-WIDER. https://doi.org/10.35188/UNU-WIDER/2020/832-0

MDS and PNUD (Programa de las Naciones Unidas Para el Desarrollo) (2020). Evolución de La Pobreza 1990–2017 ¿Cómo Ha Cambiado Chile? Santiago: MDS, Gobierno de Chile.

Messina, J., and J. Silva (2019). 'Twenty Years of Wage Inequality in Latin America'. IDB Working Paper 1041. Washington, DC: Inter-American Development Bank (IDB). https://doi.org/10.18235/0001806

Michaels, G., A. Natraj, and J. Van Reenen (2013). 'Has ICT Polarized Skill Demand? Evidence from Eleven Countries over Twenty-Five Years'. The Review of Economics and Statistics, 96(1): 60–77. https://doi.org/10.1162/REST_a_00366

O*NET (2003). 'O*NET 5.0 Database, September 2003 Release'. Washington, DC: US Department of Labor. Available at: https://www.onetcenter.org (accessed 3 July 2019).

OECD (2014/15). 'Survey of Adult Skills (PIAAC) Second Round (2014–15)'. Paris: OECD. Available at: http://www.oecd.org/skills/piaac/data (accessed 3 July 2019).

OECD (2018). OECD Economic Surveys: Chile. Overview. Paris: OECD. https://doi.org/10.1787/eco_surveys-can-2018-en

OECD (2020). 'Income Inequality'. OECD Data. Available at: http://data.oecd.org/inequality/income-inequality.htm (accessed 10 November 2020).

Perticará, M., and P. Celhay. 2010. 'Informalidad Laboral y Políticas Públicas En Chile'. *Ilades-Georgetown University Working Papers* (257). https://fen.uahurtado.cl/wp-content/uploads/2010/07/I-257Perticara-y-Celhay-informalidad.pdf

PNUD (2017). *Desiguales. Orígenes, cambios y desafíos de la brecha social en Chile.* Santiago: Programa de las Naciones Unidas Para el Desarrollo (PNUD).

Sebastian, R. (2018). 'Explaining Job Polarisation in Spain from a Task Perspective'. *SERIEs*, 9(2): 215–48. https://doi.org/10.1007/s13209-018-0177-1

Shorrocks, A. (2013). 'Decomposition Procedures for Distributional Analysis: A Unified Framework based on the Shapley Value'. *Journal of Economic Inequality*, 11: 99–126. https://doi.org/10.1007/s10888-011-9214-z

Solimano, A., and G. Zapata-Román (2019). 'Structural Transformations and the Lack of Inclusive Growth: The Case of Chile'. WIDER Working Paper 118/2019. Helsinki: UNU-WIDER. https://doi.org/10.35188/UNU-WIDER/2019/754-5

Torche, F. (2014). 'Intergenerational Mobility and Inequality: The Latin American Case'. *Annual Review of Sociology*, 40(1): 619–42. https://doi.org/10.1146/annurev-soc-071811-145521

UNDP (2019). 'Human Development Reports'. UN Development Programme (UNDP). Available at: http://hdr.undp.org (accessed 6 July 2019).

WID (World Inequality Database) (2020). 'Income Inequality, Chile, 2000–2019'. *WID—World Inequality Database.* Available at: https://wid.world/country/chile (accessed 13 November 2020).

World Bank (2020a). 'GDP per Capita Growth—Chile'. Available at: https://data.worldbank.org/indicator/NY.GDP.MKTP.KD.ZG?locations=CL (accessed 30 April 2020).

World Bank (2020b). 'Gini Index (World Bank Estimate): Chile'. Data Bank Microdata Catalog. Available at: https://data.worldbank.org/indicator/SI.POV.GINI?locations=CL (accessed 10 November 2020).

Zapata-Román, G. (2021). 'The Role of Skills and Tasks in Changing Employment Trends and Income Inequality in Chile'. WIDER Working Paper 48/2021. https://doi.org/10.35188/UNU-WIDER/2021/986-0.

15

Peru

Employment and Inequality Trends

Jorge Dávalos and Paola Ballon

15.1 Introduction

Peru's latest trade liberalization episode started in the early 2000s and, as in many Latin American countries, it benefited from a favourable commodities prices cycle that lasted until the mid-2010s. The commodities boom, together with China's growing foreign demand, boosted economic growth across the region. As a consequence, poverty rates in Peru decreased substantially from around 40 per cent in the mid-2000s to 20 per cent in 2018, and inequality only reduced slightly (Herrera 2017). The modest improvement in inequality puzzles standard economic frameworks. Hence, this chapter aims to explore and identify structural drivers that shaped Peru's inequality reduction under the scope of two complementary literature strands: international economics and skill-biased technological change (SBTC).

The inequality implications of trade liberalization policies have been studied extensively during the last decade and go beyond the traditional (and frictionless) Heckscher–Ohlin–Samuelson (HOS) frameworks, which argue for the equalizing effects of trade liberalization. As Pavcnik (2017) summarizes, such a relationship is context-specific and depends substantially on the ability of workers to move across industries, firms, and locations. As such, better-educated workers will find it less costly to move to alternative sectors and occupations to materialize the potential gains or cope with the risks induced by trade shocks.[1] This is illustrated by Caselli and Michaels (2013) in Brazil and Loayza and Rigolini (2016) in Peru, who assess the effect of the commodities boom on poverty and inequality and find that mining and oil exploitation activities led to medium- and high-skilled job creation, which could not be fulfilled by the local labour force, which was mostly low-skilled. This, in turn, triggered skilled labour immigration with a consequent rise in inequality. From this perspective, in this chapter we assess distributional changes in skills and

---

[1] See Artuc et al. (2015) for an assessment of labour mobility costs in the context of trade policy interventions.

Jorge Dávalos and Paola Ballon, *Peru: Employment and Inequality Trends*. In: *Tasks, Skills, and Institutions*. Edited by Carlos Gradín, Piotr Lewandowski, Simone Schotte, and Kunal Sen, Oxford University Press. © UNU-WIDER (2023). DOI: 10.1093/oso/9780192872241.003.0015

education levels, factors that are key to the assessment of the equalizing effects of the latest trade liberalization episode in Peru.

The SBTC provides an alternative explanation to the limitations of a traditional (HOS) framework. The availability of investment capital in a high-skill, labour-intensive sector that opens up to trade may trigger technological changes, thus increasing high-skilled labour demand and relative wages (Pavcnik 2003). The latter implies lower relative wages (and compensation packages) for low-skilled workers, leading to higher inequality. A more nuanced and contemporaneous view suggests that SBTC may shift downward the demand for occupations that could be substituted through automation or outsourced abroad through improvements in communication technologies (Acemoglu and Restrepo 2020). We search for such patterns to diagnose whether this mechanism was a main driver of Peru's modest inequality improvements for the labour force during the last decades.

Alternative channels emphasize the role of labour market institutions over the above-mentioned drivers—that is, labour market deregulation has been suggested to favour pro-poor growth (Besley and Burgess 2004; Botero et al. 2004). In this regard, the Peruvian labour market has been characterized by weak labour market institutions: its informal employment rate—a proxy of compliance with labour regulations—declined only slightly from almost 80 per cent in 2004 to 73 per cent in 2017 (INEI 2018); between 2005 and 2015, minimum wage (MW) interventions were rather moderate as per the cumulated MW growth of about 21 per cent, far from their most active neighbours (i.e. Brazil, Bolivia, and Uruguay, who cumulated 58, 106, and 107 per cent, respectively, during the same period (ILO 2017)). Although institutional factors could have been related to inequality determination, we acknowledge the lack of structural reforms since the mid-2000s and consider that institutional factors stayed relatively constant during the period of analysis.

The empirical analysis presented in this chapter builds on the Peruvian household surveys for 2004–18 (Encuesta Nacional de Hogares (ENAHO)) matched with the skill content of job indicators at the occupational level (ISCO-88) obtained from the Programme for the International Assessment of Adult Competencies (PIAAC), published by the OECD (Ballon and Dávalos 2020).

We find evidence of structural shifts in skills, education, and earnings distributions. This is verified by the clear downsizing trends of the more routine low-skilled occupations such as elementary occupations and 'skilled' agriculture and fishery workers, to the benefit of less routine, medium-skilled occupations such as service, shop, and market workers, and plant and machine operators and assemblers, among others. The shift from low- to medium-skilled occupations comes along with an improvement in workers' levels of education. The share of tertiary-educated workers grew from 24 per cent in 2004 to 34 per cent in 2018.

Similarly, real earnings grew the most for the lowest paid and more routine occupations. This is particularly the case for the lowest-educated male population, who exhibited the highest earnings growth due to the expansion of the construction sector throughout the period of analysis. Our complementary microsimulation analysis of the relative importance of the commodities boom shows that its effect on inequality reduction is not negligible.

15.2 Inequality trends

Real earnings distribution has shown a slight improvement as per the Gini index that decreased from 0.53 to 0.47 between 2004 and 2018. This trend maybe initially depicted by exploring key productivity proxies. Specifically, the evolution of returns on education, and the distribution of workers' level of education by gender. An analysis of returns of education shows that they have stayed relatively constant, although its implied gender gap which favours men has been narrowing significantly for the better educated (see Ballon and Dávalos 2020: Figure 3). This suggest that education premia could have played a role in inequality reduction as long as the female labour force had shifted to higher educational levels during the period of analysis. An opposite trend verifies that, among the least educated, men's earnings increased at a faster pace, thus widening the gender gap within this segment of the labour force. This is likely to be explained by a boom in the construction sector that incentivized the demand for male labour during the period of analysis.

The employment distribution by education level (Table 15.1) shows a regular trend towards a better-educated labour force in 2018. The share of workers with tertiary education has increased unambiguously, while low-education categories (no schooling and primary education) decreased for men and women. The systematic improvement in women's education and the narrowing of the wage gender gap at the highest levels of education may have contributed to the overall reduction in inequality.

The foregoing suggests that inequality improvements were associated with higher earnings growth for the lowest-educated male and better educated female populations. To better understand the channels driving such growth, we identified the specific occupations that concentrate workers of different education levels, we then grouped the occupations in low-, medium-, and high-skill worker categories based on Peru's statistical office assessment (INEI 2015). Our classification confirms the previous findings. Among low-skilled occupations, male workers' earnings grew above those of their female counterparts (see Ballon and Dávalos 2020: Figure 5). With regards to the high-skilled occupations, male and female cumulated similar earnings trends, except for legislators, senior officials, and managers, where women's earnings grew the most (see Ballon and Dávalos 2020: Figure 6).

Table 15.1 Employment distribution by education level and gender (%)

	2004	2011	2018	Average
Men's education				
No schooling	1.89	1.30	0.87	1.31
Primary	25.97	20.56	17.55	21.05
Secondary	47.00	46.88	47.90	47.29
Tertiary	25.14	31.26	33.68	30.34
Total	100.00	100.00	100.00	100.00
Women's education				
No schooling	9.18	5.59	3.91	5.99
Primary	30.23	25.19	23.01	25.81
Secondary	37.25	37.28	38.37	37.68
Tertiary	23.34	31.95	34.70	30.52
Total	100.00	100.00	100.00	100.00

Source: Authors' compilation based on data from ENAHO.

In accordance with the above-mentioned educational profile trends, low-skill occupations (elementary occupations and skilled agriculture) systematically reduced their employment share between 2004 and 2018. Interestingly, for women their share in elementary occupations diminished from 50 to 40 per cent, while their participation as service, shop, and market workers (medium skilled) increased from 20 to 27 per cent in the period of analysis (see Ballon and Dávalos 2020: Figures 8 and 9).

A look into the employment distribution across economic sectors confirms the previous trends as the employment share in agriculture—fundamentally low skilled—has decreased for both men and women. Conversely, employment in the services sector (medium skilled) has increased steadily. The expansion in the construction sector during the period of analysis explains the rise in its employment share (see Ballon and Dávalos 2020: Figure 10).

15.2.1 Changes in employment distribution and earnings

Inequality reduction requires that the least favoured segments of the labour force receive the greatest improvement. We identify these patterns by relating the changes in occupational employment shares between 2004, 2011, and 2018 to occupations ranked by their mean earnings in the baseline period, either 2004 or 2011. We notice that lower-paid (in 2004) occupations reduced their employment share between 2004 and 2011. These occupations are mainly classified as low skilled. In contrast, average-paid and high-paid occupations increased their employment share, with the former doing so by more than the latter. These changes would partly explain the inequality reduction from 2004 to 2011. Changes in employment shares between 2011 and 2018 exhibit a similar pattern as poorer occupations reduced their employment shares the most. With regards to changes in the earnings distribution, we found a similar equalizing pattern between 2004 and 2011 as lower- and middle-paid occupations experienced the highest increase in earnings, while the better-paid occupations improved their earnings to a lesser extent. During 2011–18, earnings changed homogeneously across occupations irrespective of their baseline (2011) mean earnings. Overall, the 2004–18 occupational changes in employment and earnings were dominated by shifts during the 2004–11 period.

A simple regression may estimate this apparent negative relationship between changes in occupational employment and earnings. We follow Autor and Dorn (2013) and estimate the model:

$$d \ln E_{jt} = \gamma d \ln R_{jt} + u_{jt}$$

where γ is the elasticity that relates the employment (E_{jt}) and earnings (R_{jt}) change per occupation (ISCO-88, two-digit level) at a given point in time (t). To identify this elasticity, the equation is estimated by OLS (ordinary least squares) for three periods of analysis: 2004–11, 2011–18, and 2004–18, where the dependent variable is the change in the log of the occupational employment share and the explanatory variable is the change in the log of the mean real earnings for a given occupation. Note that the γ parameter has no causal interpretation, being only a correlation measure. We verify a negative elasticity parameter (-0.268) for 2004–11, which then fades (0.12) in 2011–18.

To go beyond the relationship between occupation and earnings changes, we now verify for the presence of polarization effects. This is motivated by the fact that in developed economies the SBTC explains the increasing inequality effects that result from technological change through polarization. Polarization is described as an increase in employment shares at both tails of the occupational earnings distribution. Even though our previous findings do not suggest its presence, we formally test for it through regression analysis.

Employment and earnings polarization

To formally test for earnings polarization effects, we follow Goos and Manning (2007) and estimate the quadratic relationship:

$$\Delta \ln E_{jt} = \beta_0 + \beta_1 \ln R_{jt-1} + \theta \ln^2 R_{jt-1} + u_{jt}$$

The model is estimated for our two periods of analysis (2004–11 and 2011–18) and for 2004–18. Overall, our 2004–18 estimates (see Table 15.2, left panel) do not

Table 15.2 Employment polarization regressions at alternative time lags

Variables	(1)	(2)	(3)	(4)	(5)	(6)
	log(empl. share)			log(earnings)		
	2004–11	2011–18	2004–18	2004–11	2011–18	2004–18
Log(earnings)	84.4***	−18.0*	−4,402*	−25.5***	23.1	207.1
$t-1$	(23.2)	(10.1)	(2,223)	(6.7)	(14.9)	(1,416)
Log(earnings)	−8.2***	1.8*	410.5*	2.7***	−2.3	−38.4
$t-1$ squared	(2.2)	(0.9)	(208)	(0.6)	(1.3)	(122.8)
Constant	−213***	44.6	11,528*	57.8***	−58.3	−252.1
	(59.7)	(26.7)	(5,829)	(17.5)	(40.8)	(3,899)
Observations	25.0	25	25	25	25	25
R-squared	0.63	0.26	0.22	0.68	0.14	0.06
Adj. R-squared	0.59	0.19	0.15	0.66	0.07	−0.02
F-test (p-val)	0.004	0.099	0.164	0.000	0.108	0.173

Note: Standard errors in parentheses. *$p<0.1$, **$p<0.05$, ***$p<0.01$.
Source: Authors' compilation based on data from ENAHO.

provide statistical evidence of polarization. Only the 2004–11 employment polarization specification unveils some statistically significant patterns, suggesting that this period was characterized by inequality improvements—that is, employment shares diminished and earnings increased for the poorer and richer occupations. No polarization effects are detected during the 2011–18 sub-period.

To further check for this relationship, we estimate the previous model with the log of real earnings as the dependent variable. As with the employment polarization tests, there is no evidence of polarization in earnings (see Table 15.2, right panel).

Our results confirm Herrera's (2017) polarization analysis for household consumption expenditure and income over the 2004–15 period, using the Foster and Wolfson (2010) polarization index. Furthermore, Maloney and Molina (2016) and Messina and Silva (2017) provide similar conclusions regarding the absence of employment polarization effects in many Latin American countries (Brazil, Peru, and Mexico). It is argued that forces other than technological change, such as commodities boom spillover effects or labour supply elasticities, may have taken a leading role in the determination of labour force dynamics.

15.2.2 Distributional changes and routine-task content of occupations

Technological change is expected to increase the productivity of non-routine occupations that require cognitive skills and/or higher levels of education, while it can also displace workers from occupations that are intensive in routine tasks

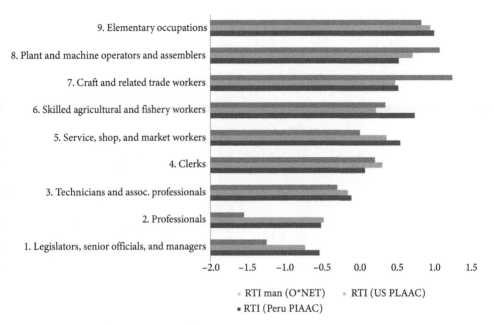

Figure 15.1 Alternative RTI indicators
Source: Authors' compilation based on data from ENAHO.

through automation or by outsourcing of those tasks abroad. Hence, focusing on the routine-task content of occupations rather than its 'skills' may provide an alternative view of SBTC inequality effects in the Peruvian context.

Three alternative measures for the routine-task content of ISCO-88 (two-digit level) occupations were available for our analysis. These are (1) the US O*NET statistics; (2) the US PIAAC survey gathered from Lewandowski et al. (2020); and (3) Peru's country-specific PIAAC survey. As can be seen in Figure 15.1, the occupational routine-task intensities (RTIs) exhibit similar rankings across definitions, except for agricultural and fishery workers (code 6, ISCO-88, one-digit level). According to Peru's PIAAC survey, this occupation is ranked as having the second highest RTI among the nine (one-digit) ISCO-88 occupations, whereas the O*NET RTI ranks it fourth. Similarly, ranking the ISCO-88 (one-digit level) occupations by their historical mean incomes and by years of education shows that this occupation has the lowest historical mean in earnings and in years of education, which is best proxied by the PIAAC RTI ranking. Due to the similarity between options (2) and (3), our analysis presents some robustness checks based on both O*NET (1) and PIAAC (3) RTIs only.

The raw RTI indicators at two- or three-digit breakdowns are time invariant (they are only observed for a given year), thus, 1-digit aggregated RTIs trends are determined by shifts in the distribution of occupations at two- or three-digit

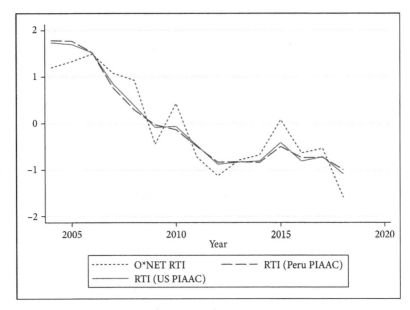

Figure 15.2 Average RTI indicator trends

Note: The average RTIs have been normalized (by their historical mean and standard deviations) for comparability purposes.
Source: Authors' compilation based on data from ENAHO.

levels. The 1-digit aggregated RTI indicators (Figure 15.2) exhibit an unambiguous downward trend until 2011–12 and stay relatively constant up to 2018, which suggests the presence of structural shifts in the distribution of occupations from highly routine to less routine occupations during the first period of our analysis (2004–11).

Figure 15.3 (left) relates the occupational employment changes between 2004–11, 2011–18, and 2004–18 to the ISCO-88 (two-digit level) occupations, presented in descending order of their PIAAC RTI (on the horizontal axis). Elementary occupations (92, 91) characterized by their high RTI, are those that reduced their employment share the most. In contrast, occupations with mid-valued RTIs and low RTIs increased their employment shares, with the mid-valued ones increasing more than low-valued ones. This pattern supports our skill reallocation findings, as there seems to be an employment shift from highly routine occupations to moderately routine ones. Earnings evolution with respect to occupations' RTIs seem to exhibit a slight relationship where high RTI occupations increased their earnings the most during 2004–11 (Figure 15.3, right). Interestingly, the RTI (PIAAC) approach suggests the presence of inequality improvements in occupational employment changes even after 2011.

Performing the previous analysis and building on the O*NET RTI as a robustness check yields similar results regarding the changes in (log) earnings. In

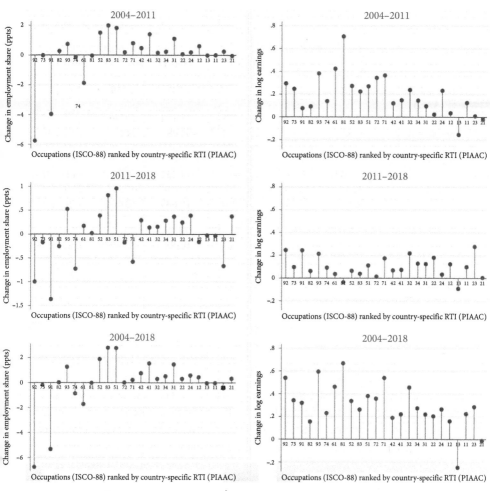

Figure 15.3 Changes in employment shares and earnings by occupation (ranked by their PIAAC RTI)

Source: Authors' compilation based on data from ENAHO.

contrast, changes in employment seem not to be improving inequality as they are not concentrated in the most routine occupations as was the case with the RTI (PIAAC) (see Ballon and Dávalos 2020: Figure 17). This is explained by the heterogeneity of Peru's country-specific RTI (PIAAC) and the O*NET alternative indicator for occupations 91 and 92. Since the country-specific RTI exhibits a more coherent correlation with historical educational and earnings levels, we consider it our preferred RTI classification.

A formal assessment of the potential polarization effects is provided by a regression analysis that accounts for the specific weight of each occupation in the

Table 15.3 Change in earnings and employment (RTI PIAAC)

	Change in empl. share			Change in log earnings		
	2004–11	2011–18	2004–18	2004–11	2011–18	2004–18
Baseline RTI (PIAAC)	−0.580	−1.416	185.823	−1.941	0.719	153.206
	(1.468)	(0.998)	(116.795)	(1.174)	(0.746)	(121.081)
Baseline RTI (PIAAC) squared	−0.283	−0.682	−312.067**	−0.708	−0.862	−108.773
	(1.504)	(0.914)	(114.669)	(1.251)	(0.854)	(141.707)
Constant	0.518	1.039	60.172	1.399*	−0.236	−21.839
	(0.940)	(0.688)	(47.203)	(0.689)	(0.474)	(79.280)
Observations	25	25	25	25	25	25
R-squared	0.022	0.217	0.166	0.288	0.030	0.033

Note: Clustered standard errors in parentheses. Clustered at the ISCO-88 two-digit level. $^*p<0.1$, $^{**}p<0.05$, $^{***}p<0.01$.
Source: Authors' compilation based on data from ENAHO.

employed labour force (Sebastian 2018). The regression analysis relates the change in the employment share at a given occupation and its baseline RTI (PIAAC) (Table 15.3). We do not find evidence of polarization (statistically significantly negative and positive linear and quadratic sign on the RTI) for any period of analysis under the country-specific RTI (PIAAC) definition. The regression on the change in (log) earnings with respect to the RTI (PIAAC) verifies the absence of polarization. Performing the same regression analysis based on our alternative definition (O*NET RTI) yields the same results (see Ballon and Dávalos 2020: Table A11).

15.3 Inequality drivers

The preceding analyses allowed us to look at factors that could explain the reduction in inequality between 2004 and 2018. Considering these factors as potential drivers of inequality, in this section we assess the specific weight that each of them may have in explaining the decrease in inequality for the period 2004–18. To do so we implement a Shapley decomposition of the Gini index and the RIF decomposition on quantiles and the Gini index (cf. Fortin et al. 2011). In addition, to appraise the effect of the mining commodities boom we specify a regression approach to measure the average effect of the shock on the Gini index using input–output technical coefficients.

The *Shapley decomposition* allows for an additive decomposition of a given inequality statistic. We implement it to identify the contribution of occupational earnings and employment shares heterogeneity to Peru's inequality trends.

Table 15.4 presents this decomposition for the observed wage distribution (actual) and two alternative counterfactual distributions—shares constant and means constant—that assume constant occupational shares and constant occupational mean earnings, respectively. The inequality improvements between 2004–11 and 2011–18 are similar (around 0.03), yet, between-occupations inequality improved the most from 0.199 in 2004 to 0.153 in 2011, staying constant until 2018. The within-occupation component played a negligible role as it stayed relatively constant between 2004 and 2018.

Whether the between-occupation improvement in inequality is explained by shifts in the labour force composition across occupations (employment shares) or their received wages (mean earnings distributions) across occupations (or both) is elucidated by the counterfactual decompositions. Keeping the employment shares constant at 2004 levels unveils that the evolution of occupational earnings alone would have reduced the Gini index to levels that are almost identical to the current ones—that is, from 0.533 to 0.504 and 0.469 in 2011 and 2018, respectively. This suggests that shifts in occupational earnings were the key determinants of the inequality trends. Similarly, keeping occupational earnings constant at 2004 levels keeps inequality constant up to 2011 and reduces it only slightly up to 2018. This confirms that shifts in occupational earnings were the main drivers of the inequality improvements during 2004–18.

Assessing between-occupations inequality by sorting occupations according to their RTI instead of their average mean earnings shows a strong relationship between occupational earnings and routine intensity for the more relevant country-specific RTI (PIAAC). The latter concentration index[2] is above 0.9, larger than the O*NET RTI that is below 0.7 during the period of analysis, both staying relatively constant up to 2018.

Additional insights are provided by the *RIF decomposition*, a regression-based approach in which the main outcome in this context is the quantile/Gini statistic obtained from workers' real earnings. The explanatory variables/drivers are workers' characteristics comprising education, age, gender, and the routine-task content of occupations (RTI PIAAC). As such, the RIF decomposition shares the spirit of the Oaxaca–Blinder decomposition by allowing us to disentangle the 'explained' and 'unexplained' factors behind inequality. To perform the RIF decomposition on an aggregate measure such as a quantile or the Gini index, one needs to compute a counterfactual distribution. Following DiNardo et al. (1996; henceforth DFL), we estimate this counterfactual by reweighting the 2004 data to have the same distribution of covariates as in 2018.

From a decomposition of the Gini index between 2004–11, 2011–18, and 2004–18, we identify that in both periods (2004–11 and 2011–18) the returns

---

[2] The relative importance of the RTI on the between-occupation Gini is proxied by the concentration indices ratio.

Table 15.4 Gini decomposition: occupation and task content

Gini	Actual			Shares constant			Means constant		
	2004	2011	2018	2004	2011	2018	2004	2011	2018
1. Overall	0.533	0.504	0.469	0.533	0.504	0.469	0.533	0.533	0.502
Shapley decomposition									
2. Between-occupation contribution	0.199	0.153	0.152	0.199	0.149	0.148	0.199	0.201	0.202
Between-occ. relative contribution (2/1)	37%	30%	32%	37%	30%	32%	37%	38%	40%
3. Within-occupation contribution	0.334	0.351	0.351	0.334	0.355	0.321	0.334	0.333	0.300
Within-occ. relative contribution (3/1)	63%	70%	75%	63%	70%	68%	63%	62%	60%
4. Gini between occupations	0.316	0.254	0.249	0.316	0.247	0.241	0.316	0.320	0.315
5a. Concentration index (RTI O*NET)	0.210	0.166	0.166	0.210	0.155	0.149	0.210	0.222	0.220
Relative concentration index (5a/4)	67%	65%	67%	67%	63%	62%	67%	69%	70%
5b. Concentration index (RTI PIAAC)	0.289	0.242	0.234	0.289	0.234	0.220	0.289	0.298	0.295
Relative concentration index (5b/4)	92%	95%	94%	92%	95%	91%	92%	93%	94%

Source: Authors' compilation based on data from ENAHO.

on workers' characteristics (earnings structure effect) played a homogeneous role in the reduction of inequality, whereas workers' characteristics themselves (composition effect) contributed to a slight inequality rise during 2004–11 (see Ballon and Dávalos (2020: Appendix A6). This is confirmed by the RIF aggregate decomposition (Figures 15.4a and 15.4b).

Breaking down the equality-enhancing earnings structure effects (returns on characteristics) into specific determinants suggests that most of the drivers remain hidden (in the constant term). This should be interpreted as the aggregate effect of unidentified factors leading to a sustained equalizing effect in real earnings throughout the overall labour force (Figure 15.4d). A second factor driving the equality-enhancing trend is gender, mostly during the 2004–11 period, which can be interpreted as the consequence of the narrowing of the real earnings gender gap illustrated earlier in the chapter. Similarly, we identify workers' returns on experience as a main inequality-increasing characteristic, mainly during the 2004–11 period. This relates to a widening wage gap between the younger and older labour force.

With regards to the role of workers' characteristics on the inequality rise mentioned above (the composition effect), we find evidence that the main inequality-increasing characteristic was the occupational task content proxied by the RTI (PIAAC) during 2004–11 only. This is likely due to the average reduction in the routine-task content of occupations shown above (Figure 15.1), which must have affected less routine occupations the most to lead to an inequality increase. Similarly, workers' experience acted as an inequality-increasing characteristic during the whole 2004–18 period (Figure 15.4c). This, again, relates to a widening wage gap between the younger and older labour force.

The DFL reweighting decomposition across deciles provides a more insightful assessment than the Gini decomposition. These results show that workers' characteristics (composition effect) are less important than unexplained factors (earnings structure effect) at every level (decile) or earnings distribution. Most importantly, the relative importance of workers' characteristics tends to increase as we move into the upper quantiles. In other words, workers at the right tail of the labour earnings distribution rely more on their own characteristics to improve their earnings in opposition to workers at lower deciles. This is confirmed by the RIF aggregate decomposition (see Ballon and Dávalos 2020: Figure A4).

15.3.1 Mining commodities boom

In the latest decades around 60 per cent of exports from Peru were mining commodities. In 2017, copper, gold, and zinc alone accounted for 89 per cent of total mining exports (Belapatiño et al. 2019). Although mining activities are known to be capital intensive, they may induce indirect effects on the rest of the economy

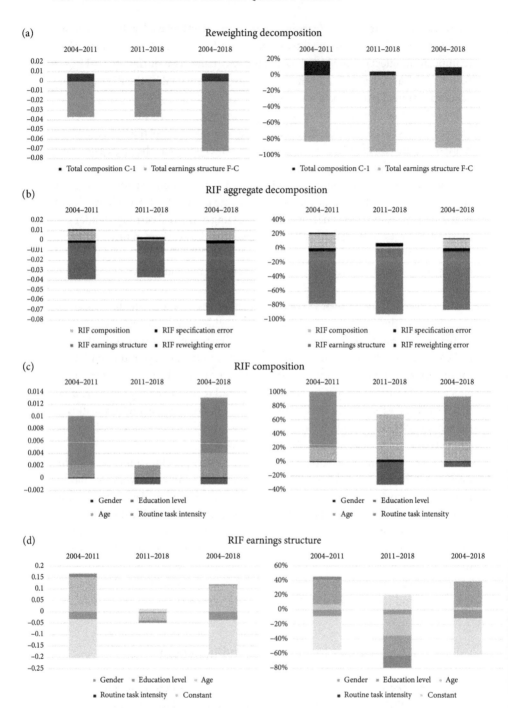

Figure 15.4 RIF: deciles and inequality decomposition
Source: Authors' compilation based on data from ENAHO.

through the demand for intermediate goods and services, and also through the demand for investment in infrastructure.

Thus, a key potential determinant of inequality in Peru is the mining commodities boom,[3] a factor we did not include in the RIF decomposition as the variation in commodity prices between 2004 and 2018 was significant. As such, it was not possible to reweight the 2004 data to obtain a counterfactual distribution that exhibits similar average values as the original one.

To account for this driver, we rely on the exogenous variation of international commodities prices that impacted the economy through spillover effects proxied by an input–output microsimulation analysis and estimate the effect of the commodities prices shocks on real labour earnings (Gini index) for 2004–18. To do so we make use of the Leontief technical relationship and construct two sectoral-level indices that reflect the commodity price effects through mining (intermediate demand) and construction (final demand) on all economic activities. Then, both indices are used as explanatory variables in a real earnings regression-based microsimulation analysis allowing the estimation of the average effect of the commodity price shocks on the Gini index (see Ballon and Dávalos 2020: section 3.1 for technical details).

The microsimulation approach

The effects of the mining commodities boom on inequality at the individual level (i) are identified from a linear model where real earnings are explained by exogenous characteristics. We use the pooled household cross-sections of 2004–18 and merge them with the longitudinal series of indices of commodity shocks by sector (j) computed previously. To account for the observed heterogeneity across education levels and gender, we specify a regression model of real earnings for every combination of gender and education level.[4] The covariates included in the x_{it} vector comprise the individual's age, age squared, and routine-task content:

$$y_{ijt} = x'_{it}\beta + \gamma_1 \tilde{q}_{jt} + \gamma_2 q_{jt} + u_j + u_c + u_r + u_t + \varepsilon_{ijt}$$

The commodity shock index from the mining sector to the j-th sector is noted q_{jt}, whereas the shock channelled from the construction to the j-th sector is noted $\tilde{q}_{jt}$. Both are indices of international price shocks (multiplier effects) obtained from an input–output analysis and were normalized to 1 for 2004. To account for unobserved characteristics that remain invariant across individuals in a given sector, we include fixed effects of economic sector (u_j), occupation (u_c), geographic location (u_r), and time (u_t). Our terms of interest are $\gamma_1 \tilde{q}_{jt}$ and $\gamma_2 q_{jt}$ and measure the (log) real earnings effects of the mining commodities shock channelled throughout the

---

[3] See, for instance, Loayza and Rigolini (2016) and Ticci and Escobal (2015).
[4] No schooling, primary, secondary, and tertiary education.

Table 15.5 Mineral prices effects (average treatment effect) on inequality (Gini)

	Observed	Counterfactual	Diff.	P value
2011	0.502	0.576	0.074	0.000
2018	0.469	0.524	0.054	0.000

Note: Counterfactual distribution assumes mineral prices of 2004.
Source: Authors' compilation based on data from ENAHO.

sectors by gender and education. From this specification we obtain a counterfactual outcome y_{ijt}, defined as the (log) real earnings given the commodity prices of 2004.[5]

Table 15.5 presents the Gini index under the observed and counterfactual distributions. The latter represents a situation without an increase in commodity prices and points to a statistically significant difference across our period of analysis.[6] Labour income inequality was expected to rise up to 0.52 compared to the current 0.47 in 2018 without the commodities boom. This suggest that alternative redistributive mechanisms have been triggered beyond the *mining canon*, a mining tax that is redistributed across the mining regions in the form of public expenditures and subsidies to households[7]. This finding contradicts some studies providing evidence of increased inequality effects at the local level that result from the medium- and high-skilled labour supply migration attracted by the mining regions (Loayza and Rigolini 2016). However, those studies ignore the spillover employment effects caused by the strong demand of infrastructure from the construction sector by the mining sector. Construction is a labour-intensive economic activity whose workers (mostly low skill male) benefited from the highest real earnings increases among the many occupations during our period of analysis.

15.4 Concluding remarks

In this chapter we looked for SBTC patterns that may have driven Peru's inequality dynamics during its latest trade liberalization episode, from the mid-2000s to 2018, with a particular focus on labour market earnings. Our results using

---

[5] In practice we calculate the counterfactual by partialling out the effect of international commodity prices after 2004: $y_{ijt} = y_{ijt} - (\gamma_1(\tilde{q}_{jt} - \tilde{q}_{j0}) + \gamma_2(q_{jt} - q_{j0}))$. Since both indices are normalized to 1 in 2004, $\tilde{q}_{j0} = q_{j0} = 1$.

[6] Statistical inference is performed using using the delta method and the survey sampling weights using Distributive Analysis Stata Package (DASP) (Araar and Duclos 2007).

[7] A similar result is found by Ballon and Cuesta (2023) when studying the profile of multidimensional exclusion in mining predominant regions in Peru.

labour income are in line with other studies' findings performed over alternative welfare indicators (household expenditure and total income), which show that inequality has improved slightly during the period of analysis. By exploring the structural changes in labour market characteristics, we identify concurrent shifts that explain the inequality dynamics. Specifically, the labour force skill level distribution exhibits a clear trend towards shifting from low- to medium-skill levels. Furthermore, this 'transition' correlates with labour earnings increasing the most for the lowest-paid occupations, thus supporting the equalizing dynamics in labour earnings distribution, in particular during the 2004–11 period. Considering a more nuanced approach to the potential SBTC effects by focusing on the routine-task content of occupations (RTI PIAAC) leads to similar conclusions; this labour structural change is characterized by a clear transition from routine to less routine (and better paid) occupations.[8]

The shift from low- to medium-skilled occupations comes with an improvement in workers' levels of education. Tertiary-educated workers shifted from 24 per cent in 2004 to 34 per cent in 2018, while primary-educated workers fell from 27 per cent to 20 per cent in the same period. Our DFL (reweighting) and RIF decomposition analyses shed light on the specific contribution of such structural changes (skills and education) on inequality. We find that workers' characteristics are less important than unexplained factors (earnings structure) and that the relative importance of workers' characteristics tends to increase for better paid workers (higher deciles). Despite the minor role of observed characteristics in earnings growth, we find that the routine-task content of occupations is a main component of the latter. Specifically, its importance increases as we move from 'poorer' to 'richer' workers.

Our findings are in line with other studies seeking to identify SBTC links in Latin American countries' inequality trends, Peru among them (Maloney and Molina 2016; Messina and Silva 2017). We argue that technological change complementarities (with high-skilled, non-routine occupations) and substitution patterns (with low-skilled, routine occupations) might not be the main drivers of the inequality dynamics in these developing economies. These countries were mainly affected by a commodities boom in specific economic sectors (agriculture and mining) that are rather intensive in medium- or low-skilled workers rather than high-skilled, and for whom technological change might not play a main role. From an additional investigation whose purpose was to identify the potential effect of the mining commodities boom on inequality, we find that mineral prices effects on income inequality may have contributed to the inequality reduction trend

---

[8] From elementary occupations and 'skilled' agriculture and fishery workers to less routine occupations such as service, shop, and market workers, and plant and machine operators and assemblers, among others.

between 2004–18. This finding is supported by the RIF earnings structure analysis which suggests that the main source of inequality reductions remained hidden i.e. it could not be attributed to shifts in workers' characteristics.

Acknowledgement

We thank Brian Daza for the excellent research assistance.

References

Acemoglu, D., and P. Restrepo (2020). 'Robots and Jobs: Evidence from US Labor Markets'. *Journal of Political Economy*, 128(6): 2188–244. https://doi.org/10.1086/705716

Araar, A., and J.-Y. Duclos (2007). *DASP: Distributive Analysis Stata Package*. Quebec City: PEP, World Bank, UNDP, and Université Laval.

Artuc, E., D. Lederman, and G. Porto (2015). 'A Mapping of Labor Mobility Costs in the Developing World'. *Journal of International Economics*, 95(1): 28–41.

Autor, D.H., and D. Dorn (2013). 'The Growth of Low-Skill Service Jobs and the Polarization of the US Labor Market'. *American Economic Review*, 103(5): 1553–97. https://doi.org/10.1257/aer.103.5.1553

Ballon, P., and J. Cuesta (2023). Multidimensional Exclusion and Exposure to Air Pollution in Peruvian Cities. In M., Mukim and M., Roberts (Eds). *Thriving: Making Cities Green, Resilient, and Inclusive in a Changing Climate*. Washington, D.C.: World Bank.

Ballon, P., and J. Dávalos (2020). 'Inequality and the changing nature of work in Peru'. UNU-WIDER Working Paper 168/2020. Helsinki: UNU-WIDER. https://doi.org/10.35188/UNU-WIDER/2020/925-9

Belapatiño, V., Y. Crispin, and F. Grippa (2019). 'Perú: situación del sector minero'. Report. Available at: www.bbvaresearch.com/publicaciones/peru-situacion-del-sector-minero-febrero-2019

Besley, T., and R. Burgess (2004). 'Can Labor Regulation Hinder Economic Performance? Evidence from India'. *Quarterly Journal of Economics*, 119(1): 91–134. https://doi.org/10.1162/003355304772839533

Botero, J.C., S. Djankov, R.L. Porta, F. Lopez-de-Silanes, and A. Shleifer (2004). 'The Regulation of Labor'. *Quarterly Journal of Economics*, 119(4): 1339–82. https://doi.org/10.1162/0033553042476215

Caselli, F., and G. Michaels (2013). 'Do Oil Windfalls Improve Living Standards? Evidence from Brazil'. *American Economic Journal: Applied Economics*, 5(1): 208–38. https://doi.org/10.1257/app.5.1.208

DiNardo, J., N.M. Fortin, and T. Lemieux (1996). 'Labor Market Institutions and the Distribution of Wages, 1973–1992: A Semiparametric Approach'. *Econometrica*, 64(5): 1001–44. https://doi.org/10.2307/2171954

Fortin, N., T. Lemieux, and S. Firpo (2011). 'Decomposition Methods in Economics'. In O. Ashenfelter and D. Card (eds), *Handbook of Labor Economics*, vol. 4, pp. 1–102. Amsterdam: Elsevier.

Foster, J.E., and M.C. Wolfson (2010). 'Polarization and the Decline of the Middle Class: Canada and the US'. *Journal of Economic Inequality*, 8(2): 247–73. https://doi.org/10.1007/s10888-009-9122-7

Goos, M., and A. Manning (2007). 'Lousy and Lovely Jobs: The Rising Polarization of Work in Britain'. *Review of Economics and Statistics*, 89(1): 118–33. https://doi.org/10.1162/rest.89.1.118

Herrera, J. (2017). 'Poverty and Economic Inequalities in Peru during the Boom in Growth: 2004–14'. *International Development Policy| Revue internationale de politique de développement*, 9(9): 138–73. https://doi.org/10.4000/poldev.2363

ILO (2017). 'Panorama Laboral 2017'. Technical Report. Geneva: International Labour Organization.

INEI (2015). 'Clasificador Nacional De Ocupaciones'. Technical Report. Lima: Instituto Nacional de Estadística e Informática.

INEI (2018). 'Producción y empleo informal en el Perú'. Technical Report. Lima: Instituto Nacional de Estadística e Informática.

Lewandowski, P., A. Park, and S. Schotte (2020). 'The Global Distribution of Routine and Non-Routine Work'. UNU-WIDER Working Paper 75/2020. Helsinki: UNU-WIDER. https://doi.org/10.35188/UNU-WIDER/2020/832-0

Loayza, N., and J. Rigolini (2016). 'The Local Impact of Mining on Poverty and Inequality: Evidence from the Commodity Boom in Peru'. *World Development*, 84: 219–34. https://doi.org/10.1016/j.worlddev.2016.03.005

Maloney, W.F., and C. Molina (2016). 'Are Automation and Trade Polarizing Developing Country Labor Markets, Too?' Policy Research Working Paper 7922. Washington, DC: World Bank. https://doi.org/10.1596/1813-9450-7922

Messina, J., and J. Silva (2017). *Wage Inequality in Latin America: Understanding the Past to Prepare for the Future*. Washington, DC: World Bank.

Pavcnik, N. (2003). 'What Explains Skill Upgrading in Less Developed Countries?' *Journal of Development Economics*, 71(2): 311–28. https://doi.org/10.1016/S0304-3878(03)00031-2

Pavcnik, N. (2017). 'The Impact of Trade on Inequality in Developing Countries'. Working Paper 23878. Cambridge, MA: National Bureau of Economic Research. https://doi.org/10.3386/w23878

Sebastian, R. (2018). 'Explaining Job Polarisation in Spain from a Task Perspective'. *SERIEs*, 9(2): 215–48. https://doi.org/10.1007/s13209-018-0177-1

Ticci, E., and J. Escobal (2015). 'Extractive Industries and Local Development in the Peruvian Highlands'. Environment and Development *Economics*, 20(1): 101–26. https://doi.org/10.1017/S1355770X13000685

PART IV
CONCLUSIONS

16

Conclusions and Policy Implications

Carlos Gradín, Piotr Lewandowski, Simone Schotte, and Kunal Sen

One of the growing fields of labour and development economics is the study of the interactions between routine-replacing technologies such as robots and software, globalization, and labour markets. The majority of research has focused on high-income countries (HICs), particularly the US. To some extent, this is due to data availability, as information on technology use, worker skills, and occupational tasks is more readily available in rich countries than in the Global South. This book fills this gap by studying the role of skills and occupational tasks in the evolution of earnings inequality in 11 developing countries. Its findings have important policy implications for understanding the drivers of labour market outcomes and wage inequality, as well as identifying the winners and losers of technological progress and globalization.

In past research, the measurements from high-income countries have often been applied to study the labour market effects of technology and globalization in low- and middle-income countries (LICs and MICs). The American dataset of occupational tasks, O*NET, is the most commonly used source of such data. However, as demonstrated in Chapter 3, assuming that the task content of occupations is the same in all countries leads to an overly optimistic view of the nature of work in the Global South and its evolution over time. It implies that the average routine-task intensity (RTI) has declined similarly across countries at all levels of development, which is implausible. It also leads to the absurd conclusion that by 2017, LICs and MICs had surpassed the developed countries as the leading global supplier of high-skilled, non-routine work.

Measuring country-specific occupational task content is now possible as a result of global data collection efforts (Lewandowski et al. 2022). It yields three stylized facts about the differences in the nature of work around the world. For starters, work in certain occupations is more routine intensive in developing countries. Second, in LICs and MICs, the gross reallocation of labour away from routine work and towards non-routine work has occurred more slowly than in HICs. Since the early 2000s, the gaps between these country groups have grown wider. Third, HICs have continued to be the primary source of non-routine work, while LICs and MICs have continued to be the primary source of routine work.

The country case studies presented in this book show that in low- and middle-income countries, job and wage polarization has been much less common than in

Carlos Gradín et al., *Conclusions and Policy Implications*. In: *Tasks, Skills, and Institutions*. Edited by Carlos Gradín, Piotr Lewandowski, Simone Schotte, and Kunal Sen, Oxford University Press. © UNU-WIDER (2023).
DOI: 10.1093/oso/9780192872241.003.0016

high-income countries, where it has emerged as a critical force behind earnings inequality. The shares and wage premia associated with the best-paid occupations that require high skill levels have increased in many countries covered by this volume. However, the occupations in the middle have declined only in some cases, such as in South Africa. Occupational upgrading—the transition from low-skilled jobs to middle-skilled jobs—has been more common, mostly due to declining shares of agriculture. In some countries, this pattern follows a typical path of structural change, with workers moving to manufacturing. In others, it has involved rising employment in construction and services. In any case, the pace of the deroutinization of work in the Global South is slower than in the OECD countries, and the related occupational change appears less disequalizing. At the same time, changes in the returns to education, especially rising premia associated with higher education, have been an important driver of earnings inequality in the countries studied in this book. In this respect, the recent developments in countries of the Global South have resembled changes in the developed countries in the 1970s and 1980s, when the so-called skill-biased technological change contributed to rising wage inequality (Card and DiNardo 2002).

The discovery of disparities in routine work intensity levels and distinct trajectories in developed and developing countries has significant policy implications. Cross-country variation in work content is much greater than cross-country variation in skill supply. Investments in education and skills are frequently cited as being necessary for convergence in the nature of work and income, as well as to avoid the negative labour market effects of technology adoption in the Global South (World Bank 2019). These investments are doubtlessly required to achieve these goals. Still, they are unlikely to be sufficient, given that technological adoption and participation in global value chains are key factors driving cross-country differences in occupational task content. Improving technology adoption should accompany investments in skills and education. Moreover, education systems should enable students to gain basic skills in solving practical problems in an ICT-rich environment. It is likely that the Global South will follow the developed countries and, in the future, such skills will be required even in low-skilled, elementary jobs. The less educated workers without such skills will be at risk of being left behind. More research is needed to fully understand how the challenges created by technological change are shaping inequalities in countries engaged in structural transformation.

In a range of countries studied in this book, labour market institutions such as a minimum wage have played an important role in taming earnings inequality. Their importance will likely increase when technology adoption accelerates and returns to skill rise further. The minimum wage systems need to balance the conflicting goals of improving low incomes and ensuring compliance, and avoiding disemployment effects. The labour market information and public employment services should support workers in relocating to more productive firms, which is a key mechanism to minimize disemployment effects and to facilitate productivity gains from minimum wage hikes (Engbom and Moser 2022).

Finally, the transmission of earnings inequality into household income inequality and poverty depends on at least three mechanisms: household composition, redistribution via tax-benefit systems, and safety nets. Policy makers can barely influence the first, but do control the second and third mechanisms. Progressive income taxation and income support for the poor are important tools to address challenges resulting from disequalizing technological and occupational change.

References

Card, D., and J.E. DiNardo (2002). 'Skill-Biased Technological Change and Rising Wage Inequality: Some Problems and Puzzles'. *Journal of Labor Economics*, 20(2): 733–83. https://doi.org/10.1086/342055

Engbom, N., and C. Moser (2022). 'Earnings Inequality and the Minimum Wage: Evidence from Brazil'. *American Economic Review*, 112(12), 3803–47. https://doi.org/10.1257/aer.20181506

Lewandowski, P., A. Park, W. Hardy, Y. Du, and S. Wu (2022). 'Technology, Skills, and Globalization: Explaining International Differences in Routine and Nonroutine Work Using Survey Data'. *The World Bank Economic Review*, 36(3): 687–708. https://doi.org/10.1093/wber/lhac005

World Bank (2019). *World Development Report 2019: The Changing Nature of Work*. Washington, DC: World Bank. https://doi.org/10.1596/978-1-4648-1328-3

Index

Please note that page references to Figures will be followed by the letter 'f', to Tables by the letter 't'.